STUDY GUIDE

STUDY GUIDE

Richard O. Straub
University of Michigan, Dearborn

to accompany

The Developing Person
Through the Life Span
NINTH EDITION

Kathleen Stassen Berger

WORTH PUBLISHERS
Macmillan Education

Study Guide
by Richard O. Straub
to accompany
Berger: **The Developing Person Through the Life Span**, Ninth Edition

ISBN 10: 1-4292-8394-7
ISBN 13: 978-1-4292-8394-6

Second printing

Worth Publishers
41 Madison Avenue
New York, NY 10010
www.worthpublishers.com

CONTENTS

PREFACE

This Study Guide is designed for use with *The Developing Person Through the Life Span*, Ninth Edition, by Kathleen Stassen Berger. It is intended to help you to evaluate your understanding of that material, and then to review any problem areas. "How to Manage Your Time Efficiently, Study More Effectively, and Think Critically" provides detailed instructions on how to use the textbook and this Study Guide for maximum benefit. It also offers additional study suggestions based on principles of time management, effective note-taking, evaluation of exam performance, and an effective program for improving your comprehension while studying from textbooks.

Each chapter of the Study Guide includes a Chapter Overview, What Will You Know? questions from the text, a Chapter Review section to be completed after you have read the text chapter, and two review tests. The Chapter Review also includes practical study tips and applications. These tips and applications are designed to help you evaluate your understanding of the text chapter's broader concepts, and make the text material more meaningful by relating it to your own life. For both review tests, the correct answers are given and complete explanations not only of why the answer is correct but also of why the other choices are incorrect.

I would like to thank Ellen Stein and Jill Hawes of Ohlinger Publishing Services for their assistance in the preparation of this Study Guide. My thanks also to Betty and Don Probert for their continuing support and fine work, and to Catherine Michaelsen, Stacey Alexander, and Julio Espin for their skillful assistance in the preparation of this Study Guide. We hope that our efforts will help you to achieve your highest level of academic performance in this course and to acquire a keen appreciation of human development.

Richard O. Straub

How to Manage Your Time Efficiently, Study More Effectively, and Think Critically

How effectively do you study? Good study habits make the job of being a college student much easier. Many students, who *could* succeed in college, fail or drop out because they have never learned to manage their time efficiently. Even the best students can usually benefit from an in-depth evaluation of their current study habits.

There are many ways to achieve academic success, of course, but your approach may not be the most effective or efficient. Are you sacrificing your social life or your physical or mental health in order to get A's on your exams? Good study habits result in better grades *and* more time for other activities.

Evaluate Your Current Study Habits

To improve your study habits, you must first have an accurate picture of how you currently spend your time. Begin by putting together a profile of your present living and studying habits. Answer the following questions by writing *yes* or *no* on each line.

_____ 1. Do you usually set up a schedule to budget your time for studying, recreation, and other activities?

_____ 2. Do you often put off studying until time pressures force you to cram?

_____ 3. Do other students seem to study less than you do, but get better grades?

_____ 4. Do you usually spend hours at a time studying one subject, rather than dividing that time between several subjects?

_____ 5. Do you often have trouble remembering what you have just read in a textbook?

_____ 6. Before reading a chapter in a textbook, do you skim through it and read the section headings?

_____ 7. Do you try to predict exam questions from your lecture notes and reading?

_____ 8. Do you usually attempt to paraphrase or summarize what you have just finished reading?

_____ 9. Do you find it difficult to concentrate very long when you study?

_____ 10. Do you often feel that you studied the wrong material for an exam?

Thousands of college students have participated in similar surveys. Students who are fully realizing their academic potential usually respond as follows: (1) yes, (2) no, (3) no, (4) no, (5) no, (6) yes, (7) yes, (8) yes, (9) no, (10) no.

Compare your responses to those of successful students. The greater the discrepancy, the more you could benefit from a program to improve your study habits. The questions are designed to identify areas of weakness. Once you have identified your weaknesses, you will be able to set specific goals for improvement and implement a program for reaching them.

Manage Your Time

Do you often feel frustrated because there isn't enough time to do all the things you must and want to do? Take heart. Even the most productive and successful people feel this way at times. But they establish priorities for their activities and they learn to budget time for each of them. There's much in the saying "If you want something done, ask a busy person to do it." A busy person knows how to get things done.

If you don't now have a system for budgeting your time, develop one. Not only will your academic accomplishments increase, but you will actually find more time in your schedule for other activities. And you won't have to feel guilty about "taking time off," because all your obligations will be covered.

Establish a Baseline

As a first step in preparing to budget your time, keep a diary for a few days to establish a summary, or baseline, of the time you spend in studying, socializing, working, and so on. If you are like many students, much of your "study" time is nonproductive; you may sit at your desk and leaf through a book, but the time is actually wasted. Or you may procrastinate. You are always getting ready to study, but you rarely do.

Besides revealing where you waste time, your time-management diary will give you a realistic picture of how much time you need to allot for meals, commuting, and other fixed activities. In addition, careful records should indicate the times of the day when you are consistently most productive. Table 1 shows a sample time-management diary.

Plan the Term

Having established and evaluated your baseline, you are ready to devise a more efficient schedule. Buy a calendar that covers the entire school term and has ample space for each day. Using the course outlines provided by your instructors, enter the dates of all exams, term paper deadlines, and other important academic obligations. If you have any long-range personal plans (concerts, weekend trips, etc.), enter the dates on the calendar as well. Keep your calendar up to date and refer to it often. I recommend carrying it with you at all times.

Develop a Weekly Calendar

Now that you have a general picture of the school term, develop a weekly schedule that includes all of your activities. Aim for a schedule that you can live with for the entire school term. A sample weekly schedule, incorporating the following guidelines, is shown in Table 2.

1. Enter your class times, work hours, and any other fixed obligations first. *Be thorough.* Using information from your time-management diary, allow plenty of time for such things as commuting, meals, laundry, and the like.

Table 1   Sample Time-Management Diary

Activity	Time Completed	Duration Hours: Minutes
Monday		
Sleep	7:00	7:30
Dressing	7:25	:25
Breakfast	7:45	:20
Commute	8:20	:35
Coffee	9:00	:40
French	10:00	1:00
Socialize	10:15	:15
Videogame	10:35	:20
Coffee	11:00	:25
Psychology	12:00	1:00
Lunch	12:25	:25
Study Lab	1:00	:35
Psych. Lab	4:00	3:00
Work	5:30	1:30
Commute	6:10	:40
Dinner	6:45	:35
TV	7:30	:45
Study Psych.	10:00	2:30
Socialize	11:30	1:30
Sleep		

Prepare a similar chart for each day of the week. When you finish an activity, note it on the chart and write down the time it was completed. Then determine its duration by subtracting the time the previous activity was finished from the newly entered time.

2. Set up a study schedule for each of your courses. The study habits survey and your time-management diary will direct you. The following guidelines should also be useful.

(a) Establish regular study times for each course. The 4 hours needed to study one subject, for example, are most profitable when divided into shorter periods spaced over several days. If you cram your studying into one 4-hour block, what you attempt to learn in the third or fourth hour will interfere with what you studied in the first 2 hours. Newly acquired knowledge is like wet cement. It needs some time to "harden" to become memory.

(b) Alternate subjects. The type of interference just mentioned is greatest between similar topics. Set up a schedule in which you spend time on several *different* courses during each study session. Besides reducing the potential for interference, alternating subjects will help to prevent mental fatigue with one topic.

(c) Set weekly goals to determine the amount of study time you need to do well in each course. This will

Table 2   Sample Weekly Schedule

Time	Mon.	Tues.	Wed.	Thurs.	Fri.	Sat.
7–8	Dress Eat	Dress Eat	Dress Eat	Dress Eat	Dress Eat	
8–9	Psych.	Study Psych.	Psych.	Study Psych.	Psych.	Dress Eat
9–10	Eng.	Study Eng.	Eng.	Study Eng.	Eng.	Study Eng.
10–11	Study French	Free	Study French	Open Study	Study French	Study Stats.
11–12	French	Study Psych. Lab	French	Open Study	French	Study Stats.
12–1	Lunch	Lunch	Lunch	Lunch	Lunch	Lunch
1–2	Stats.	Psych. Lab	Stats.	Study or Free	Stats.	Free
2–3	Bio.	Psych. Lab	Bio.	Free	Bio.	Free
3–4	Free	Psych.	Free	Free	Free	Free
4–5	Job	Job	Job	Job	Job	Free
5–6	Job	Job	Job	Job	Job	Free
6–7	Dinner	Dinner	Dinner	Dinner	Dinner	Dinner
7–8	Study Bio.	Study Bio.	Study Bio.	Study Bio.	Free	Free
8–9	Study Eng.	Study Stats.	Study Psych.	Open Study	Open Study	Free
9–10	Open Study	Open Study	Open Study	Open Study	Free	Free

This is a sample schedule for a student with a 16-credit load and a 10-hour-per-week part-time job. Using this chart as an illustration, make up a weekly schedule, following the guidelines outlined here.

depend on, among other things, the difficulty of your courses and the effectiveness of your methods. Many professors recommend studying at least 1 to 2 hours for each hour in class. If your time-management diary indicates that you presently study less time than that, do not plan to jump immediately to a much higher level. Increase study time from your baseline by setting weekly goals [see (4)] that will gradually bring you up to the desired level. As an initial schedule, for example, you might set aside an amount of study time for each course that matches class time.

(d) Schedule for maximum effectiveness. Tailor your schedule to meet the demands of each course. For the course that emphasizes lecture notes, schedule time for a daily review soon after the class. This will give you a chance to revise your notes and clean up any hard-to-decipher shorthand while the material is still fresh in your mind. If you are evaluated for class participation (for example, in a language course), allow time for a review just before the class meets. Schedule study time for your most difficult (or least motivat-

ing) courses during hours when you are the most alert and distractions are fewest.

(e) Schedule open study time. Emergencies, additional obligations, and the like could throw off your schedule. And you may simply need some extra time periodically for a project or for review in one of your courses. Schedule several hours each week for such purposes.

3. After you have budgeted time for studying, fill in slots for recreation, hobbies, relaxation, household errands, and the like.

4. Set specific goals. Before each study session, make a list of specific goals. The simple note "7–8 PM: study psychology" is too broad to ensure the most effective use of the time. Formulate your daily goals according to what you know you must accomplish during the term. If you have course outlines with advance assignments, set systematic daily goals that will allow you, for example, to cover fifteen chapters before the exam. And be realistic: Can you actu-

ally expect to cover a 78-page chapter in one session? Divide large tasks into smaller units; stop at the most logical resting points. When you complete a specific goal, take a 5- or 10-minute break before tackling the next goal.

5. Evaluate how successful or unsuccessful your studying has been on a daily or weekly basis. Did you reach most of your goals? If so, reward yourself immediately. You might even make a list of five to ten rewards to choose from. If you have trouble studying regularly, you may be able to motivate yourself by making such rewards contingent on completing specific goals.

6. Finally, until you have lived with your schedule for several weeks, don't hesitate to revise it. You may need to allow more time for chemistry, for example, and less for some other course. If you are trying to study regularly for the first time and are feeling burned out, you probably have set your initial goals too high. Don't let failure cause you to despair and abandon the program. Accept your limitations and revise your schedule so that you are studying only 15 to 20 minutes more each evening than you are used to. The point is to identify a regular schedule with which you can achieve some success. Time management, like any skill, must be practiced to become effective.

Techniques for Effective Study

Knowing how to put study time to best use is, of course, as important as finding a place for it in your schedule. Here are some suggestions that should enable you to increase your reading comprehension and improve your note-taking. A few study tips are included as well.

Using SQ3R to Increase Reading Comprehension

How do you study from a textbook? If you are like many students, you simply read and reread in a *passive* manner. Studies have shown, however, that most students who simply read a textbook cannot remember more than half the material ten minutes after they have finished. Often, what is retained is the unessential material rather than the important points upon which exam questions will be based.

This *Study Guide* employs a program known as SQ3R (*Survey, Question, Read, Retrieve,* and *Review*) to facilitate, and allow you to assess, your comprehension of the important facts and concepts in *The Developing Person Through the Life Span*, Ninth Edition, by Kathleen Stassen Berger.

Research has shown that students using SQ3R achieve significantly greater comprehension of textbooks than students reading in the more traditional passive manner. Once you have learned this program, you can improve your comprehension of any textbook.

Survey Before reading a chapter, determine whether the text or the study guide has an outline or list of objectives. Read this material and the summary at the end of the chapter. Next, read the textbook chapter fairly quickly, paying special attention to the major headings and subheadings. This survey will give you an idea of the chapter's contents and organization. You will then be able to divide the chapter into logical sections in order to formulate specific goals for a more careful reading of the chapter.

In this Study Guide, the *Chapter Overview* summarizes the major topics of the textbook chapter. This section also provides a few suggestions for approaching topics you may find difficult.

Question You will retain material longer when you have a use for it. If you look up a word's definition in order to answer a multiple-choice question, for example, you will remember it longer than if you merely guess at what seems to be the most logical answer. Surveying the chapter will allow you to generate important questions that the chapter will proceed to answer. These question correspond to "mental files" into which knowledge will be sorted for easy access.

As you survey, jot down several questions for each chapter section. One simple technique is to generate questions by rephrasing a section heading. For example, the "Preoperational Thought" head could be turned into "What is preoperational thought?" Good questions will allow you to focus on the important points in the text. Examples of good questions are those that begin as follows: "List two examples of . . .." "What is the function of . . .?" "What is the significance of . . .?" Such questions give a purpose to your reading. Similarly, you can formulate questions based on the chapter outline.

The *What Will You Know?* section of this Study Guide provides the types of questions you might formulate while surveying each chapter. This section is a detailed set of objectives covering the points made in the text.

Read When you have established "files" for each section of the chapter, review your first question, begin reading, and continue until you have discovered its answer. If you come to material that seems to answer an important question you don't have a file for, stop and write down the question.

Using this Study Guide, read the chapter one section at a time. First, preview the section by skimming it, noting headings and boldface items. as you read the chapter section, search for the answer to each of your questions.

Be sure to read everything. Don't skip photo or art captions, graphs, marginal notes. In some cases, what may seem vague in reading will be made clear by a simple graph. Keep in mind that test questions are sometimes drawn from illustrations and charts.

Retrieve When you have found the answer to one of your questions, close your eyes and mentally recite the question and its answer. Then write the answer next to the question in your own words. Trying to explain something in your own words will help you figure out where there are gaps in your understanding. These kinds of opportunities to practice retrieving develop the skills you will need when you are taking exams. If you study without ever putting your book and notes aside, you may develop false confidence about what you know. With the material available, you may be able to recognize the correct answer to your questions. But will you be able to recall it later, when you take an exam without having your mental props in sight?

Test your understanding as often as you can. Testing yourself is part of successful learning, because the act of testing forces your brain to work at remembering, thus establishing the memory more permanently (so you can find it later for the exam!)

After you have retrieved and written your answer, continue with your next question. Read, retrieve, and so on.

Review When you have answered the last question on the material you have designated as a study goal, go back and review. Read over each question and your written answer to it. Your review might also include a brief written summary that integrates all of your questions and answers. This review need not take longer than a few minutes, but it is important. It will help you retain the material longer and will greatly facilitate a final review of each chapter before the exam.

In this Study Guide, the *Chapter Review* section contains fill-in and one- or two-sentence essay questions for you to complete after you have finished reading the text and have written answers to your questions. The correct answers are given at the end of the chapter. Generally, your answer to a fill-in question should match exactly (as in the case of important terms, theories, or people). In some cases, the answer is not a term or name, so a word close in meaning will suffice. You should go through the *Chapter Review*

several times before taking an exam, so it is a good idea to mentally fill in the answers until you are ready for a final pretest review.

Also provided to facilitate your review are two *Progress Tests* that include multiple-choice questions and, where appropriate, matching or true–false questions. These tests are not to be taken until you have read the chapter, written answers to your questions, and completed the *Chapter Review*. Correct answers, along with explanations of why each alternative is correct or incorrect, are provided at the end of the chapter. If you miss a question, read these explanations and, if necessary, review the text material to further understand why. The *Progress Tests* do not test every aspect of a concept, so you should treat an incorrect answer as an indication that you need to review the concept.

The chapter concludes with *Key Terms*. It is important that the answers be written from memory, and in list form, in your own words. The *Answers* section at the end of the chapter gives a definition of each term, sometimes along with an example of its usage and/or a tip to help you remember its meaning.

One final suggestion: Incorporate SQ3R into your time-management calendar. Set specific goals for completing SQ3R with each assigned chapter. Keep a record of chapters completed, and reward yourself for being conscientious. Initially, it takes more time and effort to "read" using SQ3R, but with practice, the steps will become automatic. More importantly, you will comprehend significantly more material and retain what you have learned longer than passive readers do.

Taking Lecture Notes

Are your class notes as useful as they might be? One way to determine their worth is to compare them with those taken by other good students. Are yours as thorough? Do they provide you with a comprehensible outline of each lecture? If not, then the following suggestions might increase the effectiveness of your note-taking.

1. Keep a separate notebook for each course. Use standard notebook pages. Consider using a ring binder, which would allow you to revise and insert notes while still preserving lecture order.

2. Take notes in the format of a lecture outline. Use roman numerals for major points, letters for supporting arguments, and so on. Some instructors will make this easy by delivering organized lectures and, in some cases, by outlining their lectures on the board. If a lecture is disorganized, you will probably want to reorganize your notes soon after the class.

3. As you take notes in class, leave a wide margin on one side of each page. After the lecture, expand or clarify any shorthand notes while the material is fresh in your mind. Use this time to write important questions in the margin next to notes that answer them. This will facilitate later review and will allow you to anticipate similar exam questions.

Evaluate Your Exam Performance

How often have you received a grade on an exam that did not do justice to the effort you spent preparing for the exam? This is a common experience that can leave one feeling bewildered and abused. "What do I have to do to get an A?" "The test was unfair!" "I studied the wrong material!"

The chances of this happening are greatly reduced if you have an effective time-management schedule and use the study techniques described here. But it can happen to the best-prepared student and is most likely to occur on your first exam with a new professor.

Remember that there are two main reasons for studying. One is to learn for your own general academic development. Many people believe that such knowledge is all that really matters. Of course, it is possible, though unlikely, to be an expert on a topic without achieving commensurate grades, just as one can, occasionally, earn an excellent grade without truly mastering the course material. During a job interview or in the workplace, however, your A in HTML won't mean much if you can't actually program a computer.

In order to keep career options open after you graduate, you must know the material and maintain competitive grades. In the short run, this means performing well on exams, which is the second main objective in studying.

Probably the single best piece of advice to keep in mind when studying for exams is to *try to predict exam questions*. This means ignoring the trivia and focusing on the important questions and their answers (with your instructor's emphasis in mind).

A second point is obvious. How well you do on exams is determined by your mastery of both lecture and textbook material. Many students (partly because of poor time management) concentrate too much on one at the expense of the other.

To evaluate how well you are learning lecture and textbook material, analyze the questions you missed on the first exam. If your instructor does not review exams during class, you can easily do it yourself. Divide the questions into two categories: those drawn primarily from lectures and those drawn primarily from the textbook. Determine the percentage of questions you missed in each category. If your errors are evenly distributed and you are satisfied with your grade, you have no problem. If you are weaker in one area, you will need to set future goals for increasing and/or improving your study of that area.

Similarly, note the percentage of test questions drawn from each category. Although exams in most courses cover both lecture notes and the textbook, the relative emphasis of each may vary from instructor to instructor. While your instructors may not be entirely consistent in making up future exams, you may be able to tailor your studying for each course by placing additional emphasis on the appropriate area.

Exam evaluation will also point out the types of questions your instructor prefers. Does the exam consist primarily of multiple-choice, true–false, or essay questions? You may also discover that an instructor is fond of wording questions in certain ways. For example, an instructor may rely heavily on questions that require you to draw an analogy between a theory or concept and a real-world example. Evaluate both your instructor's style and how well you do with each format. Use this information to guide your future exam preparation.

Important aids, not only in studying for exams but also in determining how well prepared you are, are the Progress Tests provided in this Study Guide. If these tests don't include all of the types of questions your instructor typically writes, make up your own practice exam questions. Spend extra time testing yourself with question formats that are most difficult for you. There is no better way to evaluate your preparation for an upcoming exam than by testing yourself under the conditions most likely to be in effect during the actual test.

A Few Practical Tips

Even the best intentions for studying sometimes fail. Some of these failures occur because students attempt to work under conditions that are simply not conducive to concentrated study. To help ensure the success of your time-management program, here are a few suggestions that should assist you in reducing the possibility of procrastination or distraction.

1. If you have set up a schedule for studying, make your roommate, family, and friends aware of this commitment, and ask them to honor your quiet study time. Close your door and post a "Do Not Disturb" sign.

2. Set up a place to study that minimizes potential distractions. Use a desk or table, not your bed or an extremely comfortable chair. Keep your desk and the walls around it free from clutter. If you need a place other than your room, find one that meets as many of the above requirements as possible—for example, in the library stacks.

3. Do nothing but study in this place. It should become associated with studying so that it "triggers" this activity, just as a mouth-watering aroma elicits an appetite.

4. Never study with the television on or with other distracting noises present. If you must have music in the background in order to mask outside noise, for example, play soft instrumental music. Don't pick vocal selections; your mind will be drawn to the lyrics.

5. Study by yourself. Other students can be distracting or can break the pace at which your learning is most efficient. In addition, there is always the possibility that group studying will become a social gathering. Reserve that for its own place in your schedule.

If you continue to have difficulty concentrating for very long, try the following suggestions.

6. Study your most difficult or most challenging subjects first, when you are most alert.

7. Start with relatively short periods of concentrated study, with breaks in between. If your attention starts to wander, get up immediately and take a break. It is better to study effectively for 15 minutes and then take a break than to fritter away 45 minutes out of an hour. Gradually increase the length of study periods, using your attention span as an indicator of successful pacing.

Critical Thinking

Having discussed a number of specific techniques for managing your time efficiently and studying effectively, let us now turn to a much broader topic: What exactly should you expect to learn as a student of developmental psychology?

Most developmental psychology courses have two major goals: (1) to help you acquire a basic understanding of the discipline's knowledge base, and (2) to help you learn to think like a psychologist. Many students devote all of their efforts to the first of these goals, concentrating on memorizing as much of the course's material as possible.

The second goal—learning to think like a psychologist—has to do with critical thinking. Critical thinking has many meanings. On one level, it refers to an attitude of healthy skepticism that should guide your study of psychology. As a critical thinker, you learn not to accept any explanation or conclusion about behavior as true until you have evaluated the evidence. On another level, critical thinking refers to a systematic process for examining the conclusions and arguments presented by others. In this regard, many of the features of the SQ3R technique for improving reading comprehension can be incorporated into an effective critical thinking system.

To learn to think critically, you must first recognize that psychological information is transmitted through the construction of persuasive arguments. An argument consists of three parts: an assertion, evidence, and an explanation (Mayer and Goodchild, 1990).

An assertion is a statement of relationship between some aspect of behavior, such as intelligence, and another factor, such as age. Learn to identify and evaluate the assertions about behavior and mental processes that you encounter as you read your textbook, listen to lectures, and engage in discussions with classmates. A good test of your understanding of an assertion is to try to restate it in your own words. As you do so, pay close attention to how important terms and concepts are defined. When a researcher asserts that "intelligence declines with age," for example, what does he or she mean by "intelligence"? Assertions such as this one may be true when a critical term ("intelligence") is defined one way (for example, "speed of thinking"), but not when defined in another way (for example, "general knowledge"). One of the strengths of psychology is the use of *operational* definitions that specify how key terms and concepts are measured, thus eliminating any ambiguity about their meaning. "Intelligence," for example, is often operationally defined as performance on a test measuring various cognitive skills. Whenever you encounter an assertion that is ambiguous, be skeptical of its accuracy.

When you have a clear understanding of an argument's assertion, evaluate its supporting evidence, the second component of an argument. Is it *empirical*? Does it, in fact, support the assertion? Psychologists accept only *empirical (observable) evidence* that is based on direct measurement of behavior. Hearsay, intuition, and personal experiences are not acceptable evidence. Chapter 1 discusses the various research methods used by developmental psychologists to gather empirical evidence. Some examples include surveys, observations of behavior in natural settings, and experiments.

As you study developmental psychology, you will become aware of another important issue in evaluating evidence—determining whether or not the research on which it is based is faulty. Research can be faulty for many reasons, including the use of an unrepresentative sample of subjects, experimenter bias, and inadequate control of unanticipated factors that might influence results. Evidence based on faulty research should be discounted.

The third component of an argument is the explanation provided for an assertion, which is based on the evidence that has been presented. While the argument's assertion merely *describes* how two things (such as intelligence and age) are related, the explanation tells *why*, often by proposing some theoretical mechanism that causes the relationship. Empirical evidence that thinking speed slows with age (the assertion), for example, may be explained as being caused by age-related changes in the activity of brain cells (a physiological explanation).

Be cautious in accepting explanations. In order to think critically about an argument's explanation, ask yourself three questions: (1) Can I restate the explanation in my own words?; (2) Does the explanation make sense based on the stated evidence?; and (3) Are there alternative explanations that adequately explain the assertion? Consider this last point in relation to our sample assertion: It is possible that the slower thinking speed of older adults is due to their having less recent experience than younger people with tasks that require quick thinking (a disuse explanation).

Because psychology is a relatively young science, its theoretical explanations are still emerging, and often change. For this reason, not all psychological arguments will offer explanations. Many arguments will only raise additional questions for further research to address.

Some Suggestions for Becoming a Critical Thinker

1. Adopt an attitude of healthy skepticism in evaluating psychological arguments.

2. Insist on unambiguous operational definitions of an argument's important concepts and terms.

3. Be cautious in accepting supporting evidence for an argument's assertion.

4. Refuse to accept evidence for an argument if it is based on faulty research.

5. Ask yourself if the theoretical explanation provided for an argument "makes sense" based on the empirical evidence.

6. Determine whether there are alternative explanations that adequately explain an assertion.

7. Use critical thinking to construct your own effective arguments when writing term papers, answering essay questions, and speaking.

8. Polish your critical-thinking skills by applying them to each of your college courses, and to other areas of life as well. Learn to think critically about advertising, political speeches, and the material presented in popular periodicals.

Some Closing Thoughts

I hope that these suggestions help make you more successful academically, and that they enhance the quality of your college life in general. Having the necessary skills makes any job a lot easier and more pleasant. Let me repeat my warning not to attempt to make too drastic a change in your life-style immediately. Good habits require time and self-discipline to develop. Once established they can last a lifetime.

STUDY GUIDE

The Science of Human Development

Chapter Overview

Chapter 1 introduces the study of human development. The first section defines development, briefly describing the how, why, and who of this definition. This section also identifies five characteristics of the scientific method and discusses the interaction of nature and nurture in human development.

The second section introduces the life-span perspective, leading to a new understanding of human development as multidirectional, multicultural, plastic, and best understood from the perspective of multiple disciplines. The story of David illustrates the importance of human plasticity. The ecological-systems approach is Bronfenbrenner's description of how the individual is affected by, and affects, many other individuals, groups of individuals, and other environmental contexts.

The third section discusses the strategies developmentalists use in their research, including scientific observation, experiments, surveys, and case studies. To study people over time, developmentalists have created several research designs: cross-sectional, longitudinal, and cross-sequential.

The final section discusses several common mistakes that can be made in interpreting research, including the mistake of confusing correlation with causation and the ethics of research with humans. In addition to ensuring confidentiality and safety, developmentalists who study children are especially concerned that the benefits of research outweigh the risks.

What Will You Know?

The text chapter should be studied one section at a time. Before you read, preview each section by skimming it, noting headings and boldface items. Then read the sections, one at a time, keeping these questions in mind.

1. What are the complexities of studying growth over the life span?
2. What research methods do developmentalists use to study change over time?
3. Why do scientific conclusions need to be interpreted with caution?

Chapter Review

When you have finished reading the chapter, work through the material that follows to review it. Completing the sentences and answering the questions will enable you to answer the "What Have You Learned?" questions at the end of the text chapter. In some cases, Study Tips explain how best to learn a difficult concept, while Think About It and Applications help you to know how well you understand the material. Check your understanding of the material by consulting the answers at the end of this chapter. Do not continue with the next section until you understand each answer. If you need to, review or reread the appropriate section in the textbook before continuing.

Understanding How and Why

1. The scientific study of human development can be defined as the science that seeks to understand

   _____ .

2. In order, the basic steps of the scientific method are

   a. _____

   b. _____

   c. _____

   d. _____

   e. _____

3. A specific, testable prediction that forms the basis of a research project is called a _____ . In testing a prediction, research must be based on _____ _____ , meaning that it is based on observation or experimentation.

4. To repeat an experimental test procedure and obtain the same results is to _____ the test of the hypothesis.

5. The question of how much of any characteristic is the result of genes and how much is the result of experience is the _____– _____ debate. In this debate, _____ refers to environmental influences and _____ refers to the influence of genes that people inherit.

6. Genes and environment _____ (affect/do not affect) every aspect of development.

STUDY TIP Developmental science's biggest and most enduring debate concerns the *nature–nurture issue*—the controversy over the relative contributions of genes and experience to the development of psychological traits and behavior. Developmental psychologists explore the issue by asking, for example, how differences in intelligence, personality, and psychological disorders are influenced by heredity and by environment. As a simple way to think about current views regarding this issue, remember this brief statement: *Nurture works on what nature endows.* Our species is biologically endowed with an enormous capacity to learn and to adapt. Moreover, every psychological event is simultaneously a biological event.

APPLICATIONS:

7. Professor Cohen predicts that because "baby boomers" grew up in an era that promoted independence and assertiveness, people in their 60s will respond differently to a political survey than will people in their 30s and 40s. The professor's prediction regarding political attitudes is an example of a _____ .

8. Professor Stefik warns her students to be skeptical of the results of a controversial study because it has not been replicated. By this, she means that
   a. the researcher did not predict the results.
   b. the researcher did not specify whether nature or nurture would be the primary influence.
   c. the study has not yet been repeated by other researchers in order to verify the original findings.
   d. the results are statistically insignificant.

The Life-Span Perspective

9. The approach to the study of human development that takes into account all phases of life is the _____- _____ perspective.

10. The five developmental characteristics embodied within the life-span perspective are that development is
   a. _____
   b. _____
   c. _____
   d. _____
   e. _____

11. An important insight emerging from the fact that development is multidirectional is that human development does not always follow a straight, _____ growth pattern. One way to express this variability is to note that some characteristics are stable over time, called _____ , and other characteristics are not stable over time, called _____ .

12. A time when a particular type of developmental growth must happen if it is ever going to happen is called a _____ _____ . More common in human development are _____ _____ , when a certain type of development is most likely to happen or happens most easily. An example of this type of time period is the development of _____ .

APPLICATIONS:

34. Professor Jorgenson believes development is plastic. By this she means that
    a. change in development occurs in every direction, not always in a straight line.
    b. human lives are embedded in many different contexts.
    c. many cultures influence development.
    d. every individual, and every trait within each individual, can be altered at any point in the life span.

35. Dr. Ahmed is conducting research that takes into consideration the relationship between the individual and the environment. Evidently, Dr. Ahmed is using the _____-_____ approach.

36. Jahmal is writing a paper on the role of the social context in development. He would do well to consult the writings of _____ .

37. Son Yi's mother is puzzled by the many differences between the developmental psychology textbook she used in 1976 and her daughter's contemporary text. Son Yi explains that the differences are the result of _____ _____ .

Using the Scientific Method

38. When researchers observe and record, in a systematic and objective manner, what research participants do, they are using _____ _____ .

39. In the science of human development, people may be observed in a _____ setting or in a _____ . Observation may also involve searching _____ data.

40. A chief limitation of observation is that it does not indicate the _____ of the behavior being observed.

41. The method that allows a scientist to determine cause and effect is the _____ . In this method, researchers manipulate a(n) _____ variable to determine its effect on a(n) _____ variable.

42. In an experiment, the participants who receive a particular treatment constitute the _____ _____ ; the participants who do not receive the treatment constitute the _____ _____ .

43. In a(n) _____ , scientists collect information from a large group of people by personal interview, written questionnaire, or some other means. One drawback to this method is that participants' answers are influenced by the _____ and _____ of the questions.

44. An in-depth study of one person is called a _____ _____ . Limitations of this method are that the researcher's assumptions may _____ the results and that the person being studied may be _____ other people.

45. Research that involves the comparison of people of different ages is called a _____-_____ research design.

46. With cross-sectional research, it is very difficult to ensure that the various groups differ only in their _____ . In addition, every cross-sectional study will, to some degree, reflect _____ differences in addition to age effects.

47. Research that follows the same people over a relatively long period is called a _____ research design.

State the drawbacks of this type of research design.

48. The research method that combines the longitudinal and cross-sectional methods is the _____-_____ research method.

STUDY TIP To distinguish between independent variables and dependent variables, remember that independent variables are manipulated (controlled) directly by the researcher to determine how they affect dependent variables. Dependent variables are the behaviors and mental processes that psychologists are striving to understand. In a sense, dependent variables depend on the actions of independent variables. When you are struggling to distinguish two variables, try the following exercise. Ask yourself, "Which of these two variables can affect the other?" Consider, for example, a researcher investigating caffeine and reaction time. After randomly assigning students either to a group that drinks a highly caffeinated drink or to a group that drinks a weakly caffeinated drink, she measures each student's speed in pushing a button in response to a signal light. Which variable is the independent variable, and which is the dependent variable? If the answer is not obvious, try the test question, "Which variable can affect the other?" Clearly, reaction time cannot affect caffeine. So, in this example, the dose of caffeine is the independent variable and reaction time is the dependent variable.

APPLICATIONS:

49. To study the effects of temperature on mood, Dr. Sanchez had students fill out questionnaires in very warm or very cool rooms. In this study, the independent variable consisted of
    a. the number of students assigned to each group.
    b. the students' responses to the questionnaire.
    c. the room temperature.
    d. the subject matter of the questions.

50. Esteban believes that high doses of caffeine slow a person's reaction time. To test his belief, he has five friends each drink three 8-ounce cups of coffee and then measures their reaction time on a learning task. What is wrong with Esteban's research strategy?
    a. No independent variable is specified.
    b. No dependent variable is specified.
    c. There is no comparison condition.
    d. There is no provision for replication of the findings.

51. In an experiment testing the effects of group size on individual effort in a tug-of-war task, the amount of individual effort is the _____ variable.

52. Dr. Weston is comparing research findings for a group of 30-year-olds with findings for the same individuals at age 20, as well as with findings for groups who were 30 in 1990. Which research method is she using? _____

53. To find out whether people's attitudes regarding an issue vary with their ages, Karen distributes the same survey to groups of people in their 20s, 30s, 40s, 50s, and 60s. Karen is evidently conducting _____ research.

Cautions and Challenges from Science

54. A number that indicates the degree of relationship between two variables is a _____ . To say that two variables are related in this way _____ (does/does not) necessarily imply that one caused the other. A correlation is _____ if both variables tend to _____ together; a correlation is _____ if one variable tends to _____ when the other _____ ; a correlation is _____ if there is no evident connection between the two variables.

55. Developmental researchers work from a set of moral principles that constitute their _____ _____ _____ . Researchers who study humans must obtain _____ _____ , which refers to written permission, and ensure that their participants are not _____ and that they are allowed to stop at any time. The guidelines for research are set by the _____ _____ _____ at most medical and educational institutions.

56. To ensure that research is not unintentionally slanted, it must be _____ , so _____ is possible.

STUDY TIP A common mistake in understanding correlation is the belief that a negative correlation indicates a weak or absent relationship between two variables. Remember that correlation does not prove causation; it indicates only the degree to which you can predict changes in one variable from another. The strength of a correlation, indicated by its numerical value, is independent of the direction (positive or negative) of the relationship. A negative correlation simply means that two variables change in opposite directions, such as when sales of hot chocolate decrease as the average daily temperature increases.

APPLICATION:

57. If height and body weight are correlated, which of the following is true?
    a. There is a cause-and-effect relationship between height and weight.
    b. Knowing a person's height, we can predict his or her weight.
    c. All people of the same height will weigh the same amount.
    d. None of these facts is true.

Progress Test 1

Multiple-Choice Questions

Circle your answers to the following questions and check them against the answers at the end of this chapter. If your answer is incorrect, read the explanation for why it is incorrect and then consult the text.

1. The *science of human development* is defined as the study of
   a. how and why people change or remain the same over time.
   b. psychosocial influences on aging.
   c. individual differences in learning over the life span.
   d. all of these factors.

2. The research method that involves the use of open-ended questions and obtains answers that are not easily translated into categories is
   a. the survey.
   b. qualitative research.
   c. cross-sectional study.
   d. quantitative research.

3. Nature is to nurture as
   a. environment is to genes.
   b. genes are to environment.
   c. continuity is to discontinuity.
   d. discontinuity is to continuity.

4. Dynamic-systems theory emphasizes the idea(s) that
   a. human development is always changing and that change in one area affects all others.
   b. developmental science should emphasize quantitative data.
   c. a person's position in society is determined primarily by social factors such as income and education.
   d. concepts such as race are based on social perceptions.

5. The ecological-systems approach to developmental psychology focuses on the
   a. biochemistry of the body systems.
   b. macrosystems only.
   c. internal thinking processes.
   d. overall environment of development.

6. The science of development focuses on
   a. the sources of continuity from the beginning of life to the end.
   b. the sources of discontinuity throughout life.
   c. the "nonlinear" character of human development.
   d. all of this information.

7. A hypothesis is a
   a. conclusion.
   b. prediction to be tested.
   c. statistical test.
   d. correlation.

8. A developmentalist who is interested in studying the influences of a person's immediate environment on his or her behavior is focusing on which system?
   a. mesosystem   c. microsystem
   b. macrosystem   d. exosystem

9. Socioeconomic status is determined by a combination of variables, including
   a. age, education, and income.
   b. income, ethnicity, and occupation.
   c. income, education, and occupation.
   d. age, ethnicity, and occupation.

10. To say that developmental science is empirical means that it
    a. is theoretical in nature.
    b. is hypothetical in nature.
    c. is based on observation, experience, or experiment.
    d. has all of these characteristics.

11. In an experiment that tests the effects of group size on individual effort in a tug-of-war task, the number of people in each group is the
    a. hypothesis.
    b. independent variable.
    c. dependent variable.
    d. level of significance.

12. Which research method would be most appropriate for investigating the relationship between parents' religious beliefs and their attitudes toward middle-school sex education?
    a. experimentation
    b. longitudinal research
    c. naturalistic observation
    d. the survey

13. To establish cause, which type of research study would an investigator conduct?
    a. an experiment
    b. a survey
    c. scientific observation
    d. cross-sectional research

14. Developmentalists who carefully observe the behavior of schoolchildren during recess are using a research method known as
    a. the case study.
    b. cross-sectional research.
    c. scientific observation.
    d. cross-sequential research.

15. An example of longitudinal research would be an investigator comparing the performance of
    a. several different age groups on a memory test.
    b. the same group of people, at different ages, on a test of memory.
    c. an experimental group and a comparison group on a test of memory.
    d. several different age groups on a test of memory as each group is tested repeatedly over a period of years.

True or False Items

Write T (*true*) or F (*false*) on the line in front of each statement.

_____ 1. Scientists rarely repeat an experiment.
_____ 2. The case study of David clearly demonstrates that for some children only nature (or heredity) is important.
_____ 3. Observation usually indicates a clear relationship between cause and effect.
_____ 4. Each social context influences development independently.
_____ 5. Cohort differences are an example of the impact of the social context on development.
_____ 6. Every trait of an individual can be molded into different forms and shapes.
_____ 7. People of different ethnic groups can all share one culture.

_____ 8. The influences between and within Bronfenbrenner's systems are unidirectional and independent.
_____ 9. Longitudinal research is particularly useful in studying development over a long age span.
_____ 10. The concepts of critical periods and sensitive periods do not apply to human development.

Progress Test 2

Progress Test 2 should be completed during a final chapter review. Answer the following questions after you thoroughly understand the correct answers for the Chapter Review and Progress Test 1.

Multiple-Choice Questions

1. An individual's personal sphere of development refers to his or her
    a. microsystem and mesosystem.
    b. exosystem.
    c. macrosystem.
    d. microsystem, mesosystem, exosystem, macrosystem, and chronosystem.

2. The most important principle of the developmental research code of ethics is
    a. never physically or psychologically harm those who are involved in research.
    b. maintain confidentiality at all costs.
    c. obtain informed consent from all participants.
    d. ensure that participants do not understand the true purpose of their research study.

3. The difference-equals-deficit error occurs when a person falsely believes that
    a. genes exert a stronger influence on developmental abnormalities than the environment.
    b. the environment exerts a stronger influence on developmental abnormalities than genes.
    c. nature and nurture contribute equally to deviations from average development.
    d. deviations from average development are necessarily inferior.

4. According to the ecological-systems approach, the macrosystem would include
    a. the peer group.
    b. the community.
    c. cultural values.
    d. the family.

5. An idea that is built more on shared perceptions than on objective reality is
   a. a cohort effect.
   b. empirical.
   c. a social construction.
   d. a hypothesis.

6. In an experiment, the treatment of interest is given to the _____ group; the no-treatment group is the _____ group.
   a. experimental; control
   b. control; experimental
   c. dependent; independent
   d. independent; dependent

7. A cohort is defined as a group of people
   a. of similar national origin.
   b. who share a common language.
   c. born within a few years of one another.
   d. who share the same religion.

8. In a test of the effects of noise, groups of students performed a proofreading task in a noisy or a quiet room. To what group were students in the noisy room assigned?
   a. experimental
   b. comparison
   c. randomly assigned
   d. dependent

9. In differentiating ethnicity and culture, we note that
   a. ethnicity is an exclusively biological phenomenon.
   b. an ethnic group is a group of people who were born within a few years of one another.
   c. people of many ethnic groups can share one culture, yet maintain their ethnic identities.
   d. racial identity is always an element of culture.

10. If developmentalists discovered that poor people are happier than wealthy people, this would indicate that wealth and happiness are
    a. unrelated.
    b. correlated.
    c. examples of nature and nurture, respectively.
    d. causally related.

11. The plasticity of development refers to the fact that
    a. development is not always linear.
    b. each human life must be understood as embedded in many contexts.
    c. there are many reciprocal connections between childhood and adulthood.
    d. human characteristics can be molded into different forms and shapes.

12. In an experiment that tests the effects of noise level on mood, mood is the
    a. hypothesis.
    b. independent variable.
    c. dependent variable.
    d. scientific observation.

13. Which of the following statements concerning ethnicity and culture is not true?
    a. Ethnicity is determined genetically.
    b. Race is a social construction.
    c. Racial identity is an element of ethnicity.
    d. Ethnic identity provides people with shared values and beliefs.

14. From ages 2 to 10, children ordinarily gain a few pounds each year. This is an example of
    a. continuity in development.
    b. discontinuity in development.
    c. multidirectional development.
    d. developmental plasticity.

15. Maya explains to her friend that experts today view race as a social construction. By this, she means that race is
    a. a valid biological category.
    b. a meaningless concept.
    c. an idea created by society.
    d. none of these answers.

Matching Items

Match each definition or description with its corresponding term.

Terms

_____ 1. independent variable
_____ 2. dependent variable
_____ 3. culture
_____ 4. replicate
_____ 5. chronosystem
_____ 6. exosystem
_____ 7. mesosystem
_____ 8. socioeconomic status
_____ 9. cohort
_____ 10. ethnic group
_____ 11. cross-sectional research
_____ 12. longitudinal research
_____ 13. continuity
_____ 14. discontinuity

Definitions or Descriptions

a. group of people born within a few years of one another
b. determined by a person's income, education, occupation, and so on
c. research study comparing people of different ages at the same time
d. the historical conditions that affect development
e. collection of people who share certain attributes, such as national origin
f. shared values, patterns of behavior, and customs maintained by people in a specific setting
g. local institutions such as schools
h. the variable manipulated in an experiment
i. connections between microsystems
j. to repeat a study and obtain the same findings
k. the variable measured in an experiment
l. research study retesting one group of people at several different times
m. stability in development
n. lack of stability in development

Key Terms

Using your own words, write a brief definition or explanation of each of the following terms on a separate piece of paper.

1. science of human development
2. scientific method
3. hypothesis
4. empirical evidence
5. replication
6. nature
7. nurture
8. life-span perspective
9. critical period
10. sensitive period
11. ecological-systems approach
12. cohort
13. socioeconomic status (SES)
14. culture

15. social construction
16. difference-equals-deficit error
17. ethnic group
18. race
19. epigenetic
20. dynamic-systems approach
21. differential sensitivity
22. scientific observation
23. experiment
24. independent variable
25. dependent variable
26. survey
27. case study
28. cross-sectional research
29. longitudinal research
30. cross-sequential research
31. correlation

ANSWERS

CHAPTER REVIEW

1. how and why people—all people, everywhere, of every age—change or remain the same over time
2. **a.** begin with curiosity and pose a question
   b. develop a hypothesis
   c. test the hypothesis, conducting research to gather empirical evidence
   d. draw conclusions
   e. report the results
3. hypothesis; empirical evidence
4. replicate
5. nature–nurture; nurture; nature
6. affect
7. hypothesis
8. **c.** is the answer. Although any of the other points may be true, none has anything to do with replication.
9. life-span
10. **a.** multidirectional
    b. multicontextual
    c. multicultural
    d. multidisciplinary
    e. plastic
11. linear; continuity; discontinuity
12. critical period; sensitive periods; language
13. ecological-systems; Urie Bronfenbrenner; bioecological
14. microsystem
15. exosystem
16. macrosystem
17. chronosystem
18. mesosystem
19. cohort; the same way
20. socioeconomic status; SES
21. culture; social construction
22. do not necessarily indicate; difference-equals-deficit; study all kinds of people, of every age and background
23. Lev Vygotsky; education; guided participation
24. ethnic group
25. race
26. biological; society; social construction
27. multidisciplinary; genetic analysis; Human Genome Project
28. epigenetic; methylation
29. depression; increases and decreases; genetic; biochemical; neurological; experience; cognition
30. plasticity
31. dynamic-systems; body; mind; individual; environment
32. rubella; plasticity
33. differential sensitivity; nature; nurture; sensitive periods
34. **d.** is the answer.
    a. describes the multidirectional nature of development.
    b. describes the multicontextual nature of development.
    c. describes the multicultural nature of development.
35. ecological-systems. Bronfenbrenner, who recommended this approach, argued that developmentalists need to examine all the systems that surround the development of each person.
36. Bronfenbrenner. He advocated an ecological-systems approach.
37. changing social conditions and cohort effects
38. scientific observation
39. natural; laboratory; archival
40. cause
41. experiment; independent; dependent
42. experimental group; comparison group (control group)
43. survey; wording; sequence
44. case study; bias; unlike
45. cross-sectional
46. ages; cohort
47. longitudinal

Longitudinal studies require much more time and effort than cross-sectional research, and that limits the number of participants. Probably the biggest problem comes from the historical context.

48. cross-sequential
49. **c.** is the answer. Room temperature is the variable being manipulated.
50. **c.** is the answer. To determine the effects of caffeine on reaction time, Esteban needs to measure reaction time (the dependent variable) in a comparison group that does not receive caffeine (the independent variable).
51. dependent. The group size would be the independent variable. A hypothesis for this experiment might be that the larger the group, the less effort each person exerts.
52. cross-sequential research. Dr. Weston's research combines the features of cross-sectional research

(comparing people of different ages who share certain characteristics) and longitudinal research (comparing the same group of people over time).

53. cross-sectional. Karen is surveying people of different ages about a particular issue.

54. correlation; does not; positive; increase; negative; increase; decreases; zero

55. code of ethics; informed consent; harmed; Institutional Review Board

56. published; replication

57. **b.** is the answer. Correlation does not imply causation, but it does allow prediction.

PROGRESS TEST 1

Multiple-Choice Questions

1. **a.** is the answer.

   b. & c. The study of development is concerned with a broader range of phenomena, including physical aspects of development, than these answers specify.

2. **b.** is the answer.

   a. In this research method, many people are studied using interviews and/or questionnaires.

   c. In this research method, groups of people who differ in age are compared.

   d. This type of research provides data that can be expressed with numbers.

3. **b.** is the answer.

4. **a.** is the answer.

5. **d.** is the answer. This approach sees development as occurring within five interacting levels, or environments.

6. **d.** is the answer.

7. **b.** is the answer.

8. **c.** is the answer.

   a. This refers to systems that link one system to another.

   b. This refers to cultural values, political philosophies, economic patterns, and social conditions.

   d. This includes the community structures that affect the functioning of smaller systems.

9. **c.** is the answer.

10. **c.** is the answer.

11. **b.** is the answer.

a. A possible hypothesis for this experiment would be that the larger the group, the less hard a given individual will pull.

c. The dependent variable is the measure of individual effort.

d. Significance level refers to the numerical value specifying the possibility that the results of an experiment could have occurred by chance.

12. **d.** is the answer.

   a. Experimentation is appropriate when one is seeking to uncover cause-and-effect relationships; in this example, the researcher is only interested in determining whether the parents' beliefs *predict* their attitudes.

   b. Longitudinal research would be appropriate if the researcher sought to examine the development of these attitudes over a long period.

   c. Mere observation would not allow the researcher to determine the attitudes of the participants.

13. **a.** is the answer.

   b. & c. These research methods do not indicate what causes people to do what they do.

   d. This is a research design to study change over time.

14. **c.** is the answer.

   a. In this method, *one* person is studied over time.

   b. & d. In these research methods, two or more groups of participants are studied and compared.

15. **b.** is the answer

True or False Items

1. F Just the opposite. Scientists always try to replicate their or other people's work.

2. F The case study of David shows that both nature and nurture are important in affecting outcome.

3. F A disadvantage of observation is that the variables are numerous and uncontrolled, and therefore cause-and-effect relationships are difficult to pinpoint.

4. F Each social context affects the way a person develops, and each is affected by the other contexts.

5. T

6. T

7. T

8. F The reverse is true.

9. T

10. F These terms apply to all animals, including humans.

PROGRESS TEST 2

Multiple-Choice Questions

1. **d.** is the answer.

2. **a.** is the answer.

   b. & c. Although these are important aspects of the code of ethics, protecting participants from harm is the most important.

3. **d.** is the answer.

4. **c.** is the answer.

   a. & d. These are part of the microsystem.

   b. This is part of the exosystem.

5. **c.** is the answer.

6. **a.** is the answer.

   c. & d. Independent and dependent refer to treatments and behaviors, respectively.

7. **c.** is the answer.

   a., b., & d. These are attributes of an ethnic group.

8. **a.** is the answer. The experimental group is the one in which the variable or treatment—in this case, noise—is present.

   b. Students in the quiet room would be in the comparison condition.

   c. Presumably, all students in both groups were randomly assigned to their groups.

   d. The word *dependent* refers to a kind of variable in experiments; groups are either experimental or control.

9. **c.** is the answer.

   a. & d. Ethnicity refers to shared attributes, such as ancestry, national origin, religion, and language.

   b. This describes a cohort.

10. **b.** is the answer.

    a. Wealth and happiness clearly *are* related.

    c. For one thing, poverty is clearly an example of nurture, not nature.

    d. Correlation does not imply causation.

11. **d.** is the answer.

12. **c.** is the answer.

    a. Hypotheses make *specific,* testable predictions.

    b. Noise level is the independent variable.

    d. Scientific observation is a research method in which participants are watched, while their behavior is recorded unobtrusively.

13. **a.** is the answer. Ethnic identity is a product of the social environment and the individual's consciousness.

14. **a.** is the answer.

15. **c.** is the answer.

Matching Items

1. h	6. g	11. c
2. k	7. i	12. l
3. f	8. b	13. m
4. j	9. a	14. n
5. d	10. e	

KEY TERMS

1. The **science of human development** seeks to understand how and why all people, everywhere, of every age, change or remain the same over time.

2. The **scientific method** is a way to answer questions that requires empirical research and data-based conclusions. The five basic steps of the scientific method are (1) pose a research question; (2) develop a hypothesis; (3) test the hypothesis; (4) draw conclusions; and (5) report the results, allowing for replication.

3. In the scientific method, a **hypothesis** is a specific, testable prediction.

4. To say that the science of human development relies on **empirical evidence** means that it is based on observation and experimentation, rather than theory alone.

5. **Replication** means to repeat a test of a research hypothesis and to try to obtain the same results using different participants.

6. **Nature** refers to all the traits that a person inherits genetically from his or her parents.

7. **Nurture** refers to all the environmental influences that affect development.

8. The **life-span perspective** is an approach to the study of human development that focuses on all phases of life.

9. A **critical period** is a time when a particular type of developmental growth must happen for normal development to occur.

10. A **sensitive period** is a time when a particular type of development happens most easily.

11. The **ecological-systems approach** to developmental research takes into consideration all the influences from the various contexts of development. (Later renamed *bioecological theory*.)

12. A **cohort** is a group of people who, because they were born within a few years of one another, experience many of the same historical events and cultural shifts.

13. An individual's **socioeconomic status (SES)** is a person's position in society determined by his or her income, education, place of residence, and occupation.

14. A **culture** is a system of shared beliefs, norms, behaviors, and expectations that persist over time and prescribe social behavior and assumptions.

15. A **social construction** is an idea that is based on shared perceptions, not on objective reality.

16. The **difference-equals-deficit error** is the mistaken belief that deviations from average development are always inferior.

17. An **ethnic group** is a collection of people whose ancestors were born in the same region, usually sharing a language, culture, and religion.

18. **Race** is a misleading social construction for a group of people who are regarded (by themselves or others) as distinct on the basis of physical appearance.

19. **Epigenetic** refers to the effects of environmental forces on the expressions of genes.

20. The **dynamic-systems approach** views human development as an ongoing, ever-changing interaction between the body and mind and between the individual and every aspect of the environment.

21. **Differential sensitivity** is the idea that some people are more vulnerable than others to certain experiences.

22. **Scientific observation** is a method of testing a hypothesis by unobtrusively watching and recording participants' behavior in a systematic and objective manner, in the laboratory, in a natural setting, or in searches of archival data.

23. The **experiment** is a research method in which a researcher seeks to determine a cause-and-effect relationship between two variables by manipulating one (the independent variable) while observing changes in the other (the dependent variable).

24. The **independent variable** is the variable that is manipulated in an experiment to observe what effect it has on the dependent variable.

25. The **dependent variable** is the variable that may change as a result of whatever new condition or situation is added in an experiment.

    Example: In the study of the effects of a new drug on memory, the participants' memory is the dependent variable.

26. The **survey** is the research method in which information is collected from a large number of people, either through written questionnaires, personal interviews, or some other means.

27. A **case study** is a research method in which one person is studied in depth.

28. In **cross-sectional research,** groups of people who differ in age but share other important characteristics are compared with regard to the variable under investigation.

29. In **longitudinal research,** the same group of individuals is studied over time to measure both change and stability as they age.

30. **Cross-sequential research** follows a group of people of different ages over time, thus combining the strengths of the cross-sectional and longitudinal methods; also called cohort-sequential research or time-sequential research.

31. **Correlation** is a number between +1.0 and −1.0 indicating the degree of relationship between two variables, such that one is likely (or unlikely) to occur when the other occurs or one is likely to increase (or decrease) when the other increases (or decreases).

Theories of Development

Chapter Overview

After explaining the value of theories in general, this chapter describes and evaluates six theories—psychoanalytic theory, behaviorism, cognitive theory, sociocultural theory, humanism, and evolutionary theory—that will be used throughout the book to present information and to provide a framework for interpreting events and issues in human development. Each theory or perspective has developed a unique vocabulary with which to describe and explain events as well as to organize ideas into a cohesive system of thought.

Three of the theories presented—psychoanalytic theory, behaviorism, and cognitive theory—are "grand theories" that are comprehensive in scope but inadequate in the face of recent research findings. Two of the theories—sociocultural and universal (humanism and evolutionary theory)—are multicultural and multidisciplinary, which makes them particularly pertinent to current developmental science. Together, these developmental theories provide a coherent framework for understanding how and why people change as they grow older. Rather than adopt any one theory exclusively, most developmentalists therefore take an eclectic perspective and use many or all of the theories.

What Will You Know?

The text chapter should be studied one section at a time. Before you read, preview each section by skimming it, noting headings and boldface items. Then read the sections, one at a time, keeping these questions in mind.

1. How does a theory differ from a fact?

2. Does development occur in stages, or more gradually, day by day?

3. What limitations do Freud, Erikson, Watson, Skinner, and Piaget share?

4. Why is it better to use several theories to understand human development rather than just one?

Chapter Review

When you have finished reading the chapter, work through the material that follows to review it. Completing the sentences and answering the questions will enable you to answer the "What Have You Learned?" questions at the end of the text chapter. In some cases, Study Tips explain how best to learn a difficult concept, while Think About It and Applications help you to know how well you understand the material. As you proceed, evaluate your performance for each section by consulting the answers at the end of the chapter. Do not continue with the next section until you understand each answer. If you need to, review or reread the appropriate section in the textbook before continuing.

What Theories Do

1. A systematic statement of principles and generalizations that provides a coherent framework for understanding how and why people change as they grow older is called a

   _____ _____ .

2. Developmental theories form the basis for educated guesses, or

   _____ , about behavior; they generate_____ , and they offer

   _____ guidance.

3. An average measurement of many individuals within a specific group is a _____ .

STUDY TIP As you study this chapter, consider what each of the theories has to say about your own development, as well as that of friends and relatives in other age groups. It is also a good idea to keep the following questions in mind as you study each theory: Which of the theory's principles are generally accepted by contemporary developmentalists? How has the theory been criticized? In what ways does this theory agree with the other theories? In what ways does it disagree?

Grand Theories

4. Psychoanalytic theory interprets human development in terms of inner _____ and _____ , which are_____ (conscious/unconscious) and originate in _____ .

5. According to Freud's _____ theory, children experience sexual pleasures and desires during the first six years as they pass through three stages. From infancy to early childhood to the preschool years, these stages are the_____ stage, the _____ stage, and the _____ stage.

6. One of Freud's most influential ideas was that each stage includes its own potential _____ .

Specify the focus of sexual pleasure and the major developmental need associated with each of Freud's stages.

oral _____

_____

anal _____

_____

phallic _____

_____

genital _____

_____

7. Erik Erikson's theory of development, which focuses on social and cultural influences, describes _____ (number) developmental stages, each characterized by a particular developmental_____

related to the person's relationship to the social and cultural environment. Unlike Freud, Erikson proposed stages of development that _____ (span/do not span) a person's lifetime.

Complete the following chart regarding Erikson's stages of psychosocial development.

Age Period	Stage
Birth to 1 yr.	trust vs. _____
1–3 yrs.	autonomy vs. _____
3–6 yrs.	initiative vs. _____
6–11 yrs.	_____ vs. inferiority
Adolescence	identity vs. _____
Young adulthood	_____ vs. isolation
Middle adulthood	_____ vs. stagnation
Older adulthood	_____ vs. despair

8. A major theory in American psychology, which opposed psychoanalytic theory, was _____ . This theory, which emerged early in the twentieth century under the influence of _____ , is also called _____ theory because of its emphasis on learning behavior step by step.

9. Behaviorists have formulated laws of behavior that are believed to apply _____ (only at certain ages/at all ages). The learning process, which is called _____ , takes two forms: _____ and _____ _____ .

10. In classical conditioning, which was discovered by the Russian scientist _____ and is also called _____ conditioning, a person or an animal learns to associate a(n) _____ stimulus with a meaningful one.

11. According to _____ , the learning of more complex responses is the result of _____ conditioning, in which a person learns that a particular behavior produces a particular _____ , such as a reward. This type of learning is also called _____ conditioning.

12. The process of repeating a consequence to make it more likely that the behavior in question will recur is called _____ .

13. The extension of behaviorism that emphasizes the ways that people learn new behaviors by observing others is called _____ _____ theory. The process whereby a child patterns his or her behavior after a parent or teacher, for example, is called _____ (also called _____ _____).

14. This process is most likely to occur when an observer is_____ or _____ and when the model is _____ .

15. The structure and development of thought processes and the way those thought processes shape our attitudes, beliefs, values, assumptions, and behaviors are the focus of _____ theory. An important pioneer of cognitive theory is _____ .

16. In Piaget's first stage of development, the _____ stage, children experience the world through their senses and motor abilities. This stage occurs between birth and age _____ .

17. According to Piaget, during the preschool years (up to age _____), children are in the _____ stage. A hallmark of this stage is that children begin to think magically and poetically. Another hallmark is that sometimes the child's thinking is _____ , or focused on seeing the world solely from his or her own perspective.

18. Piaget believed that children begin to think logically in a consistent way at about _____ years of age. At this time, they enter the _____ _____stage.

19. In Piaget's final stage, the _____ stage, reasoning expands from the purely concrete to encompass _____

thinking. Piaget believed most children enter this stage by age _____ .

20. According to Piaget, cognitive development is guided by the need to maintain a state of mental balance, called _____ _____ .

21. When new experiences challenge existing understanding, creating a kind of imbalance, the individual experiences_____ _____ , which eventually leads to cognitive growth.

22. According to Piaget, people adapt to new experiences either by reinterpreting them to fit into, or _____ with, old ideas. Some new experiences force people to revamp old ideas so that they can _____ new experiences.

23. A newer approach to cognitive theory, called _____ _____ , compares human thinking to the way a _____ _____ _____ .

24. According to this approach, cognition begins with _____ from the five senses; proceeds to _____ reactions, connections, and stored _____; and concludes with some form of _____ .

STUDY TIP The best way to differentiate between classical conditioning and operant conditioning is to ask yourself two questions: (1) Is the behavior voluntary (operant conditioning) or involuntary (classical conditioning)? (2) Does the learning involve an association between two stimuli (classical conditioning) or between a response and an outcome (operant conditioning)? Test your understanding on the following examples.

---

25. **a.** After receiving a mild shock from the "invisible fence" surrounding his yard, a dog no longer crosses the boundary.

_____

b. You flinch when someone yells, "Duck!"

_____

c. You ask more questions in class after the professor praises you for a good question.

_____

d. The pupil of your eye dilates (opens wider) after you enter a darkened theater.

_____

APPLICATIONS:

26. A pigeon is rewarded for producing a particular response, and so learns to produce that response to obtain rewards. Psychologists describe this chain of events as

_____ _____ .

27. Professor Swenson believes that much of our learning involves associating neutral stimuli with meaningful stimuli. He would most likely agree with the writings of _____ .

28. A confirmed neo-Freudian, Dr. Thomas strongly endorses the views of Erik Erikson. She would most likely disagree with Freud regarding the importance of
a. unconscious forces in development.
b. irrational forces in personality formation.
c. early childhood experiences.
d. sexual urges in development.

29. After watching several older children climbing around a new jungle-gym, 5-year-old Jennie decides to try it herself. Which of the following best accounts for her behavior?
a. modeling
b. plasticity
c. cohort effect
d. classical conditioning

30. I am 8 years old. Although I understand some logical principles, I have trouble thinking about hypothetical concepts. According to Piaget, I am in the _____ _____ stage of development.

31. Two-year-old Jamail has a simple understanding for "Dad." Each time he encounters a man with a child, he calls him "Dad." When he learns that these other men are not "Dad," Jamail experiences _____ .

32. Four-year-old Bjorn takes great pride in successfully undertaking new activities. Erikson would probably say that Bjorn is capably meeting the psychosocial challenge of _____

_____ _____ .

33. Dr. Bazzi believes that development is a life-long process of gradual and continuous growth. Based on this information, with which of the following theories would Dr. Bazzi most likely agree?
a. Piaget's cognitive theory
b. Erikson's psychosocial theory
c. Freud's psychoanalytic theory
d. behaviorism

Newer Theories

Identify several background variables that limited the perspectives of the grand theorists.

34. In contrast to the grand theories, the newer theories draw from the findings of _____ (one/many) discipline(s). They are also _____ .

35. Sociocultural theory sees human development as the result of _____ _____ between developing persons and the surrounding _____ and _____ forces.

36. The pioneer of this perspective was _____ , who was primarily interested in the development of _____ competencies.

37. Vygotsky believed that these competencies result from the interaction between _____ and more skilled members of the society, acting as _____ .

38. In Vygotsky's view, the best way to accomplish the goals of learning is through a(n) _____ _____ _____ , in which the tutor engages the learner in joint activities.

39. According to Vygotsky, a tutor draws a child into the _____ _____ _____ _____ ,

which is defined as the range of skills that a person can acquire with _____ but cannot master independently.

40. Psychoanalytic theory is limited by its emphasis on the_____ _____ . Behaviorism is limited by failure to recognize the existence of _____ _____ . The limits of these theories were apparent to _____ and_____ , who founded the theory called _____ .

41. According to Maslow, all people have the same basic _____ , which form a _____ . In order, these are _____ , _____ _____ _____ , _____ _____ _____ , and _____ .

42. Rogers thought people should give each other _____ _____ _____ .

43. Humanists emphasize _____ (what people have in common/national, ethic, and cultural differences). Humanism flourished during the decade of the_____ .

Cite several criticisms of humanism.

44. The application of Darwin's _____ theory to the study of human development is relatively recent. According to this theory, two long-standing and _____ based drives for

every species are _____ and _____ . Through the process of _____ _____ , genes that enhance survival and reproductive ability are selected, over generations, to become more frequent.

45. One controversial idea stemming from evolutionary theory is that women and men are selected for _____ (the same/different) patterns of mating and sexual behavior. According to this argument, women benefit by seeking _____ (one steady mate/multiple sexual partners), while men spread their genes more widely if they have _____ (one/many) sexual partners and dozens of offspring. Critics of this idea contend that a _____ explanation rather than a biological one accounts for these differences.

STUDY TIP A helpful way to distinguish the grand theories of development (psychoanalytic theory, behaviorism, and cognitive theory) from the newer theories (sociocultural theory and the universal perspective [humanism and evolutionary theory]) is to remember that while each of the grand theories emphasizes a single factor in development (unconscious processes in the case of psychoanalytic theory, for example), the newer theories are broader in scope in that each draws upon multiple factors in explaining development. Evolutionary theory, for example, emphasizes inherited genetic tendencies that fostered survival of the human species, while sociocultural theory focuses on how each person's development is shaped by unique interactions with tutors and other environmental experiences. Humanism focuses on the shared impulses and common needs of all humanity.

APPLICATIONS:

46. Dr. Ivey's research focuses on the genetic tendencies that shape each child's characteristic way of reacting to environmental experiences. Evidently, Dr. Ivey is working from a(n) _____ perspective.

47. Which of the following is the best example of an apprenticeship in thinking?

    a. After watching her mother change her baby sister's diaper, 4-year-old Brandy changes her doll's diaper.

    b. To help her son learn to pour liquids, Sandra engages him in a bathtub game involving pouring water from cups of different sizes.

    c. Seeing his father shaving, 3-year-old Kyle pretends to shave by rubbing whipped cream on his face.

    d. After reading a recipe in a magazine, Jack gathers ingredients from the cupboard.

48. Dr. Mickelson is an evolutionary psychologist. She notes that people in Sweden are lactose tolerant because of _____ .

49. The school psychologist believes that each child's developmental needs can be understood only by taking into consideration the child's broader social and cultural background. Evidently, the school psychologist is working within the _____ perspective.

What Theories Contribute

50. Which major theory of development emphasizes

    a. the importance of culture in fostering development? _____

    b. the ways in which thought processes affect actions? _____

    c. environmental influences?

    _____

    d. the impact of unconscious impulses on development? _____

    e. the interaction of genes and the environment?

    _____

    f. needs and impulses shared by all humans?

    _____

51. Which major theory of development has been criticized for

    a. being too mechanistic?

    _____

    b. undervaluing emotions?

    _____

    c. being too subjective?

    _____

    d. neglecting the human differences?

    _____

    e. neglecting individual initiative?

    _____

    f. placing too much emphasis on personal freedom?

    _____

52. Because no one theory can encompass all human behavior, most developmentalists prefer a(n) _____ perspective, which capitalizes on the strengths of all the theories.

STUDY TIP Most students come to class with a bias or predisposition toward one or more of the basic theories of development presented in this chapter. As you read through the descriptions of the theories, which makes the most sense to you? Why? Think about some specific aspect of your own biosocial, cognitive, or psychosocial development. Which theoretical perspective(s) seem to offer the best account of your developmental history? Do you find yourself drawing from different theories?

To reinforce your understanding of the key differences in the various theories, consider the following questions.

53. a. Which of the theories are stage theories?

    b. Which theory(ies) emphasize(s) conscious organization of experience? Unconscious urges? Observable behavior? Individuality?

    c. Which theory(ies) emphasize(s) the impact of early experiences on development?

    d. How does each theory view the child?

e. Do the theories use the same methodology? How does each make use of the scientific method?

f. How do the theories view adult development?

APPLICATION:

54. Dr. Cleaver's developmental research draws upon insights from several theoretical perspectives. Evidently, Dr. Cleaver is working from a(n) _____ perspective.

Progress Test 1

Multiple-Choice Questions

Circle your answers to the following questions and check them with the answers at the end of the chapter. If your answer is incorrect, read the explanation for why it is incorrect and then consult the text.

1. The purpose of a developmental theory is to
    a. provide a broad and coherent view of the complex influences on human development.
    b. offer guidance for practical issues encountered by parents, teachers, and therapists.
    c. generate testable hypotheses about development.
    d. accomplish all of these goals.

2. Which developmental theory emphasizes the influence of unconscious drives and motives on behavior?
    a. psychoanalytic
    b. behaviorism
    c. cognitive
    d. sociocultural

3. Which of the following is the correct order of the psychosexual stages proposed by Freud?
    a. oral stage; anal stage; phallic stage; latency; genital stage
    b. anal stage; oral stage; phallic stage; latency; genital stage
    c. oral stage; anal stage; genital stage; latency; phallic stage
    d. anal stage; oral stage; genital stage; latency; phallic stage

4. Erikson's psychosocial theory of human development describes
    a. eight crises all people are thought to face.
    b. four psychosocial stages and a latency period.
    c. the same number of stages as Freud's, but with different names.
    d. a stage theory that is not psychoanalytic.

5. Which of the following theories does NOT belong with the others?
    a. psychoanalytic
    b. behaviorism
    c. sociocultural
    d. cognitive

6. An American psychologist who explained complex human behaviors in terms of operant conditioning was
    a. Lev Vygotsky.
    b. Ivan Pavlov.
    c. B. F. Skinner.
    d. Jean Piaget.

7. Pavlov's dogs learned to salivate at the sound of a tone because they associated the tone with food. Pavlov's experiment with dogs was an early demonstration of
    a. classical conditioning.
    b. operant conditioning.
    c. positive reinforcement.
    d. social learning.

8. A child who calls all furry animals "doggie" will experience cognitive _____ when she encounters a hairless breed for the first time. This may cause her to revamp her concept of "dog" in order to _____ the new experience.
   a. disequilibrium; accommodate
   b. disequilibrium; assimilate
   c. equilibrium; accommodate
   d. equilibrium; assimilate

9. Modeling, an integral part of social learning theory, is so called because it
   a. follows the scientific model of learning.
   b. molds character.
   c. follows the immediate reinforcement model.
   d. involves people's patterning their behavior after that of others.

10. Which developmental theory suggests that each person is born with genetic tendencies that direct development?
    a. sociocultural   c. behaviorism
    b. cognitive   d. evolutionary

11. Which grand theory of development focuses on emotions?
    a. psychoanalytic   c. cognitive
    b. behaviorism   d. sociocultural

12. Which is the correct sequence of stages in Piaget's theory of cognitive development?
    a. sensorimotor, preoperational, concrete operational, formal operational
    b. sensorimotor, preoperational, formal operational, concrete operational
    c. preoperational, sensorimotor, concrete operational, formal operational
    d. preoperational, sensorimotor, formal operational, concrete operational

13. When an individual's existing understanding no longer fits his or her present experiences, the result is called
    a. a psychosocial crisis.
    b. equilibrium.
    c. disequilibrium.
    d. negative reinforcement.

14. Children with ADHD have a functional deficit in which part of the brain?
    a. temporal lobe
    b. occipital lobe
    c. hypothalamus
    d. fronto-striatal

15. The zone of proximal development refers to
    a. a stage during which the child exhibits preoperational thinking.
    b. the influence of a pleasurable stimulus on behavior.
    c. the range of skills a learner can exercise with assistance but cannot perform independently.
    d. the tendency of a child to model an admired adult's behavior.

True or False Items

Write T (true) or F (false) on the line in front of each statement.

_____ 1. Behaviorists study what people actually do, not what they might be thinking.

_____ 2. Erikson's eight developmental stages are centered not on a body part but on each person's relationship to the social environment.

_____ 3. Sociocultural theory arose from the fields of archeology, biology, and ethology.

_____ 4. Few developmental theorists today believe that humans have instincts or abilities that arise from our species' biological heritage.

_____ 5. Of the major developmental theories, cognitive theory gives the most emphasis to the interaction of genes and experience in shaping development.

_____ 6. According to Piaget, a state of cognitive equilibrium must be attained before cognitive growth can occur.

_____ 7. In part, cognitive theory examines how an individual's understandings and expectations affect his or her behavior.

_____ 8. According to Piaget, children begin to think only when they reach preschool age.

_____ 9. Most contemporary researchers have adopted an eclectic perspective on development.

_____ 10. The central idea of humanism is that all people have the same basic needs.

Progress Test 2

Progress Test 2 should be completed during a final chapter review. Answer the following questions after you thoroughly understand the correct answers for the Chapter Review and Progress Test 1.

Multiple-Choice Questions

1. Which developmental theorist has been criticized for suggesting that every child, in every culture, in every nation, passes through certain fixed stages?
   a. Freud
   b. Erikson
   c. Piaget
   d. all of these theorists

2. Of the following terms, the one that does NOT describe a stage of Freud's theory of childhood sexuality is
   a. phallic.
   b. oral.
   c. anal.
   d. sensorimotor.

3. We are more likely to imitate the behavior of others if we particularly admire and identify with them. This belief finds expression in
   a. stage theory.
   b. sociocultural theory.
   c. social learning theory.
   d. Pavlov's experiments.

4. Dr. Iverson believes the computer, and how it processes data, is an excellent model for studying human thinking. Dr. Iverson is evidently a proponent of which theory?
   a. information processing
   b. humanism
   c. evolutionary theory
   d. behaviorism

5. According to Erikson, an adult who has difficulty establishing a secure, mutual relationship with a life partner might never have resolved the crisis of
   a. initiative versus guilt.
   b. autonomy versus shame and doubt.
   c. intimacy versus isolation.
   d. trust versus mistrust.

6. Who would be most likely to agree with the statement, "Anything can be learned"?
   a. Jean Piaget
   b. Lev Vygotsky
   c. John Watson
   d. Erik Erikson

7. Classical conditioning is to _____ as operant conditioning is to _____ .
   a. Skinner; Pavlov
   b. Watson; Vygotsky
   c. Pavlov; Skinner
   d. Vygotsky; Watson

8. Behaviorists have found that they can often solve a person's seemingly complex psychological problem by
   a. analyzing the patient.
   b. admitting the existence of the unconscious.
   c. altering the environment.
   d. administering well-designed punishments.

9. According to Piaget, an infant first comes to know the world through
   a. senses and motor abilities.
   b. naming and counting.
   c. preoperational thought.
   d. instruction from parents.

10. According to Piaget, the stage of cognitive development that generally characterizes preschool children (2 to 6 years old) is the
    a. preoperational stage.
    b. sensorimotor stage.
    c. oral stage.
    d. psychosocial stage.

11. In Piaget's theory, cognitive equilibrium refers to
    a. a state of mental balance.
    b. a kind of imbalance that leads to cognitive growth.
    c. the ultimate stage of cognitive development.
    d. the first stage in the processing of information.

12. You teach your dog to "speak" by giving her a treat each time she does so. This is an example of
    a. classical conditioning.
    b. respondent conditioning.
    c. reinforcement.
    d. modeling.

13. A child who must modify an old idea in order to incorporate a new experience is using the process of
    a. assimilation.
    b. accommodation.
    c. cognitive equilibrium.
    d. unconditional positive regard.

14. Children with ADHD have a functional deficit in a part of the brain that makes it hard for them to
    a. understand language.
    b. interpret emotions from facial expressions.
    c. stay awake.
    d. walk normally.

15. A major pioneer of the sociocultural perspective was
    a. Jean Piaget.
    b. Albert Bandura.
    c. Lev Vygotsky.
    d. Ivan Pavlov.

Matching Items

Match each theory or term with its corresponding description or definition.

Theories or Terms

_____ 1. psychoanalytic theory
_____ 2. humanism
_____ 3. behaviorism
_____ 4. social learning theory
_____ 5. cognitive theory
_____ 6. unconditional positive regard
_____ 7. sociocultural theory
_____ 8. conditioning
_____ 9. newer theories
_____ 10. modeling
_____ 11. evolutionary theory

Descriptions or Definitions

a. emphasizes the impact of the immediate environment on behavior
b. sociocultural, evolutionary, humanism
c. emphasizes that people learn by observing others
d. seeing others with appreciation and without conditions
e. a process of learning, as described by Pavlov or Skinner
f. emphasizes the "hidden dramas" that influence behavior
g. emphasizes the cultural context in development
h. emphasizes how our thoughts shape our actions
i. the process whereby a person learns by imitating someone else's behavior
j. emphasizes inherited tendencies that foster species' survival and reproduction
k. theory that genes determine every aspect of development

Key Terms

Using your own words, write a brief definition or explanation of each of the following terms on a separate piece of paper.

1. developmental theory
2. norm
3. psychoanalytic theory
4. behaviorism
5. conditioning
6. classical conditioning
7. operant conditioning
8. reinforcement
9. social learning theory
10. modeling
11. cognitive theory
12. cognitive equilibrium
13. assimilation
14. accommodation
15. information processing theory
16. sociocultural theory
17. apprenticeship in thinking
18. guided participation
19. humanism
20. selective adaptation
21. eclectic perspective

ANSWERS

CHAPTER REVIEW

1. developmental theory
2. hypotheses; discoveries; practical
3. norm
4. motives; drives; unconscious; childhood
5. psychoanalytic; oral; anal; phallic
6. conflicts

Oral stage: The mouth is the focus of pleasurable sensations, and sucking is the most stimulating activity.

Anal stage: The anus is the focus of pleasurable sensations, and toilet training is the most important activity.

Phallic stage: Pleasure is derived from genital stimulation.

Genital stage: Mature sexual interests that last throughout adulthood emerge.

7. eight; crisis (challenge); span

Age Period	Stage
Birth to 1 yr.	trust vs. mistrust
1–3 yrs.	autonomy vs. shame and doubt
3–6 yrs.	initiative vs. guilt
6–11 yrs.	industry vs. inferiority
Adolescence	identity vs. role confusion
Young adulthood	intimacy vs. isolation
Middle adulthood	generativity vs. stagnation
Older adulthood	integrity vs. despair

8. behaviorism; John B. Watson; learning

9. at all ages; conditioning; classical conditioning; operant conditioning

10. Ivan Pavlov; respondent; neutral

11. B. F. Skinner; operant; consequence; instrumental

12. reinforcement

13. social learning; modeling; observational learning

14. uncertain; inexperienced; admirable and powerful, nurturing, or similar to the observer

15. cognitive; Jean Piaget

16. sensorimotor; 2

17. 6; preoperational; egocentric

18. 6; concrete operational

19. formal operational; abstract (hypothetical); 12

20. cognitive equilibrium

21. cognitive disequilibrium

22. assimilate; accommodate

23. information processing; computer processes data

24. input; brain; memories; output

25. The examples in a. and c. are operant conditioning because a response's recurrence is determined by its consequences. The answers to b. and d. are classical conditioning because two stimuli are associated.

   a. operant

   b. classical

   c. operant

   d. classical

26. operant conditioning. This is an example of operant conditioning because a response recurs due to its consequences.

27. Pavlov. In classical conditioning, developed by Pavlov, an organism comes to associate a neutral stimulus with a meaningful one and then responds to the former stimulus as if it were the latter.

28. d. is the answer. Unlike Freud, who emphasized sexual urges in development, Erikson put more emphasis on family and culture.

29. a. is the answer. Evidently, Jennie has learned by observing the other children at play, which is key to social learning theory.

30. concrete operational. During Piaget's concrete operational stage, children can understand and apply logical operations but only to what they personally see, hear, touch, and experience.

31. disequilibrium. When Jamail experiences something that conflicts with his existing understanding, he experiences disequilibrium. Piaget believed that this could lead to cognitive growth.

32. initiative vs. guilt. Children at this stage feel either adventurous or guilty.

33. d. is the answer. Each of the other theories emphasizes that development is a discontinuous process that occurs in stages.

The grand theorists were all men, born more than a hundred years ago, whose ancestors were from Western Europe and North America.

34. many; multicultural

35. dynamic interaction; societal; cultural

36. Lev Vygotsky; cognitive

37. novices; tutors (or mentors)

38. apprenticeship in thinking

39. zone of proximal development; help

40. animalistic id; free will; Abraham Maslow; Carl Rogers; humanism

41. needs; hierarchy; physiological, safety and security, love and belonging, respect and esteem, self-actualization

42. unconditional positive regard

43. what people have in common; 1960s

During the 1960s, humanism was blamed for the abuse of psychedelic drugs, for sexual liberation, and for New Age philosophy. Humanism is also criticized for not appreciating the diverse cultures of people.

44. evolutionary; biologically; survival; reproduction; selective adaptation

45. different; one steady mate; many; sociocultural

46. evolutionary. Although based in the disciplines of biology, genetics, and chemistry, evolutionary theory also emphasizes the influence of the environment on genes.

47. **b.** is the answer. An apprenticeship in thinking involves coaching by a tutor. a. and c. are both examples of modeling. In d., Jack is simply following written directions.

48. selective adaptation. People with the gene that allows for easy digestion of cow's milk were more likely to survive and reproduce in cattle-raising locations.

49. sociocultural. This theory emphasizes a dynamic interaction in which mentors provide an apprenticeship in thinking in a zone of proximal development.

50. **a.** sociocultural
    b. cognitive
    c. behaviorism
    d. psychoanalytic
    e. evolutionary
    f. humanism (universal perspective)

51. **a.** behaviorism
    b. cognitive
    c. psychoanalytic
    d. evolutionary (and to some extent behaviorism)
    e. sociocultural
    f. humanism (universal perspective)

52. eclectic

53. **a.** Psychoanalytic and cognitive theories are stage theories.
    b. Conscious experience: behaviorism, sociocultural, evolutionary, humanism
    Unconscious urges: psychoanalytic
    Observable behavior: behaviorism
    Individuality: humanism
    c. Freud's psychoanalysis emphasizes early experiences. Erikson considers childhood an important period, but extends development through old age.

d. Freud's psychoanalysis viewed childhood as all-important. Erikson extends development through adulthood. Piaget considered childhood a major learning period. The nonstage theories consider childhood important but do not limit development to that period.

e. Freud, Erikson, Piaget, Rogers, Maslow, and Vygotsky all used more qualitative methodology than the behaviorists, social learning theorists, and evolutionary theorists. They focused on observation rather than quantitative research.

f. Freud believed that development occurred during childhood and that nothing significant occurred during adulthood. Erikson believed that development was lifelong. The nonstage theorists also believed that development continued throughout the life span.

54. eclectic. Eclectic theorists draw from any of the many theories as the situation dictates.

PROGRESS TEST 1

Multiple-Choice Questions

1. **d.** is the answer

2. **a.** is the answer.
   b. Behaviorism emphasizes the influence of the immediate environment on behavior.
   c. Cognitive theory emphasizes the impact of *conscious* thought processes on behavior.
   d. Sociocultural theory emphasizes the influence on development of social interaction in a specific cultural context.

3. **a.** is the answer.

4. **a.** is the answer.
   b. & c. Whereas Freud identified four stages of psychosexual development, Erikson proposed eight psychosocial stages.
   d. Although his theory places greater emphasis on social and cultural forces than Freud's did, Erikson's theory is nevertheless classified as a psychoanalytic theory.

5. **c.** is the answer. Sociocultural theory is a newer theory.
   a., b., & d. Each of these is an example of a grand theory.

6. **c.** is the answer.

7. **a.** is the answer. In classical conditioning, a neutral stimulus—in this case, the bell—is associated with a meaningful stimulus—in this case, food.

b. In operant conditioning, the consequences of a voluntary response determine the likelihood of its being repeated. Salivation is an involuntary response.

c. & d. Positive reinforcement and social learning pertain to voluntary, or operant, responses.

8. **a.** is the answer.

   b. Because the dog is not furry, the child's concept of dog cannot incorporate (assimilate) the discrepant experience without being revamped.

   c. & d. Equilibrium exists when ideas (such as what a dog is) and experiences (such as seeing a hairless dog) do not clash.

9. **d.** is the answer.

   a. & c. These can be true in all types of learning.

   b. This was not discussed as an aspect of developmental theory.

10. **d.** is the answer.

    a. & c. Sociocultural theory and behaviorism focus almost entirely on environmental factors (nurture) in development.

    b. Cognitive theory emphasizes the developing person's own mental activity but ignores genetic differences in individuals.

11. **a.** is the answer.

    b. Behaviorism focuses on actions.

    c. Cognitive theory focuses on thoughts.

    d. This is not a grand theory.

12. **a.** is the answer.

13. **c.** is the answer.

    a. This refers to the core of Erikson's psychosocial stages, which deals with people's interactions with the environment.

    b. Equilibrium occurs when existing schemes *do* fit a person's current experiences.

    d. Negative reinforcement is the removal of a stimulus as a consequence of a desired behavior.

14. **d.** is the answer.

15. **c.** is the answer.

    a. This is a stage of Piaget's cognitive theory.

    b. This describes positive reinforcement.

    d. This is an aspect of social learning theory.

True or False Items

1. T

2. T

3. F   This is true of evolutionary theory. Sociocultural theory draws on research in education, anthropology, and history.

4. F   This assumption lies at the heart of evolutionary theory.

5. F   Evolutionary theory emphasizes the interaction of genes and experience.

6. F   On the contrary, *dis*equilibrium often fosters greater growth.

7. T

8. F   The hallmark of Piaget's theory is that, at every age, individuals think about the world in unique ways.

9. T

10. T

PROGRESS TEST 2

Multiple-Choice Questions

1. **d.** is the answer.

2. **d.** is the answer. This is one of Piaget's stages of cognitive development.

3. **c.** is the answer.

4. **a.** is the answer.

   b. This term was not used to describe development.

   c. & d. These terms describe the processes by which cognitive concepts incorporate (assimilate) new experiences or are revamped (accommodated) by them.

5. **d.** is the answer.

6. **c.** is the answer.

   a. Piaget formulated a cognitive theory of development.

   b. Vygotsky formulated a sociocultural theory of development.

   d. Erikson formulated a psychoanalytic theory of development.

7. **c.** is the answer.

8. **c.** is the answer.

   a. & b. These are psychoanalytic approaches to treating psychological problems.

   d. Behaviorists generally do not recommend the use of punishment.

9. **a.** is the answer. These behaviors are typical of infants in the sensorimotor stage.

   b., c., & d. These are typical of older children.

10. **a.** is the answer.

   b. The sensorimotor stage describes development from birth until 2 years of age.

   c. This is a psychoanalytic stage described by Freud.

   d. This is not the name of a stage; "psychosocial" refers to Erikson's stage theory.

11. **a.** is the answer.

   b. This describes *dis*equilibrium.

   c. This is formal operational thinking.

   d. Piaget's theory does not propose stages of information processing.

12. **c.** is the answer.

   a. & b. Teaching your dog in this way is an example of operant, rather than classical (respondent), conditioning.

   d. Modeling involves learning by imitating others.

13. **b.** is the answer.

   a. Assimilation occurs when new experiences do *not* clash with existing ideas.

   c. Cognitive equilibrium is mental balance, which occurs when ideas and experiences do *not* clash.

   d. This is Rogers' term for how people should accept others without conditions.

14. **b.** is the answer.

   a., c., & d. These deficits are not observed in children with ADHD.

15. **c.** is the answer.

Matching Items

1. f	5. h	9. b
2. k	6. d	10. i
3. a	7. g	11. j
4. c	8. e	

KEY TERMS

1. *A* **developmental theory** is a systematic statement of principles and generalizations that provides a coherent framework for understanding how and why people change as they grow older.

2. A **norm** is an average, typical, or standard level of development among a large group of individuals.

3. **Psychoanalytic theory,** a grand theory, interprets human development in terms of inner drives and motives, many of which are irrational and unconscious.

4. **Behaviorism,** a grand theory, emphasizes the laws and processes by which behavior is learned; also called *learning theory.*

5. **Conditioning** is the learning process that occurs either through the association of two stimuli (classical conditioning) or through the use of positive or negative reinforcement or punishment (operant conditioning).

6. **Classical conditioning** is the process by which a neutral stimulus becomes associated with a meaningful one so that both are responded to in the same way; also called *respondent conditioning.*

7. **Operant conditioning** is the process by which a response is gradually learned through reinforcement or punishment; also called *instrumental conditioning.*

8. **Reinforcement** is the process by which a particular action is followed by something desired (which makes the person or animal more likely to repeat the action).

9. An extension of behaviorism, **social learning theory** emphasizes that people often learn new behaviors through observation and imitation of other people.

10. **Modeling** refers to the process by which we observe other people's behavior and then copy it.

11 **Cognitive theory,** a grand theory, emphasizes that the way people think and understand the world shapes their attitudes, beliefs, and behaviors.

12. In Piaget's theory, **cognitive equilibrium** is a state of mental balance, in which a person's thoughts about the world seem not to clash with each other or with his or her experiences.

13. In Piaget's theory, **assimilation** is the process by which new experiences are reinterpreted to fit into old ideas.

14. In Piaget's theory, **accommodation** is the process in which old ideas are restructured to incorporate new experiences.

15. **Information processing** is a perspective that compares human thinking processes to the way a computer analyzes data.

16. **Sociocultural theory** seeks to explain development as the result of a dynamic interaction

between developing persons and the surrounding social and cultural forces.

17. In Vygotsky's view, an **apprenticeship in thinking** is the process by which each person develops new competencies by learning from skilled mentors or tutors.

18. In sociocultural theory, **guided participation** is the process by which people learn from others who guide their efforts.

19. **Humanism** is a theory that stresses the shared basic needs of all people, and the potential of all humans for good.

20. **Selective adaptation** is the process by which humans and other species gradually adjust to their environment. Whether a genetic trait increases or decreases over generations depends on whether it contributes to survival and reproductive ability.

21. Developmentalists who work from an **eclectic perspective** accept elements from several theories, instead of adhering to only a single perspective.

Heredity and Environment

Chapter Overview

Conception occurs when the male and female reproductive cells—the sperm and ovum, respectively—come together to create a new, one-celled zygote with its own unique combination of genetic material. The genetic material furnishes the instructions for development—not only for obvious physical characteristics, such as sex, coloring, and body shape, but also for certain psychological characteristics, such as bashfulness, moodiness, and vocational aptitude.

Every year, scientists make new discoveries and reach new understandings about genes and their effects on the development of individuals. This chapter presents some of their findings, including that most human characteristics are polygenic and multifactorial—the result of the interaction of many genetic and environmental influences—and that all important human characteristics are epigenetic. Perhaps the most important findings have come from research into the causes of genetic and chromosomal abnormalities. The chapter discusses the most common of these abnormalities and concludes with a section on genetic counseling. Genetic testing before and after conception can help predict whether a couple will have a child with a genetic problem.

What Will You Know?

The text chapter should be studied one section at a time. Before you read, preview each section by skimming it, noting headings and boldface items. Then read the sections, one at a time, keeping these questions in mind.

1. What is the relationship between genes and chromosomes?

2. Do sex differences result from chromosomes or culture?

3. How can a child have genetic traits that are not obvious in either parent?

4. If both parents are alcoholics, will their children be alcoholics too?

5. Why are some children born with Down syndrome, and what can be done for them?

Chapter Review

When you have finished reading the chapter, work through the material that follows to review it. Completing the sentences and answering the questions will enable you to answer the "What Have You Learned?" questions at the end of the text chapter. Scattered throughout the Chapter Review are Study Tips, which explain how best to learn a difficult concept, and Think About It discussions and Applications, which help you to know how well you understand the material. Check your understanding of the material by consulting the answers at the end of the chapter. Do not continue with the next section until you understand each answer. If you need to, review or reread the appropriate section in the textbook before continuing.

STUDY TIP This chapter contains a lot of technical material that you might find difficult to master. Not only are there many terms for you to remember, but you must also understand the basic principles of how genes interact with environmental influences to affect development. Learning this material will require a great deal of rehearsal. Working the chapter review several times, making flash cards, and mentally reciting terms are all useful techniques for rehearsing this type of material.

The Genetic Code

1. The human reproductive cells, which are
   called _____ , include
   the male's_____ and the
   female's _____ . When the
   gametes' nuclei fuse, a living cell called a

_____ is formed.

2. The work of body cells is done by
_____ , under the direction
of instructions stored in molecules of
_____ , which are stored on
_____ .

3. Each normal person inherits
_____ chromosomes,
_____ from each parent.
The genetic instructions in chromosomes are
organized into units called _____ ,
each of which contains instructions for a
specific _____ , which in turn
is composed of chemical building blocks called
_____ _____ .

   Some genes come in several slight, normal
variations called _____ .

4. Everyone has additional _____
surrounding each gene. In the process of
_____ , this material enhances,
transcribes, connects, empowers, and otherwise
alters genes.

5. Genes with codes that vary from other versions of
that gene are called _____ .
Genes that have various versions are called
_____-_____
_____ . The sum total of these
genetic instructions to make a living organism is
called its _____ .

The Beginnings of Life

6. An organism's entire genetic inheritance is called
its _____ .

7. The chromosomes in a pair are generally
identical or similar. The 44 chromosomes that are
independent of the sex chromosomes are called
_____ . If a gene from one parent
is exactly like that from the other parent, the gene
pair is said to be _____ . If the
match is not perfect, the gene pair is said to be
_____ .

the "words," and DNA molecules are the "letters."
You can also keep the relationship among genes,
DNA, and chromosomes straight by thinking visually.
Chromosomes are the largest of the units. They are
made of up genes, which are in turn made up of
DNA.

8. The developing person's sex is determined by
the _____ pair of chromosomes.
In the female, this pair is composed of two
_____-shaped chromosomes and
is designated _____ . In the male,
this pair includes one _____ and
one _____ chromosome and is
therefore designated _____ .

9. The critical factor in the determination of a
zygote's sex is which _____
(sperm/ovum) reaches the other gamete first.

10. (Opposing Perspectives) In countries such as
China, prenatal tests that show the sex of the
child have been used to _____ .
The sex ratio can also be affected by
_____ pregnancies of the
"wrong" sex or by _____-
_____ , changing the proportion
of X and Y sperm before insemination.

11. Within hours after conception, the zygote
begins to _____ and
_____ . At about the eight-cell
stage, the cells start to _____ ,
with various cells beginning to specialize
and reproduce at different rates. As a result
of these processes, cells change from being
_____ _____ that
are able to produce any type of cell to becoming
specialized cells.

12. Identical, or monozygotic, twins, who
develop from one _____ ,
_____ (are/are not) genetically
identical. This occurs about once in every
_____ (how many?) conceptions.

13. Twins who begin life as two separate zygotes
created by the fertilization of two ova are called
_____ , or _____ ,
twins. Such twins have approximately
_____ percent of their genes in
common.

14. The incidence of dizygotic births varies by
_____ . In about 12 percent
of pregnancies, the _____
_____phenomenon occurs, in
which only one of two _____
continues to grow.

15. For infertile couples, medical intervention, or
_____ _____
_____ , can help in conceiving
and then sustaining a pregnancy.

16. One simple treatment for infertility is to use
_____ to cause ovulation.

17. Another technique, which involves fertilization in
a laboratory dish, is called _____
_____fertilization. This may
be done by inserting a sperm directly into the
ovum, a process called _____-
_____ _____
_____ .

APPLICATIONS:

18. Concluding her presentation on the hazards of
multiple births, Kirsten notes that, "the more
embryos that develop together, the"
   a. larger each is.
   b. less mature and more vulnerable each is.
   c. less vulnerable each is.
   d. larger and less vulnerable each is.

19. If a dizygotic twin develops schizophrenia, the
likelihood of the other twin experiencing serious
mental illness is much lower than is the case with
monozygotic twins. This suggests that
   a. schizophrenia is caused by genes.
   b. schizophrenia is influenced by genes.
   c. environment is unimportant in the develop-
      ment of schizophrenia.
   d. monozygotic twins are especially vulnerable
      to schizophrenia.

From Genotype to Phenotype

20. The actual appearance and manifest behavior of
the person is called the _____ .

21. Most human characteristics are affected by many
genes, and so they are _____ ,
and by many factors, and so they are
_____ .

22. All important human characteristics are
_____ . This idea emphasizes the
interaction between _____ and
the _____ .

23. The prefix "epi" refers to the various
_____ factors that affect
the expression of _____
_____ . These include
factors that can slow development such as
_____ _____ .
Others are facilitating factors such as
_____ .

24. The international effort to map the complete
human genetic code, the _____
_____ _____ ,
was completed in 2001. This effort found that
humans have _____ (many
more/far fewer) genes than previously thought.

25. A phenotype that reflects the sum of the
contributions of all the genes involved
in its determination illustrates the
_____ pattern of genetic
interaction. Examples include genes
that affect _____ and
_____ _____ .

26. Less often, genes interact in a
_____ fashion. In one example of
this pattern, some genes are more influential than
others; this is called the_____–
_____ pattern. In this
pattern, the more influential allele is called
_____ , and the weaker one is
called _____ .

27. A person who has a gene in his or her genotype
that is not expressed in the phenotype but that
can be passed on to the person's offspring is said
to be a _____ of that gene.

28. Some recessive genes are located only
on the X chromosome and so are called
_____-_____ .
Examples of such genes are the ones that
determine _____
_____ .

Because they have only one X chromosome,
_____ (females/males) are
more likely to have these characteristics in their
phenotype.

29. Almost every disease involves

_____ _____

_____ , which are genes with
repeats or deletions of base pairs.

30. When genes function differently depending on
which parent they came from, the phenomenon
known as _____
_____ occurs. Examples of this
phenomenon include Prader-Willi syndrome and
Angelman syndrome.

APPLICATIONS:

31. If your mother is much taller than your father, it
is most likely that your height will be
   a. about the same as your mother's because the
   X chromosome determines height.
   b. about the same as your father's because the
   Y chromosome determines height.
   c. somewhere between your mother's and
   father's heights because the genes for height
   are additive.
   d. greater than both your mother's and father's
   because of your grandfather's dominant
   gene.

32. Some men are color-blind because they inherit
a particular recessive gene from their mothers.
That recessive gene is carried on the
_____ chromosome.

33. Winona inherited a gene from her mother that,
regardless of her father's contribution to her
genotype, will be expressed in her phenotype.
Evidently, the gene Winona received from her
mother is a _____ gene.

Nature and Nurture

34. Certain _____ traits encourage
drinking and drug taking. These traits include
_____ .

35. Two other factors in alcoholism are
_____ and _____
_____ . Women become drunk
on _____ (less/more) alcohol
than men do.

36. The percentage of the variation in a trait within
a particular population, in a particular context
and era, that can be traced to genes is called its
_____ .

37. Like alcoholism, vision is also affected by
_____ , _____ ,
and _____ . The alarming
increase in the rate of the vision problem of
_____ among children in
East Asia has been attributed to the increasing
amount of time spent by children in the
_____ . In other parts of the
world, this problem may be caused by genes or
by poor _____ , especially lack of
_____ _____ .

STUDY TIP A common mistake in trying to
understand the concept of heritability is to apply
this statistic to the traits of an individual person.
You need to remember that heritability refers to
the variation in a trait that occurs within a large
group of individuals that can be traced to genetic
influences, not to the traits of an individual person.
As an example, although research studies may
demonstrate that the heritability of a particular
trait is 60 percent, it is incorrect to conclude that
there is a 60 percent probability that an individual
who manifests that trait in his or her phenotype
will inherit the trait. Remember that heritability is a
general statistic that applies only to populations, not
individuals.

APPLICATIONS:

38. Genetically, Claude's potential height is 6'0.
Because he did not eat a balanced diet, however,
he grew to only 5'9". Claude's actual height is an
example of a _____ .

39. A person's skin turns yellow-orange as a result of
a carrot-juice diet regimen. This is an example of
   a. an environmental influence.
   b. an alteration in genotype.
   c. polygenic inheritance.
   d. incomplete dominance.

40. Laurie and Brad, who both have a history of alcoholism in their families, are concerned that the child they hope to have will inherit a genetic predisposition to alcoholism. Based on information presented in the text, what advice should you offer them?

    a. "Stop worrying, alcoholism is only weakly genetic."
    b. "It is almost certain that your child will abuse alcohol."
    c. "Social influences, such as the family and peer environment, play a critical role in determining whether alcoholism is expressed."
    d. "Wait to have children until you are both middle aged, in order to see if the two of you become alcoholic."

Chromosomal and Genetic Problems

41. Researchers study genetic and chromosomal abnormalities for three major reasons. State them.

    a. _____
       _____
    b. _____
       _____
    c. _____
       _____

42. Chromosomal abnormalities occur during the formation of the _____ , producing a sperm or ovum that does not have the normal complement of chromosomes.

43. One variable that correlates with chromosomal abnormalities is _____
    _____ .

44. Many fetuses with chromosomal abnormalities are _____
    _____ . Nevertheless, about 1 in every _____ newborns has one chromosome too few or one too many, leading to a cluster of characteristics called a _____ .

45. The most common extra-chromosome syndrome is _____ _____ , which is also called _____-
    _____ . People with this syndrome are usually slower to develop _____ , especially in _____ .

List several of the physical and psychological characteristics associated with Down syndrome.

46. About 1 in every 500 infants is either missing a _____ chromosome or has three or more such chromosomes. Having an odd number of these chromosomes impairs _____ and psychosocial development as well as _____
    _____ .

47. Most of the known single-gene disorders are _____ (dominant/recessive). Genetic disorders usually _____ (are/are not) seriously disabling. Severe dominant disorders are _____ (common/rare) because people with these disorders usually _____ (do/do not) have children.

48. One exception is the central nervous system disease called _____
    _____ . Another is a rare but severe form of _____ disease that causes dementia before age 60.

49. In some individuals, part of the X chromosome is attached by such a thin string of molecules that it seems about to break off; this abnormality is called _____
    _____ syndrome.

50. Three common recessive disorders that are not sex-linked are _____
    _____ , _____ , and _____-
    _____ .

THINK ABOUT IT About 1 baby in 30 is born with a serious genetic problem. If this is so, you will have encountered many people who have such problems. Indeed, in any population of 30 people you might expect to encounter 1 person who has a serious genetic problem. Remember, however, that "serious" does not mean "disabling." Think back to your elementary school days. About how many children were in your fifth- or sixth-grade class? Were you aware that any of these children had a serious genetic problem?

APPLICATIONS:

51. Which of the following is an inherited abnormality that quite possibly could develop into a recognizable syndrome?
   a. Just before dividing to form a sperm or ovum, corresponding gene segments of a chromosome pair break off and are exchanged.
   b. Just before conception, a chromosome pair splits imprecisely, resulting in a mixture of cells.
   c. A person inherits an X chromosome in which part of the chromosome is attached to the rest of it by a very slim string of molecules.
   d. A person inherits a recessive gene on his Y chromosome.

52. Sixteen-year-old Joey experiences some mental slowness and hearing and heart problems, yet he is able to care for himself and is unusually sweet-tempered. Joey probably has

   _____ _____ .

53. Jason, who is 40 years old, has just been diagnosed with an inherited, dominant disorder of the central nervous system. Jason most likely would be diagnosed with _____

   _____ .

Genetic Counseling and Testing

54. Through _____

   _____ , couples today can learn more about their genes and about their chances of conceiving a child with chromosomal or other genetic abnormalities.

55. List five situations in which genetic counseling is especially useful.

   a. _____

   _____

   b. _____

   _____

   c. _____

   _____

   d. _____

   _____

   e. _____

   _____

THINK ABOUT IT Genetic testing and counseling have made wondrous strides in recent years. At the same time, these advances have created potential new dilemmas that earlier cohorts of parents-to-be were less likely to face. Consider, for example, the following question: If your unborn child were fated to develop a life-threatening chronic illness, would you want him or her to know? Would you want to know? Why or why not?

Progress Test 1

Multiple-Choice Questions

Circle your answers to the following questions and check them against the answers at the end of the chapter. If your answer is incorrect, read the explanation for why it is incorrect and then consult the text.

1. When a sperm and an ovum merge, a one-celled _____ is formed.
   a. zygote
   b. reproductive cell
   c. gamete
   d. monozygote

2. Genes are separate units that provide the chemical instructions that each cell needs to become
   a. a zygote.
   b. a chromosome.
   c. a specific part of a functioning human body.
   d. deoxyribonucleic acid.

3. In the male, the 23rd pair of chromosomes is designated; in the female, this pair is designated _____ .
   a. XX; XY   c. XO; XXY
   b. XY; XX   d. XXY; XO

4. Because the 23rd pair of chromosomes in females is XX, each ovum carries an
   a. XX zygote.
   b. X zygote.
   c. XY zygote.
   d. X chromosome.

5. When a zygote splits, the two identical, independent clusters that develop become
   a. dizygotic twins.
   b. monozygotic twins.
   c. fraternal twins.
   d. trizygotic twins.

6. During adulthood, genetic influences on development
   a. generally increase.
   b. generally decrease.
   c. remain steady.
   d. vary from individual to individual.

7. Most of the known single-gene disorders are
   a. dominant.
   b. recessive.
   c. seriously disabling.
   d. sex-linked.

8. When we say that a characteristic is multifactorial, we mean that
   a. many genes are involved.
   b. many environmental factors are involved.
   c. many genetic and environmental factors are involved.
   d. the characteristic is polygenic.

9. Genes are segments of molecules of
   a. genotype.
   b. deoxyribonucleic acid (DNA).
   c. karyotype.
   d. phenotype.

10. The form of assisted reproduction in which a single sperm cell is injected into an ovum is
   a. intra-cytoplasmic injection.
   b. in vitro fertilization.
   c. assisted reproductive technology.
   d. fragile X therapy.

11. A genetic disorder that is "dominant" is one that is
   a. always expressed.
   b. expressed only when other risk factors are present.
   c. more common in women than in men.
   d. more common in men than in women.

12. Some developmentalists believe that the epidemic increase in nearsightedness among children in Hong Kong, Singapore, and Taiwan is partly the result of
   a. the recent epidemic of rubella.
   b. vitamin A deficiency.
   c. the increasing amount of time spent by children in close study.
   d. mutations in the Pax6 gene.

13. Babies born with trisomy-21 (Down syndrome) are often
   a. born to older parents.
   b. unusually aggressive.
   c. abnormally tall by adolescence.
   d. blind.

14. To say that a trait is polygenic means that
   a. many genes make it more likely that the individual will inherit the trait.
   b. several genes must be present for the individual to inherit the trait.
   c. the trait is multifactorial.
   d. most people carry genes for the trait.

15. Some genetic diseases are recessive, so the child cannot inherit the condition unless both parents
   a. have Huntington disease.
   b. carry the same recessive gene.
   c. are older than 40.
   d. have the disease.

Matching Items

Match each term with its corresponding description or definition.

Terms

_____ 1. gametes

_____ 2. chromosome

_____ 3. genotype

_____ 4. phenotype

_____ 5. monozygotic

_____ 6. dizygotic

_____ 7. additive

_____ 8. fragile X syndrome

_____ 9. carrier

_____ 10. zygote

_____ 11. alleles

_____ 12. XX

_____ 13. XY

Descriptions or Definitions

a. chromosome pair inherited by genetic females
b. identical twins
c. sperm and ovum
d. the first cell of the developing person
e. a person who has a recessive gene in his or her genotype that is not expressed in the phenotype
f. fraternal twins
g. a pattern in which each gene in question makes an active contribution to the final outcome
h. a DNA molecule
i. the behavioral or physical expression of genetic potential
j. a chromosomal abnormality
k. alternate versions of a gene
l. chromosome pair inherited by genetic males
m. a person's entire genetic inheritance

Progress Test 2

Progress Test 2 should be completed during a final chapter review. Answer the following questions after you thoroughly understand the correct answers for the Chapter Review and Progress Test 1.

Multiple-Choice Questions

1. Copy number variations occur when there are
   a. additions of base pairs in genes.
   b. deletions of base pairs in genes.
   c. additions or deletions of base pairs in genes.
   d. deviations in the number of chromosomes a zygote receives.

2. If a man carries the recessive gene for cystic fibrosis and his wife does not, the chances of their having a child with cystic fibrosis
   a. is one in four.
   b. is 50/50.
   c. is zero.
   d. depends on the wife's ethnic background.

3. The fatal central nervous system disorder caused by a genetic miscode is
   a. Albinism.
   b. cystic fibrosis.
   c. Huntington disease.
   d. muscular dystrophy.

4. With the exception of sperm and egg cells, each human cell contains
   a. 23 genes.
   b. 23 chromosomes.
   c. 46 genes.
   d. 46 chromosomes.

5. Most recessive disorders are
   a. not on the autosomes.
   b. sex-linked.
   c. not sex-linked.
   d. not on the autosomes and are sex-linked.

6. Dizygotic twins result when
   a. a single egg is fertilized by a sperm and then splits.
   b. a single egg is fertilized by two different sperm.
   c. two eggs are fertilized by two different sperm.
   d. either a single egg is fertilized by one sperm or two eggs are fertilized by two different sperm.

7. Molecules of DNA that in humans are organized into 23 complementary pairs are called
   a. zygotes.
   b. genes.
   c. chromosomes.
   d. ova.

8. Shortly after the zygote is formed, it begins the processes of duplication and division. Each resulting new cell has
   a. the same number of chromosomes as was contained in the zygote.
   b. half the number of chromosomes as was contained in the zygote.
   c. twice, then four times, then eight times the number of chromosomes as was contained in the zygote.
   d. all the chromosomes except those that determine sex.

9. If an ovum is fertilized by a sperm bearing a Y chromosome
   a. a female will develop.
   b. cell division will result.
   c. a male will develop.
   d. spontaneous abortion will occur.

10. When the male cells in the testes and the female cells in the ovaries divide to produce gametes, the process differs from that in the production of all other cells. As a result of the different process, the gametes have
    a. one rather than both members of each chromosome pair.
    b. 23 chromosome pairs.
    c. X but not Y chromosomes.
    d. chromosomes from both parents.

11. Most human traits are
    a. polygenic and multifactorial.
    b. determined by a single gene.
    c. determined by dominant–recessive patterns.
    d. unaffected by environmental factors.

12. Genotype is to phenotype as _____ is to _____ .
    a. genetic potential; physical expression
    b. physical expression; genetic potential
    c. sperm; ovum
    d. gamete; zygote

13. The genes that influence height and skin color interact according to the _____ pattern.
    a. dominant–recessive
    b. X-linked
    c. additive
    d. nonadditive

14. X-linked recessive genes explain why some traits seem to be passed from
    a. father to son.
    b. father to daughter.
    c. mother to daughter.
    d. mother to son.

15. In vitro fertilization is a technique
    a. in which sperm are mixed with ova that have been surgically removed from a woman's ovary.
    b. in which sperm from a donor are inserted into the woman's uterus via a syringe.
    c. for helping infertile couples conceive a pregnancy.
    d. for helping infertile couples sustain a pregnancy.

True or False Items

Write T (*true*) or F (*false*) on the line in front of each statement.

_____ 1. Most human characteristics are multifactorial, caused by the interaction of genetic and environmental factors.

_____ 2. Most dominant disorders are sex-linked.

_____ 3. Research suggests that susceptibility to alcoholism is at least partly the result of genetic inheritance.

_____ 4. The human reproductive cells (ova and sperm) are called gametes.

_____ 5. Only a very few human traits are polygenic.

_____ 6. The zygote contains all the biologically inherited information—the genes and chromosomes—that a person will have during his or her life.

_____ 7. A couple should probably seek genetic counseling if several earlier pregnancies ended in spontaneous abortion.

_____ 8. Many genetic conditions are recessive; thus, a child will have the condition even if only the mother carries the gene.

_____ 9. Two people who have the same phenotype may have a different genotype for a trait such as eye color.

_____ 10. When cells divide to produce reproductive cells (gametes), each sperm or ovum receives only 23 chromosomes, half as many as the original cell.

_____ 11. Most genes have only one function.

Key Terms

Using your own words, write on a separate piece of paper a brief definition or explanation of each of the following terms.

1. gamete
2. zygote
3. deoxyribonucleic acid (DNA)
4. chromosome
5. gene
6. allele
7. genome
8. genotype
9. homozygous
10. heterozygous
11. 23rd pair
12. XX
13. XY
14. stem cell
15. monozygotic (MZ) twins
16. dizygotic (DZ) twins
17. assisted reproductive technology (ART)
18. in vitro fertilization (IVF)
19. intra-cytoplasmic injection (ICSI)
20. phenotype
21. polygenic
22. multifactorial
23. Human Genome Project
24. dominant–recessive pattern
25. carrier
26. X-linked
27. copy number variations
28. heritability
29. Down syndrome
30. fragile X syndrome
31. genetic counseling

ANSWERS

CHAPTER REVIEW

1. gametes; sperm; ovum; zygote
2. proteins; DNA; chromosomes
3. 46; 23; genes; protein; amino acids; alleles
4. DNA; methylation

5. polymorphic; single-nucleotide polymorphisms; genome
6. genotype
7. autosomes; homozygous; heterozygous
8. 23rd; X; XX; X; Y; XY
9. sperm
10. abort female fetuses; aborting; sperm-sorting
11. duplicate; divide; differentiate; stem cells
12. zygote; are; 250
13. dizygotic; fraternal; 50
14. ethnicity; disappearing twin; embryos
15. assisted reproductive technology (ART)
16. drugs
17. in vitro; intra-cytoplasmic sperm injection (ICSI)
18. **b.** is the answer. The more fetuses that share a womb, the smaller, less mature, and more vulnerable each one is. All their lives, multiple-birth babies have higher rates of disease and disabilities.
19. **b.** is the answer. Because monozygotic twins are genetically identical, while dizygotic twins share only 50 percent of their genes, greater similarity of traits between monozygotic twins suggests that genes are an important influence.
20. phenotype
21. polygenic; multifactorial
22. epigenetic; genes; environment
23. environmental; genetic influences; injury, temperature extremes, drug abuse, and crowding; nourishing food, loving care, and freedom to play
24. Human Genome Project; far fewer
25. additive; height; skin color (or hair curliness)
26. nonadditive; dominant–recessive; dominant; recessive
27. carrier
28. X-linked; color blindness, many allergies, several diseases, and some learning disabilities; males
29. copy number variations
30. parental imprinting
31. **c.** is the answer. It is unlikely that the other factors account for height differences from one generation to the next.
32. X. Color blindness is X-linked. Since the Y chromosome is much smaller than the X, an X-linked recessive gene almost never has a dominant counterpart on the Y. Thus, color blindness most often occurs in males.

33. dominant. The dominant gene is always expressed in the person's phenotype. For a recessive gene to be expressed, the individual must inherit a recessive gene from both parents.

34. temperamental; a quick temper, sensation seeking, and high anxiety

35. gender; biological sex; less

36. heritability

37. age; genes; culture; nearsightedness; close study of books and papers; nutrition; vitamin A

38. phenotype. The phenotype is the observable characteristics of a person. Genotype is the individual's entire genetic inheritance, or genetic potential.

39. **a.** is the answer. Genotype is a person's genetic potential, established at conception. Polygenic inheritance refers to the influence of many genes on a particular trait. Incomplete dominance refers to the phenotype being influenced primarily, but not exclusively, by the dominant gene.

40. **c.** is the answer. Despite a strong genetic influence on alcoholism, the environment also plays a critical role.

41. **a.**   They provide insight into the complexities of genetic interactions.

    b.   Knowing their origins helps limit their harmful effects.

    c.   Information combats the prejudice that surrounds such problems.

42. gametes

43. maternal age

44. spontaneously aborted; 200; syndrome

45. Down syndrome; trisomy-21; intellectually; language

Most people with Down syndrome have certain facial characteristics—a thick tongue, round face, slanted eyes—as well as distinctive hands, feet, and fingerprints. Many also have hearing problems, heart abnormalities, muscle weakness, and short stature.

46. sex; cognitive; sexual maturation

47. dominant; are not; rare; do not

48. Huntington disease; Alzheimer

49. fragile X

50. cystic fibrosis, thalassemia, sickle-cell anemia

51. **c.** is the answer. This describes the fragile X syndrome. The phenomenon described in a. merely contributes to genetic diversity; b. is an example of a particular nonadditive gene interaction pattern. Regarding d., for a recessive gene to be expressed, both parents must pass it on to the child.

52. Down syndrome

53. Huntington disease

54. genetic counseling

55. Genetic counseling is recommended for (a) those who have a parent, sibling, or child with a serious genetic condition; (b) those who have a history of spontaneous abortions or stillbirths; (c) couples who are infertile; (d) couples who are from the same ethnic group, particularly if they are related to each other; and (e) women over age 35 and men age 40 or older.

PROGRESS TEST 1

Multiple-Choice Questions

1. **a.** is the answer.

   b. & c. The reproductive cells (sperm and ova), which are also called gametes, are individual entities.

   d. Monozygote refers to one member of a pair of identical twins.

2. **c.** is the answer.

   a. The zygote is the first cell of the developing person.

   b. Chromosomes are molecules of DNA that *carry* genes.

   d. DNA molecules contain genetic information.

3. **b.** is the answer.

4. **d.** is the answer. When the gametes are formed, one member of each chromosome pair splits off; because in females both are X chromosomes, each ovum must carry an X chromosome.

   a., b., & c. The zygote refers to the merged sperm and ovum that is the first new cell of the developing individual.

5. **b.** is the answer. *Mono* means "one." Thus, monozygotic twins develop from one zygote.

   a. & c. Dizygotic, or fraternal, twins develop from two (*di*) zygotes.

   d. A trizygotic birth would result in triplets (*tri*), rather than twins.

6. **a.** is the answer.

7. **a.** is the answer.

   c. & d. Most dominant disorders are neither seriously disabling nor sex-linked.

8. **c.** is the answer.

   a., b., & d. *Polygenic* means "many genes"; *multifactorial* means "many factors," which are not limited to either genetic or environmental factors.

9. **b.** is the answer.

   a. Genotype is a person's genetic potential.

   c. A karyotype is a picture of a person's chromosomes.

   d. Phenotype is the actual expression of a genotype.

10. **a.** is the answer.

11. **a.** is the answer.

   c. & d. The text does not indicate a gender difference in dominant genetic disorders.

12. **c.** is the answer.

   a. Rubella has not been mentioned as a major reason for the recent increase in nearsightedness in these countries.

   b. Vitamin A deficiencies may be a factor in the vision problems of children among certain African ethnic groups.

   d. The rapid changes in the prevalence of nearsightedness suggest that an environmental factor is the culprit.

13. **a.** is the answer.

14. **b.** is the answer.

15. **b.** is the answer.

   a. Huntington disease is a dominant-gene disorder.

   c. Age is not a factor in recessive-gene disorders.

   d. For an offspring to inherit a recessive condition, the parents need only be carriers of the recessive gene in their genotypes; they need not actually have the disease.

Matching Items

1. c	**6.** f	**11.** k
2. h	**7.** g	**12.** a
3. m	**8.** j	**13.** l
4. i	**9.** e	
5. b	**10.** d	

PROGRESS TEST 2

Multiple-Choice Questions

1. **c.** is the answer.

2. **c.** is the answer. Cystic fibrosis is a recessive-gene disorder; therefore, for a child to inherit this disease, he or she must receive the recessive gene from both parents.

3. **c.** is the answer.

   a. Albinism is a skin disorder.

   b. Cystic fibrosis affects mucous membranes,

especially in the lungs.

   d. Muscular dystrophy causes a weakening of the muscles.

4. **d.** is the answer.

   a. & c. Human cells contain thousands of genes.

5. **c.** is the answer.

   a., b., & d. Most recessive disorders are on the autosomes and are not sex-linked.

6. **c.** is the answer.

   a. This would result in monozygotic twins.

   b. Only one sperm can fertilize an ovum.

   d. A single egg fertilized by one sperm would produce a single offspring or monozygotic twins.

7. **c.** is the answer.

   a. Zygotes are fertilized ova.

   b. Genes are the smaller units of heredity that are organized into sequences on chromosomes.

   d. Ova are female reproductive cells.

8. **a.** is the answer.

9. **c.** is the answer. The ovum will contain an X chromosome; with the sperm's Y chromosome, it will produce the male XY pattern.

   a. Only if the ovum is fertilized by an X chromosome from the sperm will a female develop.

   b. Cell division will occur regardless of whether the sperm contributes an X or a Y chromosome.

   d. Spontaneous abortions are likely to occur when there are chromosomal or genetic abnormalities; the situation described is perfectly normal.

10. **a.** is the answer.

   b. & d. These are true of all body cells *except* the gametes.

   c. Gametes have either X or Y chromosomes.

11. **a.** is the answer.

12. **a.** is the answer. Genotype refers to the sum total of all the genes a person inherits; phenotype refers to the actual expression of the individual's characteristics.

13. **c.** is the answer.

14. **d.** is the answer. X-linked genes are located only on the X chromosome. Because males inherit only one X chromosome, they are more likely than females to have these characteristics in their phenotype.

15. **a.** is the answer.

   b. This describes intrauterine insemination.

c. & d. These answers, which are too general, describe all forms of assisted reproductive technology.

True or False Items

1. T
2. F Since these disorders appear in the phenotype, they would have to occur only in males to be sex-linked.
3. T
4. T
5. F Most traits are polygenic.
6. T
7. T
8. F A trait from a recessive gene will be part of the phenotype only when the person has two recessive genes for that trait.
9. T
10. T
11. F Most genes have several functions.

KEY TERMS

1. **Gametes** are the human reproductive cells.

2. The **zygote** is the single cell formed during conception by the fusing of two gametes, a sperm and an ovum.

3. **Deoxyribonucleic acid (DNA)** is the chemical composition of the molecules that contain the genes, which are the chemical instructions for cells to manufacture various proteins.

4. **Chromosomes** are molecules of DNA that contain the genes organized in precise sequences. Each cell contains 46 chromosomes (23 pairs).

5. **Genes** are segments of a chromosome, which is a DNA molecule; they are the basic units for the transmission of hereditary instructions.

6. An **allele** is one of the normal versions of a gene that has several possible sequences of base pairs.

7. The **genome** is the full set of genes that are the instructions to make an individual member of a certain species.

8. The total of all the genes a person inherits—his or her genetic potential—is called the **genotype.**

9. **Homozygous** refers to two genes of one pair that are exactly the same in every letter of their code.

10. **Heterozygous** refers to two genes of one pair that differ in some way.

11. The **23rd pair** of chromosomes, in humans, determines the individual's sex.

12. **XX** is the 23rd chromosome pair that, in humans, determines that the developing fetus will be female.

13. **XY** is the 23rd chromosome pair that, in humans, determines that the developing fetus will be male.

14. A **stem cell** is one from which any other specialized type of cell can form.

15. **Monozygotic (MZ) twins** develop from one zygote that splits apart, producing genetically identical zygotes; also called *identical twins.*

    Memory aid: Mono means "one"; **monozygotic twins** develop from one fertilized ovum.

16. **Dizygotic (DZ) twins** develop from two separate ova fertilized by different sperm at roughly the same time, and therefore are no more genetically similar than ordinary siblings; also called fraternal twins.

    Memory aid: A fraternity is a group of two (di) or more nonidentical individuals.

17. **Assisted reproductive technology (ART)** refers to the various techniques available to help infertile couples conceive and sustain a pregnancy.

18. **In vitro fertilization (IVF)** is a form of ART in which ova surgically removed from a woman are mixed with sperm. If a zygote is produced, it is inserted into the woman's uterus, where it may implant and develop into a baby.

19. **Intra-cytoplasmic injection (ICSI)** is a form of ART in which a single sperm cell is injected directly into an ovum.

20. The actual physical or behavioral expression of a genotype, the result of the interaction of the genes with each other and with the environment, is called the **phenotype.**

21. Most human traits are **polygenic;** that is, they are affected by many genes.

22. Most human traits are also **multifactorial**—that is, influenced by many factors, including genetic and environmental factors.

23. **The Human Genome Project,** an international effort to map the complete human genetic code, was essentially completed in 2001.

24. The **dominant–recessive pattern** is the interaction of a heterozygous pair of alleles in such a way

that the phenotype reveals the influence of the dominant gene more than that of the recessive gene.

25. A person who has a recessive gene that is not expressed in his or her phenotype but that can be passed on to the person's offspring is called a **carrier** of that gene.

26. **X-linked** genes are genes that are located only on the X chromosome. Because males have only one X chromosome, they are more likely than females to have the characteristics determined by these genes in their phenotype.

27. **Copy number variations,** which are correlated with most diseases, are genes with repeats or deletions of base pairs.

28. **Heritability** is a statistic that refers to the percentage of variation in a particular trait within a particular population, in a particular context and era, that can be traced to genes.

29. **Down syndrome** (*trisomy-21*) is the most common extra-chromosome condition. People with Down syndrome age faster than others, often have unusual facial features and heart abnormalities, and are usually slower to develop intellectually.

30. The **fragile X syndrome** is a single-gene disorder in which part of the X chromosome is attached by such a thin string of molecules that it seems about to break off. Although the characteristics associated with this syndrome are quite varied, some mental deficiency is relatively common.

31. **Genetic counseling** involves consultations and tests through which couples can learn more about their genes, and can thus make informed decisions about their childbearing and child-rearing future.

Prenatal Development and Birth

Chapter Overview

Prenatal development is the most dramatic and extensive transformation of the entire life span. During prenatal development, the individual changes from a one-celled zygote to a complex human baby. This development is outlined in Chapter 4, along with some of the problems that can occur—among them prenatal exposure to disease, drugs, and other hazards—and the factors that moderate the risks of teratogenic exposure.

For the developing person, birth marks the most radical transition of the entire life span. No longer sheltered from the outside world, the fetus becomes a separate human being who begins life almost completely dependent upon his or her caregivers. Chapter 4 also examines the birth process and its possible variations and problems.

The chapter concludes with a brief discussion of the parent–infant bond, including the role of the father in early development.

What Will You Know?

The text chapter should be studied one section at a time. Before you read, preview each section by skimming it, noting headings and boldface items. Then read the sections, one at a time, keeping these questions in mind.

1. What are the three stages of pregnancy, and what are the major developmental changes in each stage?

2. What usually occurs in the first few minutes of a newborn's life?

3. What factors determine whether a potentially harmful substance or circumstance will actually have detrimental effects on the developing fetus? What are the causes and consequences of anoxia?

4. What kinds of changes does the birth of a child cause in family relationships, and what can couples do to help ensure they adjust to these changes in ways that are best for the child?

Chapter Review

When you have finished reading the chapter, work through the material that follows to review it. Completing the sentences and answering the questions will enable you to answer the "What Have You Learned?" questions at the end of the text chapter. Scattered throughout the Chapter Review are Study Tips, which explain how best to learn a difficult concept, and Think About It discussions and Applications, which help you to know how well you understand the material. Check your understanding of the material by consulting the answers at the end of the chapter. Do not continue with the next section until you understand each answer. If you need to, review or reread the appropriate section in the textbook before continuing.

Prenatal Development

1. Prenatal development is divided into

   _____ main periods. The
   first two weeks of development are called
   the _____ period; from the
   _____ week through the
   _____ week is known as the
   _____ period; and from this
   point until birth is the _____
   period.

2. About one week after conception, the multiplying cells separate into outer cells that will become the_____ and inner cells form the nucleus that will become the

   _____ .

3. The next significant event is the burrowing of the zygote into the lining of the uterus, a process called _____ . This process _____ (is/is not) automatic.

4. At the beginning of the period of the embryo, a thin line down the middle of the developing individual forms a structure that will become the _____ _____ , which becomes the _____ _____ and eventually will develop into the _____ _____ _____ .

Briefly describe the major features of development during the second month.

5. At the end of the eighth week after conception, the embryo weighs about _____ and is about _____ in length. From the start of the ninth week after conception until birth, the organism is called the _____ .

6. If the fetus has a(n) _____ chromosome, the _____ gene on this chromosome sends a signal that triggers development of the _____ (male/female) sex organs. Without that gene, no signal is sent and the fetus begins to develop _____ (male/female) sex organs.

7. Prenatal development is_____ , meaning that it proceeds from "head to tail," and _____ , or from "near to far." By the end of the _____ month, the sex organs are visible on a(n) _____ (also called a(n) _____).

8. By the end of the third month, the fetus weighs approximately_____ and is about _____ long. These figures _____ (vary/do not vary) from fetus to fetus.

9. During the fourth, fifth, and sixth months, the brain increases in size by a factor of _____ . The brain develops new neurons in a process called _____ and new connections between them (synapses) in a process called _____ . This neurological maturation is essential to the regulation of such basic body functions as _____ and _____ .

10. The age at which a fetus has at least some chance of surviving outside the uterus is called the _____ _____ _____ , which occurs about _____ weeks after conception. This barrier _____ (has/has not) been reduced by advances in neonatal care, probably because maintaining life depends on some _____ response.

11. Three crucial aspects of development in the last months of prenatal life are maturation of the _____ , _____ , and _____ systems.

12. By full term, brain growth is so extensive that the brain's advanced outer layer, called the _____ , forms several folds in order to fit into the skull.

13. In the final _____ (how many?) months, the fetus hears many sounds, including the mother's _____ and _____ .

THINK ABOUT IT Compared with the gestation periods of other mammals, the nine-month gestation period in humans is relatively long. Compared with how slowly human development proceeds in other aspects of the life span, however, nine months seems a little on the short side. In fact, some evolutionary biologists have suggested that humans ought to be in utero 15 or 16 months! What sorts of evolutionary pressures might have contributed to this "compromise" in the time allotted for prenatal development?

_____

APPLICATIONS:

14. My brain is developing well as a result of the processes of _____ and _____. I am a _____ .

15. Karen and Brad report to their neighbors that, six weeks after conception, an utrasound of their child-to-be revealed female sex organs. The neighbors are skeptical of their statement because
    a. ultrasounds are never administered before the ninth week.
    b. ultrasounds only reveal the presence or absence of male sex organs.
    c. the fetus does not begin to develop female sex organs until about the eighth week.
    d. it is impossible to determine that a woman is pregnant until seven weeks after conception

Birth

16. About _____ (how many?) weeks after conception, the fetal brain signals the release of certain _____ , specifically _____ , that signal the fetal brain for delivery and starts labor. The normal birth process begins when contractions become regular. The average length of labor is _____ hours for first births and _____ hours for subsequent births.

17. Worldwide, the newborn is usually rated on the

    _____ _____ , which assigns a score of 0, 1, or 2 to each of the following five characteristics:

    _____ _____ ,
    _____ , _____ ,
    _____ , _____ ,
    and _____ . A score below _____ indicates that the newborn is in critical condition and requires immediate attention; if the score is _____ or better, all is well. This rating is made twice, at

_____ minute(s) after birth and again at _____ minutes.

18. In more than _____ (how many?) of U.S. births, a surgical procedure called a _____ _____ is performed.

19. (Thinking Critically) Planned home births are much more common in many nations in _____ than they are in the _____ _____ . In the poorest nations, most babies are born _____ (at home/in the hospital).

20. A traditional custom incorporated into a modern birth is the presence of a professional birth coach, or _____ , to assist in the birth process.

Problems and Solutions

21. Harmful agents and conditions that can result in birth defects, called _____ , include _____ .

22. Substances that impair the child's action and intellect by harming the brain are called _____ _____ . Approximately _____ percent of all children are born with behavioral difficulties that could be connected to damage done during the prenatal period.

23. Three crucial factors that determine whether a specific teratogen will cause harm, and of what nature, are the _____ of exposure, the _____ of exposure, and the developing organism's _____ _____ to damage from the substance.

24. The time when a particular part of the body is most susceptible to teratogenic damage is called its _____ _____ . For physical structure and form, this is the entire period of the _____ . However, for _____ teratogens, the entire prenatal period is critical.

25. Some teratogens have a _____ effect—that is, the substances are harmless until exposure reaches a certain level.

26. Other teratogens, when taken together, _____ and so are more harmful than when taken separately.

27. Genes are also known to affect the likelihood of neural-tube defects such as_____ _____ or _____ . These defects occur more commonly in certain _____ groups, which led researchers to discover the allele that prevents the normal utilization of _____ _____ .

28. Women are advised to avoid all _____ before becoming pregnant. Prenatal development can also be impaired by _____ .

29. High doses of alcohol during pregnancy may cause _____ _____ _____ . It later causes _____ _____ _____ , leading to hyperactivity, poor concentration, impaired spatial reasoning, and slow learning.

STUDY TIP To emphasize the variety of teratogens to which pregnant women may be exposed every day, imagine that you have decided to become a parent. If you are a male, some teratogens to which you are exposed may affect your unborn child. Make a list of all the teratogens you have experienced recently that you would want to avoid to ensure that your body is teratogen-free for the year during which fertilization and gestation occur. If you are stumped, check the Internet for ideas.

APPLICATIONS:

30. Five-year-old Benjamin can't sit quietly and concentrate on a task for more than a minute at a time. Dr. Simmons, who is a teratologist, suspects that Benjamin may have been exposed to _____ during prenatal development.
    a. HIV
    b. a behavioral teratogen
    c. rubella
    d. lead

31. Which of the following is an example of a threshold effect?
    a. Some teratogens are virtually harmless until exposure reaches a certain level.
    b. Maternal use of alcohol and tobacco together does more harm to the developing fetus than either teratogen would do alone.
    c. Some teratogens cause damage only on specific days during prenatal development.
    d. All of these are examples of threshold effects.

32. Suppose a woman drinks heavily during pregnancy, and her baby is born with fetal alcohol syndrome. Although alcohol is a proven teratogen, research indicates that the cause of the baby's condition may be
    a. the woman's genetic history.
    b. the level of exposure to the teratogen.
    c. the timing of exposure to the teratogen.
    d. any of these factors.

33. Sylvia and Stan, who are of British descent, are hoping to have a child. Dr. Caruthers asks for a complete nutritional history and is particularly concerned when she discovers that Sylvia may have a deficiency of folic acid in her diet. Dr. Caruthers is probably worried about the risk of _____ - _____ _____ in the couple's offspring.

34. Newborns who weigh less than _____ are classified as _____ - _____ babies. Below 3 pounds, 5 ounces, they are called _____ - _____ - _____ babies; at less than 2 pounds, 3 ounces, they are _____ - _____ - _____ babies. Worldwide, rates of this condition _____ (vary/do not vary) from nation to nation.

35. Babies who are born 3 or more weeks before the standard 38 weeks have elapsed are called _____ .

36. Infants who weigh substantially less than they should, given how much time has passed since conception, are called_____ _____ _____ _____ .

37. Causes of SGA include maternal or fetal
_____ . However, maternal
_____ use is a more common
reason. About 25 percent of all LBW births are
linked to maternal use of _____ .

38. Another other common reason for low
birthweight is maternal _____ .
In addition, _____ births are
more likely to result in LBW. Consequently,
the rate of LBW has increased dramatically
with the use of_____

_____ .

39. LBW babies are more likely to become adults
who have higher rates of _____ ,
_____ disease, and
_____ .

40. The disorder_____
_____ , which affects motor
centers in the brain, often results from
_____ vulnerability, worsened
by exposure to _____ and a
preterm birth that involves_____ , a
temporary lack of _____ during
birth.

APPLICATIONS:

41. Three-year-old Kenny was born underweight
and premature. Today, he is small for his age.
What would be the most likely reason for
Kenny's small size? _____

42. Which of the following newborns would be most
likely to have problems in body structure and
functioning?
   a. Anton, whose Apgar score is 6
   b. Debora, whose Apgar score is 7
   c. Sheila, whose Apgar score is 3
   d. Simon, whose Apgar score is 5

43. At birth, Clarence was classified as small for gestational age. It is likely that Clarence
   a. was born in a rural hospital.
   b. suffered several months of prenatal malnutrition.
   c. was born in a large city hospital.
   d. comes from a family with a history of such
births.

44. Of the following, who is most likely to give birth
to a low-birthweight child?
   a. 21-year-old Janice, who was herself a low-
birthweight baby
   b. 25-year-old May Ling, who gained 25 pounds
during her pregnancy
   c. 16-year-old Donna, who diets frequently
despite being underweight
   d. 30-year-old Maria, who has already given
birth to four children

45. An infant is born 38 weeks after conception,
weighing 4 pounds. How would that infant be
classified in terms of weight and timing?

_____

_____

46. An infant who was born at 35 weeks, weighing 6
pounds, would be called a _____
infant.

47. One minute and five minutes after he was born,
Malcolm was tested using the Apgar scale. The
characteristics of a newborn tested by the scale
are _____

_____ .

The New Family

48. The test that measures behavioral responsiveness
in newborns is the _____

_____ _____

_____ .

49. An involuntary response to a stimulus is called a
_____ .

50. The involuntary response that causes a newborn
to take the first breath even before the umbilical
cord is cut is called the _____
_____ . Other reflexive
behaviors that maintain oxygen are
_____ , _____ ,
and _____ .

51. Shivering, crying, and tucking the legs close
to the body are examples of reflexes that
help to maintain _____
_____ _____ .

52. A third set of reflexes manages
    _____ . One of these is the
    tendency of the newborn to suck anything that
    touches the lips; this is the _____
    reflex. Another is the tendency of newborns
    to turn their heads and start to suck when
    something brushes against their cheek; this
    is the _____ reflex. Other
    important reflexes that facilitate this behavior are

    _____ , _____ ,

    _____ , and

    _____ _____ .

STUDY TIP "Going metric" will help you remember
the differences among low birthweight (LBW),
very low birthweight (VLBW), and extremely
low birthweight (ELBW) babies. Remember two
numbers: 2,500 (grams) and 500 (grams). The
LBW threshold is a weight below 2,500 grams.
Two decreases of 500 grams each are the criteria
for VLBW (2,500 grams minus [2 Ð 500] equals
1,500 grams). For ELBW, it's three decreases of 500
grams each (2,500 grams minus (3 Ð 500 grams)
equals 1,000 grams). To remember the criterion for
a preterm birth, think of "3 (weeks)," which rhymes
with "pre." Thus, a preterm birth is one that occurs 3
or more weeks early. Small for gestational age (SGA)
is self-defining. An SGA baby is one who gained
weight too slowly during gestation (pregnancy).

THINK ABOUT IT Thanks to recent medical
breakthroughs, even extremely-low-birthweight
infants have a decent chance of surviving. As a
result, ethical and social dilemmas often arise
regarding the rights of the fetus as a separate
individual. For example, judges have ordered
pregnant women who were close to term to have
blood transfusions and surgical births, even when
those procedures were unwanted by the women.
How do you feel about this? Who should have the
authority to decide in such cases?

---

53. At birth, the presence of the
    _____ reduces complications.
    This may explain the _____
    _____ , which says that
    although immigrants to the United States are
    _____ and have less adequate
    _____ care, they have
    _____ (healthier/less healthy)
    newborns than native-born mothers of the same
    ethnic background.

54. Many fathers experience symptoms of
    pregnancy, including _____

    _____ , _____ ,

    and _____ _____

    _____ . These experiences are

    called _____ .

55. A crucial factor in the birth experience is the
    formation of a strong _____
    _____ between the prospective
    parents.

56. Some new mothers experience a profound
    feeling of sadness called _____

    _____ .

57. The term used to describe the close relationship
    that begins within the first hours after birth is the

    _____-_____

    _____ . Research on monkeys
    using the strategy of _____-
    _____ suggests that bonding
    need not occur immediately.

58. For vulnerable infants, parents are encouraged
    to help with early caregiving in the hospital.
    This _____ stress in both infant
    and parents. One example of early caregiving is
    _____ _____ , in
    which mothers of low-birthweight infants spend
    extra time holding their infants between their
    breasts.

STUDY TIP Infants have a number of reflexes that
are critical for survival and others that indicate
normal body and brain functioning. Filling in the
missing information in the table on the next page will
provide you with a handy summary of those reflexes.
In some cases, the description is provided; in other
cases, the reflex name is given. First, try to complete
the following table from memory; then check text
page 117.

59. Reflex(es)

Reflex(es)	Description
a.	breathing, hiccupping, sneezing, and thrashing
b. Maintaining constant body temperature	
c.	Sucking, rooting, swallowing
d. Babinski	
e.	Infants move their legs as if to walk when they are held upright and their feet touch a flat surface
f. Swimming	
g.	Infants grip things that touch their palms
h. Moro	

60. Your sister and brother-in-law, who are about to adopt a 6-month-old, are worried that the child will never bond with them. What advice should you offer?

a. Tell them that, unfortunately, this is true; they would be better off waiting for a younger child who has not yet bonded.

b. Tell them that, although the first year is a biologically determined critical period for attachment, there is a 50/50 chance that the child will bond with them.

c. Tell them that bonding is a long-term process between parent and child that is determined by the nature of interaction throughout infancy, childhood, and beyond.

d. Tell them that if the child is female, there is a good chance that she will bond with them, even at this late stage.

Progress Test 1

Multiple-Choice Questions

Circle your answers to the following questions and check them with the answers at the end of the chapter. If your answer is incorrect, read the explanation for why it is incorrect and then consult the text.

1. The third through the eighth week after conception is called the
   a. embryonic period.
   b. ovum period.
   c. fetal period.
   d. germinal period.

2. The primitive streak develops into the
   a. respiratory system.
   b. umbilical cord.
   c. brain and spinal column.
   d. circulatory system.

3. To say that a teratogen has a *threshold effect* means that it is
   a. virtually harmless until exposure reaches a certain level.
   b. harmful only to low-birthweight infants.
   c. harmful to certain developing organs during periods when these organs are developing most rapidly.
   d. harmful only if the pregnant woman's weight does not increase by a certain minimum amount during her pregnancy.

4. By the eighth week after conception, the embryo has almost all the basic organs EXCEPT the
   a. skeleton.
   b. elbows and knees.
   c. male and female sex organs.
   d. fingers and toes.

5. The most critical factor in attaining the age of viability is development of the
   a. placenta.
   b. eyes.
   c. brain.
   d. skeleton.

6. An important nutrient that many women do not get in adequate amounts from the typical diet is
   a. vitamin A.   c. guanine.
   b. zinc.   d. folic acid.

7. An embryo begins to develop male sex organs if
   _____ , and female sex organs if
   _____ .
   a. genes on the Y chromosome send a signal; no signal is sent from an X chromosome
   b. genes on the Y chromosome send a signal; genes on the X chromosome send a signal
   c. genes on the X chromosome send a signal; no signal is sent from an X chromosome
   d. genes on the X chromosome send a signal; genes on the Y chromosome send a signal

8. A teratogen
   a. cannot cross the placenta during the period of the embryo.
   b. is usually inherited from the mother.
   c. can be counteracted by good nutrition most of the time.
   d. may be a virus, a drug, a chemical, or environmental pollutants.

9. Among the characteristics of babies born with fetal alcohol syndrome are
   a. slowed physical growth and behavior problems.
   b. addiction to alcohol and methadone.
   c. deformed arms and legs.
   d. blindness.

10. The birth process begins
    a. when the fetus moves into the right position.
    b. when the uterus begins to contract at regular intervals to push the fetus out.
    c. about eight hours (for firstborns) after the uterus begins to contract at regular intervals.
    d. when the baby's head appears at the opening of the vagina.

11. The Apgar scale is administered
    a. only if the newborn is in obvious distress.
    b. once, just after birth.
    c. twice, one minute and five minutes after birth.
    d. repeatedly during the newborn's first hours.

12. Most newborns weigh about
    a. 5 pounds.
    b. 6 pounds.
    c. $7\frac{1}{2}$ pounds.
    d. $8\frac{1}{2}$ pounds.

13. Low-birthweight babies born near the due date but weighing substantially less than they should
    a. are classified as preterm.
    b. are called small for gestational age.
    c. usually have no sex organs.
    d. show many signs of immaturity.

14. Approximately one out of every four low-birthweight births in the United States is caused by maternal use of
    a. alcohol.
    b. tobacco.
    c. crack cocaine.
    d. household chemicals.

15. A newborn is classified as preterm if he or she is born
    a. one or more weeks early.
    b. two or more weeks early
    c. three or more weeks early.
    d. four or more weeks early.

16. A reflex is best defined as a(n)
    a. fine motor skill.
    b. motor ability mastered at a specific age.
    c. involuntary response to a given stimulus.
    d. gross motor skill.

Matching Items

Match each definition or description with its corresponding term.

Terms

_____ 1. embryonic period

_____ 2. fetal period

_____ 3. placenta

_____ 4. preterm

_____ 5. teratogens

_____ 6. anoxia

_____ 7. doula

_____ 8. critical period

_____ 9. primitive streak

_____ 10. fetal alcohol syndrome

_____ 11. germinal period

_____ 12. couvade

Definitions or Descriptions

a. term for the period during which a developing baby's body parts are most susceptible to damage

b. agents and conditions that can damage the developing organism

c. the age when viability is attained

d. the precursor of the central nervous system

e. lack of oxygen, which, if prolonged during the birth process, may lead to brain damage

f. characterized by abnormal facial characteristics, slowed growth, behavior problems, and mental retardation

g. symptoms of pregnancy experienced by fathers

h. the life-giving organ that nourishes the embryo and fetus

i. when implantation occurs

j. the prenatal period when all major body structures begin to form

k. a baby born three or more weeks early

l. a woman who helps with the birth process

Progress Test 2

Progress Test 2 should be completed during a final chapter review. Answer the following questions after you thoroughly understand the correct answers for the Chapter Review and Progress Test 1.

Multiple-Choice Questions

1. The phenomenon in which fathers experience the symptoms of pregnancy is called
   a. doula.
   b. anoxia.
   c. kangaroo care.
   d. couvade.

2. In order, the correct sequence of prenatal stages of development is
   a. embryo; germinal; fetus
   b. germinal; fetus; embryo
   c. germinal; embryo; fetus
   d. ovum; fetus; embryo

3. Monika is preparing for the birth of her first child. If all proceeds normally, she can expect that her labor will last about
   a. 7 hours.
   b. 8 hours.
   c. 10 hours.
   d. 12 hours.

4. (Table 4.5) Tetracycline and retinoic acid
   a. can be harmful to the human fetus.
   b. have been proven safe for pregnant women after the embryonic period.
   c. will prevent spontaneous abortions.
   d. are safe when used before the fetal period.

5. (Table 4.5) The teratogen that, if not prevented by immunization, could cause deafness, blindness, and brain damage in the fetus is
   a. rubella (German measles).
   b. anoxia.
   c. acquired immune deficiency syndrome (AIDS).
   d. neural-tube defect.

6. Kangaroo care refers to
   a. the rigid attachment formed between mothers and offspring in the animal kingdom.
   b. the fragmented care that the children of single parents often receive.
   c. a program of increased involvement by mothers of low-birthweight infants.
   d. none of these.

7. Among the characteristics rated on the Apgar scale are
   a. shape of the newborn's head and nose.
   b. presence of body hair.
   c. interactive behaviors.
   d. muscle tone and color.

8. A newborn is classified as low birthweight if he or she weighs less than
   a. 7 pounds.
   b. 6 pounds.
   c. $5\frac{1}{2}$ pounds.
   d. 4 pounds.

9. A critical problem for preterm babies is
   a. the immaturity of the sex organs—for example, undescended testicles.
   b. spitting up or hiccupping.
   c. infection from intravenous feeding.
   d. breathing difficulties.

10. Which of the following is NOT true regarding alcohol use and pregnancy?
    a. Alcohol in high doses is a proven teratogen.
    b. Not every pregnant woman who drinks heavily has a newborn with fetal alcohol syndrome.
    c. Most doctors in the United States advise pregnant women to use alcohol in moderation during pregnancy.
    d. Only after a fetus is born does fetal alcohol syndrome become apparent.

11. Neurogenesis refers to the process by which
    a. the fetal brain develops new neurons.
    b. new connections between neurons develop.
    c. the neural tube forms during the middle trimester.
    d. the cortex folds into layers in order to fit into the skull.

12. Which Apgar score indicates that a newborn is in normal health?
    a. 4
    b. 5
    c. 6
    d. 7

13. Synaptogenesis refers to the process by which
    a. the fetal brain develops new neurons.
    b. new connections between neurons develop.
    c. the neural tube forms during the middle trimester.
    d. the cortex folds into layers in order to fit into the skull.

14. When there is a strong parental alliance
    a. mother and father cooperate because of their mutual commitment to their children.
    b. the parents agree to support each other in their shared parental roles.
    c. children are likely to thrive.
    d. all of these answers are true.

15. The critical period for preventing physical defects appears to be the
    a. zygote period.
    b. embryonic period.
    c. fetal period.
    d. entire pregnancy.

16. Some infant reflexes are critical for survival. Hiccups and sneezes help the infant maintain _____ , and leg tucking maintains_____ .
    a. feeding; oxygen supply
    b. feeding; a constant body temperature
    c. the oxygen supply; feeding
    d. the oxygen supply; a constant body temperature

True or False Items

Write T (*true*) or F (*false*) on the line in front of each statement.

_____ 1. The fetus becomes aware of the mother's voice.

_____ 2. Eight weeks after conception, the embryo has formed almost all the basic organs.

_____ 3. Less than 1 percent of births in the United States take place in the home.

_____ 4. In general, behavioral teratogens have the greatest effect during the embryonic period.

_____ 5. The effects of cigarette smoking during pregnancy remain highly controversial.

_____ 6. The Apgar scale is used to measure vital signs such as heart rate, breathing, and reflexes.

_____ 7. Newborns usually breathe on their own, moments after birth.

_____ 8. Research has shown that immediate mother–infant contact at birth is necessary for the normal emotional development of the child.

_____ 9. Low birthweight is often correlated with maternal malnutrition.

_____ 10. Cesarean sections are rarely performed in the United States today because of the resulting danger to the fetus.

_____ 11. Reflexive hiccups, sneezes, and thrashing are signs that the infant's reflexes are not functioning properly.

Key Terms

Using your own words, write a brief definition or explanation of each of the following terms on a separate piece of paper.

1. germinal period
2. embryonic period
3. fetal period
4. implantation
5. embryo
6. fetus
7. ultrasound
8. age of viability
9. Apgar scale
10. cesarean section (c-section)
11. doula
12. teratogens
13. behavioral teratogens
14. threshold effect
15. fetal alcohol syndrome (FAS)
16. false positive
17. low birthweight (LBW)
18. very low birthweight (VLBW)
19. extremely low birthweight (ELBW)
20. preterm
21. small for gestational age (SGA)
22. cerebral palsy
23. anoxia

24. Brazelton Neonatal Assessment Scale (NBAS)
25. reflex
26. couvade
27. postpartum depression
28. parental alliance
29. parent–infant bond
30. kangaroo care

ANSWERS

CHAPTER REVIEW

1. three; germinal; third; eighth; embryonic; fetal
2. placenta; embryo
3. implantation; is not
4. primitive streak; neural tube; central nervous system

The head begins to take shape as eyes, ears, nose, and mouth start to form. A tiny blood vessel that will become the heart begins to pulsate. By the fifth week, buds that will become arms and legs emerge. The upper arms, then the forearms, palms, and webbed fingers appear. Legs, feet, and webbed toes follow. At the end of the eighth week, the embryo has all the basic organs and body parts, except the sex organs.

5. one-thirtieth of an ounce (1 gram); 1 inch (2.5 centimeters); fetus
6. Y; SRY; male; female
7. cephalocaudal; proximodistal; third; ultrasound; sonogram
8. 3 ounces (87 grams); 3 inches (7.5 centimeters); vary
9. six; neurogenesis; synaptogenesis; breathing; sucking
10. age of viability; 22; has not; brain
11. neurological; respiratory; cardiovascular
12. cortex
13. three; heartbeat; voice
14. neurogenesis; synaptogenesis; fetus. Brain maturity is the key to reaching the age of viability.
15. c. is the answer. Male and female sex organs do not develop until the ninth week.
16. 38; hormones; oxytocin; 12; 7
17. Apgar scale; heart rate, breathing, muscle tone, color, and reflexes; 4; 7; one; five

18. one-third; cesarean section

19. Europe; United States; at home

20. doula

21. teratogens; viruses, drugs, chemicals, pollutants, extreme stress, and malnutrition

22. behavioral teratogens; 20

23. timing; amount; genetic vulnerability

24. critical period; embryo; behavioral

25. threshold

26. interact

27. spina bifida; anencephaly; ethnic; folic acid

28. drugs, chemicals in pesticides, cleaning fluids, and cosmetics; medications

29. fetal alcohol syndrome; fetal alcohol effects

30. **b.** is the answer. HIV is the virus that causes AIDS. Rubella may cause blindness, deafness, and brain damage. In small doses, lead may be harmless; large doses may produce brain damage in the fetus.

31. **a.** is the answer. Some teratogens are virtually harmless until they reach a certain level. For example, too much vitamin A can cause some abnormalities.

32. **d.** is the answer. Researchers do not yet know which of these factors are necessary for alcohol to be teratogenic.

33. neural-tube defects. Folic acid is needed for the fetus to develop normally.

34. 2,500 grams (5^1/$_2$ pounds); low-birthweight; very-low-birthweight; extremely-low-birthweight; vary

35. preterm

36. small for gestational age

37. illness; drug; tobacco

38. malnutrition; multiple; assisted reproduction

39. obesity; heart; diabetes

40. cerebral palsy; genetic; teratogens; anoxia; oxygen

41. Kenny's mother smoked heavily during her pregnancy. Although every psychoactive drug slows prenatal growth, tobacco is the worst and most prevalent cause of SGA.

42. **c.** is the answer. If a newborn's Apgar score is below 4, the infant is in critical condition and needs immediate medical attention.

43. **b.** is the answer. Where a baby is born generally will not affect its size at birth. And certainly size is not hereditary.

44. **c.** is the answer. Donna's risk factor for having an LBW baby is her weight (teens tend not to eat well and can be undernourished).

45. low-birthweight; small-for-gestational age. Thirty-eight weeks is full term, so a baby at 4 pounds would be small-for-gestational age and, of course, low birthweight.

46. preterm. Any birth before 38 weeks is preterm.

47. reflexes, breathing, muscle tone, heart rate, and color

48. Brazelton Neonatal Assessment Scale

49. reflex

50. breathing reflex; hiccups; sneezes; thrashing

51. constant body temperature

52. feeding; sucking; rooting; swallowing; crying; spitting up

53. father; immigration paradox; poorer; prenatal; healthier

54. weight gain, indigestion, pain during labor; couvade

55. parental alliance

56. postpartum depression

57. parent–infant bond; cross-fostering

58. reduces; kangaroo care

59. **a.** reflexes that maintain oxygen supply
    b. crying, shivering, tucking in their legs, pushing blankets away
    c. reflexes that facilitate feeding
    d. infants' toes fan upward when their feet are stroked
    e. stepping reflex
    f. infants stretch out their arms and legs when they are held on their stomachs
    g. Palmar grasping reflex
    h. infants fling their arms outward and then clutch them against their chests in response to a loud noise

60. **c.** is the answer.

PROGRESS TEST 1

Multiple-Choice Questions

1. **a.** is the answer.

   b. This term, which refers to the germinal period, is not used in the text.

   c. The fetal period is from the ninth week until birth.

   d. The germinal period covers the first two weeks.

2. **c.** is the answer.

3. **a.** is the answer.

   b., c., & d. Although low birthweight (b.), critical periods of organ development (c.), and maternal malnutrition (d.) are all hazardous to the developing person during prenatal development, none is an example of a threshold effect.

4. **c.** is the answer. The sex organs do not begin to take shape until the fetal period.

5. **c.** is the answer.

6. **d.** is the answer.

7. **a.** is the answer.

8. **d.** is the answer.

   a. In general, teratogens can cross the placenta at any time.

   b. Teratogens are agents in the environment, not heritable genes (although *susceptibility* to individual teratogens has a genetic component).

   c. Although nutrition is an important factor in healthy prenatal development, the text does not suggest that nutrition alone can usually counteract the harmful effects of teratogens.

9. **a.** is the answer.

10. **b.** is the answer.

11. **c.** is the answer.

12. **c.** is the answer.

13. **b.** is the answer.

14. **b.** is the answer.

15. **c.** is the answer.

16. **c.** is the answer.

Matching Items

1. j	5. b	9. d
2. c	6. e	10. f
3. h	7. l	11. i
4. k	8. a	12. g

PROGRESS TEST 2

Multiple-Choice Questions

1. **d.** is the answer.

   a. A doula is a woman who assists the mother-to-be through labor, delivery, and newborn care.

   b. Anoxia is a temporary lack of oxygen during the birth process.

   c. Kangaroo care occurs when the mother of a low-birthweight infant spends at least one hour a day holding her infant.

2. **c.** is the answer.

3. **d.** is the answer.

   a. The average length of labor for subsequent births is 7 hours.

4. **a.** is the answer.

5. **a.** is the answer.

6. **c.** is the answer.

7. **d.** is the answer.

8. **c.** is the answer.

9. **d.** is the answer.

10. **c.** is the answer. Most doctors in the United States advise pregnant women to abstain completely from alcohol.

11. **a.** is the answer.

12. **d.** is the answer.

13. **b.** is the answer.

14. **d.** is the answer.

15. **c.** is the answer.

16. **d.** is the answer.

True or False Items

1. T
2. T
3. T
4. F Behavioral teratogens can affect the fetus at any time during the prenatal period.
5. F There is no controversy about the damaging effects of smoking during pregnancy.
6. T
7. T

8. F Though highly desirable, mother–infant contact at birth is not necessary for the child's normal development or for a good parent–child relationship. Many opportunities for bonding occur throughout childhood.

9. T

10. F About 32 percent of births in the United States are now cesarean.

11. F Hiccups, sneezes, and thrashing are common during the first few days, and they are entirely normal reflexes.

KEY TERMS

1. The first two weeks of development after conception, characterized by rapid cell division and the beginning of cell differentiation, are called the **germinal period.**

   Memory aid: A *germ cell* is one from which a new organism can develop. The **germinal period** is the first stage in the development of the new organism.

2. The **embryonic period** is approximately the third through the eighth week of prenatal development, when the basic forms of all body structures develop.

3. From the ninth week after conception until birth is the **fetal period,** when the organs grow in size and mature in functioning.

4. **Implantation** is the process by which the zygote burrows into the placenta that lines the uterus, where it can be nourished and protected during growth.

5. **Embryo** is the name given to the developing human organism from about the third through the eighth week after conception.

6. **Fetus** is the name for the developing human organism from the start of the ninth week after conception until birth.

7. An **ultrasound** is an image of an unborn fetus (or an internal organ) produced with high-frequency sound waves; all called *sonogram.*

8. About 22 weeks after conception, the fetus attains the **age of viability,** at which point it has at least some slight chance of survival outside the uterus if specialized medical care is available.

9. Newborns are rated at one minute and then at five minutes after birth according to the **Apgar scale.** This scale assigns a score of 0, 1, or 2 to each of five characteristics: heart rate, breathing, muscle tone, color, and reflexes. A score of 7 or better indicates that all is well.

10. In a **cesarean section (c-section),** the fetus is removed from the mother surgically. (Also called simply *section.*)

11. A **doula** is a woman who works alongside medical staff to assist a woman through labor, delivery, breast-feeding, and newborn care.

12. **Teratogens** are agents and conditions, such as viruses, drugs, chemicals, extreme stress, and malnutrition, that can impair prenatal development and lead to birth defects or even death.

13. **Behavioral teratogens** are agents and conditions that can damage the prenatal brain, impairing the future child's intellectual and emotional functioning.

14. A **threshold effect** is the harmful effect of a substance that occurs when exposure to it reaches a certain level.

15. Prenatal alcohol exposure may cause **fetal alcohol syndrome (FAS),** a cluster of birth defects that includes abnormal facial characteristics, slow physical growth, behavior problems, and retarded mental development.

16. A false positive is the result of a prenatal diagnostic test that reports something as true when in fact it is not true.

17. A birthweight of less than 5 1/2 pounds (2,500 grams) is called **low birthweight (LBW).** Low-birthweight infants are at risk for many immediate and long-term problems.

18. A birthweight of less than 3 pounds, 5 ounces (1,500 grams) is called **very low birthweight (VLBW).**

19. A birthweight of less than 2 pounds, 5 ounces (1,000 grams) is called **extremely low birthweight (ELBW).**

20. When an infant is born 3 or more weeks before the due date, it is said to be a **preterm** birth.

21. Infants who weigh substantially less than they should, given how much time has passed since conception, are called **small for gestational age (SGA),** or small-for-dates.

22. **Cerebral palsy** is a muscular control disorder caused by damage to the brain's motor centers during or before birth.

23. **Anoxia** is a temporary lack of oxygen during the birth process that, if prolonged, can cause brain damage or death to the baby.

24. The **Brazelton Neonatal Behavioral Assessment Scale (NBAS)** is a test of newborn responsiveness that measures 46 behaviors, including 20 reflexes.

25. A **reflex** is an unlearned, involuntary action or movement emitted in response to a specific stimulus.

26. **Couvade** refers to the phenomenon in which some fathers experience symptoms of pregnancy and birth.

27. **Postpartum depression** is a new mother's feeling of sadness and inadequacy in the days and weeks after giving birth.

28. **Parental alliance** refers to the cooperation and mutual support between mother and father because of their mutual commitment to their children.

29. The term **parent–infant bond** describes the strong feelings of attachment between parent and child in the early moments of their relationship together.

30. **Kangaroo care** occurs when the mother of a low-birthweight infant spends at least one hour a day holding her infant between her breasts.

The First Two Years: Biosocial Development

Chapter 5: The First Two Years: Chapter Overview

Chapter 5 is the first of a three-chapter unit that describes the developing person from birth to age 2 in terms of biosocial, cognitive, and psychosocial development.

The chapter begins with observations on the overall growth of infants, including information on infant sleep patterns. Following is a discussion of brain growth and development and the importance of experience and sleep in healthy development. The chapter then turns to a discussion of sensory, perceptual, and motor abilities and the ages at which the average infant acquires them. Preventive medicine, the importance of immunizations, and good nutrition during the first two years, including the consequences of severe malnutrition, are discussed next.

What Will You Know?

The text chapter should be studied one section at a time. Before you read, preview each section by skimming it, noting headings and boldface items. Then read the sections, one at a time, keeping these questions in mind.

1. What part of an infant grows most in the first two years?
2. How do newborn humans differ from newborn kittens?
3. Does immunization protect or harm babies?

Chapter Review

When you have finished reading the chapter, work through the material that follows to review it. Completing the sentences and answering the questions will enable you to answer the "What Have You Learned?" questions at the end of the text chapter. Scattered throughout the Chapter Review are Study Tips, which explain how best to learn a difficult concept, and Think About It discussions and Applications, which help you to know how well you understand the material. Check your understanding of the material by consulting the answers at the end of the chapter. Do not continue with the next section until you understand each answer. If you need to, review or reread the appropriate section in the textbook before continuing.

Growth in Infancy

1. By age 2, the typical child weighs about _____ and measures _____ . The typical 2-year-old is almost _____ percent of his or her adult weight and _____ percent of his or her adult height.

2. To compare a child's growth to that of other children, we determine _____ , a point on a ranking scale of _____ (what number?) to _____ (what number?).

3. When nutrition is temporarily inadequate, the body stops growing but the brain does not. This is called _____-_____ .

4. The brain's communication system consists primarily of nerve cells called _____ . About _____ percent of these cells are in the brain's outer layer called the _____ .

5. The last part of the brain to mature is the

_____ _____ ,

which is the area for _____ ,

_____ , and

_____ _____ .

6. Each neuron has many _____ but only a single _____ .

7. Neurons communicate with one another at intersections called _____ .
While traveling down the length of the _____ , the electrical impulses become chemicals called _____ that carry information across the _____ _____ to the _____ of a "receiving" neuron. The transmission of neural impulses is speeded up in axons covered by _____ .

8. During the first months of life, brain development is most noticeable in the _____ .
The growth of _____ is the major reason that brain weight triples in the first two years.

9. From birth until age 2, the density of dendrites in the cortex _____ (increases/ decreases) by a factor of _____ .
The phenomenal temporary increase in neural connections over the first two years has been called _____ _____ . Following this growth process, some neurons wither in the process called _____ because _____ does not activate those brain areas.

10. Brain functions that require basic common experiences in order to develop normally are called _____ - _____ brain functions; those that depend on particular, variable experiences in order to develop are called _____ - _____ brain functions.

11. A life-threatening condition that occurs when an infant is held by the shoulders and quickly

shaken back and forth is _____

_____ _____ .

Crying stops because of ruptured

_____ _____

in the brain, which result in broken

_____ connections.

12. The inborn drive to remedy a developmental deficit is called _____ -

_____ .

13. (A View From Science) The part of the brain that is adept at face recognition is the

_____ _____

_____ . This area of the brain,

which is _____ (experience-expectant/experience-dependent/both experience-expectant and experience-dependent),

_____ (is active/is not active) in newborns. Before their first birthday, infants more readily notice differences among faces from their own _____ and

their own _____ group. This

phenomenon, called the _____ -

_____ effect, is the result of

limited _____ experience.

THINK ABOUT IT The text cites several lines of research evidence that environmental events after birth can shape the development of a child's brain and affect overall cognitive functioning in the years beyond infancy. In the face of this evidence, many parents wonder how far they should go in providing their babies with enriched environmental experiences. Based on your reading of this section of the text chapter, what practical advice would you offer to prospective parents?

14. Over the first months of life, the relative amount of time spent in the different

_____ of sleep changes. The stage of sleep characterized by flickering eyes behind closed lids and _____ is called

_____ _____ .

During this stage of sleep, brain waves are fairly

_____ (slow/rapid). This stage

of sleep _____ (increases/ decreases) over the first months, as does the dozing stage called _____

_____ .

15. Quiet sleep, also called _____-_____ sleep, increases markedly at about _____ months of age.

16. (Opposing Perspectives) In most Western cultures, children _____ (do/do not) sleep with their parents. In contrast, parents in _____ , _____ , and _____ _____ traditionally practice _____ with their infants. This practice _____ (does/does not) seem to be harmful unless the adult is _____ .

THINK ABOUT IT Growth in early infancy is astoundingly rapid. You can begin to appreciate just how rapid this growth is by projecting the growth patterns of the infant onto an adult, such as yourself. If you were gaining weight at the rate of an infant, your weight would be tripled one year from today. How much would you weigh? If you were growing at the rate of an infant during the first year, you would add an inch each month. What would your height be a year from today?

STUDY TIP As you can see from the list of Key Terms, this chapter introduces many important new words for you to remember. You will need to spend extra time committing these terms to memory. Many students find flash cards and quizzing a study partner helpful for learning new terminology. To help remember the key parts of a neuron, you might find it useful to practice drawing and labeling dendrites, axons, myelin, and synapses.

APPLICATIONS:

17. I am a chemical that carries information between nerve cells in the brain. What am I?

_____

18. Sharetta's pediatrician informs her parents that Sharetta's 1-year-old brain is exhibiting transient exuberance. In response to this news, Sharetta's parents
    a. smile, because they know their daughter's brain is developing new neural connections.
    b. worry, because this may indicate increased vulnerability to a later learning disability.
    c. know that this process, in which axons become coated, is normal.
    d. are alarmed, because this news indicates that the frontal area of Sharetta's cortex is immature.

19. Trying to impress his professor, Erik explains that we know humans have a critical period for learning certain skills because the brain cannot form new synapses after age 13. Should the professor be impressed with Erik's knowledge of biosocial development?
    a. Yes, although each neuron may have already formed as many as 15,000 connections with other neurons.
    b. Yes, although the branching of dendrites and axons does continue through young adulthood.
    c. No. Although Erik is correct about neural development, the brain attains adult size by about age 7.
    d. No. Synapses form throughout life.

20. Two-year-old Rafael weighs 28 pounds and is 34 inches tall. He is considered average because his height and weight are in the _____ percentile for 2-year-olds.

21. The Farbers, who are first-time parents, are wondering whether they should be concerned because their 12-month-old daughter, who weighs 22 pounds and measures 30 inches, is not growing quite as fast as she did during her first 11 months. You should tell them that
    a. any slowdown in growth during the second year is a cause for immediate concern.
    b. their daughter's weight and height are well below average for her age.
    c. growth patterns for a first child are often erratic.
    d. physical growth is somewhat slower in the second year.

22. Concluding her presentation on sleep, Lakshmi notes each of the following EXCEPT
    a. dreaming occurs during REM sleep.
    b. quiet sleep increases markedly at about 3 or 4 months.
    c. the dreaming brain is characterized by slow brain waves.
    d. regular and ample sleep is an important factor in a child's emotional regulation.

Perceiving and Moving

23. The process by which the visual, auditory, and other sensory systems detect stimuli is called _____ ; _____ occurs when the brain tries to make sense out of a stimulus so that the individual becomes aware of it. At birth, only _____ is apparent; _____ requires experience. In the process called _____ , a person thinks about

and interprets what he or she has perceived. This process _____ (can/cannot) occur without sensation.

24. Generally speaking, newborns' hearing _____ (is/is not) very acute at birth. Newborns _____ (can/cannot) perceive differences in voices, rhythms, and cadences long before they achieve comprehension of _____ . Infants also become accustomed to the rules of their _____ .

25. The least mature of the senses at birth is _____ . Newborns' visual focusing is best for objects between _____ and _____ inches away.

26. Experience and increasing maturation of the visual cortex accounts for improvements in other visual abilities, such as the infant's ability to see _____ and then notice _____ . By 2 months, they look more intently at a human _____ . The ability to use both eyes in a coordinated manner to focus on one object, which is called _____ _____ , develops at about _____ of age.

27. Taste, smell, and touch _____ (function/do not function) at birth. The ability to be comforted by the human _____ is a skill tested in the _____ Neonatal Behavioral Assessment Scale.

28. The infant's early sensory abilities seem organized for two goals: _____ _____ and _____ .

29. The most visible and dramatic advances of infancy involve _____ _____ .

30. Large movements such as walking and running are called _____ _____ skills.

31. Most infants are able to crawl on all fours (sometimes called creeping) between

_____ and _____ months of age. Three factors in the development of walking are _____

_____ , _____ , and _____ .

List the major hallmarks in children's mastery of walking.

32. Abilities that require more precise, small movements, such as picking up a coin, are called _____ _____ skills. By _____ months of age, most babies can reach for, grab, and hold onto almost any object of the right size.

33. Although the _____ in which motor skills are mastered is the same in all healthy infants, the _____ of acquisition of skills varies greatly.

34. Motor skill norms vary from one _____ group to another.

35. Motor skill acquisition in identical twins _____ (is/is not) more similar than in fraternal twins, suggesting that genes _____ (do/do not) play an important role. Another influential factor is the _____ _____ of infant care.

APPLICATIONS:

36. Sensation is to perception as _____ is to _____ .
    a. hearing; seeing
    b. detecting a stimulus; making sense of a stimulus
    c. making sense of a stimulus; detecting a stimulus
    d. tasting; smelling

37. Like all newborns, Serena is able to
  a. differentiate one sound from another.
  b. see objects more than 30 inches from her face quite clearly.
  c. use her mouth to recognize objects by taste and touch.
  d. do all of these things.

38. Three-week-old Nathan should have the least difficulty focusing on the sight of
  a. stuffed animals on a bookshelf across the room from his crib.
  b. his mother's face as she holds him in her arms.
  c. the checkerboard pattern in the wallpaper covering the ceiling of his room.
  d. the family dog as it dashes into the nursery.

Surviving in Good Health

39. Without public health practices, the number of children who die would be _____ (how much?) the number who did die between 1950 and 2010. One method, _____ _____ _____ (giving restorative liquids to children who are sick and have diarrhea), saves 3 million children a year.

40. Globally, today most children _____ (do/do not) live to adulthood. A key factor in reducing the childhood death rate was the development of _____ , a process that stimulates the body's _____ system to defend against contagious diseases. This process has met with stunning success in eradicating or reducing diseases such as _____ , _____ , _____ , and _____ . Other reasons for a decrease in infant mortality are _____ .

41. The ideal infant food is _____ _____ , beginning with the thick, high-calorie fluid called _____ . The only situations in which formula may be healthier for the infant than breast milk are when _____ .

State several advantages of breast milk over cow's milk for the developing infant.

42. Most doctors recommend exclusive breast-feeding for the first _____ (how many?) months.

43. The serious nutritional problem in which a person does not consume sufficient food is _____ - _____ _____ . Chronic malnutrition of this type causes children to be short for their age (called _____) in about _____ (what proportion?) of the world's children. Malnutrition also causes _____ , in which children are severely underweight for their age.

44. Chronically malnourished infants suffer in three ways: Their _____ may not develop normally, they may have no _____ _____ to protect them against disease, and they may develop the diseases _____ or _____ .

45. Severe protein-calorie deficiency in early infancy causes _____ . If malnutrition begins after age 1, protein-calorie deficiency is more likely to cause the disease called _____ , which involves swelling or bloating of the face, legs, and abdomen.

46. Crib death, or _____ _____ _____ _____ , most often affects infants between _____ and _____ months of age. Placing infants on their _____ while sleeping protects against SIDS.

APPLICATIONS:

47. To promote optimal nutrition for her new baby, Emma's pediatrician recommends exclusive breast-feeding for the first _____ (how many months?).

48. Before she became pregnant, Nell had a bout of the measles. After the baby was born, her pediatrician recommended breast-feeding because

_____

_____ .

Progress Test 1

Multiple-Choice Questions

Circle your answers to the following questions and check them with the answers at the end of the chapter. If your answer is incorrect, read the explanation for why it is incorrect and then consult the text.

1. *Stunting* refers to the tendency of children who are
   a. overfed to be shorter than average for their age.
   b. chronically malnourished to be shorter than average for their age.
   c. chronically malnourished to be underweight for their age.
   d. overfed to have fewer dendrites in their brain.

2. Compared with growth during the first year, growth during the second year
   a. proceeds at a slower rate.
   b. continues at about the same rate.
   c. includes more insulating fat.
   d. includes more bone and muscle.

3. The major motor skill most likely to be mastered by an infant by 4 months is
   a. sitting without support.
   b. sitting with head steady.
   c. turning the head in search of a nipple.
   d. grabbing a small object within arm's reach.

4. The last part of the brain to mature is the
   a. auditory cortex.
   b. visual cortex.
   c. brain stem.
   d. prefrontal cortex.

5. Head-sparing is the phenomenon in which
   a. the brain continues to grow even though the body stops growing as a result of malnutrition.
   b. the infant's body grows more rapidly during the second year.
   c. axons develop more rapidly than dendrites.
   d. dendrites develop more rapidly than axons.

6. Dreaming is characteristic of
   a. slow-wave sleep.
   b. transitional sleep.
   c. REM sleep.
   d. quiet sleep.

7. For a pediatrician, the most important factor in assessing a child's healthy growth is
   a. height in inches.
   b. weight in pounds.
   c. body fat percentage.
   d. the percentile rank of a child's height or weight.

8. Brain functions that depend on babies' having things to see and hear, and people to feed and carry them, are called
   a. experience-dependent.
   b. experience-expectant.
   c. pruning functions.
   d. transient exuberance.

9. Compared with formula-fed infants, breast-fed infants tend to have
   a. greater weight gain.
   b. fewer allergies and stomach upsets.
   c. less frequent feedings during the first few months.
   d. more social approval.

10. Marasmus and kwashiorkor are caused by
    a. bloating.
    b. protein-calorie deficiency.
    c. living in a developing country.
    d. poor family food habits.

11. The brain's communication system consists primarily of nerve cells called
    a. axons.
    b. dendrites.
    c. synapses.
    d. neurons.

12. Which of the following is said to have had the greatest impact on human mortality reduction and population growth?
    a. improvements in infant nutrition
    b. oral rehydration therapy
    c. medical advances in newborn care
    d. childhood immunization

13. Which of the following is true of motor-skill development in healthy infants?
    a. It follows the same basic sequence the world over.
    b. It occurs at different rates from individual to individual.
    c. It follows norms that vary from one ethnic group to another.
    d. All of these statements are true.

14. Most of the nerve cells a human brain will ever need are present
    a. at conception.
    b. about one month following conception.
    c. at birth.
    d. at age 5 or 6.

15. Chronically malnourished children suffer in which of the following ways?
    a. They have no body reserves to protect them.
    b. Their brains may not develop normally.
    c. They may die from marasmus.
    d. All of these conditions are true of malnourished children.

Matching Items

Match each definition or description with its corresponding term.

Terms

_____ 1. neurons
_____ 2. dendrites
_____ 3. kwashiorkor
_____ 4. marasmus
_____ 5. gross motor skill
_____ 6. fine motor skill
_____ 7. protein-calorie malnutrition
_____ 8. transient exuberance
_____ 9. prefrontal cortex
_____ 10. self-righting
_____ 11. pruning

Definitions or Descriptions

a. protein deficiency during the first year in which growth stops and body tissues waste away
b. picking up an object
c. the most common serious nutrition problem of infancy
d. protein deficiency during toddlerhood
e. process by which unused brain connections atrophy and die
f. walking or running
g. the phenomenal increase in neural connections over the first two years
h. nerve cells
i. the brain area that specializes in anticipation, planning, and impulse control
j. the inborn drive to correct a developmental deficit
k. communication networks among nerve cells

Progress Test 2

Progress Test 2 should be completed during a final chapter review. Answer the following questions after you thoroughly understand the correct answers for the Chapter Review and Progress Test 1.

Multiple-Choice Questions

1. Dendrite is to axon as neural _____ is to neural _____ .
   a. input; output
   b. output; input
   c. myelin; synapse
   d. synapse; myelin

2. *Wasting* refers to the tendency of children who are
   a. overfed to be shorter than average for their age.
   b. chronically malnourished to be shorter than average for their age.
   c. chronically malnourished to be underweight for their age.
   d. overfed to have fewer dendrites in their brain.

3. Regarding the debate over the potential benefits and dangers of immunization, most developmentalists agree that
   a. the benefits have consistently been shown to outweigh the risks.
   b. the risks have consistently been shown to outweigh the benefits.
   c. immunization is advisable only for children who are not malnourished.
   d. much more research is needed before any conclusions can be drawn.

4. The ability to use both eyes to focus on an object is called
   a. marasmus.
   b. kwashiorkor.
   c. binocular vision.
   d. perception.

5. Regarding the brain's cortex, which of the following is NOT true?
   a. The cortex houses about 70 percent of the brain's neurons.
   b. The cortex is the brain's outer layer.
   c. The cortex is the location of most thinking, feeling, and sensing.
   d. Only primates have a cortex.

6. During the first weeks of life, babies seem to focus reasonably well on
   a. little in their environment.
   b. objects at a distance of 4 to 30 inches.
   c. objects at a distance of 1 to 3 inches.
   d. objects several feet away.

7. Which sleep stage increases markedly at about 3 or 4 months?
   a. REM
   b. transitional
   c. fast-wave
   d. slow-wave

8. An advantage of breast milk over formula is that it
   a. is always sterile and at body temperature.
   b. contains traces of medications ingested by the mother.
   c. can be given without involving the father.
   d. contains more protein and vitamin D than does formula.

9. Synapses are
   a. nerve fibers that receive electrochemical impulses from other neurons.
   b. nerve fibers that transmit electrochemical impulses to other neurons.
   c. intersections between the axon of one neuron and the dendrites of other neurons.
   d. chemical signals that transmit information from one neuron to another.

10. Transient exuberance and pruning demonstrate that
    a. the pace of acquisition of motor skills varies markedly from child to child.
    b. newborns sleep more than older children because their immature nervous systems cannot handle the higher, waking level of sensory stimulation.
    c. the specifics of brain structure and growth depend partly on the infant's experience.
    d. good nutrition is essential to healthy biosocial development.

11. Jumping is to using a crayon as _____ is to _____ .
    a. fine motor skill; gross motor skill
    b. gross motor skill; fine motor skill
    c. reflex; fine motor skill
    d. reflex; gross motor skill

12. Over the first two years, the brain increases to about what percentage of its adult weight?
    a. 25 percent
    b. 50 percent
    c. 75 percent
    d. 100 percent

13. (A View from Science) Compared with the brains of laboratory rats that were raised in barren cages, those of rats raised in stimulating, toy-filled cages
    a. were better developed and had more dendrites.
    b. had fewer synaptic connections.
    c. showed less transient exuberance.
    d. displayed all of these characteristics.

14. In determining a healthy child's growth, a pediatrician focuses on
    a. the child's past growth.
    b. the growth of others the same age.
    c. growth changes from earlier rankings.
    d. all of these factors.

15. Infant sensory and perceptual abilities appear to be especially organized for
    a. obtaining adequate nutrition and comfort.
    b. comfort and social interaction.
    c. looking.
    d. touching and smelling.

True or False Items

Write T (true) or F (false) on the line in front of each statement.

_____ 1. Imaging studies have identified a specific area of the brain that specializes in recognizing faces.

_____ 2. Sudden infant death is less common when babies sleep beside their parents.

_____ 3. Infants of all ethnic backgrounds develop the same motor skills at approximately the same age.

_____ 4. The typical 2-year-old is almost one-fifth its adult weight and one-half its adult height.

_____ 5. Vision is better developed than hearing in most newborns.

_____ 6. Today, most infants in industrialized nations are breast-fed up to 6 months.

_____ 7. Certain basic sensory experiences seem necessary to ensure full brain development in the human infant.

_____ 8. Dendrite growth is the major reason that brain weight increases so dramatically in the first two years.

_____ 9. The only motor skills apparent at birth are reflexes.

_____ 10. The prefrontal cortex is one of the first brain areas to mature.

Key Terms

Using your own words, write a brief definition or explanation of each of the following terms on a separate piece of paper.

1. percentile
2. head-sparing
3. neuron
4. cortex
5. prefrontal cortex
6. axon
7. dendrite
8. synapse
9. neurotransmitter
10. synaptic gap
11. transient exuberance
12. pruning
13. experience-expectant brain functions
14. experience-dependent brain functions
15. shaken baby syndrome
16. self-righting
17. REM sleep
18. co-sleeping
19. sensation
20. perception
21. binocular vision
22. motor skill
23. gross motor skill
24. fine motor skill
25. immunization
26. protein-calorie malnutrition
27. stunting
28. wasting
29. marasmus
30. kwashiorkor
31. sudden infant death syndrome (SIDS)

ANSWERS

CHAPTER REVIEW

1. 28 pounds (13 kilograms); 34 inches (86 centimeters); 20; 50

2. percentile; zero; 100

3. head-sparing

4. neurons; 70; cortex

5. prefrontal cortex; anticipation; planning; impulse control

6. dendrites; axon

7. synapses; axon; neurotransmitters; synaptic gap; dendrite; myelin

8. cortex; dendrites

9. increases; five; transient exuberance; pruning; experience

10. experience-expectant; experience-dependent

11. shaken baby syndrome; blood vessels; neural

12. self-righting

13. fusiform face area; both experience-expectant and experience-dependent; is active; species; ethnic; own-race; multiethnic

14. stages; dreaming; REM sleep; rapid; decreases; transitional sleep

15. slow-wave; 3 or 4

16. do not; Asia; Africa; Latin America; co-sleeping; does not; drugged or drunk

17. neurotransmitter

18. a. is the answer. Transient exuberance results in a proliferation of neural connections during infancy, some of which will disappear because they are not used; that is, they are not needed to process information.

19. d. is the answer. Although synapses do form more rapidly in infancy than at any other time, they do not stop forming after infancy.

20. 50th. The 50th percentile is the midpoint in a ranking from 0 to 100, which means Rafael is exactly average.

21. d. is the answer. Although slowdowns in growth during infancy are often a cause for concern, their daughter's weight and height are typical of 1-year-old babies.

22. c. is the answer. The dreaming brain is characterized by rapid brain waves.

23. sensation; perception; sensation; perception; cognition; can

24. is; can; meaning; language

25. vision; 4; 30

26. shapes; details; face; binocular vision; 14 weeks

27. function; touch; Brazelton

28. social interaction; comfort

29. motor skills

30. gross motor

31. 8; 10; muscle strength; practice; brain maturation within the motor cortex

Some children can walk while holding a hand at 9 months, can stand alone momentarily at 10 months, and can walk well, unassisted, at 12 months.

32. fine motor; 6

33. sequence; age

34. ethnic

35. is; do; cultural pattern

36. b. is the answer. Answers a. and d. are incorrect because sensation and perception operate in all of these sensory modalities.

37. a. is the answer. Objects more than 30 inches away are out of focus for newborns. The ability to recognize objects by taste or touch does not emerge until about 1 month of age.

38. b. is the answer. This is true because, at birth, focusing is best for objects between 4 and 30 inches away.

39. twice; oral rehydration therapy

40. do; immunization; immune; smallpox; polio; measles; rotavirus; advances in prenatal and newborn care, better nutrition, and access to clean water

41. breast milk; colostrum; the mother is HIV-positive or using toxic or addictive drugs

Breast milk is always sterile and at body temperature; it contains more iron, vitamins, and other nutrients; it contains antibodies that provide the infant some protection against disease; and it is more digestible than any formula.

42. four to six

43. protein-calorie malnutrition; stunting; one-third; wasting

44. brains; body reserves; marasmus; kwashiorkor

45. marasmus; kwashiorkor

46. sudden infant death syndrome; 2; 6; backs

47. four to six months

48. having had measles, Nell has developed an immunity to the disease. With breast milk, she will pass the resulting antibodies on to her newborn.

PROGRESS TEST 1

Multiple-Choice Questions

1. **b.** is the answer.

    a. Stunting is caused by underfeeding, not overfeeding.

    c. This describes wasting.

2. **a.** is the answer.

3. **b.** is the answer.

    a. The age norm for this skill is 6–7 months.

    c. This is a reflex, not an acquired motor skill.

    d. This skill is acquired between 6 and 9 months.

4. **d.** is the answer.

5. **a.** is the answer.

6. **c.** is the answer.

7. **d.** is the answer.

8. **b.** is the answer.

    a. Experience-dependent functions depend on particular, variable experiences in order to develop.

    c. Pruning refers to the process by which some neurons wither because experience does not activate them.

    d. This refers to the great increase in the number of neurons, dendrites, and synapses that occurs in an infant's brain over the first two years of life.

9. **b.** is the answer. This is because breast milk is more digestible than cow's milk or formula.

    a., c., & d. Breast- and bottle-fed babies do not differ in these attributes.

10. **b.** is the answer.

11. **d.** is the answer.

    a. Axons are nerve fiber extensions that send impulses from one neuron to the dendrites of other neurons.

    b. Dendrites are nerve fiber extensions that receive impulses from other neurons.

    c. Synapses are the points at which the axon of one neuron meets the dendrites of other neurons.

12. **d.** is the answer.

13. **d.** is the answer.

14. **c.** is the answer.

15. **d.** is the answer.

Matching Items

1. h	6. b	11. e
2. k	7. c	
3. d	8. g	
4. a	9. i	
5. f	10. j	

PROGRESS TEST 2

Multiple-Choice Questions

1. **a.** is the answer.

2. **c.** is the answer.

    a. Wasting is caused by underfeeding, not overfeeding.

    b. This describes stunting.

3. **a.** is the answer.

4. **c.** is the answer.

5. **d.** is the answer. All mammals have a cortex.

6. **b.** is the answer.

    a. Although focusing ability seems to be limited to a certain range, babies do focus on many objects in this range.

    c. This is not within the range at which babies *can* focus.

    d. Babies have very poor distance vision.

7. **d.** is the answer.

8. **a.** is the answer.

    b. If anything, this is a potential *disadvantage* of breast milk over formula.

    c. So can formula.

    d. Breast milk contains more iron, certain vitamins, and other nutrients than cow's milk; it does not contain more protein and vitamin D, however.

9. **c.** is the answer.

    a. These are dendrites.

    b. These are axons.

    d. These are neurotransmitters.

10. **c.** is the answer.

11. **b.** is the answer.

12. **c.** is the answer.

13. **a.** is the answer.

14. **d.** is the answer.

15. **b.** is the answer.

True or False Items

1. T

2. F   In fact, just the opposite is true..

3. F   Although all healthy infants develop the same motor skills in the same sequence, the age at which these skills are acquired can vary greatly from infant to infant.

4. T

5. F   Vision is relatively poorly developed at birth, whereas hearing is well developed.

6. F   Only 36 percent of all babies are breast-fed up to 6 months.

7. T

8. T

9. T

10. F   In fact, the prefrontal cortex is probably the last area of the brain to attain maturity.

KEY TERMS

1. A **percentile** is any point on a ranking scale of 0 to 100; percentiles are often used to compare a child's development to group norms and to his or her own prior development.

2. **Head-sparing** is a biological mechanism in which the brain continues to grow even though the body stops growing in a malnourished child.

3. **Neurons,** or nerve cells, are the main components of the central nervous system, especially the brain.

4. The **cortex** is the outer layers of the brain that is involved in most thinking, feeling, and sensing.

    Memory aid: Cortex in Latin means "bark." As bark covers a tree, the cortex is the "bark of the brain."

5. The **prefrontal cortex** is the brain area that specializes in anticipation, planning, and impulse control.

6. An **axon** is the nerve fiber that sends electrochemical impulses from one neuron to the dendrites of other neurons.

7. A **dendrite** is a nerve fiber that receives the electrochemical impulses transmitted from other neurons via their axons.

8. A **synapse** is the point at which the axon of a sending neuron meets the dendrites of a receiving neuron.

9. **Neurotransmitters** are chemicals in the brain that carry messages from the axon of a sending neuron to the dendrite of a receiving neuron.

10. A **synaptic gap** is the pathway across which neurotransmitters carry information between neurons.

11. **Transient exuberance** is the dramatic but temporary increase in the number of dendrites that occurs in an infant's brain over the first two years of life.

12. **Pruning** is the process by which unused connections in the brain atrophy and die.

13. **Experience-expectant brain functions** are those that require basic common experiences (such as having things to see and hear) in order to develop normally.

14. **Experience-dependent brain functions** are those that depend on particular, and variable, experiences (such as experiencing language) in order to develop.

15. **Shaken baby syndrome** is a life-threatening condition in which blood vessels in an infant's brain have been ruptured because the infant has been forcefully shaken back and forth.

16. **Self-righting** is the inborn drive to remedy a deficit in development.

17. **REM sleep,** or rapid eye movement sleep, is a stage of sleep characterized by flickering eyes behind closed eyelids, dreaming, and rapid brain waves.

18. **Co-sleeping** is the custom in which parents and their infants sleep together in the same room.

19. **Sensation** is the response of a sensory system when it detects a stimulus.

20. **Perception** is the process by which the brain tries to make sense of a stimulus such that the individual becomes aware of it.

21. **Binocular vision** is the ability to use both eyes in a coordinated fashion in order to see one image.

    Memory aid: Bi- indicates "two"; ocular means something pertaining to the eye. Binocular vision is vision for "two eyes."

22. **Motor skills** are learned abilities to move specific parts of the body.

23. **Gross motor skills** are physical abilities that demand large body movements, such as walking, jumping, and running.

24. **Fine motor skills** are physical abilities that require precise, small movements, such as picking up a coin.

25. **Immunization** (also called vaccination) is the process by which the developing person's immune system becomes fortified, via antibodies, to resist a specific contagious disease.

26. **Protein-calorie malnutrition** results when a person does not consume enough food.

27. **Stunting** is the failure of children who are chronically malnourished to grow to a normal height for their age.

28. **Wasting** is the tendency for malnourished children to be severely underweight for their age.

29. **Marasmus** is a disease caused by severe protein-calorie deficiency during the first year of life. Growth stops, body tissues waste away, and the infant eventually dies.

30. **Kwashiorkor** is a disease caused by protein-calorie deficiency during childhood. The child's face, legs, and abdomen swell with fluid; the child becomes more vulnerable to other diseases. Other body parts are degraded, including the hair, which becomes thin, brittle, and colorless.

31. **Sudden infant death syndrome** (SIDS) occurs when a seemingly healthy infant, usually between 2 and 6 months of age, suddenly stops breathing and dies while sleeping.

The First Two Years: Cognitive Development

Chapter Overview

Chapter 6 explores the ways in which the infant comes to learn about, think about, and adapt to his or her surroundings. It focuses on the various ways in which infant intelligence is revealed: through sensorimotor intelligence, perception, memory, and language development. The chapter begins with a description of Jean Piaget's theory of sensorimotor intelligence, which maintains that infants think exclusively with their senses and motor skills. Piaget's six stages of sensorimotor intelligence are examined.

The second section discusses the information-processing theory, which compares cognition to the ways in which computers analyze data. Eleanor and James Gibson's influential theory is also described. Central to this theory is the idea that infants gain cognitive understanding of their world through the affordances of objects, that is, the activities they can do with them.

The text also discusses the key cognitive elements needed by the infant to structure the environment discovered through his or her newfound perceptual abilities. Using the habituation procedure, researchers have found that the speed with which infants recognize familiarity and seek something novel is related to later cognitive skill. It points out the importance of memory to cognitive development.

Finally, the chapter turns to the most remarkable cognitive achievement of the first two years: the acquisition of language. Beginning with a description of the infant's first attempts at language, the chapter follows the sequence of events that leads to the child's ability to utter two-word sentences. The chapter concludes with an examination of three classic theories of language acquisition and a fourth, hybrid theory that combines aspects of each.

What Will You Know?

The text chapter should be studied one section at a time. Before you read, preview each section by skimming it, noting headings and boldface items. Then read the sections, one at a time, keeping these questions in mind.

1. Why did Piaget compare 1-year-olds to scientists?

2. Why isn't Piaget's theory of sensorimotor intelligence universally recognized as insightful?

3. What factors influence whether infants remember what happens to them before they can talk?

4. When and how do infants learn to talk?

Chapter Review

When you have finished reading the chapter, work through the material that follows to review it. Completing the sentences and answering the questions will enable you to answer the "What Have You Learned?" questions at the end of the text chapter. Scattered throughout the Chapter Review are Study Tips, which explain how best to learn a difficult concept, and Think About It discussions and Applications, which help you to know how well you understand the material. Check your understanding of the material by consulting the answers at the end of the chapter. Do not continue with the next section until you understand each answer. If you need to, review or reread the appropriate section in the textbook before continuing.

Sensorimotor Intelligence

1. The first major theorist to realize that infants are active learners was _____ .

2. When infants begin to explore the environment through sensory and motor skills, they are displaying what Piaget called _____ intelligence. In number,

Piaget described _____ stages of development of this type of intelligence.

3. The first two stages of sensorimotor intelligence are examples of _____

_____ _____ .

Stage one begins with newborns' reflexes, such as _____ and _____ ,

and also the _____ . It lasts from birth to _____ of age.

4. Stage two begins when newborns show signs of _____ of their

_____ and senses to the specifics of the environment. This process involves _____ and

_____ .

Describe the development of the sucking reflex during stages one and two.

5. In stages three and four, development switches to _____ _____

_____ , involving the baby with an object or with another person. During stage three, which occurs between _____ and_____

months of age, infants repeat a specific action that has just elicited a pleasing response.

Describe a typical stage-three behavior.

6. In stage four, which lasts from _____ to _____

months of age, infants can better _____ events. At this stage, babies also engage in purposeful actions, or _____-directed behavior.

7. A major cognitive accomplishment of infancy is the ability to understand that objects exist even when they are _____ .

This awareness is called _____

_____ . To test for this awareness, Piaget devised a procedure to observe whether an infant will _____

for a hidden object. Using this test, Piaget concluded that this awareness does not develop until about _____ of age. More recent research studies have shown that this ability actually begins to emerge at _____ months.

8. During stage five, which lasts from _____ to _____

months, infants begin experimenting in thought and deed. They do so through

_____ _____

_____ , which involve taking in experiences and trying to make sense of them.

Explain what Piaget meant when he described the stage-five infant as a "little scientist."

9. Stage six, which lasts from _____ to _____ months, is the stage of anticipating and solving simple problems by using _____

_____ . One sign that children have reached stage six is_____

_____ , which is their emerging ability to imitate behaviors they noticed earlier.

10. Two research tools that have become available since Piaget's time are _____ studies and _____ , which reveals brain activity as cognition occurs. Neurological research has revealed the existence of brain cells called _____

_____ that may be the basis by which babies learn by observing the actions of others.

STUDY TIP Jean Piaget was the first major theorist to realize that each stage of life has its own characteristic way of thinking. To deepen your understanding of Jean Piaget's stages of sensorimotor development, fill in the missing information in the following chart. See how much you can fill in without reviewing the textbook. To get you started, the first stage has been completed.

11. Typical Age Range	Stage	Behavior Indicating a Child Is in This Stage
0–1 month	reflexes	reflexive cries
a. 1–4 months		
b. 4–8 months		
c. 8–12 months		
d. 12–18 months		
e. 18–24 months		

APPLICATIONS:

12. A 9-month-old repeatedly reaches for his sister's doll, even though he has been told "no" many times. This is an example of _____-

    _____ _____ .

13. Before putting her dolly to bed, 18-month-old Jessica sings her a song. According to Piaget, Jessica's behavior is an example of the use of
    a. new means through active experimentation.
    b. mental combinations.
    c. new adaptation and anticipation.
    d. first acquired adaptations.

14. Nine-month-old Akshay, who looks out of his crib for a toy that has fallen, is clearly demonstrating an understanding of

    _____ _____ .

15. Six-month-old Calysta sucks harder on a nipple, evidences a change in heart rate, or stares longer at one image than at another when presented with a change of stimulus. This indicates that she
    a. is annoyed by the change.
    b. is both hungry and angry.
    c. has become habituated to the new stimulus.
    d. perceives some differences between stimuli.

16. A 20-month-old girl who is able to try out various actions mentally without actually having to perform them is learning to solve simple problems by using _____ _____ .

17. Seven-month-old Francisca is attempting to interact with her smiling mother. She is demonstrating an ability that typically occurs in stage _____ of sensorimotor development.

18. Angelo realizes that sucking a pacifier is different from sucking a nipple. Angelo is in stage _____ of cognitive development.

Information Processing

19. A perspective on human cognition that is modeled on how computers analyze data is the

    _____-_____

    theory. Two aspects of this theory as applied to human development are _____ , which concern perception and so are analogous to computer input, and _____ , which involves storage and retrieval of ideas, or output.

20. Much of the current research in perception and cognition has been inspired by the work of the Gibsons, who stress that perception is a(n) _____ (active/passive/automatic) cognitive phenomenon.

21. According to the Gibsons, any object in the environment offers diverse opportunities for interaction; this property of an object is called a(n) _____ .

22. Which properties an individual perceives in an object depends on the individual's _____ _____ and _____ _____ , on his or her _____ _____ , and on his or her _____ _____ of what the object might be used for.

23. A firm surface that appears to drop off is called a _____ _____ .

    Although perception of this dropoff was once linked to _____ maturity, later research found that infants as young as _____ are able to perceive the dropoff, as evidenced by changes in their _____ _____ and their wide-open eyes.

24 Babies have great difficulty storing new memories in their first _____ (how long?).

25. The term _____ _____ refers to the mistaken belief that infants remember nothing before about age 2.

26. Research has revealed, however, that babies can show that they remember when three conditions are met:

    a. _____

    b. _____

    c. _____

27. When these conditions are met, infants as young as _____ months "remembered" events from two weeks earlier if they experienced a _____ _____ prior to retesting.

28. After about _____ months, infants become capable of retaining information for longer periods of time, with less training, repetition, or reminding.

29. PET scans and fMRI studies reveal that one region of the _____ is devoted to memory for _____ and other regions to memory for _____ . Memory for routines that remains hidden until a stimulus triggers it is called _____ _____ .

30. Memories that can be recalled on demand are referred to as _____ _____ . The region of the brain that this latter type of memory depends on is the _____ . This brain region remains immature until about age _____ .

STUDY TIP According to Eleanor and James Gibson, which of the many affordances people perceive in a given object depends on their developmental level and past experiences, their present needs and motivation, and their sensory awareness of what that object might be used for. To increase your appreciation of the fact that infants are capable of learning about their worlds only by attempting to apply new experiences to a limited repertoire of existing reflexes, conduct a simple observational study with a lollipop. As you employ the sensorimotor reflex of sucking on the treat, consider variations in sucking—for example, licking, chewing—that represent elaborations of the basic action. Consider, too, how the sucking reflex can be adapted to many other objects (just as infants discover), including a finger, toy, or bottle. Why did Piaget consider such adaptations to be examples of intelligent behavior?

APPLICATIONS:

31. Eighteen-month-old Emma sees a large, round raised area on her mother's computer modem. She immediately presses the area with her fingers. James Gibson would say that Emma has perceived the modem button's _____ .

32. Professor Norman frequently uses examples of how computers analyze data to help the class understand how human memory works. Professor Norman evidently is a fan of
    a. Jean Piaget.
    b. James Gibson.
    c. information-processing theory.
    d. dynamic perception theory.

Language: What Develops in the First Two Years?

33. Children the world over _____ (follow/do not follow) the same sequence of early language development. The timing of this sequence and depth of ability _____ (vary/do not vary).

34. Newborns show a preference for hearing _____ over other sounds, including the high-pitched, simplified adult speech called _____- _____ speech, which is sometimes called _____ _____ .

35. By 4 months of age, most babies' verbal repertoire consists of _____ .

36. Between _____ and _____ months of age, babies begin to repeat certain syllables, a phenomenon referred to as _____ .

37. Babbling is _____- _____ , so although deaf babies babble at first, they stop because they can't hear responses. Deaf babies may also use _____ _____ to babble.

38. The average baby speaks a few words at about _____ of age. They understand _____ (more/fewer) words than they speak.

39. Another characteristic of infant language development is the use of the _____ , in which a single word expresses a complete thought. Variations of tone and pitch, called _____ , are extensive in babbling and in this later form of speech.

40. When vocabulary reaches approximately 50 expressed words, it suddenly begins to build rapidly, at a rate of _____ or more words a month. This language spurt is called the _____ _____ because toddlers learn a disproportionate number of _____ .

41. Language acquisition may be shaped by our _____ , as revealed by the fact that English-speaking infants learn more _____ than Chinese or Korean infants, who learn more _____ . Alternatively, the entire _____ may determine language acquisition.

42. Children begin to produce their first two-word sentences at about _____ months, showing a clearly emerging understanding of _____ , which refers to all the methods that languages use to communicate meaning, apart from the words themselves. A child's grammar correlates with the size of his or her _____ . One measure of language development is _____ , defined as the _____ .

43. Reinforcement and other conditioning processes account for language development, according to the learning theory of _____ . One study that followed mother–infant pairs over time found that the frequency of early _____ _____ predicted the child's rate of language acquisition many months later.

44. According to the _____- _____ theory, infants communicate because they are _____ beings. Thus, _____ _____ , not explicit _____ , lead infants to learn language.

45. The theorist who stressed that language is too complex to be mastered so early and easily through conditioning is _____ . Because all young children _____ (master/do not master) basic grammar at about the same age, there is, in a sense, a

_____ _____ .

This theorist also maintained that all children are born with an LAD, or _____

_____ _____ ,

that enables children to quickly derive the rules of grammar from the speech they hear.

Summarize the research support for theory three.

46. A new _____ theory combines aspects of several theories. A fundamental aspect of this theory is that _____

_____ .

STUDY TIP To review the sequences of sensorimotor and language development, and to deepen your understanding of their interrelationship, see if you can fill in the missing information in the chart below. For each listed age (column 1), write down the corresponding sensorimotor stage (column 2) and hallmarks or milestones of language development (column 3).

47. Age	Sensorimotor Stage	Language Milestones
a. 0–1 month		
b. 1–4 months		
c. 4–8 months		
d. 8–12 months		
e. 12–18 months		
f. 18–24 months		

APPLICATIONS:

48. At about 21 months, Darrell, who is typical of his age group, will
   a. have a vocabulary of between 250 and 350 words.
   b. begin to speak in holophrases.
   c. put words together to form rudimentary sentences.
   d. be characterized by all of these abilities.

49. As an advocate of the social-pragmatic theory, Professor Caruso believes that
   a. infants communicate in every way they can because they are social beings.
   b. biological maturation is a dominant force in language development.
   c. infants' language abilities mirror those of their primary caregivers.
   d. language develops in many ways for many reasons.

50. As soon as her babysitter arrives, 21-month-old Christine holds on to her mother's legs and, in a questioning manner, says "bye-bye." Because Christine clearly is "asking" her mother not to leave, her utterance can be classified as a

_____ .

51. Six-month-old Lars continually repeats a variety of sound combinations such as "ba-ba-ba." This form of language is called _____ .

52. Monica firmly believes that her infant daughter "taught" herself language because of the seemingly effortless manner in which she has mastered new words and phrases. Monica is evidently a proponent of the theory proposed by

    _____ .

53. Like most Korean toddlers, Noriko has acquired a greater number of _____ (nouns/verbs) in her vocabulary than her North American counterparts, who tend to acquire more _____ (nouns/verbs).

Progress Test 1

Multiple-Choice Questions

Circle your answers to the following questions and check them with the answers at the end of the chapter. If your answer is incorrect, read the explanation for why it is incorrect and then consult the text.

1. In general terms, the Gibsons' concept of affordances emphasizes the idea that the individual perceives an object in terms of its
   a. economic importance.
   b. physical qualities.
   c. function or use to the individual.
   d. role in the larger culture or environment.

2. According to Piaget, when a baby repeats an action that has just triggered a pleasing response from his or her caregiver, a stage _____ behavior has occurred.
   a. one   c. three
   b. two   d. six

3. Sensorimotor intelligence begins with a baby's first
   a. attempt to crawl.
   b. reflexes.
   c. auditory perception.
   d. adaptation of a reflex.

4. Piaget and the Gibsons would most likely agree that
   a. perception is largely automatic.
   b. language development is biologically predisposed in children.

   c. learning and perception are active cognitive processes.
   d. it is unwise to "push" children too hard academically.

5. Toward the end of the first year, infants usually learn how to
   a. accomplish simple goals.
   b. manipulate various symbols.
   c. solve complex problems.
   d. pretend.

6. When an infant begins to understand that objects exist even when they are out of sight, she or he has begun to understand the concept of object
   a. displacement.   c. permanence.
   b. importance.   d. location.

7. Today, most cognitive psychologists view language acquisition as
   a. primarily the result of imitation of adult speech.
   b. a behavior that is determined primarily by biological maturation.
   c. a behavior determined entirely by learning.
   d. determined by both biological maturation and learning.

8. Despite cultural differences, children all over the world attain very similar language skills
   a. according to ethnically specific timetables.
   b. in the same sequence according to a variable timetable.
   c. according to culturally specific timetables.
   d. according to timetables that vary from child to child.

9. The average baby speaks a few words at about
   a. 6 months.   c. 12 months.
   b. 9 months.   d. 24 months.

10. A single word used by toddlers to express a complete thought is
    a. a holophrase.
    b. child-directed speech.
    c. babbling.
    d. an affordance.

11. A distinctive form of language, with a particular pitch, structure, etc., that adults use in talking to infants is called
    a. a holophrase.
    b. the LAD.
    c. child-directed speech.
    d. conversation.

12. Habituation studies reveal that most infants detect the difference between a *pah* sound and a *bah* sound at
    a. birth.
    b. 1 month.
    c. 3 months.
    d. 6 months.

13. The imaging technique in which the brain's magnetic properties indicate activation in various parts of the brain is called a(n)
    a. PET scan.
    b. EEG.
    c. fMRI.
    d. MRI.

14. A toddler who taps on the computer's keyboard after observing her mother sending e-mail the day before is demonstrating
    a. assimilation.
    b. accommodation.
    c. deferred imitation.
    d. dynamic perception.

15. In Piaget's theory of sensorimotor intelligence, reflexes that involve the infant's own body are examples of
    a. primary circular reactions.
    b. secondary circular reactions.
    c. tertiary circular reactions.
    d. none of these reactions.

Matching Items

Match each definition or description with its corresponding term.

Terms

_____   1. mirror neurons
_____   2. affordances
_____   3. object permanence
_____   4. Noam Chomsky
_____   5. B. F. Skinner
_____   6. sensorimotor intelligence
_____   7. babbling
_____   8. holophrase
_____   9. habituation
_____   10. deferred imitation
_____   11. MLU

Definitions or Descriptions

a. getting used to an object or event after repeated exposure to it
b. repetitive utterance of certain syllables
c. the average number of words used in a typical sentence
d. the ability to witness, remember, and later copy a behavior
e. the realization that something that is out of sight continues to exist
f. brain cells that respond to actions observed in another person
g. opportunities for interaction that an object offers
h. theorist who believed that verbal behavior is conditioned
i. a single word used to express a complete thought
j. theorist who believed that language ability is innate
k. thinking through the senses and motor skills

Progress Test 2

Progress Test 2 should be completed during a final chapter review. Answer the following questions after you thoroughly understand the correct answers for the Chapter Review and Progress Test 1.

Multiple-Choice Questions

1. Stage five (12 to 18 months) of sensorimotor intelligence is best described as
   a. first acquired adaptations.
   b. the period of the "little scientist."
   c. procedures for making interesting sights last.
   d. new means through symbolization.

2. Piaget referred to the shift in an infant's behavior from reflexes to deliberate actions as the shift from
   a. secondary circular reactions to primary circular reactions.
   b. first acquired adaptations to secondary circular reactions.
   c. primary circular reactions to tertiary circular reactions.
   d. stage one primary circular reactions to stage two primary circular reactions.

3. (text and A View from Science) Research suggests that the concept of object permanence
   a. fades after a few months.
   b. is a skill some children never acquire.
   c. may occur earlier and more gradually than Piaget recognized.
   d. involves pretending as well as mental combinations.

4. Which of the following is an example of a secondary circular reaction?
   a. a 1-month-old infant stares at a mobile suspended over her crib
   b. a 2-month-old infant sucks a pacifier
   c. realizing that rattles make noise, a 4-month-old infant laughs with delight when his mother puts a rattle in his hand
   d. a 12-month-old toddler licks a bar of soap to learn what it tastes like

5. An 18-month-old toddler puts a collar on a stuffed dog, then pretends to take it for a walk. The infant's behavior is an example of a
   a. primary circular reaction.
   b. secondary circular reaction.
   c. tertiary circular reaction.
   d. first acquired adaptation.

6. According to Piaget, the use of deferred imitation is an example of stage _____ behavior.
   a. three   c. five
   b. four   d. six

7. For Noam Chomsky, the language acquisition device refers to
   a. the human predisposition to acquire language.
   b. the portion of the human brain that processes speech.
   c. the vocabulary of the language to which the child is exposed.
   d. all of these.

8. The first stage of sensorimotor intelligence lasts until
   a. infants can anticipate events that will fulfill their needs.
   b. infants begin to adapt their reflexes to the environment.
   c. infants interact with objects to produce exciting experiences.
   d. infants are capable of thinking about past and future events.

9. Whether an infant perceives certain characteristics of objects, such as "suckability" or "graspability," seems to depend on
   a. his or her prior experiences.
   b. his or her needs.
   c. his or her sensory awareness.
   d. all of these factors.

10. (A View from Science) Piaget was INCORRECT in his belief that infants younger than 8 months do not have
    a. object permanence.
    b. intelligence.
    c. goal-directed behavior.
    d. any of these abilities.

11. The purposeful actions that begin to develop in sensorimotor stage four are called
    a. reflexes.
    b. affordances.
    c. goal-directed behaviors.
    d. mental combinations.

12. What is the correct sequence of stages of language development?
    a. crying, babbling, cooing, first word
    b. crying, cooing, babbling, first word
    c. crying, babbling, first word, cooing
    d. crying, cooing, first word, babbling

13. Compared with hearing babies, deaf babies
    a. are less likely to babble.
    b. are more likely to babble.
    c. typically never babble.
    d. are more likely to babble using hand signals.

14. According to Skinner, children acquire language
    a. as a result of an inborn ability to use the basic structure of language.
    b. through reinforcement and other aspects of conditioning.
    c. mostly because of biological maturation.
    d. in a fixed sequence of predictable stages.

15. A fundamental idea of the hybrid model of language acquisition is that
    a. all humans are born with an innate language acquisition device.
    b. learning some aspects of language is best explained by one theory at one age, by other theories at another age.
    c. language development occurs too rapidly and easily to be entirely the product of conditioning.
    d. imitation and reinforcement are crucial to the development of language.

Matching Items

Match each definition or description with its corresponding term.

Terms

_____ 1. goal-directed behavior

_____ 2. visual cliff

_____ 3. primary circular reaction

_____ 4. child-directed speech

_____ 5. new adaptation and anticipation

_____ 6. "little scientist"

_____ 7. mental combinations

_____ 8. secondary circular reaction

_____ 9. tertiary circular reaction

_____ 10. LAD

_____ 11. grammar

Definitions or Descriptions

a. a device for studying depth perception

b. understanding how to reach a goal

c. able to put two ideas together

d. a feedback loop involving the infant's own body

e. a feedback loop involving people and objects

f. a hypothetical device that facilitates language development

g. also called baby talk or motherese

h. Piaget's term for the stage-five toddler

i. purposeful actions

j. a feedback loop involving active exploration and experimentation

k. all the methods used by a language to communicate meaning

Key Terms

Using your own words, write a brief definition or explanation of each of the following terms on a separate piece of paper.

1. sensorimotor intelligence
2. primary circular reactions
3. secondary circular reactions
4. object permanence
5. tertiary circular reactions
6. "little scientist"
7. deferred imitation
8. habituation
9. mirror neurons
10. fMRI
11. information-processing theory
12. affordance
13. visual cliff
14. reminder session
15. implicit memory
16. explicit memory
17. child-directed speech
18. babbling
19. holophrase
20. naming explosion
21. grammar

22. mean length of utterance (MLU)
23. language acquisition device (LAD)

ANSWERS

CHAPTER REVIEW

1. Jean Piaget
2. sensorimotor; six
3. primary circular reactions; sucking; grasping; senses; 1 month
4. adaptation; reflexes; assimilation; accommodation

Stage-one infants suck everything that touches their lips. By about 1 month, they start to adapt their reflexive sucking. After several months, they have organized the world into objects to be sucked to soothe hunger, objects to be sucked for comfort, and objects not to be sucked at all.

5. secondary circular reactions; 4; 8

A stage-three infant may squeeze a duck, hear a quack, and squeeze the duck again.

6. 8; 12; anticipate; goal
7. no longer in sight; object permanence; search; 8 months; $4\frac{1}{2}$
8. 12; 18; tertiary circular reactions

The stage-five "little scientist" uses trial and error in creative and active exploration.

9. 18; 24; mental combinations; deferred imitation

10. habituation; fMRI; mirror neurons

11. 0–1 month: reflexes (Stage 1); reflexive cries

    a. 1–4 months: first acquired adaptations (Stage 2); sucking a thumb for comfort but not sucking a whole hand

    b. 4–8 months: making interesting sights last (Stage 3); shaking a doll that says "Mama"

    c. 8–12 months: new adaptation and anticipation (Stage 4); pointing at a toy to get Dad to bring it to him or her

    d. 12–18 months: new means through active experimentation (Stage 5); pushing all the buttons on the remote control

    e. 18–24 months: new means through mental combinations (Stage 6); learning that the furry little teddy bear isn't real but can be used for cuddling and security

12. goal-directed behavior

13. **b.** is the answer. Jessica realizes the doll isn't real, but she also knows she can do "real things" with the doll.

14. object permanence. Akshay knows that out of sight doesn't mean the object ceases to exist.

15. **d.** is the answer. In these habituation studies, the infant's increased attention indicates she perceives a difference from the previous stimulus.

16. mental combinations. The child is able to think about something before actually doing anything, a major advance in cognitive development.

17. four. This is the stage of new adaptation and anticipation. The infant becomes more deliberate and purposeful in responding to people and objects.

18. two. This is the stage of first acquired adaptations, when the infant accommodates and coordinates reflexes.

19. information-processing; affordances; memory

20. active

21. affordance

22. past experience; current development; immediate motivation; sensory awareness

23. visual cliff; visual; 3 months; heart rate

24. year

25. infant amnesia

26. (a) experimental conditions are similar to real life; (b) motivation is high; (c) retrieval is strengthened by reminders and repetition

27. 3; reminder session

28. 6

29. brain; faces; sounds, events, sights, phrases, and much more; implicit memory

30. explicit memory; hippocampus; 5 or 6

31. affordance

32. **c.** is the answer. Information-processing theory compares human thinking processes, by analogy, to computer analysis of data.

33. follow; vary

34. speech; child-directed; baby talk (or motherese)

35. squeals, growls, gurgles, grunts, croons, and yells

36. 6; 9; babbling

37. experience-expectant; hand gestures

38. 1 year; more

39. holophrase; intonation

40. 50 to 100; naming explosion; nouns

41. culture; nouns; verbs; social context

42. 21; grammar; vocabulary; mean length of utterance (MLU); average number of words a child uses in a typical sentence

43. B. F. Skinner; maternal responsiveness

44. social-pragmatic; social; social impulses; teaching

45. Noam Chomsky; master; universal grammar; language acquisition device

Support for this theory comes from the fact that all babies babble ma-ma and da-da sounds. No reinforcement is needed. Infants merely need dendrites to grow, mouth muscles to strengthen, neurons to connect, and speech to be heard.

46. hybrid; some learning of language is best explained by one theory at one age and other aspects by another perspective at another age

47. **a.** 0–1 month: reflexes (Stage 1); crying, facial expressions

    b. 1–4 months: first acquired adaptations (Stage 2); cooing, laughing, squealing, growling, crooning, vowel sounds

    c. 4–8 months: making interesting sights last (Stage 3); babbling at 6 months

    d. 8–12 months: new adaptation and anticipation (Stage 4); at 10 months, comprehension of simple words; speechlike intonations

    e. 12–18 months: new means through active experimentation (Stage 5); first spoken words at 12 months; vocabulary growth up to about 50 words

    f. 18–24 months: new means through mental combinations (Stage 6); three or more words learned per day, first two-word sentence at 21 months, multiword sentences at 24 months

48. **c.** is the answer. The first two-word sentence is uttered at about 21 months.

49. **a.** is the answer. **b.** is more consistent with Noam Chomsky's theory, **c.** would be based on B. F. Skinner's learning theory, and **d.** is consistent with the hybrid theory.

50. holophrase. These are one-word utterances that express a complete, meaningful thought.

51. babbling. This form of speech, which begins between 6 and 9 months of age, is characterized by the extended repetition of certain syllables (such as "ma-ma").

52. Noam Chomsky. Chomsky and his followers believe that language is too complex to be learned through reinforcement alone.

53. verbs; nouns. Korean is considered a verb-friendly language, because verbs appear at the beginning of sentences. North Americans use nouns first in their sentences.

PROGRESS TEST 1

Multiple-Choice Questions

1. **c.** is the answer.

2. **c.** is the answer.

3. **b.** is the answer. This was Piaget's most basic contribution to the study of infant cognition— that intelligence is revealed in behavior at every age.

4. **c.** is the answer.

    b. This is Chomsky's position.

    d. This issue was not discussed in the text.

5. **a.** is the answer.

    b. & c. These abilities are not acquired until children are much older.

    d. Pretending is associated with stage six (18 to 24 months).

6. **c.** is the answer.

7. **d.** is the answer.

8. **b.** is the answer.

    a., c., & d. Children the world over follow the same sequence, but the timing of their accomplishments may vary considerably.

9. **c.** is the answer.

10. **a.** is the answer.

    b. Child-directed speech is the speech adults use with infants.

    c. Babbling refers to the first syllables a baby utters.

d. An affordance is an opportunity for perception and interaction.

11. **c.** is the answer.

    a. A holophrase is a single word uttered by a toddler to express a complete thought.

    b. According to Noam Chomsky, the LAD, or language acquisition device, is an innate ability in humans to acquire language.

    d. These characteristic differences in pitch and structure are precisely what distinguish child-directed speech from regular conversation.

12. **b.** is the answer.

13. **c.** is the answer.

14. **c.** is the answer

    a. & b. In Piaget's theory, these refer to processes by which mental concepts incorporate new experiences (assimilation) or are modified in response to new experiences (accommodation).

    d. Dynamic perception is not discussed in the chapter.

15. **a.** is the answer.

    b. Secondary circular reactions involve the baby with an object or with another person.

    c. Tertiary circular reactions involve active exploration and experimentation, rather than mere reflexive action.

Matching Items

1. f	5. h	9. a
2. g	6. k	10. d
3. e	7. b	11. c
4. j	8. i	

PROGRESS TEST 2

Multiple-Choice Questions

1. **b.** is the answer.

    a. & c. These are stages two and three.

    d. This is not one of Piaget's stages of sensorimotor intelligence.

2. **d.** is the answer. Thinking is more innovative in stage four because adaptation is more complex.

3. **c.** is the answer.

4. **c.** is the answer.

    a. & b. These are examples of primary circular reactions.

d. This is an example of a tertiary circular reaction.

5. **c.** is the answer.

6. **d.** is the answer.

7. **a.** is the answer. Chomsky believed that this device is innate.

8. **b.** is the answer.

   a. & c. Both of these occur later than stage one.

   d. This is a hallmark of stage six.

9. **d.** is the answer.

10. **a.** is the answer.

11. **c.** is the answer.

   a. Reflexes are involuntary (and therefore unintentional) responses.

   b. Affordances are perceived opportunities for interaction with objects.

   d. Mental combinations are actions that are carried out mentally, rather than behaviorally. Moreover, mental combinations do not develop until a later age, during sensorimotor stage six.

12. **b.** is the answer.

13. **d.** is the answer.

   a. & b. Hearing and deaf babies do not differ in the overall likelihood that they will babble.

   c. Deaf babies definitely babble.

14. **b.** is the answer.

   a., c., & d. These views on language acquisition describe the theory offered by Noam Chomsky.

15. **b.** is the answer.

   a. & c. These ideas are consistent with Noam Chomsky's theory.

   d. This is the central idea of B. F. Skinner's theory.

Matching Items

1. i	5. b	9. j
2. a	6. h	10. f
3. d	7. c	11. k
4. g	8. e	

KEY TERMS

1. Piaget's stages of **sensorimotor intelligence** (from birth to about 2 years old) are based on his theory that infants think exclusively with their senses and motor skills.

2. In Piaget's theory, **primary circular reactions** are a type of feedback loop in sensorimotor intelligence involving the infant's own body, in which infants take in experiences (such as sucking and grasping) and try to make sense of them.

3. **Secondary circular reactions** are a type of feedback loop in sensorimotor intelligence involving the infant's responses to objects and other people.

4. **Object permanence** is the understanding that objects (including people) continue to exist even when they cannot be seen, touched, or heard.

5. In Piaget's theory, **tertiary circular reactions** are the most sophisticated type of infant feedback loop in sensorimotor intelligence, involving active exploration and experimentation.

6. **"Little scientist"** is Piaget's term for the stage-five toddler (12 to 18 months) who learns about the properties of objects in his or her world through active experimentation.

7. **Deferred imitation** is the ability of infants to perceive and later copy a behavior they noticed hours or days earlier.

8. **Habituation** is the process of getting used to an object or event through repeated exposure to it.

9. **Mirror neurons** are brain cells that respond to an action performed by another person in the same way they would if the observer were performing the action.

10. The **fMRI** (functional magnetic resonance imaging) is a measuring technique in which the brain's electrical excitement indicates activation anywhere in the brain.

11. **Information-processing theory** is a theory of human cognition that compares thinking to the ways in which a computer analyzes data, through the processes of sensory input, connections, stored memories, and output.

12. **Affordances** are perceived opportunities for interacting with people, objects, or places in the environment. Infants perceive sucking, grasping, noisemaking, and many other affordances of objects at an early age.

13. A **visual cliff** is an experimental apparatus that provides the illusion of a sudden dropoff between one horizontal surface and another.

14. A **reminder session** is any perceptual experience that helps people recollect an idea, a thing, or an experience.

15. **Implicit memory** is unconscious or automatic memory that is usually stored via habits, emotional responses, routine procedures, and various sensations.

16. **Explicit memory** is memory that is easy to retrieve on demand, usually with words.

17. **Child-directed speech** is a form of speech used by adults when talking to infants. It is simplified, it has a higher pitch, and it is repetitive; it is also called *baby talk* or *motherese*.

18. **Babbling,** which begins between 6 and 9 months of age, is characterized by the extended repetition of certain syllables (such as "ma-ma").

19. Another characteristic of infant speech is the use of the **holophrase,** in which a single word is used to convey a complete, meaningful thought.

20. The **naming explosion** refers to the dramatic increase in the infant's vocabulary that begins at about 18 months of age.

21. The **grammar** of a language includes rules of word order, verb forms, and all other methods used to communicate meaning, apart from the words themselves.

22. A measure of language development, **mean length of utterance** (MLU) is the average number of words used by a child in a typical sentence.

23. According to Chomsky, children possess an innate **language acquisition device (LAD),** which is a hypothesized mental structure that enables them to acquire language, including the basic aspects of grammar, vocabulary, and intonation.

The First Two Years: Psychosocial Development

Chapter Overview

Chapter 7 describes the emotional and social life of the developing person during infancy. It begins with a description of the infant's emerging emotions and how they reflect mobility and social awareness. Two emotions, pleasure and pain, are apparent at birth and are soon joined by anger and fear. As self-awareness develops, many new emotions emerge, including embarrassment, shame, guilt, and pride.

The second and third sections explore the impact of brain development on emotions, and the social context in which emotions develop, respectively. Emotions and relationships are then examined from the perspective of parent–infant interaction. Videotaped studies of parents and infants, combined with laboratory studies of attachment, have greatly expanded our understanding of psychosocial development. By referencing their caregivers' signals, infants learn when and how to express their emotions. This section concludes by exploring the impact of day care on infants.

The final section explores theories of infant psychosocial development. These include the psychoanalytic theories of Freud and Erikson along with behaviorist, cognitive, and sociocultural theories, which help us understand how the infant's emotional and behavioral responses begin to take on the various patterns that form personality. Temperament, which affects later personality and is primarily inborn, is influenced by the individual's interactions with the environment.

What Will You Know?

The text chapter should be studied one section at a time. Before you read, preview each section by skimming it, noting headings and boldface items. Then read the sections, one at a time, keeping these questions in mind.

1. How do smiles, tears, anger, and fear change from birth to age 2?

2. Does a baby's temperament predict lifelong personality?

3. What are the signs of a healthy parent–infant relationship?

4. Do human cultures differ in their understanding of infant emotions and caregiving practices

Chapter Review

When you have finished reading the chapter, work through the material that follows to review it. Completing the sentences and answering the questions will enable you to answer the "What Have You Learned?" questions at the end of the text chapter. Scattered throughout the Chapter Review are Study Tips, which explain how best to learn a difficult concept, and Think About It discussions and Applications, which help you to know how well you understand the material. Check your understanding of the material by consulting the answers at the end of the chapter. Do not continue with the next section until you understand each answer. If you need to, review or reread the appropriate section in the textbook before continuing.

Introduction and Emotional Development

1. Psychosocial development includes
   _____ development and
   _____ development.

2. The first emotions that can be reliably discerned
   in infants are _____ and
   _____ . Other early infant
   emotions include _____ and
   _____ . Infants' pleasure
   in seeing faces is first expressed by the

   _____ _____ ,

   which appears at about _____
   weeks.

3. Anger becomes evident at about
_____ months. During
infancy, anger _____ (is/is
not) a healthy response, and usually occurs in
response to _____ . In contrast,
sadness indicates _____ and
is accompanied by an increase in the stress
hormone _____ .

4. Fully formed fear emerges at about
_____ months. One expression
of this new emotion is _____
_____ ; another is
_____ _____ ,
or fear of abandonment, which is normal at age
_____ year(s) and intensifies
by age _____ year(s). During
the second year, anger and fear typically
_____ (increase/decrease) and
become more _____ toward
specific things.

5. Toward the end of the second year, the
new emotions of _____ ,
_____ , _____ ,
_____ , and
_____ become apparent.
These emotions require an awareness of
_____ _____ .

6. An important foundation for emotional
growth is _____-
_____ ; very young infants
have no sense of _____ . This
emerging sense of "me" and "mine" leads to
a new _____ of others. This
sense usually emerges at the same time as
advances in _____ and using
_____-_____
pronouns.

7. Pride may be linked with the infant's maturing
_____ _____ .

Brain and Emotions

8. Emotional development depends
partly on maturation of the developing
_____ , along with having varied

_____ , which promote specific
connections between _____ and
emotions. In particular, maturation of the area
of the cortex called the _____
_____ _____ is
connected to emotional self-regulation.

9. In a study of adults born either in the United
States or in China, the _____
_____ _____ of
the brain was activated when the adult judged
whether certain adjectives applied to them.

10. For many people, _____
_____ is stronger than any
other anxieties. Two factors in the development
of this anxiety are _____ and
_____ _____ .

11. Excessive stress increases _____
and can harm the developing brain, in particular
the _____ .

12. Each infant is born with a _____
predisposition to develop certain emotional
traits. Among these are the traits of
_____ .

13. These traits may overlap with
_____ . Although these traits
are not learned, as _____
traits are, their expression is influenced by the
_____ .

14. The classic long-term study of children's
temperament is the _____
_____ _____
_____ . The study found
that by 3 months, infants manifested
_____ temperamental
traits that can be clustered into four types:
_____ , _____ ,
_____ _____
_____ _____ ,
and _____ _____
_____ .

15. Later research showed that only three
dimensions of temperament are clearly present
in early childhood: _____

_____ , _____

_____ , and

_____ .

_____

STUDY TIP/APPLICATION Most students (in fact, most people) find it difficult to understand how young children cannot be self-aware. To enhance your understanding of this limitation in young children, first briefly describe the nature and findings of the classic rouge-and-mirror experiment on self-awareness in infants. Then, try it out with young children of different ages.

_____

APPLICATION:

16. Chella and David are planning a night out for the first time since their infant was born nine months ago. As they prepare to leave, baby Lili begins to cry, indicating _____

_____ . Then, when the unfamiliar babysitter approaches her, she cries and clings tightly to her mother, a sign of _____

_____ .

The Development of Social Bonds

17. The coordinated interaction of response between infant and caregiver is called _____ . Partly through this interaction, infants learn to _____ and to develop some of the basic skills of _____ _____ . Synchrony usually begins with _____ (infants/parents) imitating _____ (infants/parents).

18. To study the importance of synchrony in development, researchers use an experimental device, called the _____-_____ technique, in which the caregiver _____ (does/does not) show any facial expression.

19. The emotional bond that develops between slightly older infants and their caregivers is called _____ .

20. Approaching and following the caregiver are signs of _____-_____ behaviors, while snuggling, touching, and holding are signs of _____-_____ behaviors.

21. An infant who derives comfort and confidence from the secure base provided by the caregiver is displaying _____ _____ (type B). In this type of relationship, the caregiver acts as a _____ _____ _____ from which the child is willing to venture forth. Approximately _____ (what proportion?) of all normal infants tested with this procedure demonstrate secure attachment.

22. By contrast, _____ _____ is characterized by an infant's fear, anger, anxiety, or indifference. Two extremes of this type of relationship are _____-_____ _____ (type A) and _____-_____/_____ _____ (type C). When infant–caregiver interactions are inconsistent, infants are classified as _____ (type D).

(text and Table 7.2) Briefly describe the two types of insecure attachment as well as disorganized attachment.

23. The procedure developed by Mary Ainsworth to measure attachment is called the

_____ _____ .

24. Securely attached infants are more likely to become socially _____ preschoolers, _____-_____ schoolchildren, and _____ parents. However, attachment status _____ (can/cannot) change.

25. The search for information about another person's feelings is called _____ _____ .

26. In _____ (most/some/a few) nations and ethnic groups, fathers spend much less time with infants than mothers do.

27. Close father–infant relationships can teach infants appropriate expressions of _____ . They also help the men, reducing the risk of_____ . Fathers provide _____; mothers _____ , _____ , and sing.

STUDY TIP Most students find it easier to remember the characteristics associated with secure and insecure attachment and their consequences if they are neatly summarized in a table. Complete the table below as a way of organizing the information.

28. Attachment Style	Characteristic Behavior of Infant	Characteristics of Parents
Secure (type B)	Infant plays happily and comfortably, sometimes glancing at Mom for reassurance.	Parent is sensitive and responsive to infant's needs; synchrony is high; parents are not stressed; parents have a working model from their own parents.
Insecure-avoidant (type A)		
Insecure-resistant/ ambivalent (type C)		
Disorganized (type D)		

APPLICATIONS:

29. One-year-old Kirsten and her Mom are participating in a laboratory test of attachment. When Mom returns to the playroom after a short absence, Kirsten, who is securely attached, is most likely to
   a. cry and protest her Mom's return.
   b. climb into her Mom's arms, then leave to resume play.
   c. climb into her Mom's arms and stay there.
   d. continue playing without acknowledging her Mom.

30. After a scary fall, 18-month-old Miguel looks to his mother to see if he should cry or laugh. Miguel's behavior is an example of

   _____ _____ .

31. Which of the following is a clear sign of Isabel's attachment to her grandmother, her full-time caregiver?
   a. She turns to her grandmother when distressed.
   b. She protests when Grandma leaves a room.
   c. She may cry when strangers appear.
   d. These are all signs of infant attachment.

32. Concluding her report on the impact of day care on young children, Deborah notes that infants are likely to become insecurely attached if
    a. their own mothers are insensitive caregivers.
    b. the quality of day care is poor.
    c. more than 20 hours per week are spent in day care.
    d. all of these conditions exist.

33. Kalil's mother left him alone in the room for a few minutes. When she returned, Kalil seemed indifferent to her presence. According to Mary Ainsworth's research with children in the Strange Situation, Kalil is probably
    a. a normal, independent infant.
    b. an abused child.
    c. insecurely attached.
    d. securely attached.

34. Two-year-old Anita and her mother spend many hours together in well-coordinated mutual responding: When Anita smiles, her mother smiles. When Anita pouts, her mother shows distress. Their behavior illustrates

    _____ .

Theories of Infant Psychosocial Development

35. In Freud's theory, development begins with the _____ stage, so named because the _____ is the infant's prime source of gratification and pleasure.

36. According to Freud, in the second year, the prime focus of gratification comes from stimulation and control of the bowels. Freud referred to this period as the _____ stage.

37. Freud believed that the potential conflicts of these stages had _____ (short-term/long-term) consequences. If the conflicts are not resolved, the child may become an adult with, for example, an _____
    _____ .

38. The theorist who believed that development occurs through a series of psychosocial crises is _____ . According to his theory, the crisis of infancy is one of
    _____ _____
    _____ , whereas the crisis of toddlerhood is one of _____
    _____ _____
    _____ _____ .

39. According to the perspective of _____ , personality is molded through the processes of _____ and _____ of the child's spontaneous behaviors.

40. Later theorists incorporated the role of _____ learning, that is, infants' tendencies to observe and _____ the personality traits of their parents. The theorist most closely associated with this type of learning is _____ .

41. (Opposing Perspectives) Researchers have found that physically close, _____ parenting predicts toddlers who later are less _____ and more _____ , in comparison to physically far, _____ parenting, which produces children with the opposite traits.

42. According to cognitive theory, a person's _____ and _____ determine his or her perspective on the world. Early experiences are important because
    _____ , _____ , and _____ make them so. Infants use their early relationships to build a
    _____ _____ that becomes a frame of reference for organizing perceptions and experiences.

43. According to _____ theory, attachment promoted our species' survival because _____-
    _____ and
    _____-_____ behaviors kept toddlers safe.

44. The care of children by people other than their biological parents is called _____ . In the United States, about _____ percent of infants are cared for exclusively by their mothers throughout the first year.

45. (Table 7.4) Researchers have identified five factors that are essential to high-quality day care:

a. _____

b. _____

c. _____

d. _____

e. _____

STUDY TIP Several theories of development have provided different explanations for how infants' emotions and temperaments develop. To help you remember the theories, complete the chart below and use it as a study aid. Some elements are filled in to give you a head start.

46.

Theory	Stages or Continuous	Important Concepts	Effects on Emotional Development
Psychoanalytic Theory Freud	stages	Oral and anal stages Sexual impulses and unconscious conflicts	If conflicts not resolved, fixation may occur.
Erikson			
Behaviorism	continuous		
Cognitive Theory			
Sociocultural Theory			

APPLICATIONS:

47. Professor Kipketer believes that infants' emotions are molded as their parents reinforce or punish their behaviors. Professor Kipketer evidently is a proponent of _____ .

48. Dr. Hidalgo believes that infants use their early relationships to develop a set of assumptions that become a frame of reference for later experiences. Dr. Hidalgo evidently is a proponent of

_____ _____ .

49. Felix has an unusually strong need to regulate all aspects of his life. Freud would probably say that Felix is

a. demonstrating the temperament he developed during infancy.

b. fixated at the anal stage.

c. fixated in the oral stage.

d. experiencing the crisis of trust versus mistrust.

Progress Test 1

Multiple-Choice Questions

Circle your answers to the following questions and check them with the answers at the end of the chapter. If your answer is incorrect, read the explanation for why it is incorrect and then consult the text.

1. Newborns have two identifiable emotions:
   a. shame and embarrassment.
   b. pleasure and pain.
   c. anger and joy.
   d. pride and guilt.

2. Parenting that results in children who are self-aware but less obedient is called
   a. proximal parenting.
   b. distal parenting.
   c. synchrony.
   d. scaffolding.

3. An infant's fear of being left by the mother or other caregiver, called _____ , is most obvious at about _____ .
   a. separation anxiety; 2 to 4 months
   b. stranger wariness; 2 to 4 months
   c. separation anxiety; 9 to 14 months
   d. stranger wariness; 9 to 14 months

4. Social referencing refers to
   a. parenting skills that change over time.
   b. changes in community values regarding, for example, the acceptability of using physical punishment with small children.
   c. the support network for new parents provided by extended family members.
   d. the infant response of looking to trusted adults for emotional cues in uncertain situations.

5. A key difference between temperament and personality is that
   a. temperamental traits are learned.
   b. personality includes traits that are primarily learned.
   c. personality is more stable than temperament.
   d. personality does not begin to form until much later, when self-awareness emerges.

6. The concept of a working model is most consistent with
   a. psychoanalytic theory.
   b. behaviorism.
   c. cognitive theory.
   d. sociocultural theory.

7. Freud's oral stage corresponds to Erikson's crisis of
   a. orality versus anality.
   b. trust versus mistrust.
   c. autonomy versus shame and doubt.
   d. secure versus insecure attachment.

8. Erikson believed that the development of a sense of trust in early infancy depends on
   a. the quality of the infant's food.
   b. the child's genetic inheritance.
   c. consistency, continuity, and sameness of experience.
   d. the introduction of toilet training.

9. Keisha is concerned that her 15-month-old daughter, who no longer seems to enjoy face-to-face play, is showing signs of insecure attachment. You tell her
   a. not to worry; face-to-face play almost disappears toward the end of the first year.
   b. she may be right to worry, because face-to-face play typically increases throughout infancy.
   c. not to worry; attachment behaviors are unreliable until toddlerhood.
   d. that her child is typical of children who spend more than 20 hours in day care each week.

10. "Easy," "slow to warm up," and "difficult" are descriptions of different
    a. forms of attachment.
    b. types of temperament.
    c. types of parenting.
    d. toddler responses to the Strange Situation.

11. The more physical play of fathers has been described as
    a. proximal parenting.
    b. distal parenting.
    c. disorganized parenting.
    d. insecure parenting.

12. *Synchrony* is a term that describes
    a. the carefully coordinated interaction between caregiver and infant.
    b. a mismatch of the temperaments of caregiver and infant.
    c. a research technique involving videotapes.
    d. the concurrent evolution of different species.

13. The emotional tie that develops between an infant and his or her primary caregiver is called
    a. self-awareness.   c. affiliation.
    b. synchrony.   d. attachment.

14. Research studies using the still-face technique have demonstrated that
    a. a parent's responsiveness to an infant aids development.
    b. babies become more upset when a parent leaves the room than when the parent's facial expression is not synchronized with the infant's.
    c. beginning at about 2 months, babies become very upset by a still-faced caregiver.
    d. beginning at about 10 months, babies become very upset by a still-faced caregiver.

15. Interest in people, as evidenced by the social smile, appears for the first time when an infant is _____ weeks old.
    a. 3   c. 9
    b. 6   d. 12

True or False Items

Write T (true) or F (false) on the line in front of each statement.

_____ 1. The major developmental theories all agree that maternal care is better for children than nonmaternal care.

_____ 2. Approximately 25 percent of infants display secure attachment.

_____ 3. A baby at 11 months is likely to display both stranger wariness and separation anxiety.

_____ 4. Emotional development is affected by maturation of conscious awareness.

_____ 5. A securely attached toddler is most likely to stay close to his or her mother even in a familiar environment.

_____ 6. Current research shows that the majority of infants in day care are slow to develop cognitive skills.

_____ 7. In their play with infants, fathers provide more excitement; mothers caress more.

_____ 8. Temperament is genetically determined and is unaffected by environmental factors.

_____ 9. Self-awareness enables toddlers to feel pride as well as guilt.

_____ 10. In the United States, most infants are cared for exclusively by their mothers throughout their first year.

Progress Test 2

Progress Test 2 should be completed during a final chapter review. Answer the following questions after you thoroughly understand the correct answers for the Chapter Review and Progress Test 1.

Multiple-Choice Questions

1. Infant–caregiver interactions that are marked by inconsistency are usually classified as
   a. disorganized.
   b. insecure-avoidant.
   c. insecure-resistant.
   d. insecure-ambivalent.

2. Freud's anal stage corresponds to Erikson's crisis of
   a. autonomy versus shame and doubt.
   b. trust versus mistrust.
   c. orality versus anality.
   d. identity versus role confusion.

3. Not until the sense of self begins to emerge do babies realize that they are seeing their own faces in the mirror. This realization usually occurs
   a. shortly before 3 months.
   b. at about 6 months.
   c. between 15 and 24 months.
   d. after 24 months.

4. Excessive stress during the first two years increases _____ levels and may impair development of the brain's

   _____ .

   a. serotonin; cortex
   b. dopamine; thalamus
   c. cortisol; hypothalamus
   d. ghrelin; pineal gland

5. Emotions such as shame, guilt, embarrassment, and pride emerge at the same time that
   a. the social smile appears.
   b. aspects of the infant's temperament can first be discerned.
   c. self-awareness begins to emerge.
   d. parents initiate toilet training.

6. Research by the NYLS on temperamental characteristics indicates that
   a. temperament is probably innate.
   b. the interaction of parent and child determines later personality.
   c. parents pass their temperaments on to their children through modeling.
   d. self-awareness contributes to the development of temperament.

7. In the second six months, stranger wariness is a
   a. result of insecure attachment.
   b. result of social isolation.
   c. normal emotional response.
   d. setback in emotional development.

8. The caregiving environment can affect a child's temperament through
   a. the child's temperamental pattern and the demands of the home environment.
   b. parental expectations.
   c. both a. and b.
   d. neither a. nor b.

9. While observing mothers playing with their infants in a playroom, you notice one mother who often teases her son, ignores him when he falls down, and tells him to "hush" when he cries. Mothers who display these behaviors usually have infants who exhibit which type of attachment?
   a. secure
   b. insecure-avoidant
   c. insecure-resistant
   d. disorganized

10. The later consequences of secure attachment and insecure attachment for children are
    a. balanced by the child's current rearing circumstances.
    b. irreversible, regardless of the child's current rearing circumstances.
    c. more significant in girls than in boys.
    d. more significant in boys than in girls.

11. The attachment pattern marked by anxiety and uncertainty is
    a. insecure-avoidant.
    b. insecure-resistant/ambivalent.
    c. disorganized.
    d. type B.

12. Compared with mothers, fathers are more likely to
    a. engage in more imaginative, exciting play.
    b. encourage intellectual development in their children.
    c. encourage social development in their children.
    d. read to their toddlers.

13. Like Freud, Erikson believed that:
    a. problems arising in early infancy last a lifetime.
    b. inability to resolve a conflict in infancy may result in later fixation.
    c. human development can be viewed in terms of psychosexual stages.
    d. all of these are true.

14. Which of the following is an example of social learning?
    a. Sue discovers that a playmate will share a favorite toy if she asks politely.
    b. Jon learns that other children are afraid of him when he raises his voice.
    c. Zach develops a hot temper after seeing his father regularly display anger and, in turn, receive respect from others.
    d. All of these are examples of social learning.

15. Which of the following is NOT true regarding synchrony?
    a. There are wide variations in the frequency of synchrony from baby to baby.
    b. Synchrony appears to be uninfluenced by cultural differences.
    c. The frequency of mother–infant synchrony has varied over historical time.
    d. Parents and infants spend about one hour a day in face-to-face play.

Matching Items

Match each theorist, term, or concept with its corresponding description or definition.

Theorists, Terms, or Concepts

_____ 1. temperament
_____ 2. Erikson
_____ 3. Strange Situation
_____ 4. synchrony
_____ 5. trust versus mistrust
_____ 6. Freud
_____ 7. social referencing
_____ 8. autonomy versus shame and doubt
_____ 9. self-awareness
_____ 10. Ainsworth
_____ 11. proximity-seeking behaviors
_____ 12. contact-maintaining behaviors

Descriptions or Definitions

a. looking to caregivers for emotional cues
b. the crisis of infancy
c. the crisis of toddlerhood
d. approaching and following
e. theorist who described psychosexual stages of development
f. researcher who devised a laboratory procedure for studying attachment
g. laboratory procedure for studying attachment
h. a person's relatively consistent inborn traits
i. touching, snuggling, and holding
j. coordinated interaction between parent and infant
k. theorist who described psychosocial stages of development
l. a person's sense of being distinct from others

Key Terms

Using your own words, write a brief definition or explanation of each of the following terms on a separate piece of paper.

1. social smile
2. cortisol
3. separation anxiety
4. stranger wariness
5. self-awareness
6. temperament
7. synchrony
8. still-face technique
9. attachment
10. secure attachment (type B)
11. insecure-avoidant attachment (type A)
12. insecure-resistant/ambivalent attachment (type C)
13. disorganized attachment (type D)
14. Strange Situation
15. social referencing
16. trust versus mistrust
17. autonomy versus shame and doubt
18. social learning
19. proximal parenting
20. distal parenting
21. working model
22. allocare

ANSWERS

CHAPTER REVIEW

1. emotional; social
2. pleasure; pain; curiosity; happiness; social smile; 6
3. 6; is; frustration; withdrawal; cortisol
4. 9; stranger wariness; separation anxiety; 1; 2; decrease; targeted (focused)
5. pride; shame; embarrassment; guilt; disgust; other people
6. self-awareness; self; consciousness; pretending; first-person
7. social awareness
8. brain; experiences; neurons; anterior cingulate gyrus
9. medial prefrontal cortex
10. social anxiety; genes; parenting behavior
11. cortisol; hypothalamus
12. genetic; temperament
13. personality; personality; environment

14. New York Longitudinal Study (NYLS); nine; easy; difficult; slow to warm up; hard to classify

15. effortful control; negative mood; exuberant

Study Tip: In the classic self-awareness experiment, babies look in a mirror after a dot of rouge is put on their nose. If the babies react to the mirror image by touching their noses, it is clear they know they are seeing their own faces. Most babies demonstrate this self-awareness between 15 and 24 months of age.

16. separation anxiety; stranger wariness

17. synchrony; read other people's emotions; social interaction; parents; infants

18. still-face; does not

19. attachment

20. proximity-seeking; contact-maintaining

21. secure attachment; base for exploration; two-thirds

22. insecure attachment; insecure-avoidant attachment; insecure-resistant/ambivalent attachment; disorganized

Some infants are avoidant: They engage in little interaction with their mothers before and after her departure. Others are anxious and resistant: They cling nervously to their mothers, are unwilling to explore, become very upset when she leaves, and refuse to be comforted when she returns. Others are disorganized: They show an inconsistent mixture of behaviors toward their mothers.

23. Strange Situation

24. competent; high-achieving; capable; can

25. social referencing

26. most

27. emotion; depression; excitement; caress; read

28. Insecure-avoidant: They have less confidence and play independently without maintaining contact with the parent. Parents are neglectful, stressed, intrusive, and controlling, and father is an active alcoholic.

    Insecure-resistant/ambivalent: This child is unwilling to leave the parent's lap. Parent is abusive and depressed.

    Disorganized: This type has elements of the other types; the infant shifts between hitting and kissing the parent, from staring to crying. The most troubled children are classified as type D. The parent is abusive, paranoid, and stressed. The mother is an active alcoholic.

29. b. is the answer. Securely attached infants use their caregiver as a secure base. Kirsten returns to her mother for reassurance, so she can then resume play.

30. social referencing. Miguel is asking his mother how he should react by looking at her after the fall.

31. d. is the answer.

32. d. is the answer.

33. c. is the answer. Insecure-resistant/ambivalent infants usually become upset when the caregiver leaves but may resist or seek contact when she returns.

34. synchrony. Synchrony is a coordinated and smooth exchange of responses between a caregiver and an infant. Usually, it begins with the caregiver imitating the infant's behavior.

35. oral; mouth

36. anal

37. long-term; oral fixation

38. Erik Erikson; trust versus mistrust; autonomy versus shame and doubt

39. behaviorism; reinforcement; punishment

40. social; imitate; Albert Bandura

41. proximal; self-aware; compliant; distal

42. values; thoughts; beliefs; perceptions; memories; working model

43. evolutionary; proximity-seeking; contact-maintaining

44. allocare; 20

45. a. adequate attention to each infant
    b. encouragement of sensorimotor and language development
    c. attention to health and safety
    d. well-trained and professional caregivers
    e. warm and responsive caregivers

46. Only Freud and Erikson proposed stage theories. Other theories see development as continuous throughout the lifespan.

    Erikson emphasized psychosocial conflicts at each stage. If the conflicts are not resolved, the effects could last a lifetime, for example, creating a suspicious and pessimistic adult (mistrusting).

    Behaviorism emphasizes that emotions and personality are molded as parents reinforce or punish a child's spontaneous behavior. The result can last a lifetime if no other reinforcement or punishment changes the behavior.

    Cognitive theory believes that infants develop a working model that serves as a frame of reference later in life. They use this model to organize their perceptions and experiences.

Sociocultural theory contends that social and cultural factors have a significant influence on development and continue throughout the life span.

47. behaviorism. Behaviorists focus on learning through reinforcement or punishment and by observing others.

48. cognitive theory. Cognitive theory holds that thoughts and values determine a person's perspective.

49. **b.** is the answer. According to Freud, if the conflict at a particular stage is not resolved, the person becomes fixated at that stage. So, being fixated at the anal stage, Felix has a strong need for self-control.

PROGRESS TEST 1

Multiple-Choice Questions

1. **b.** is the answer.

   a., c., & d. These emotions emerge later in infancy, at about the same time as self-awareness emerges.

2. **b.** is the answer.

3. **c.** is the answer.

4. **d.** is the answer.

5. **b.** is the answer.

6. **c.** is the answer.

7. **b.** is the answer.

   a. Orality and anality refer to personality traits that result from fixation in the oral and anal stages, respectively.

   c. According to Erikson, this is the crisis of toddlerhood, which corresponds to Freud's anal stage.

   d. This is not a developmental crisis in Erikson's theory.

8. **c.** is the answer.

9. **a.** is the answer.

   c. Attachment behaviors are reliably found during infancy.

   d. There is no indication that the child attends day care.

10. **b.** is the answer. Another type is "hard to classify."

    a. "Secure" and "insecure" are different forms of attachment.

    c. The chapter does not describe different types of parenting.

d. The Strange Situation is a test of attachment rather than of temperament.

11. **a.** is the answer.

    c. & d. These terms were not used to describe parenting styles.

12. **a.** is the answer.

13. **d.** is the answer.

    a. Self-awareness refers to the infant's developing sense of "me and mine."

    b. Synchrony describes the coordinated interaction between infant and caregiver.

    c. Affiliation describes the tendency of people at any age to seek the companionship of others.

14. **a.** is the answer.

    b. In fact, just the opposite is true.

    c. & d. Not usually at 2 months, but clearly at 6 months, babies become very upset by a still-faced caregiver.

15. **b.** is the answer.

True or False Items

1. F   Sociocultural theorists contend that the entire social context can have an impact on the infant's development.

2. F   About two-thirds of infants display secure attachment.

3. T

4. T

5. F   A securely attached toddler is most likely to explore the environment, with the mother's presence being enough to give him or her the courage to do so.

6. F   Researchers believe that high-quality day care is not likely to harm the child. In fact, it is thought to be beneficial to the development of cognitive and social skills.

7. T

8. F   Temperament is a product of both genes and experience.

9. T

10. F   Only 20 percent of infants in the United States are cared for exclusively by their mothers throughout their first year.

PROGRESS TEST 2

Multiple-Choice Questions

1. **a.** is the answer.

2. **a.** is the answer.

3. **c.** is the answer.

4. **c.** is the answer.

5. **c.** is the answer.

   a. & b. The social smile, as well as temperamental characteristics, emerge well before the first signs of self-awareness.

   d. Contemporary developmentalists link these emotions to self-consciousness, rather than any specific environmental event such as toilet training.

6. **a.** is the answer.

   b. & c. Although environment, especially parents, affects temperamental tendencies, the study noted that temperament was established within three months of birth.

   d. Self-awareness is not a temperamental characteristic.

7. **c.** is the answer.

8. **c.** is the answer.

9. **d.** is the answer.

10. **a.** is the answer.

    c. & d. The text does not suggest that the consequences of secure and insecure attachment differ in boys and girls.

11. **b.** is the answer.

    a. Insecure-avoidant attachment is marked by behaviors that indicate an infant is uninterested in a caregiver's presence or departure.

    c. Disorganized attachment is marked only by the inconsistency of infant–caregiver behaviors.

    d. Type B, or secure attachment, is marked by behaviors that indicate an infant is using a caregiver as a base from which to explore the environment.

12. **a.** is the answer.

13. **a.** is the answer.

    b. & c. Freud alone would have agreed with these statements.

14. **c.** is the answer.

    a. & b. Social learning involves learning by observing others. In these examples, the children are learning directly from the consequences of their own behavior.

15. **b.** is the answer.

Matching Items

1.	h	5.	b	9.	l
2.	k	6.	e	10.	f
3.	g	7.	a	11.	d
4.	j	8.	c	12.	i

KEY TERMS

1. A **social smile** occurs when an infant smiles in response to a human face; evident in infants about six weeks after birth.

2. **Cortisol** is the primary stress hormone.

3. **Separation anxiety,** which is the infant's fear of being left by a familiar caregiver, is usually strongest at 9 to 14 months.

4. A common early fear in response to an unfamiliar person, thing, or situation, **stranger wariness** is first noticeable at about 9 months.

5. **Self-awareness** refers to a person's realization that he or she is a distinct individual whose body, mind, and actions are separate from other people. Self-awareness makes possible many new self-conscious emotions, including shame, embarrassment, disgust, guilt, and pride.

6. **Temperament** refers to the "constitutionally based individual differences" in emotions, activity, and self-regulation.

7. **Synchrony** refers to a coordinated, rapid, and smooth interaction between caregiver and infant that helps infants learn to express and read emotions.

8. The **still-face technique** is an experimental device in which an adult keeps his or her face unmoving and without expression in face-to-face interaction with an infant.

9. According to Mary Ainsworth, **attachment** is the enduring emotional bond that a person forms with another.

10. A **secure attachment (type B)** is one in which the infant obtains comfort and confidence from the base of exploration provided by a caregiver.

11. **Insecure-avoidant attachment (type A)** is the pattern of attachment in which the infant seems uninterested in the caregiver's presence, departure, or return.

12. **Insecure-resistant/ambivalent attachment (type C)** is the pattern of attachment in which an infant resists active exploration, becomes very upset when the caregiver leaves, and both resists and seeks contact when the caregiver returns.

13. **Disorganized attachment (type D)** is the pattern of attachment that is neither secure nor insecure and is marked by inconsistent infant–caregiver interactions.

14. The **Strange Situation** is a laboratory procedure developed by Mary Ainsworth for assessing attachment. Infants are observed in a playroom, in several successive episodes, while the caregiver (usually the mother) and a stranger move in and out of the room.

15. When infants engage in **social referencing,** they are looking to trusted adults for emotional cues on how to react to unfamiliar or ambiguous objects or events.

16. In Erikson's theory, the psychosocial crisis of infancy is one of **trust versus mistrust,** in which the infant learns whether the world is essentially a secure place in which basic needs will be met.

17. In Erikson's theory, the psychosocial crisis of toddlerhood is one of **autonomy versus shame and doubt,** in which toddlers strive to rule their own actions and bodies.

18. **Social learning** is learning by observing others.

19. **Proximal parenting** practices involve close physical contact between child and parent.

20. **Distal parenting** practices involve remaining distant from a baby.

21. According to cognitive theory, infants use early social relationships to develop a set of assumptions called a **working model** that organizes their perceptions and experiences.

22. **Allocare** is the care of children by people other than their biological parents.

Early Childhood: Biosocial Development

Chapter Overview

Chapter 8 introduces the developing person between the ages of 2 and 6. The chapter begins by outlining growth rates and the changes in shape that occur from ages 2 through 6, as well as the toddler's eating habits. This is followed by a look at brain growth and development and its role in physical and cognitive development. The developing limbic system is also described, along with its role in the expression and regulation of emotions during early childhood. A description of the acquisition of gross and fine motor skills follows, noting that mastery of such skills develops steadily during these years along with intellectual growth.

The next section begins with a discussion of the important issues of injury control and accidents, the major cause of childhood death. This section concludes with an in-depth exploration of child maltreatment, including its prevalence, contributing factors, consequences for future development, treatment, and prevention.

What Will You Know?

The text chapter should be studied one section at a time. Before you read, preview each section by skimming it, noting headings and boldface items. Then read the sections, one at a time, keeping these questions in mind.

1. Do children eat too much, too little, or just the right amount?
2. How does brain maturation affect emotional development in early childhood?
3. What do children need for their gross motor skills to develop?
4. When and how should child abuse be prevented?

Chapter Review

When you have finished reading the chapter, work through the material that follows to review it. Completing the sentences and answering the questions will enable you to answer the "What Have You Learned?" questions at the end of the text chapter. Scattered throughout the Chapter Review are Study Tips, which explain how best to learn a difficult concept, and Think About It discussions and Applications, which help you to know how well you understand the material. Check your understanding of the material by consulting the answers at the end of the chapter. Do not continue with the next section until you understand each answer. If you need to, review or reread the appropriate section in the textbook before continuing.

Body Changes

1. In early childhood, from age

   _____ to _____ ,
   children add almost _____ in
   height and gain about _____ in
   weight per year. By age 6, the average child in a
   developed nation weighs _____
   and measures about _____ in
   height.

2. In multiethnic countries, children of

   _____ descent tend to be tallest,
   followed by _____ ,
   then _____ , and then

   _____ .

3. Height differences _____
   (between/within) groups are greater than the
   average differences _____
   (between/within) groups.

4. Household _____ also affects physical growth. In Brazil, for instance, whereas low income once correlated with _____ (undernutrition/ overnutrition), today it also correlates with more _____ (undernutrition/ overnutrition).

5. Overfed children _____ (tend/do not necessarily tend) to become overweight adults. Overweight children often have early symptoms of two chronic illnesses: _____ disease and _____ . During early childhood, children need _____ (fewer/ more) calories per pound than they did as infants.

6. The most prevalent nutritional problem in early childhood is an insufficient intake of _____ , _____ , and _____ . An additional problem for American children is that they

consume too many _____ . One result of too much sugar is _____ _____ , the most common disease of young children in developed nations.

7. Young children generally insist that a particular experience occur in an exact sequence and manner, a phenomenon called

_____ _____ . By age _____ , this rigidity fades somewhat.

_____

STUDY TIP Learning (and remembering) developmental changes in height, weight, brain maturation, and other aspects of biosocial development requires a lot of rote memorization. A good way to facilitate your learning is to design and complete a simple organizational chart. Your chart might look something like the one below. Continue adding to the chart as you work your way through the chapter.

8. Physical Changes in Early Childhood (2–6 years)

	Changes	Description
Height (in inches)	3 inches per year	The child is taller and thinner and, on average, is $3\frac{1}{2}$ feet tall by 6 years of age.
Weight (in pounds)		
Brain functions General functions		
Limbic system		
Prefrontal cortex		
Motor skills Gross motor skills		
Fine motor skills		

APPLICATION:

9. Three-year-old Kyle's parents are concerned because Kyle, who generally seems healthy, doesn't seem to have the hefty appetite he had as an infant. Should they be worried?
   a. Yes, because appetite normally increases throughout early childhood.
   b. Yes, because appetite remains as good during early childhood as it was earlier.
   c. No, because caloric need is less during early childhood than during infancy.
   d. There is not enough information to determine whether Kyle is developing normally.

Brain Development

10. By age 2, substantial _____ of the brain's connections has occurred, and the brain weighs _____ percent of its adult weight. By age 5, the brain has attained about _____ percent of its adult weight.

11. Some of the brain's increase in size during childhood is due to the proliferation of _____ pathways, but most of it occurs because of the ongoing process of _____ . This process enables greater _____ _____ _____ .

12. The long, thick band of nerve fibers that connects the right and left sides of the brain, called the _____ _____ , grows and _____ rapidly during early childhood. This helps children better coordinate functions that involve _____ .

13. The two sides of the body and brain _____ (are/are not) identical. The specialization of the two sides of the body and brain is called _____ . Throughout the world, societies are organized to favor _____-handedness. Developmentalists _____ (advise against/advise) trying to switch a child's handedness.

14. Adults who are _____ (right-/left-) handed tend to have a thicker corpus callosum, probably because as children they had a greater need to _____ both sides of the body in a right-handed world.

15. The left hemisphere of the brain controls the _____ side of the body and contains areas dedicated to _____ _____ , detailed _____ , and the basics of _____ . The right hemisphere controls the _____ side of the body and contains brain areas dedicated to generalized _____ and _____ impulses. As a rule, though, every cognitive skill requires _____ (the right/the left/both) side(s) of the brain.

16. In older children, the corpus callosum is more _____ , which partly explains why they are better at thinking and why their behaviors sometimes are less clumsy.

17. The part of the brain that shows the most prolonged period of postnatal development is the _____ _____ . Development of this brain area increases throughout _____ . This area is sometimes called the _____ because all other areas of the brain are ruled by its decisions. Maturation of this area over the years of early childhood is evident as _____ becomes more regular, _____ become more nuanced, _____ _____ subside, and uncontrollable laughter and tears become less common.

18. Two signs of an immature prefrontal cortex are poor _____ _____ and _____ , which is the tendency to stick to a thought or action for a long time.

19. The part of the brain that plays a crucial role in the expression and regulation of emotions is the _____ _____ . Within this system is the _____ , which registers emotions, particularly _____ and _____ . Next to this area is the _____ , which is a central processor of _____ , especially of _____ . Another structure in this brain region is the _____ , which

produces _____ that activate other parts of the brain and body.

THINK ABOUT IT Students, and people in general, often have difficulty understanding the limitations of the young child's thinking and emotional impulsiveness. To increase your understanding, make a list of behaviors that demonstrate the child's immaturity, then observe and compare 2- or 3-year-olds with 6-year-olds.

APPLICATIONS:

20. Rodesia is a left-handed adult. It is most likely that she
    a. has a thinner corpus callosum.
    b. has a thicker corpus callosum.
    c. experienced delayed maturation of her prefrontal cortex.
    d. experienced accelerated maturation of her prefrontal cortex.

21. Following an automobile accident, Amira developed severe problems with her speech. Her doctor believes that the accident injured the _____ _____ of her brain.

22. Yolanda, who is 5 years old, has improved dramatically in her ability to throw and catch a baseball. Which aspect of her brain development contributed most to enable these abilities by enhancing communication among the brain's various specialized areas?
    a. increasing brain weight
    b. proliferation of dendrite networks
    c. myelination
    d. increasing specialization of brain areas

Improving Motor Skills

23. Large body movements such as running, climbing, jumping, and throwing are called _____ _____ skills.

24. Most children learn specific gross motor skills best from _____ (other children/parents).

25. Environmental hazards such as _____ do more harm to young brains and bodies than to older, more developed ones. Some of the substances that have proven to be harmful are _____ .

26. (A View from Science) The symptoms of lead poisoning, which is also called _____ , include _____ .

27. Skills that involve small body movements, such as pouring liquids and cutting food, are called _____ _____ skills. Most 2-year-olds have greater difficulty with these skills primarily because they have not developed the _____ control, patience, or _____ needed—in part because of the immaturity of the _____ _____ and _____ _____ .

28. Fine motor skills are useful in almost all forms of _____ _____ , yet such skills are far from perfect. These skills typically mature _____ (earlier/later), by about _____ months, in _____ (girls/boys).

APPLICATIONS:

29. Two-year-old Ali is quite clumsy, falls down frequently, and often bumps into stationary objects. Ali most likely
    a. has a neuromuscular disorder.
    b. has an underdeveloped right hemisphere of the brain.
    c. is suffering from an iron deficiency.
    d. is a normal 2-year-old whose gross motor skills will improve dramatically during early childhood.

30. Climbing a fence is an example of a _____ _____ .

31. Which of the following activities would probably be the most difficult for a 5-year-old child?
    a. climbing a ladder
    b. catching a ball
    c. throwing a ball
    d. pouring juice from a pitcher without spilling it

32. A factor that would figure very little into the development of fine motor skills, such as drawing and writing, is
    a. strength.   c. judgment.
    b. muscular control.   d. short, fat fingers.

Injuries and Abuse

33. The leading cause of childhood death is
_____ .

34. Not until age _____ does any
disease become a greater cause of mortality.

35. Instead of *accident prevention*, many
experts speak of _____
_____ (or _____
_____), an approach based on the
belief that most accidents _____
(are/are not) preventable.

36. Preventive community actions that reduce
everyone's chance of injury are called
_____ _____
. Preventive actions that avert harm in a high-
risk situation constitute _____
_____ . Actions aimed
at minimizing the impact of an adverse
event that has already occurred constitute
_____ _____ .

37. Until about 1960, the concept of child
maltreatment was mostly limited to rare
and _____ outbursts of
a disturbed stranger. Today, it is known
that most perpetrators of maltreatment are
_____ .

38. Intentional harm to or avoidable endangerment
of someone under age 18 defines child
_____ . Actions that are
deliberately harmful to a child's well-being are
classified as _____ . A failure to
act appropriately to meet a child's basic needs is
classified as _____ .

39. Since 1993, the ratio of the number of cases of
_____ _____ ,
in which authorities have been officially
notified, to cases of _____
_____ , which have been
reported, investigated, and verified, has been
about _____ (what ratio?).

40. Often the first sign of maltreatment is
_____ _____ ,
such as slow growth or lack of curiosity.

41. Signs of maltreatment may be symptoms of
_____-_____
_____ _____ ,
which was first described in combat victims.

42. Maltreated children suffer substantial
_____ and _____
handicaps. However, deficits in their
_____ _____ are
even more apparent.
Describe other deficits of children who have been
maltreated.

43. Public policy measures and other efforts
designed to prevent maltreatment from ever
occurring are called _____
_____ . An approach that focuses
on spotting and treating the first symptoms of
maltreatment is called _____
_____ . Last-ditch measures,
such as removing a child from an abusive home,
jailing the perpetrator, and so forth, constitute
_____ _____ .

44. Once maltreatment has been substantiated
and the child legally removed from the home,
U.S. federal law requires authorities to begin
_____ _____ for
the child's long-term care.

45. Some children are officially removed from
their biological parents and placed in a
_____ _____
arrangement with another adult or family that is
paid to nurture them.

46. In another type of foster care, called
_____ _____ ,
a relative of the maltreated child becomes
the approved caregiver. A final option is
_____ .

APPLICATIONS:

47. Two-year-old Carrie is hyperactive, often confused between fantasy and reality, and jumps at any sudden noise. Her pediatrician suspects that she is suffering from
    a. perseveration.
    b. child abuse.
    c. post-traumatic stress disorder.
    d. child neglect.

48. To prevent accidental death in childhood, some experts urge forethought and planning for safety and measures to limit the damage of such accidents when they do occur. This approach is called _____ _____ .

49. After his daughter scraped her knee, Ben gently cleansed the wound and bandaged it. Ben's behavior is an example of _____ prevention.

50. Helga comes to school with large black-and-blue marks on her arm. Her teacher suspects
    a. ongoing abuse and neglect by Helga's own parents.
    b. a rare outburst from a unfamiliar perpetrator.
    c. abuse by a neighbor or friend of Helga's family.
    d. abuse by a mentally ill perpetrator.

51. A mayoral candidate is calling for sweeping policy changes to help ensure the well-being of children by promoting home ownership, high-quality community centers, and more stable neighborhoods. If these measures are effective in reducing child maltreatment, they would be classified as _____ prevention.

Progress Test 1

Multiple-Choice Questions

Circle your answers to the following questions and check them with the answers at the end of the chapter. If your answer is incorrect, read the explanation for why it is incorrect and then consult the text.

1. During early childhood, the most common disease of young children in developed nations is
   a. undernutrition.
   b. malnutrition.
   c. tooth decay.
   d. diabetes.

2. The brain center for the basics of language is usually located in the
   a. right hemisphere.
   b. left hemisphere.
   c. corpus callosum.
   d. space just below the right ear.

3. Which of the following is an example of tertiary prevention of child maltreatment?
   a. removing a child from an abusive home
   b. home visitation of families with infants by a social worker
   c. new laws establishing stiff penalties for child maltreatment
   d. public policy measures aimed at creating stable neighborhoods

4. The brain area that registers emotions is the
   a. hippocampus.
   b. hypothalamus.
   c. amygdala.
   d. prefrontal cortex.

5. Children's problems with tooth decay result primarily from their having too much _____ in their diet.
   a. iron   c. fat
   b. sugar   d. carbohydrates

6. Skills that involve large body movements, such as running and jumping, are called
   a. activity-level skills.
   b. fine motor skills.
   c. gross motor skills.
   d. left-brain skills.

7. The brain's ongoing myelination during childhood helps children
   a. control their actions more precisely.
   b. react more quickly to stimuli.
   c. control their emotions.
   d. do all of these things.

8. The leading cause of death in childhood is
   a. accidents.
   b. untreated diabetes.
   c. malnutrition.
   d. cancer.

9. Regarding lateralization, which of the following is NOT true?
   a. Some cognitive skills require only one side of the brain.
   b. Brain centers for generalized emotional impulses can be found in the right hemisphere.

   c. The left hemisphere contains brain areas dedicated to logical reasoning.

   d. The right side of the brain controls the left side of the body.

10. In young children, perseveration is a sign of

   a. immature brain functions.
   b. maltreatment.
   c. abuse.
   d. amygdala.

11. The area of the brain that directs and controls the other areas is the

   a. corpus callosum.
   b. myelin sheath.
   c. prefrontal cortex.
   d. amygdala.

12. The brain structure that produces hormones that activate other parts of the brain and body is the

   a. corpus callosum.
   b. amygdala.
   c. hippocampus.
   d. hypothalamus.

13. Which of the following is true of the corpus callosum?

   a. It enables short-term memory.
   b. It connects the two halves of the brain.
   c. It must be fully myelinated before gross motor skills can be acquired.
   d. All of these statements are correct.

14. The improvements in eye–hand coordination that allow young children to catch and then throw a ball occur, in part, because

   a. the brain areas associated with this ability become more fully myelinated.
   b. the corpus callosum begins to function.
   c. fine motor skills have matured by age 2.
   d. gross motor skills have matured by age 2.

15. During early childhood, inadequate lateralization of the brain and immaturity of the prefrontal cortex may contribute to deficiencies in

   a. cognition.
   b. peer relationships.
   c. emotional control.
   d. all of these abilities.

True or False Items

Write T (true) or F (false) on the line in front of each statement.

_____ **1.** Growth between ages 2 and 6 results in body proportions more similar to those of an adult.

_____ **2.** During childhood, the legs develop rapidly.

_____ **3.** For most people, the brain center for language is located in the left hemisphere.

_____ **4.** At age 5, the body mass index is lower than at any other age.

_____ **5.** Overweight children tend to become overweight adults.

_____ **6.** Fine motor skills are usually easier for preschoolers to master than are gross motor skills.

_____ **7.** Most serious childhood injuries truly are "accidents."

_____ **8.** Children often fare as well in kinship care as they do in conventional foster care.

_____ **9.** Tertiary prevention is generally the most effective method of injury control.

_____ **10.** Myelination is essential for basic communication between neurons.

Progress Test 2

Progress Test 2 should be completed during a final chapter review. Answer the following questions after you thoroughly understand the correct answers for the Chapter Review and Progress Test 1.

Multiple-Choice Questions

1. Each year from ages 2 to 6, the average child gains and grows, respectively,

   a. 2 pounds and 1 inch.
   b. 3 pounds and 2 inches.
   c. $4\frac{1}{2}$ pounds and 3 inches.
   d. 6 pounds and 6 inches.

2. The center for appreciation of music, art, and poetry is usually located in the brain's

   a. right hemisphere.
   b. left hemisphere.
   c. right or left hemisphere.
   d. corpus callosum.

3. Regarding handedness, which of the following is NOT true?

   a. Infants and toddlers usually show a preference for grabbing with either the right or the left hand.

   b. Some societies favor left-handed people.

   c. Experience can influence hand development.

   d. Language, customs, tools, and taboos all illustrate social biases toward right-handedness.

4. A nutritional problem of young children in developed nations is

   a. too much salt.   c. too much zinc.

   b. too little iron.   d. too much calcium.

5. Seeing her toddler reach for a brightly glowing burner on the stove, Sheila grabs his hand and says, "No, that's very hot." Sheila's behavior is an example of

   a. primary prevention.

   b. secondary prevention.

   c. tertiary prevention.

   d. none of these types of prevention.

6. When parents or caregivers do not meet a child's basic physical, educational, or emotional needs, it is referred to as

   a. abuse.

   b. neglect.

   c. endangering.

   d. maltreatment.

7. Which of the following is true of a developed nation in which many ethnic groups live together?

   a. Ethnic variations in height and weight disappear.

   b. Ethnic variations in stature persist, but are substantially smaller.

   c. Children of African descent tend to be tallest, followed by Europeans, Asians, and Latinos.

   d. Cultural patterns exert a stronger-than-normal impact on growth patterns.

8. Which of the following is an example of perseveration?

   a. 2-year-old Jason sings the same song over and over

   b. 3-year-old Kwame falls down when attempting to kick a soccer ball

   c. 4-year-old Kara pours water very slowly from a pitcher into a glass

   d. None of these is an example.

9. Which of the following is an example of a fine motor skill?

   a. kicking a ball

   b. running

   c. drawing with a pencil

   d. jumping

10. Children who have been maltreated often

    a. regard other children and adults as hostile and exploitative.

    b. are less friendly and more aggressive.

    c. are more isolated than other children.

    d. have all of these characteristics.

11. The left half of the brain contains areas dedicated to all of the following EXCEPT

    a. language.

    b. logic.

    c. analysis.

    d. creative impulses.

12. Most gross motor skills can be learned by healthy children by about age

    a. 2.   c. 5.

    b. 3.   d. 7.

13. Andrea is concerned because her 3-year-old daughter has been having nightmares. Her pediatrician tells her

    a. not to worry, because nightmares are often caused by increased activity in the amygdala, which is normal during early childhood.

    b. nightmares are a possible sign of an overdeveloped prefrontal cortex.

    c. to monitor her daughter's diet, because nightmares are often caused by too much sugar.

    d. to consult a neurologist, because nightmares are never a sign of healthy development.

14. The brain area that is a central processor for memory is the

    a. hippocampus.

    b. amygdala.

    c. hypothalamus.

    d. prefrontal cortex.

15. The appetites of young children seem _____ they were in the first two years of life.

    a. larger than

    b. smaller than

    c. about the same as

    d. erratic, sometimes smaller and sometimes larger than

Matching Items

Match each term or concept with its corresponding description or definition.

Terms or Concepts

_____   1. corpus callosum

_____   2. gross motor skills

_____   3. fine motor skills

_____   4. kinship care

_____   5. foster care

_____   6. injury control

_____   7. right hemisphere

_____   8. left hemisphere

_____   9. child abuse

_____   10. child neglect

_____   11. primary prevention

_____   12. secondary prevention

_____   13. tertiary prevention

Descriptions or Definitions

a. brain area that is primarily responsible for processing language

b. brain area that is primarily responsible for generalized creative impulses

c. legal placement of a child in the care of someone other than his or her biological parents

d. a form of care in which a relative of a maltreated child takes over from the biological parents

e. procedures to prevent unwanted events or circumstances from ever occurring

f. running and jumping

g. actions that are deliberately harmful to a child's well-being

h. actions for averting harm in the immediate situation

i. painting a picture or tying shoelaces

j. failure to appropriately meet a child's basic needs

k. an approach emphasizing accident prevention

l. actions aimed at reducing the harm that has occurred

m. band of nerve fibers connecting the right and left hemispheres of the brain

Key Terms

Using your own words, write a brief definition or explanation of each of the following terms on a separate piece of paper.

1. myelination
2. corpus callosum
3. lateralization
4. impulse control
5. perseveration
6. amygdala
7. hippocampus
8. hypothalamus
9. injury control/harm reduction
10. primary prevention
11. secondary prevention
12. tertiary prevention
13. child maltreatment
14. child abuse
15. child neglect

16. substantiated maltreatment
17. reported maltreatment
18. post-traumatic stress disorder (PTSD)
19. permanency planning
20. foster care
21. kinship care
22. adoption

ANSWERS

CHAPTER REVIEW

1. 2; 6; 3 inches (about 7 centimeters); $4\frac{1}{2}$ pounds (2 kilograms); between 40 and 50 pounds (between 18 and 22 kilograms); $3\frac{1}{2}$ feet (more than 100 centimeters)

2. African; Europeans; Asians; Latinos

3. within; between

4. income; undernutrition; overnutrition

5. tend; heart; diabetes; fewer

6. iron; zinc; calcium; sweetened cereals and drinks; tooth decay

7. just right (just so); 6

8. Weight: Children gain $4\frac{1}{2}$ pounds each year. Because they are also growing rapidly, they are actually thinner than in earlier years.

   General brain functions: Increased myelination allows for greater speed of thought and greater motor abilities, such as catching and throwing a ball.

   Limbic system: The amygdala, hippocampus, and hypothalamus in the limbic system advance during these years. The amygdala registers emotions; increased activity in this area makes the child sensitive to other people's emotions and subject to strong personal emotions, including fear.

   Prefrontal cortex: Said to be the executive of the brain, the prefrontal cortex is responsible for planning and analyzing. It continues to mature through childhood and adolescence, which enables more regular sleep, more nuanced emotions, and fewer temper tantrums and uncontrollable laughter and tears.

   Gross motor skills: These large body movements improve markedly in early childhood. Children can climb a ladder; ride a tricycle; throw, catch, and kick a ball; and sometimes ski, skate, and dive.

   Fine motor skills: These small body movements are more difficult for young children because of an immature corpus callosum and prefrontal cortex and because of short, stubby fingers. The lack of fine motor skills is one reason 3-year-olds are not allowed in first grade.

9. c. is the answer.

10. pruning; 75; 90

11. communication; myelination; speed of thought

12. corpus callosum; myelinates; both sides of the brain or body

13. are not; lateralization; right; advise against

14. left-; coordinate

15. right; logical reasoning; analysis; language; left; emotional; creative; both

16. myelinated

17. prefrontal cortex; adolescence; executive; sleep; emotions; temper tantrums

18. impulse control; perseveration

19. limbic system; amygdala; fear; anxiety; hippocampus; memory; locations; hypothalamus; hormones

20. **b.** is the answer. This is probably because, growing up in a right-handed world, left-handers have a greater need to coordinate both sides of the body.

21. left side. The left side of the brain specializes in the basics of language.

22. **c.** is the answer. The greatest myelination in early childhood occurs in the motor and sensory areas, the areas responsible for the skills that develop dramatically during this time.

23. gross motor

24. other children

25. pollutants; lead in the water and air, pesticides, BPA in plastic, and secondhand cigarette smoke

26. (A View from Science) plumbism; intellectual disability, hyperactivity, and even death

27. fine motor; muscular; judgment; corpus callosum; prefrontal cortex

28. artistic expression; earlier; 6; girls

29. **d.** is the answer. Because the child has better balance and coordination of both sides of the brain, motor skills improve greatly during this period.

30. gross motor skill

31. **d.** is the answer. Fine motor skills are more difficult for the young child, in part because of their short, stubby fingers.

32. **a.** is the answer.

33. violence

34. 40

35. injury control; harm reduction; are

36. primary prevention; secondary prevention; tertiary prevention

37. sudden; one or both of the child's own parents

38. maltreatment; abuse; neglect

39. reported maltreatment; substantiated maltreatment; 3-to-1

40. delayed development

41. post-traumatic stress disorder

42. biological; academic; social skills

Maltreated children tend to regard other people as hostile and exploitative, and thus are less friendly, more aggressive, and more isolated than other children. Adults who were severely maltreated often abuse drugs or alcohol, choose unsupportive relationships, become victims or aggressors, sabotage their own careers, eat too much or too little, and engage in self-destructive behavior.

43. primary prevention; secondary prevention; tertiary prevention

44. permanency planning

45. foster care

46. kinship care; adoption

47. **c.** is the answer. First identified in combat veterans, PTSD is now evident in some maltreated children.

48. injury control.

49. tertiary. Ben is applying medical treatment after the adverse event, his daughter scraping her knee.

50. **a.** is the answer. At one time, people thought child maltreatment was a rare situation, perpetrated by a mentally ill stranger. Today, they know it is more likely to be perpetrated by the child's own parents.

51. primary. Primary prevention refers to actions taken to prevent an adverse event from occurring to a child.

PROGRESS TEST 1

Multiple-Choice Questions

1. **c.** is the answer.

    a., b., & d. All of these conditions are much more likely to occur in infancy or in adolescence than in early childhood.

2. **b.** is the answer.

    a. & d. The right brain is the location of areas associated with generalized emotional and creative impulses.

    c. The corpus callosum helps integrate the functioning of the two halves of the brain; it does not contain areas specialized for particular skills.

3. **a.** is the answer.

    b. This is an example of secondary prevention.

    c. & d. These are examples of primary prevention.

4. **c.** is the answer.

    a. The hippocampus is a central processor of memory.

    b. The hypothalamus produces hormones that activate other parts of the brain and body.

    d. The prefrontal cortex is responsible for regulating attention, among other things. It makes formal education more possible in children.

5. **b.** is the answer.

6. **c.** is the answer.

7. **d.** is the answer.

8. **a.** is the answer.

9. **a.** is the answer.

10. **a.** is the answer.

    b., c., & d. Although maltreatment, whether in the form of abuse or neglect, may cause brain injury, perseveration is not necessarily a symptom of brain injury from those sources.

11. **c.** is the answer.

    a. The corpus callosum is the band of fibers that link the two halves of the brain.

    b. The myelin sheath is a fatty substance that surrounds some neurons in the brain.

    d. The amygdala registers emotions.

12. **d.** is the answer.

13. **b.** is the answer.

    a. The corpus callosum is not directly involved in memory.

    c. Myelination of the central nervous system is important to the mastery of *fine* motor skills.

14. **a.** is the answer.

    b. The corpus callosum begins to function long before the years between 2 and 6.

    c. & d. Neither fine nor gross motor skills have fully matured by age 2.

15. **d.** is the answer.

True or False Items

1. T

2. F   During childhood, the brain develops faster than any other part of the body.

3. T

4. T

5. T

6. F   Fine motor skills are more difficult for preschoolers to master than are gross motor skills.

7. F   Most serious accidents involve someone's lack of forethought.

8. T

9. F   Primary prevention is the most effective method of injury control.

10. F   Although myelination is not essential for basic communication between neurons, it is essential for fast and complex communication.

PROGRESS TEST 2

Multiple-Choice Questions

1. **c.** is the answer.

2. **a.** is the answer.

   b. & c. The left hemisphere of the brain contains areas associated with language development.

   d. The corpus callosum does not contain areas for specific behaviors.

3. **b.** is the answer. All societies favor right-handed people.

4. **b.** is the answer.

5. **b.** is the answer.

6. **b.** is the answer.

   a. Abuse is deliberate, harsh injury to the body.

   c. Endangerment was not discussed.

   d. Maltreatment is too broad a term.

7. **c.** is the answer.

8. **a.** is the answer.

   b. Kicking a ball is a gross motor skill.

   c. Pouring is a fine motor skill.

9. **c.** is the answer.

   a., b., & d. These are gross motor skills.

10. **d.** is the answer.

11. **d.** is the answer. Brain areas that control generalized creative and emotional impulses are found in the right hemisphere.

12. **c.** is the answer.

13. **a.** is the answer.

   b. Nightmares generally occur when activity in the amygdala overwhelms the slowly developing prefrontal cortex.

   c. There is no indication that nightmares are caused by diet.

   d. Increased activity in the amygdala is normal during early childhood, as are the nightmares that some children experience.

14. **a.** is the answer.

   b. The amygdala is responsible for registering emotions.

   c. The hypothalamus produces hormones that activate other parts of the brain and body.

   d. The prefrontal cortex is involved in planning and goal-directed behavior.

15. **b.** is the answer.

Matching Items

1. m	6. k	11. e
2. f	7. b	12. h
3. i	8. a	13. l
4. d	9. g	
5. c	10. j	

KEY TERMS

1. **Myelination** is the process by which axons become coated with myelin, a fatty substance that speeds up the transmission of nerve impulses between neurons.

2. The **corpus callosum** is a long, thick band of nerve fibers that connects the right and left hemispheres of the brain.

3. **Lateralization** refers to the specialization in certain functions by each side of the brain.

4. **Impulse control** is the ability to postpone the immediate response to an idea or behavior.

5. **Perseveration** is the tendency to stick to one thought or action for a long time. In young children, perseveration is a normal product of immature brain functions.

   Memory Aid: To *persevere* is to continue, or persist, at something.

6. A part of the brain's limbic system, the **amygdala** registers emotions, particularly fear and anxiety.

7. The **hippocampus** is the part of the brain's limbic system that is a central processor of memory, especially memory for locations.

8. The **hypothalamus** is the brain structure that responds to the amygdala and the hippocampus to produce hormones that activate other parts of the brain and body.

9. **Injury control/harm reduction** is the practice of limiting the extent of injuries by anticipating, controlling, and preventing dangerous activities.

10. **Primary prevention** refers to actions that change overall background conditions to prevent some unwanted event or circumstance.

11. **Secondary prevention** involves actions that avert harm in a high-risk situation.

12. **Tertiary prevention** involves actions taken after an adverse event occurs, aimed at reducing the

harm or preventing disability.

13. **Child maltreatment** is intentional harm to or avoidable endangerment of anyone under age 18.

14. **Child abuse** refers to deliberate actions that are harmful to a child's physical, emotional, or sexual well-being.

15. **Child neglect** refers to failure to appropriately meet a child's basic physical, educational, or emotional needs.

16. Child maltreatment that has been officially reported to authorities, investigated, and verified is called **substantiated maltreatment**.

17. Child maltreatment that has been officially reported to the police or other authorities is called **reported maltreatment**.

18. **Post-traumatic stress disorder (PTSD)** is an anxiety disorder triggered by exposure to an extreme traumatic stressor. Symptoms of PTSD include hyperactivity and hypervigilance, sleeplessness, sudden terror or anxiety, and confusion between fantasy and reality.

19. **Permanency planning** is planning for the long-term care of a child who has experienced substantiated maltreatment.

20. **Foster care** is a legally sanctioned, publicly supported arrangement in which children are removed from their biological parents and temporarily given to another adult to nurture.

21. **Kinship care** is a form of foster care in which a relative of a maltreated child becomes the child's approved caregiver.

22. **Adoption** is a legal procedure in which an adult or couple is granted the obligations and joys of being the parent(s) of an unrelated child.

Early Childhood: Cognitive Development

Chapter Overview

In countless everyday instances, as well as in the findings of numerous research studies, young children reveal themselves to be remarkably thoughtful, insightful, and perceptive thinkers whose grasp of the causes of everyday events, memory of the past, and mastery of language are sometimes astonishing. Chapter 9 begins with Piaget's and Vygotsky's views of cognitive development at this age. According to Piaget, young children's thought is prelogical: Between the ages of about 2 and 6, they are capable of symbolic thought but unable to perform many logical operations and are limited by irreversible, centered, and static thinking. Lev Vygotsky, a contemporary of Piaget's, saw learning as a social activity more than as a matter of individual discovery. Vygotsky focused on the child's zone of proximal development and the relationship between language and thought.

The next section focuses on young children's language development during early childhood. Although young children demonstrate rapid improvement in vocabulary and grammar, they have difficulty with comparisons and certain rules of grammar. A discussion of whether bilingualism in young children is useful concludes the section on language.

The chapter ends with a discussion of preschool education, including a description of quality preschool programs and an evaluation of their impact on children.

What Will You Know?

The text chapter should be studied one section at a time. Before you read, preview each section by skimming it, noting headings and boldface items. Then read the sections, one at a time, keeping these questions in mind.

1. Are young children selfish or just self-centered?
2. How should adults answer when children ask, "Why"?
3. Does it confuse young children if they hear two or more languages?
4. What do children learn in preschool?

Chapter Review

When you have finished reading the chapter, work through the material that follows to review it. Completing the sentences and answering the questions will enable you to answer the "What Have You Learned?" questions at the end of the text chapter. Scattered throughout the Chapter Review are Study Tips, which explain how best to learn a difficult concept, and Think About It discussions and Applications, which help you to know how well you understand the material. Check your understanding of the material by consulting the answers at the end of the chapter. Do not continue with the next section until you understand each answer. If you need to, review or reread the appropriate section in the textbook before continuing.

Thinking During Early Childhood

1. Piaget referred to cognitive development between the ages of 2 and 6 as _____ intelligence.

2. During this stage, children are able to think in _____ , not just via their senses and motor skills. This type of thinking is called _____ _____ .

   One example of this is _____ , the belief that natural objects are alive.

3. Young children's tendency to contemplate the world exclusively from their personal perspective is referred to as _____ . Their tendency to think about one aspect of a situation at a time is called _____ . This tendency _____ (is/is not) equated with selfishness. Children also tend to

focus on _____ to the exclusion of other attributes of objects and people.

4. Young children's understanding of the world tends to focus on _____ (static/ dynamic) reasoning, which means that they tend to think of their world as _____ . Another characteristic of preoperational thinking is _____—the inability to recognize that reversing a process will restore the original conditions from which the process began. The idea that amount is unaffected by changes in appearance is called _____ .

5. Researchers now believe that Piaget _____ (overestimated/ underestimated) conceptual ability during early childhood.

STUDY TIP When many students first read Piaget's description of the limits of preoperational thought, they have the same reaction many developmentalists did—they don't believe it. To bring to life the fact that the preoperational child sees the world from his or her own perspective (egocentrism) and has not yet mastered the principle of conservation (the idea that properties such as mass, volume, and number remain the same despite changes in appearance), you might try one of Piaget's classic tests with a younger sibling, relative, or friend—for example, cut two hot dogs into different numbers of pieces or pour milk from a tall, thin glass into a short, fat glass and ask the child which hot dog is bigger or which glass has more milk in it.

---

6. Much of the research from the sociocultural perspective on the young child's emerging cognition is inspired by the Russian psychologist _____ . According to this perspective, a child is an _____ _____ _____ , whose intellectual growth is stimulated by older and more skilled members of society.

7. Vygotsky believed that adults can most effectively help a child solve a problem by presenting _____ , by offering _____ , by adding _____ _____ , and by encouraging _____ . This

emphasizes that children's intellectual growth is stimulated by their _____ _____ in _____ experiences of their environment. The critical element in this process is that the mentor and the child _____ to accomplish a task.

8. Vygotsky suggested that for each developing individual there is a _____ _____ _____ _____ , a range of skills that the person can exercise with assistance but is not yet able to perform independently.

9. How and when new skills are developed depends, in part, on the willingness of tutors to _____ the child's participation in the learning process.

10. Children's eagerness to learn is often manifested in their _____ of adult actions that are irrelevant and inefficient.

11. Vygotsky believed that language is essential to the advancement of thinking in two crucial ways. The first is through the internal dialogue in which a person talks to himself or herself, called _____ _____ . In young children, this dialogue is likely to be _____ (expressed silently/ uttered aloud).

12. (A View From Science) A practical use of Vygotsky's theory concerns the current emphasis on education in the areas of _____ .

13. The term _____- _____ highlights the idea that children attempt to construct theories to explain everything they see and hear.

14. At about _____ years, young children acquire an understanding of others' thinking, or a _____ _____ .

Describe the theory of mind of children between the ages of 3 and 6.

15. Most 3-year-olds _____ (have/ do not have) difficulty realizing that a belief can be false.

16. Research studies reveal that theory-of-mind development depends partly on _____ maturation, particularly of the brain's _____ _____ . General _____ ability is also important in strengthening young children's theory of mind. A third helpful factor is having at least one _____ . Finally, _____ may be a factor.

THINK ABOUT IT One theory of how people acquire a theory of mind is that it is inborn. However, there are many reasons to suppose that as children grow into different cultures, their theories of mind emerge. Cultural variations in theories of mind are often revealed through language. For example, children in Samoa typically do not try to get out of trouble by saying, "I did not do it on purpose," as they often do in European American cultures; instead, they deny having done the deed at all.

APPLICATIONS:

17. An experimenter first shows a child two rows of checkers that each have the same number of checkers. Then, with the child watching, the experimenter elongates one row and asks the child if each of the two rows still has an equal number of checkers. This experiment tests the child's understanding of _____ .

18. Five-year-old Dani believes that a "party" is the one and only attribute of a birthday. She says that Daddy doesn't have a birthday because he never has a party. This thinking demonstrates the tendency Piaget called _____ .

19. Darrell understands that 6 + 3 = 9 means that 9 – 6 = 3. He has mastered the concept of _____ .

20. Which of the following terms does NOT belong with the others?
a. focus on appearances
b. static reasoning
c. reversibility
d. centration

21. In describing the limited logical reasoning of young children, a developmentalist is LEAST likely to emphasize
a. irreversibility.   c. its action-bound nature.
b. centration.   d. its static nature.

22. A young child fails to put together a difficult puzzle on her own, so her mother encourages her to try again, this time guiding her by asking questions such as, "For this space, do we need a big piece or a little piece?" With Mom's help, the child successfully completes the puzzle. Lev Vygotsky would attribute the child's success to
a. additional practice with the puzzle pieces.
b. imitation of her mother's behavior.
c. the social interaction with her mother that restructured the task to make its solution more attainable.
d. modeling and reinforcement.

23. Comparing the views of Piaget with those of Vygotsky, active learning is to guided participation as egocentrism is to
a. apprenticeship.   c. scaffold.
b. structure.   d. fast-mapping.

24. A 4-year-old tells the teacher that a clown should not be allowed to visit the class because "Pat is 'fraid of clowns." The 4-year-old thus shows that he can anticipate how another will feel. This is evidence of the beginnings of _____ .

25. When asked "Where do dreams come from?," 5-year-old Rhoda is likely to answer
a. "from God."
b. "from the sky."
c. "from my pillow."
d. "from inside my head."

Language Learning

26. Two aspects of development that make ages 2 to 6 the prime time for learning language are _____ and _____ in the language areas of the brain. Two others are _____ and the characteristic _____ interaction of early childhood.

27. Although early childhood does not appear to be a _____ period for language development, it does seem to be a _____ period for the learning of vocabulary, grammar, and pronunciation.

28. During early childhood, a dramatic increase in language occurs, with _____ increasing rapidly.

29. Through the process called _____-_____, young children often learn words after only one or two hearings. A closely related process is _____ _____ , by which children are able to apply newly learned words to other objects in the same category.

30. A meta-analysis of research studies found that both _____ and _____ predicted literacy. Five strategies and experiences that aided later reading included _____ .

31. The structures, techniques, and rules that a language uses to communicate meaning define its _____ .

32. How much a child talks is strongly influenced by _____ . The particular words and constructions a child understands is more strongly determined by the child's _____ .

33. Young children's tendency to apply rules of grammar when they should not is called _____ .

Give an example of this tendency.

34. More difficult for children to learn is _____ , which involves adjusting language according to the context in which it is used.

35. The idea that bilingualism _____ (is/is not necessarily) an asset to children in today's world has _____ (more/less) research support than the belief that children should become proficient in only one language. Even so, language-minority children are at a(n) _____ (advantage/disadvantage) if they don't speak the majority language well. Bilingual children typically process the two languages in _____ (the same/different) areas of their brains. For most people, pronunciation of a second language is particularly difficult to master after _____ .

36. Some immigrant parents are saddened when their children make a _____ and become more fluent in the school language than that of their home culture. The best solution is for children to become _____ _____ , who are fluent in both languages.

STUDY TIP To better understand the cognitive and linguistic processes of young children, you might examine several well-loved children's books. Many characteristics of preoperational thinking and language are reflected in such books. For example, much of the fun in the Amelia Bedelia books is based entirely on the main character's literal interpretation of her instructions.

APPLICATIONS:

37. Six-year-old Stefano produces sentences that follow such rules of word order as "the initiator of an action precedes the verb, the receiver of an action follows it." This demonstrates that he has a knowledge of _____ .

38. Two-year-old Amelia says, "We goed to the store." She is making a grammatical _____ .

39. Dr. Jones, who believes that children's language growth greatly contributes to their cognitive growth, evidently is a proponent of the ideas of
   a. Piaget. **c.** Flavell.
   b. Chomsky. **d.** Vygotsky.

Early-Childhood Education

40. Compared with a hundred years ago, when children didn't start school until _____ _____ , today most _____ - to _____ -year-olds are in school.

41. Many new programs use an educational model inspired by _____ that allows children to _____ . Many programs are also influenced by _____ , who believed that children learn from other _____ under the watchful guidance of adults.

42. One type of preschool was opened by _____ for poor children in Rome. This _____ - _____ school was based on the belief that children needed structured, individualized projects in order to give them a sense of _____ .

43. Another new early-childhood curriculum called _____ _____ encourages children to master skills not usually seen in North American schools until about age _____ .

44. Other preschool programs are more _____ -directed. These programs explicitly teach basic skills, including _____ , _____ , and _____ , typically using _____ _____ by a teacher.

45. In 1965, _____ _____ was inaugurated to give low-income children some form of compensatory education during early childhood.

46. Longitudinal research found that graduates of similar but more intensive, research-based programs scored _____ (higher/ no higher) on achievement tests and were more likely to attend college and less likely to go to jail.

47. No matter what the curriculum, all young children need _____ _____ , _____ , and _____ .

48. Children who develop skills in two languages are _____ _____ _____ .

STUDY TIP To help you understand why an early-education program does not succeed, refer back to Chapter 7. List several characteristics of high-quality early childhood education.

APPLICATION:

49. Noreen, a nursery school teacher, is given the job of selecting holiday entertainment for a group of young children. If Noreen agrees with the ideas of Vygotsky, she is most likely to select
   a. a simple TV show that every child can understand.
   b. a hands-on experience that requires little adult supervision.
   c. brief, action-oriented play activities that the children and teachers will perform together.
   d. holiday puzzles for children to work on individually.

Progress Test 1

Multiple-Choice Questions

Circle your answers to the following questions and check them with the answers at the end of the chapter. If your answer is incorrect, read the explanation for why it is incorrect and then consult the appropriate pages of the text if necessary.

1. Piaget believed that children are in the preoperational stage from ages
   a. 6 months to 1 year. **c.** 2 to 6 years.
   b. 1 to 3 years. **d.** 5 to 11 years.

2. Which of the following is NOT a characteristic of preoperational thinking?
   a. focus on appearance
   b. static reasoning
   c. abstract thinking
   d. centration

3. Which of the following provides evidence that early childhood is a sensitive period, rather than a critical period, for language learning?
   a. People can and do master their native language after early childhood.
   b. Vocabulary, grammar, and pronunciation are acquired especially easily during early childhood.
   c. Neurological characteristics of the young child's developing brain facilitate language acquisition.
   d. All of these abilities provide evidence.

4. According to Vygotsky, children learn because adults do all of the following except
   a. present challenges.
   b. offer assistance.
   c. encourage motivation.
   d. provide reinforcement.

5. Reggio Emilia is
   a. the educator who first opened nursery schools for poor children in Rome.
   b. the early-childhood curriculum that allows children to discover ideas at their own pace.
   c. a new form of early-childhood education that encourages children to master skills not usually seen until age 7 or so.
   d. the Canadian system for promoting bilingualism in young children.

6. The vocabulary of young children consists primarily of
   a. metaphors.
   b. self-created words.
   c. abstract nouns.
   d. verbs and concrete nouns.

7. Young children sometimes apply the rules of grammar even when they shouldn't. This tendency is called
   a. overregularization.
   b. literal language.
   c. practical usage.
   d. single-mindedness.

8. The Russian psychologist Vygotsky emphasized that
   a. language helps children form ideas.
   b. children form concepts first, then find words to express them.
   c. language and other cognitive developments are unrelated at this stage.
   d. preschoolers learn language only for egocentric purposes.

9. Private speech can be described as
   a. a way of formulating ideas to oneself.
   b. fantasy.
   c. an early learning difficulty.
   d. the beginnings of deception.

10. The child who has not yet grasped the principle of conservation is likely to
    a. insist that a tall, narrow glass contains more liquid than a short, wide glass, even though both glasses actually contain the same amount.
    b. be incapable of egocentric thought.
    c. be unable to reverse an event.
    d. do all of these things.

11. At age 10, graduates of intensive, research-based early-education programs such as High/Scope showed
    a. better report cards, but more behavioral problems.
    b. significantly higher IQ scores.
    c. higher scores on math and reading achievement tests.
    d. alienation from their original neighborhoods and families.

12. A quality preschool program is generally one that
    a. involves behavioral control.
    b. has teachers who know how to respond to the needs of children.
    c. focuses on instruction in conservation and other logical principles.
    d. has professionals demonstrate toys to the children.

13. Many preschool programs that are inspired by Piaget stress _____ , in contrast to alternative programs that stress _____ .
    a. academics; school readiness
    b. readiness; academics
    c. child development; school readiness
    d. academics; child development

14. Young children can succeed at tests of conservation when
    a. they are allowed to work cooperatively with other children.
    b. the test is presented as a competition.
    c. they are informed that they are being observed by their parents.
    d. the test is presented in a simple, nonverbal, and gamelike way.

15. Through the process called fast-mapping, children
   a. immediately assimilate new words by connecting them through their assumed meaning to categories of words they have already mastered.
   b. acquire the concept of conservation at an earlier age than Piaget believed.
   c. are able to move beyond egocentric thinking.
   d. become skilled in the practical use of language.

True or False Items

Write T (true) or F (false) on the line in front of each statement.

_____ 1. Early childhood is a prime learning period for every child.

_____ 2. In conservation problems, many young children are unable to understand the transformation because they focus exclusively on appearances.

_____ 3. Young children use private speech more selectively than older children.

_____ 4. Children typically develop a theory of mind at about age 7.

_____ 5. Preoperational children tend to focus on one aspect of a situation to the exclusion of all others.

_____ 6. Piaget focused on what children cannot do rather than what they can do.

_____ 7. With the beginning of preoperational thought, most young children can understand words that express comparison.

_____ 8. A young child who says "You comed up and hurted me" is demonstrating a lack of understanding of English grammar.

_____ 9. Successful preschool programs generally have a low adult/child ratio.

_____ 10. Vygotsky believed that cognitive growth is largely a social activity.

_____ 11. *Theory-theory* refers to the tendency of young children to see the world as an unchanging reflection of their current construction of reality.

Progress Test 2

Progress Test 2 should be completed during a final chapter review. Answer the following questions after you thoroughly understand the correct answers for the Chapter Review and Progress Test 1.

Multiple-Choice Questions

1. A balanced bilingual is
   a. a preoperational child who tends to focus only on a single aspect of a situation.
   b. an older child who is able to view the world from multiple perspectives.
   c. a person who is equally fluent in two languages.
   d. a child who uses private speech to preview a thought before it is spoken.

2. Piaget believed that preoperational children fail conservation of liquid tests because of their tendency to
   a. focus on appearance.
   b. fast-map.
   c. overregularize.
   d. exhibit all of these behaviors.

3. A young child who focuses his or her attention on only one feature of a situation is demonstrating a characteristic of preoperational thought called
   a. centration.
   b. overregularization.
   c. reversibility.
   d. egocentrism.

4. One characteristic of preoperational thought is
   a. the ability to categorize objects.
   b. the ability to count in multiples of 5.
   c. the inability to perform logical operations.
   d. difficulty adjusting to changes in routine.

5. The zone of proximal development represents the
   a. skills or knowledge that are within the potential of the learner but are not yet mastered.
   b. influence of a child's peers on cognitive development.
   c. explosive period of language development during the play years.
   d. normal variations in children's language proficiency.

6. According to Vygotsky, language advances thinking through private speech and by
   a. helping children to privately review what they know.
   b. helping children explain events to themselves.
   c. serving as a mediator of the social interaction that is a vital part of learning.
   d. facilitating the process of fast-mapping.

7. Irreversibility refers to the
   a. inability to understand that other people view the world from a different perspective than one's own.
   b. inability to think about more than one idea at a time.
   c. failure to understand that changing the arrangement of a group of objects doesn't change their number.
   d. failure to understand that undoing a process will restore the original conditions.

8. According to Piaget
   a. it is impossible for preoperational children to grasp the concept of conservation, no matter how carefully it is explained.
   b. young children fail to solve conservation problems because they center their attention on the transformation that has occurred and ignore the changed appearances of the objects.
   c. with special training, even preoperational children are able to grasp some aspects of conservation.
   d. young children fail to solve conservation problems because they have no theory of mind.

9. Scaffolding of a child's cognitive skills can be provided by
   a. a mentor.
   b. the objects or experiences of a culture.
   c. the child's past learning.
   d. all of these answers.

10. Which theorist would be most likely to agree with the statement, "Adults should focus on helping children learn rather than on what they cannot do"?
    a. Piaget   c. Montessori
    b. Vygotsky   d. Emilia

11. Children first demonstrate some understanding of grammar
    a. as soon as the first words are produced.
    b. once they begin to use language for practical purposes.
    c. through the process called fast-mapping.
    d. in their earliest sentences.

12. Seeing his cousin Jack for the first time in several months, 3-year-old Zach notices how long Jack's hair has become. "You're turning into a girl," he exclaims. Zach's comment reflects the preoperational child's
    a. egocentrism.
    b. tendency to focus on appearance.
    c. static reasoning.
    d. irreversibility.

13. Most 5-year-olds have difficulty understanding comparisons because
    a. they have not yet begun to develop grammar.
    b. they don't understand that meaning depends on context.
    c. of their limited vocabulary.
    d. of their tendency to overregularize.

14. Overregularization indicates that a child
    a. is clearly applying rules of grammar.
    b. persists in egocentric thinking.
    c. has not yet mastered the principle of conservation.
    d. does not yet have a theory of mind.

15. Regarding the value of preschool education, most developmentalists believe that
    a. most disadvantaged children will not benefit from an early preschool education.
    b. most disadvantaged children will benefit from an early preschool education.
    c. the early benefits of preschool education are likely to disappear by grade 3.
    d. the relatively small benefits of antipoverty measures such as Head Start do not justify their huge costs.

Matching Items

Match each term or concept with its corresponding description or definition.

Terms or Concepts

_____ 1. static reasoning

_____ 2. scaffold

_____ 3. theory of mind

_____ 4. zone of proximal development

_____ 5. overregularization

_____ 6. fast-mapping

_____ 7. irreversibility

_____ 8. centration

_____ 9. conservation

_____ 10. private speech

_____ 11. guided participation

_____ 12. overimitation

_____ 13. pragmatics

Descriptions or Definitions

a. the idea that amount is unaffected by changes in shape or placement

b. the tendency to see the world as an unchanging place

c. the cognitive distance between a child's actual and potential levels of development

d. the tendency to think about one aspect of a situation at a time

e. the process whereby the child learns through social interaction with a mentor

f. our understanding of mental processes in ourselves and others

g. the process by which words are learned after only one hearing

h. an inappropriate application of rules of grammar

i. the internal use of language to form ideas

j. the inability to understand that original conditions are restored by the undoing of some process

k. to structure a child's participation in learning encounters

l. adjusting language communication to the audience and context

m. imitating irrelevant adult actions

Key Terms

Using your own words, write a brief definition or explanation of each of the following terms on a separate piece of paper.

1. preoperational intelligence

2. symbolic thought

3. animism

4. centration

5. egocentrism

6. focus on appearance

7. static reasoning

8. irreversibility

9. conservation

10. zone of proximal development

11. scaffolding

12. overimitation

13. theory-theory

14. theory of mind

15. fast-mapping

16. overregularization

17. pragmatics

18. balanced bilingual

19. Montessori schools

20. Reggio Emilia

21. Head Start

22. Dual language learners (DLLs)

ANSWERS

CHAPTER REVIEW

1. preoperational

2. symbols; symbolic thought; animism

3. egocentrism; centration; is not; appearance

4. static; unchanging; irreversibility; conservation

5. underestimated

6. Lev Vygotsky; apprentice in thinking

7. challenges; assistance; crucial information; motivation; guided participation; social; interact

8. zone of proximal development

9. scaffold

10. overimitation

11. private speech; uttered aloud

12. science, technology, engineering, and math (STEM)

13. theory-theory

14. 4; theory of mind

Between the ages of 3 and 6, young children come to realize that thoughts may not reflect reality and that individuals can believe various things and, therefore, can be deliberately deceived or fooled.

15. have

16. neurological; prefrontal cortex; language; brother or sister; culture

17. conservation. This is the principle that properties such as mass, volume, and number remain the same even though they appear different. In this case, the number of checkers remains the same.

18. centration. This is the tendency to focus on one aspect of a situation while ignoring everything else. Dani equates birthday with party: No party, no birthday.

19. reversibility. Young children are unable to reverse operations, so Darrell must be older than 6 years old.

20. c. is the answer. All of the other choices are aspects of preoperational thinking.

21. c. is the answer. This is typical of cognition during the first two years, when infants think exclusively with their senses and motor skills.

22. c. is the answer. Key to Vygotsky's theory is that children are apprentices in thinking and that they learn best by working with an older and more experienced mentor.

23. c. is the answer. Piaget emphasized the young child's egocentric tendency to perceive everything from his or her own perspective; Vygotsky emphasized the young child's tendency to look to others for insight and guidance.

24. theory of mind

25. a. is the answer. In developing a theory of mind, children also understand that thoughts may not reflect reality and that individuals can believe various things.

26. maturation; myelination; scaffolding; social

27. critical; sensitive

28. vocabulary

29. fast-mapping; logical extension

30. vocabulary; phonics; code-focused teaching, book reading, parent education, language enhancement, and preschool programs

31. grammar

32. genes; experience

33. overregularization

Many English-speaking children overapply the rule of adding "s" to form the plural. Thus, they are likely to say "foots" and "snows."

34. pragmatics

35. is; more; disadvantage; the same; childhood

36. language shift; balanced bilinguals

37. grammar

38. overregularization. This shows that although Amelia is applying the rules of grammar when she should not, she has a basic understanding of those rules.

39. d. is the answer. Vygotsky believed that children used language (private speech, in the beginning) to enhance their cognitive understanding.

40. first grade; 3; 5

41. Piaget; discover ideas at their own pace; Vygotsky; children

42. Maria Montessori; child-centered; accomplishment

43. Reggio Emilia; 7

44. teacher; reading; writing; arithmetic; direct instruction

45. Head Start

46. higher

47. personal attention; consistency; continuity

48. dual language learners (DLLs)

Study Tip: In Chapter 7, high-quality preschools were described as being characterized by (a) a low adult/child ratio, (b) a trained staff (or educated parents) who are unlikely to leave the program, (c) positive social interactions among children and adults, (d) adequate space and equipment, and (e) safety. Continuity also helps, and curriculum is important.

49. c. is the answer. In Vygotsky's view, learning is a social activity. Thus, social interaction that provides motivation and focuses attention facilitates learning.

PROGRESS TEST 1

Multiple-Choice Questions

1. c. is the answer.

2. c. is the answer. Preoperational children have great difficulty understanding abstract concepts.

3. d. is the answer.

4. d. is the answer.

5. **c.** is the answer.

  a. This describes Maria Montessori.

  b. This refers to Piaget's approach.

  d. The program originated in Italy.

6. **d.** is the answer.

  a. & c. Young children generally have great difficulty understanding, and therefore using, metaphors and abstract nouns.

  b. Other than the grammatical errors of overregularization, the text does not indicate that young children use a significant number of self-created words.

7. **a.** is the answer.

  b. & d. These terms are not identified in the text and do not apply to the use of grammar.

  c. Practical usage, which also is not discussed in the text, refers to communication between one person and another in terms of the overall context in which language is used.

8. **a.** is the answer.

  b. This expresses the views of Piaget.

  c. Because he believed that language facilitates thinking, Vygotsky obviously felt that language and other cognitive developments are intimately related.

  d. Vygotsky did not hold this view.

9. **a.** is the answer.

10. **a.** is the answer.

  b., c., & d. Failure to conserve is the result of thinking that is centered on appearances. Egocentrism and irreversibility are also examples of centered thinking.

11. **c.** is the answer.

  b. This is not discussed in the text.

  a. & d. There was no indication of greater behavioral problems or alienation in graduates of this program.

12. **b.** is the answer.

13. **c.** is the answer.

14. **d.** is the answer.

15. **a.** is the answer.

True or False Items

1. T
2. T
3. F In fact, just the opposite is true.
4. F Children develop a theory of mind at about age 4.
5. T

6. T
7. F Young children have difficulty understanding words of comparison such as high and low.
8. F In adding "ed" to form a past tense, the child has indicated an understanding of the grammatical rule for making past tenses in English, even though the construction in these two cases is incorrect.
9. T
10. T
11. F This describes static reasoning; theory-theory is the idea that children attempt to construct a theory to explain all their experiences.

PROGRESS TEST 2

Multiple-Choice Questions

1. **c.** is the answer.

2. **a.** is the answer.

  b. & c. Fast-mapping and overregularization are characteristics of language development during early childhood; they have nothing to do with reasoning about volume.

3. **a.** is the answer.

  b. Overregularization is the child's tendency to apply grammatical rules even when he or she shouldn't.

  c. Reversibility is the concept that reversing an operation, such as addition, will restore the original conditions.

  d. This term is used to refer to the young child's belief that people think as he or she does.

4. **c.** is the answer. This is why the stage is called *pre*operational.

5. **a.** is the answer.

6. **c.** is the answer.

  a. & b. These are both advantages of private speech.

  d. Fast-mapping is the process by which new words are acquired, often after only one hearing.

7. **d.** is the answer.

  a. This describes egocentrism.

  b. This is the opposite of centration.

  c. This defines conservation of number.

8. **a.** is the answer.

  b. According to Piaget, young children fail to solve conservation problems because they focus on the *appearance* of objects and ignore the transformation that has occurred.

  d. Piaget did not relate conservation to a theory of mind.

9. **d.** is the answer.

10. **b.** is the answer.

   a. Piaget focused on what children cannot do.

11. **d.** is the answer. English-speaking children almost always put subject before verb in their two-word sentences.

12. **b.** is the answer.

   a., c., & d. Egocentrism, static reasoning, and irreversibility are all characteristics of preoperational thinking, but noticing the long hair is a matter of attending to appearances.

13. **b.** is the answer.

   a. By the time children are 3 years old, their grammar is quite impressive.

   c. On the contrary, vocabulary develops so rapidly that, by age 5, children seem to be able to understand and use almost any term they hear.

   d. This tendency to make language more logical by overapplying certain grammatical rules has nothing to do with understanding comparisons.

14. **a.** is the answer.

   b., c., & d. Overregularization is a *linguistic* phenomenon rather than a characteristic type of thinking (b. and d.), or a logical principle (c.).

15. **b.** is the answer.

Matching Items

1. b	5. h	9. a	13. l
2. k	6. g	10. i	
3. f	7. j	11. e	
4. c	8. d	12. m	

KEY TERMS

1. According to Piaget, thinking between the ages of about 2 and 6 is characterized by **preoperational intelligence,** meaning that children cannot yet perform logical operations; that is, they cannot use logical principles. This stage involves language and imagination.

2. **Symbolic thought** allows children to understand that words can be symbols that refer to things they cannot see.

3. **Animism** is the belief that natural objects and phenomena are alive.

4. **Centration** is the tendency of preoperational children to focus only on a single aspect of a situation or object.

5. **Egocentrism** is Piaget's term for a type of centration in which preoperational children view the world exclusively from their own perspective.

6. **Focus on appearance** refers to the preoperational child's tendency to focus only on apparent attributes and ignore all others.

7. Preoperational thinking is characterized by **static reasoning,** in which the young child sees the world as unchanging.

8. **Irreversibility** is the characteristic of preoperational thought in which the young child fails to recognize that a process can be reversed to restore the original conditions of a situation.

9. **Conservation** is the understanding that the amount or quantity of a substance or object is unaffected by changes in its appearance.

10. According to Vygotsky, each individual has a **zone of proximal development** (ZPD), which represents the skills (cognitive and physical) that are within the potential of the learner but cannot be performed independently.

11. Tutors who utilize **scaffolding** structure children's learning experiences in order to foster their emerging capabilities.

12. **Overimitation** is the common tendency of 2- to 6-year-olds to imitate adult actions that are irrelevant and inefficient.

13. **Theory-theory** is the tendency of young children to attempt to construct theories to explain everything they experience.

14. A **theory of mind** is an understanding of human mental processes, that is, of one's own or another's emotions, beliefs, intentions, motives, and thoughts.

15. **Fast-mapping** is the speedy and sometimes imprecise process by which children learn new words by tentatively connecting them to words and categories that they already understand.

16. **Overregularization** occurs when children apply rules of grammar when they should not. It is seen in English, for example, when children add "s" to form the plural even in irregular cases that form the plural in a different way.

17. **Pragmatics** refers to the practical adjusting of language according to the audience and context.

18. A **balanced bilingual** is a person who is equally fluent in two languages.

19. **Montessori schools,** which offer early-childhood education based on the philosophy of Maria Montessori, emphasize careful work and tasks that each young child can do.

20. **Reggio Emilia** is a famous program of early-childhood education that originated in the town of Reggio Emilia, Italy, and that encourages each child's creativity in a carefully designed setting.

21. **Head Start** is a federally funded early-childhood intervention program for low-income children.

22. **Dual language learners (DLLs)** are children who develop skills in two languages.

Early Childhood: Psychosocial Development

Chapter Overview

Chapter 10 explores the ways in which young children begin to relate to others in an ever-widening social environment. The chapter begins where social understanding begins, with emotional development and the emergence of the sense of self. With their increasing social awareness, children become more concerned with how others evaluate them and better able to regulate their emotions.

The next section explores how children use play to help with their emerging ability to regulate their emotions. Although play is universal, its form varies by culture and gender.

The chapter continues with a discussion of challenges facing caregivers, including parenting patterns and their effects on the developing child. The section includes a description of children's emerging awareness of male–female differences and gender identity. Five major theories of sex role development are considered.

The chapter concludes with a discussion of moral development during early childhood, focusing on the origins of helpful, prosocial behaviors in young children, as well as antisocial behaviors such as the different forms of aggressive behavior. The usefulness of the different forms of discipline, including punishment, in the child's developing morality is also considered in this section.

What Will You Know?

The text chapter should be studied one section at a time. Before you read, preview each section by skimming it, noting headings and boldface items. Then read the sections, one at a time, keeping these questions in mind.

1. Why do 2-year-olds have more sudden tempers, tears, and terrors than 6-year-olds?

2. If a child never plays, is that a problem?

3. What happens if parents let their children do whatever they want?

4. What are the long-term effects of spanking children?

Chapter Review

When you have finished reading the chapter, work through the material that follows to review it. Completing the sentences and answering the questions will enable you to answer the "What Have You Learned?" questions at the end of the text chapter. Scattered throughout the Chapter Review are Study Tips, which explain how best to learn a difficult concept, and Think About It discussions and Applications, which help you to know how well you understand the material. Check your understanding of the material by consulting the answers at the end of this chapter. Do not continue with the next section until you understand each answer. If you need to, review or reread the appropriate section in the textbook before continuing.

Emotional Development

1. The major psychosocial accomplishment of early childhood is learning _____ . This ability is called _____ _____ . This accomplishment depends on children's growing ability to regulate their emotions through effort, which is called

   _____ _____ .

2. Between 3 and 6 years of age, according to Erikson, children are in the stage of

   _____ _____

   _____ . In the process, they develop a positive _____-

   _____ and feelings of

   _____ in their accomplishments.

3. Neurological advances in the brain's

   _____

are partly responsible for the greater capacity for self-control that occurs at about age

_____ .

4. The new initiative of this age also results from _____ of the _____ system and a longer _____ span.

5. Throughout early childhood, violent outbursts, uncontrolled crying, and the irrational fears called _____ diminish.

6. For the most part, children enjoy learning, playing, and practicing for their own joy; that is, they are _____ _____ . The importance of this type of motivation is seen when children invent and converse with _____ _____ .

7. Motivation that comes from the outside is called _____ _____ .

8. Emotional regulation _____ (is/is not) valued in all cultures. Cultures _____ (differ/generally do not differ) in the emotions considered most in need of control.

9. An illness or disorder that involves the mind is called _____ . Children who have _____ problems and lash out at other people or things are said to be "_____" (overcontrolled/undercontrolled). Children who have _____ problems tend to be inhibited, fearful, and withdrawn.

10. (A View from Science) Girls generally are better than boys at regulating their _____ (internalizing/externalizing) emotions, but they are less successful with _____ (internalizing/externalizing) ones. For both sexes, though, extreme reactions predict future _____ .

11. (A View from Science) Neurological and hormonal effects may make boys more likely

to _____ and girls more likely to _____ , a difference that it is probably _____ .

THINK ABOUT IT To help you understand the difference between internalizing problems and externalizing problems in emotional regulation, you might list several examples of each type. Which have you engaged in? _____

APPLICATIONS:

12. According to Erikson, 3-year-old Samantha is incapable of feeling guilt because
   a. guilt depends on a sense of self, which is not sufficiently established in young children.
   b. she does not yet understand that she is female for life.
   c. this emotion is unlikely to have been reinforced at such an early age.
   d. guilt is associated with the resolution of the Electra complex, which occurs later in life.

13. Three-year-old Ali, who is fearful and withdrawn, is displaying signs of _____ problems, which suggests that he is emotionally _____ .

14. Summarizing her report on neurological aspects of emotional regulation, Alycia notes that young children who have externalizing problems tend to lack neurological maturity in the brain's _____ _____ .

Play

15. Young children play best with _____ , that is, people of about the same _____ and _____ _____ .

16. As children grow older, play becomes more _____ and more affected by their _____ _____ .

17. Another cultural shift that has changed the nature of children's play is the increasing prevalence of _____ _____ .

18. The developmentalist who distinguished five kinds of play is _____ . These include _____ play, in which

a child plays alone; _____
play, in which a child watches other children
play; _____ play, in which
children play together without interacting;
_____ play, in which children
interact, but their play is not yet mutual and
reciprocal; and _____ play, in
which children play together and take turns.

19. Active play correlates with _____
acceptance and a healthy _____-
_____ . The type of active play
that looks rough is called _____-
_____-_____
play. A distinctive feature of this form of play,
which _____ (occurs only in

some cultures/is universal), is the positive facial
expression that characterizes the "_____
_____ ." This type
of play advances _____ and
_____-_____ .

20. In _____ play, children act
out various roles and plots in stories of their
own creation. This type of play helps them to
explore and rehearse _____
_____ and to develop a
_____-_____ in
a nonthreatening context, for example.

STUDY TIP/APPLICATION To help you distinguish
the different types of play, complete the following
table, including the basic characteristics of each type
of play. Then, give an example of each type.

21. Type of Play	Characteristics	Examples
a. Solitary play		
b. Onlooker play		
c. Parallel play		
d. Associative play		
e. Cooperative play		
f. Rough-and-tumble play		
g. Sociodramatic play		

APPLICATION:

22. Although Juvaria and Brittany are sharing drawing materials and watching each other, their play
is not yet mutual or reciprocal. Mildred Parten
would probably classify this type of play as
_____ play.

Challenges for Caregivers

23. A significant influence on early psychosocial growth is the style of _____ that characterizes a child's family life.

24. The early research on parenting styles, which was conducted by _____ , found that parents varied in four dimensions: their expressions of _____ , their strategies for _____ , their _____ , and their expectations for _____ .

25. Parents who adopt the _____ style demand unquestioning obedience from their children. In this style of parenting, nurturance tends to be _____ (low/high), maturity demands are _____ (low/high), and parent–child communication tends to be _____ (low/high).

26. Parents who adopt the _____ style make few demands on their children and are lax in discipline. Such parents _____ (are/are not very) nurturant, communicate _____ (well/poorly), and make _____ (few/extensive) maturity demands.

27. Parents who adopt the _____ style set limits and enforce rules but also listen to their children. Such parents make _____ (high/low) maturity demands, communicate _____ (well/poorly), and _____ (are/are not) nurturant.

28. Parents who are indifferent toward their children have adopted the _____/ _____ style.

29. Although this classification is generally regarded as _____ (very useful, too simplistic), follow-up studies indicate that children raised by _____ parents are likely to be obedient but unhappy and those raised by _____ parents are likely to lack self-control. Those raised by _____ parents are more likely to be articulate, successful, happy with themselves, and generous with others.

30. An important factor in the effectiveness of parenting style is the child's _____ .

31. Culture _____ (exerts/does not exert) a strong influence on disciplinary techniques. However, discipline methods and family rules are less important than parental _____ .

STUDY TIP Students often confuse authoritarian and authoritative when studying parenting styles. Although both words have the same root noun, authority ("the power or right to give commands and enforce obedience"), their suffixes have very different meanings. The suffix –arian denotes an occupation, and the suffix –ative denotes a tendency toward something. Thus, authoritative parents don't make an occupation of enforcing obedience; rather, they tend to give commands with some margin for freedom of action.

---

32. By age _____ , children apply gender labels. By age _____ , children are convinced that certain toys are appropriate for one gender but not the other.

33. Social scientists distinguish between biological, or _____ , differences between males and females, and cultural, or _____ , differences in the _____ and behavior of males and females that are prescribed by the culture.

34. Freud called the period from age 3 to 6 the _____ _____ . According to his view, boys in this stage develop sexual feelings about their _____ and become jealous of their _____ . Freud called this phenomenon the _____ _____ . Boys also develop, in self-defense, a powerful conscience called the _____ .

35. During the phallic stage, little girls may experience the _____ _____ , in which they want to get rid of their mother and become intimate with their father.

36. According to psychoanalytic theory, children of both sexes resolve their guilt and fear through _____ with their same-sex parent.

37. According to behaviorism, young children develop a sense of gender by being _____ for behaviors deemed appropriate for their sex and _____ for behaviors deemed inappropriate.

38. Behaviorists also maintain that children learn gender-appropriate behavior not only through direct reinforcement but also through _____ _____ .

39. Cognitive theorists focus on children's _____ of male–female differences. This understanding is called a _____ _____ .

40. The theory of _____ stresses the _____ of needs, beginning with _____ , then _____ , then _____ and _____ .

41. Sexual attraction is crucial for humankind's most basic urge, reproduction, according to _____ theory.

42. The behaviors appropriate for each gender are determined by culture, not by biology, according to the _____ theory. This theory points out that some of the distinctions are tied to general patterns of _____ _____ .

43. Therefore, _____ theory would encourage male–female differences, and _____ theory would conclude that sex differences are _____ if they interfere with other values.

44. The idea that a person should combine the best of both sexes is referred to as _____ .

APPLICATIONS:

45. Yolanda and Tom are strict and aloof parents. Their children are most likely to be
    a. cooperative and trusting.
    b. obedient but unhappy.
    c. violent.
    d. withdrawn and anxious.

46. Which is NOT a feature of parenting used by Baumrind to differentiate authoritarian, permissive, and authoritative parents?
    a. maturity demands for the child's conduct
    b. efforts to control the child's actions
    c. nurturance
    d. adherence to stereotypical gender roles

47. Bonita eventually copes with the fear and anger she feels over her hatred of her mother and love of her father by
    a. identifying with her mother.
    b. copying her brother's behavior.
    c. adopting her father's moral code.
    d. competing with her brother for her father's attention.

48. A little girl who says she wants her mother to go on vacation so that she can marry her father is voicing a fantasy consistent with the _____ _____ described by Freud.

49. Leonardo believes that almost all sexual patterns are learned rather than inborn. He is clearly a strong adherent of _____ .

50. In explaining the origins of gender distinctions, Dr. Christie notes that every culture teaches its children its values and attitudes regarding preferred behavior for men and women. Dr. Christie is evidently a proponent of _____ .

Moral Development

51. The ability to truly understand the emotions of another, called _____ , often leads to sharing, helping, and other examples of _____ _____ .

    In contrast, dislike for others, or _____ , may lead to actions that are destructive or deliberately hurtful. Such actions are called _____ _____ .

52. Developmentalists distinguish four types of aggression: _____ , used to obtain or retain an object or privilege; _____ , used in angry retaliation against an intentional or accidental act committed by a peer; _____ , which takes the form of insults or social rejection; and _____ , used in an unprovoked attack on a peer.

53. (text and Table 10.2) The form of aggression that often increases from age 2 to 6 is _____ _____ . Of greater concern are _____ _____ , because it can indicate a lack of _____ _____ , and _____ _____ , which is most worrisome overall.

54. Physical punishment that hurts the body, called _____ _____ correlates with delayed _____ _____ _____ and increased _____ .

55. Another method of discipline, in which children's guilt and gratitude are used to control their behavior, is _____ _____ . This method of discipline has been linked to children's decreased _____ , _____ , and _____ acceptance.

56. The disciplinary technique most often used in North America is the _____ - _____ , in which a misbehaving child is asked to sit quietly without toys or playmates.

57. Another common practice involves the parents explaining to the child why the behavior was wrong, called _____ .

APPLICATIONS:

58. Seeking to discipline her 3-year-old son for snatching a playmate's toy, Cassandra gently says, "How would you feel if Juwan grabbed your car?" Developmentalists would probably say that Cassandra's approach
    a. is too permissive and would therefore be ineffective in the long run.

    b. would probably be more effective with a girl.
    c. will be effective in increasing prosocial behavior because it promotes empathy.
    d. will backfire and threaten her son's self-confidence.

59. When 4-year-old Seema grabs for Vincenzo's Beanie Baby, Vincenzo slaps her hand away, displaying an example of _____ aggression.

60. Five-year-old Curtis, who is above average in height and weight, often picks on children who are smaller than he is. Curtis' behavior is an example of _____ aggression.

61. Four-year-old Eboni shows signs of distrust toward strangers. Eboni's behavior is an example of _____ .

Progress Test 1

Multiple-Choice Questions

Circle your answers to the following questions and check them with the answers at the end of the chapter. If your answer is incorrect, read the explanation for why it is incorrect and then consult the text.

1. Young children have a clear (but not necessarily accurate) concept of self. Typically, they believe that they
   a. own all objects in sight.
   b. are great at almost everything.
   c. are much less competent than peers and older children.
   d. are more powerful than their parents.

2. According to Freud, the third stage of psychosexual development, during which the penis is the focus of psychological concern and pleasure, is the
   a. oral stage.
   b. anal stage.
   c. phallic stage.
   d. latency period.

3. Girls generally are better than boys at regulating their
   a. internalizing emotions.
   b. externalizing emotions.
   c. internalizing and externalizing emotions.
   d. prosocial behaviors.

4. The three *basic* patterns of parenting described by Diana Baumrind are
   a. hostile, loving, and harsh.
   b. authoritarian, permissive, and authoritative.
   c. positive, negative, and punishing.
   d. indulgent, neglecting, and traditional.

5. Authoritative parents are receptive and loving, but they also normally
   a. set limits and enforce rules.
   b. have difficulty communicating.
   c. withhold praise and affection.
   d. encourage aggressive behavior.

6. Emotional regulation is most accurately defined as
   a. the ability to control when and how emotions are expressed.
   b. the tendency of young children to feel guilty when they do not succeed at new activities.
   c. a person's understanding of who he or she is.
   d. a drive to pursue a goal that comes from inside a person.

7. Between 2 and 6 years of age, the form of aggression that is most likely to increase is
   a. reactive.   c. relational.
   b. instrumental.   d. bullying.

8. During early childhood, a child's self-concept is defined largely by his or her
   a. expanding range of skills and competencies.
   b. physical appearance.
   c. gender.
   d. relationship with family members.

9. Behaviorists emphasize the importance of _____ in the development of the preschool child.
   a. identification
   b. praise and blame
   c. initiative
   d. a theory of mind

10. Children apply gender labels and have definite ideas about how boys and girls behave as early as age
    a. 2.   c. 5.
    b. 4.   d. 7.

11. Developmentalists agree that punishment should be
    a. avoided at all costs.
    b. immediate and harsh.
    c. delayed until emotions subside.
    d. rare and limited to behaviors the child understands and can control.

12. Feelings of dislike or even hatred for another person constitute
    a. empathy.
    b. antipathy.
    c. prosocial behavior.
    d. antisocial behavior.

13. Three-year-old Jake, who lashes out at the family pet in anger, is displaying signs of _____ problems, which suggests that he is emotionally _____ .
    a. internalizing; overcontrolled
    b. internalizing; undercontrolled
    c. externalizing; overcontrolled
    d. externalizing; undercontrolled

14. Compared with North American mothers, Japanese mothers are more likely to
    a. use reasoning to control their children's social behavior.
    b. use expressions of disappointment to control their children's social behavior.
    c. express empathy for their children.
    d. use all of these techniques.

15. When her friend hurts her feelings, 6-year-old Maya shouts that she is a "mean old stinker!" Maya's behavior is an example of
    a. instrumental aggression.
    b. reactive aggression.
    c. bullying aggression.
    d. relational aggression.

True or False Items

Write T (true) or F (false) on the line in front of each statement.

_____ 1. According to Diana Baumrind, only authoritarian parents make maturity demands on their children.

_____ 2. Children of authoritative parents tend to be successful, happy with themselves, and generous with others.

_____ 3. Not until age 4 can children apply gender labels.

_____ 4. Empathy is the same as sympathy.

_____ 5. Rough-and-tumble play is more common in Western cultures than in Eastern cultures.

_____ 6. Children can be truly androgynous only if their culture promotes such ideas and practices.

_____ 7. Developmentalists do not agree about how children acquire gender roles.

_____ 8. By age 4, most children have definite ideas about what toys are appropriate for each gender.

_____ 9. Identification was defined by Freud as a means of defending one's self-concept by taking on the attitudes and behaviors of another person.

_____ 10. By adolescence, undercontrolled boys may be delinquents.

Progress Test 2

Progress Test 2 should be completed during a final chapter review. Answer the following questions after you thoroughly understand the correct answers for the Chapter Review and Progress Test 1.

Multiple-Choice Questions

1. Children of permissive parents are MOST likely to lack
   a. social skills.
   b. self-control.
   c. initiative and guilt.
   d. care and concern.

2. The major psychosocial accomplishment of early childhood is
   a. learning when and how to express emotions.
   b. developing an internalized sense of initiative.
   c. developing an identity.
   d. forging positive self-esteem.

3. Which area of the brain plays an important role in the child's greater capacity for self-control that appears at age 4 or 5?
   a. temporal lobe
   b. occipital lobe
   c. prefrontal cortex
   d. hippocampus

4. Generally speaking, the motivation of young children
   a. is intrinsic.
   b. is extrinsic.
   c. is the desire to gain praise or some other reward from someone else.
   d. varies too much from country to country to be characterized.

5. Which of the following best summarizes the current view of developmentalists regarding gender differences?
   a. Developmentalists disagree on the proportion of gender differences that are biological in origin.
   b. Most gender differences are biological in origin.
   c. Nearly all gender differences are cultural in origin.
   d. There is no consensus among developmentalists regarding the origin of gender differences.

6. According to Freud, a young boy's jealousy of his father's relationship with his mother, and the guilt feelings that result, are part of the
   a. Electra complex.
   b. Oedipus complex.
   c. phallic complex.
   d. penis envy complex.

7. The style of parenting in which the parents make few demands on children, the discipline is lax, and the parents are nurturant and accepting is
   a. authoritarian.
   b. authoritative.
   c. permissive.
   d. traditional.

8. Cooperating with a playmate is to _____ as insulting a playmate is to _____ .
   a. antisocial behavior; prosocial behavior
   b. prosocial behavior; antisocial behavior
   c. emotional regulation; antisocial behavior
   d. prosocial behavior; emotional regulation

9. Antipathy refers to a person's
   a. understanding of the emotions of another person.
   b. self-understanding.
   c. feelings of anger or dislike toward another person.
   d. tendency to internalize emotions or inhibit their expression.

10. Which of the following theories advocates the development of gender identification as a means of avoiding guilt over feelings for the opposite-sex parent?
   a. behaviorism
   b. sociocultural
   c. psychoanalytic
   d. social learning

11. A parent who wishes to use a time-out to discipline her son for behaving aggressively on the playground would be advised to
   a. have the child sit quietly indoors for a few minutes.
   b. tell her son that he will be punished later at home.
   c. tell the child that he will not be allowed to play outdoors for the rest of the week.
   d. choose a different disciplinary technique because time-outs are ineffective.

12. The young child's readiness to learn new tasks and play activities reflects his or her
   a. emerging competency and self-awareness.
   b. theory of mind.

   c. relationship with parents.
   d. growing identification with others.

13. The disciplinary technique most often used in North America is
   a. spanking.
   b. induction.
   c. time-out.
   d. psychological control.

14. In which style of parenting is the parents' word law and misbehavior strictly punished?
   a. permissive
   b. authoritative
   c. authoritarian
   d. traditional

15. Erikson noted that young children eagerly begin many new activities but are vulnerable to criticism and feelings of failure; they experience the crisis of
   a. identity versus role confusion.
   b. initiative versus guilt.
   c. basic trust versus mistrust.
   d. efficacy versus helplessness.

Matching Items

Match each term or concept with its corresponding description or definition.

Terms or Concepts

_____ 1. empathy
_____ 2. androgyny
_____ 3. antipathy
_____ 4. prosocial behavior
_____ 5. antisocial behavior
_____ 6. Electra complex
_____ 7. Oedipus complex
_____ 8. authoritative
_____ 9. authoritarian
_____ 10. identification
_____ 11. instrumental aggression

Descriptions or Definitions

a. forceful behavior that is intended to get or keep something that another person has
b. Freudian theory that every daughter secretly wishes to replace her mother
c. parenting style associated with high maturity demands and low parent–child communication
d. an action performed for the benefit of another person without the expectation of reward
e. Freudian theory that every son secretly wishes to replace his father
f. parenting style associated with high maturity demands and high parent–child communication
g. understanding the feelings of others
h. an action that is intended to harm someone else
i. dislike of others
j. the way children cope with their feelings of guilt during the phallic stage
k. a balance of traditional male and female characteristics in an individual

Key Terms

Using your own words, write a brief definition or explanation of each of the following terms on a separate piece of paper.

1. emotional regulation
2. effortful control
3. initiative versus guilt
4. self-concept
5. intrinsic motivation
6. extrinsic motivation
7. imaginary friends
8. psychopathology
9. externalizing problems
10. internalizing problems
11. rough-and-tumble play
12. sociodramatic play
13. authoritarian parenting
14. permissive parenting
15. authoritative parenting
16. neglectful/uninvolved parenting
17. sex differences
18. gender differences
19. phallic stage
20. Oedipus complex
21. superego
22. Electra complex
23. identification
24. gender schema
25. empathy
26. antipathy
27. prosocial behavior
28. antisocial behavior
29. instrumental aggression
30. reactive aggression
31. relational aggression
32. bullying aggression
33. psychological control
34. time-out

ANSWERS

CHAPTER REVIEW

1. when and how to express emotions; emotional regulation; effortful control

2. initiative versus guilt; self-concept; pride
3. prefrontal cortex; 4 or 5
4. myelination; limbic; attention
5. phobias
6. intrinsically motivated; imaginary friends
7. extrinsic motivation
8. is; differ
9. psychopathology; externalizing; undercontrolled; internalizing
10. externalizing; internalizing; psychopathology
11. externalize; internalize; genetic
12. **a.** is the answer. Erikson did not equate gender constancy with the emergence of guilt (**b**); (**c**) and (**d**) reflect the viewpoints of learning theory and Freud, respectively.
13. internalizing; overcontrolled. Usually, with maturity, extreme fears and shyness diminish.
14. prefrontal cortex. Emotional regulation requires thinking before acting, which is the province of the prefrontal cortex. Lack of maturity there results in externalizing problems.
15. peers; age; social status
16. social; physical setting
17. electronic media
18. Mildred Parten; solitary; onlooker; parallel; associative; cooperative
19. peer; self-concept; rough-and-tumble; is universal; play face; planning; self-control
20. sociodramatic; social roles; self-concept
21. There are many possible answers. Some examples follow.
    a. Solitary play: playing alone. A girl playing with her doll in her room or a boy with his truck.
    b. Onlooker play: watching other children play. Sitting on a bench in the playground watching children on the see-saw.
    c. Parallel play: playing with similar toys in similar ways, but not together. Two girls playing with their own dolls in different areas of a dollhouse or two boys building blocks.
    d. Associative play: interactive play, but not yet mutual and reciprocal. A group of children drawing with crayons.
    e. Cooperative play: playing together. Playing tag.
    f. Rough-and-tumble play: mimicking aggression but without intent to harm. Imitating a boxing match.

g. Sociodramatic play: acting out various roles and themes in stories they create. Pretend-racing cars or playing house.

22. parallel
23. parenting
24. Diana Baumrind; warmth; discipline; communication; maturity
25. authoritarian; low; high; low
26. permissive; are; well; few
27. authoritative; high; well; are
28. neglectful/uninvolved
29. too simplistic; authoritarian; permissive; authoritative
30. temperament
31. exerts; warmth, support, and concern
32. 2; 4
33. sex; gender; roles
34. phallic stage; mothers; fathers; Oedipus complex; superego
35. Electra complex
36. identification
37. reinforced; punished
38. social learning
39. understanding; gender schema
40. humanism; hierarchy; survival; safety; love; belonging
41. evolutionary
42. sociocultural; social organization
43. evolutionary; sociocultural; changeable
44. androgyny
45. b. is the answer. Authoritarian parents have behavior standards and require obedience without question. So, their children tend to be obedient but unhappy.
46. d. is the answer. Baumrind's categories have nothing to do with gender roles.
47. a. is the answer. According to psychoanalytic theory, children identify with the same-sex parents because of their guilt in hating that parent.
48. Electra complex. Resolution of this complex results in the identification noted in question 47.
49. behaviorism. Behaviorists believe that children learn through rewards and punishments.
50. sociocultural theory. Sociocultural theorists contend that children learn from their culture, not biology.

51. empathy; prosocial behaviors; antipathy; antisocial behavior
52. instrumental; reactive; relational; bullying
53. instrumental aggression; reactive aggression; emotional regulation; bullying aggression
54. corporal punishment; theory of mind; aggression
55. psychological control; achievement; creativity; social
56. time-out
57. induction
58. c. is the answer.
59. instrumental. This kind of aggression involves trying to get or keep something someone else has, as Seema is doing here.
60. bullying. This kind of aggression involves repeated, unprovoked physical or verbal attacks on other people.
61. antipathy.

PROGRESS TEST 1

Multiple-Choice Questions

1. b. is the answer.
2. c. is the answer.

   a. & b. In Freud's theory, the oral and anal stages are associated with infant development.

   d. In Freud's theory, the latency period is associated with development during the school years.
3. b. is the answer.
4. b. is the answer.

   d. Traditional is a variation of the basic styles. Indulgent and neglecting are abusive styles and clearly harmful, unlike the styles initially identified by Baumrind.
5. a. is the answer.

   b. & c. Authoritative parents communicate very well and are quite affectionate.

   d. This is not typical of authoritative parents.
6. a. is the answer.
7. b. is the answer.
8. a. is the answer.
9. b. is the answer.

   a. This is the focus of Freud's phallic stage.

   c. This is the focus of Erikson's psychosocial theory.

   d. This is the focus of cognitive theorists.

10. **a.** is the answer.

11. **d.** is the answer.

12. **b.** is the answer.

   a. This is the ability to understand the emotions and concerns of another person.

   c. This refers to feelings and actions that are helpful and kind but are of no obvious benefit to oneself.

   d. This refers to feelings and actions that are deliberately hurtful or destructive to another person.

13. **d.** is the answer.

   a. & b. Children who display internalizing problems are withdrawn and bottle up their emotions.

   c. Jake is displaying an inability to control his negative emotions.

14. **d.** is the answer.

15. **d.** is the answer.

True or False Items

1. F All parents make some maturity demands on their children; maturity demands are high in both the authoritarian and authoritative parenting styles.

2. T

3. F Children can apply gender labels by age 2.

4. F Sympathy is feeling sorry *for* someone; empathy is feeling sorry *with* someone.

5. F Rough-and-tumble play is universal.

6. T

7. T

8. T

9. T

10. T

PROGRESS TEST 2

Multiple-Choice Questions

1. **b.** is the answer.

2. **a.** is the answer.

   b. & d. Developing a sense of initiative and positive self-esteem are aspects of emotional regulation.

   c. Developing a sense of identity is the task of adolescence.

3. **c.** is the answer.

4. **a.** is the answer.

5. **a.** is the answer.

6. **b.** is the answer.

   a. & d. These are Freud's versions of phallic-stage development in little girls.

   c. There is no such thing as the "phallic complex."

7. **c.** is the answer.

   a. & b. Both authoritarian and authoritative parents make high demands on their children.

   d. This is not one of the three parenting styles. Traditional parents could be any one of these types.

8. **b.** is the answer.

9. **c.** is the answer.

   a. This describes empathy.

   b. This describes self-concept.

   d. This describes an internalizing problem.

10. **c.** is the answer.

   a. & d. Behaviorism, which includes social learning, emphasizes that children learn about gender by rewards and punishments and by observing others.

   b. Sociocultural theory focuses on the impact of the environment on gender identification.

11. **a.** is the answer.

   b. & c. Time-outs involve removing a child from a situation in which misbehavior has occurred. Moreover, these threats of future punishment would likely be less effective because of the delay between the behavior and the consequence.

   d. Although developmentalists stress the need to prevent misdeeds instead of punishing them and warn that time-outs may have unintended consequences, they nevertheless can be an effective form of discipline.

12. **a.** is the answer.

   b. This viewpoint is associated only with cognitive theory.

   c. Although parent–child relationships are important to social development, they do not determine readiness.

   d. Identification is a Freudian defensive behavior.

13. **c.** is the answer.

14. **c.** is the answer.

15. **b.** is the answer.

   a. & c. According to Erikson, these are the crises of adolescence and infancy, respectively.

   d. This is not a crisis described by Erikson.

Matching Items

1. g	**5.** h	**9.** c
2. k	**6.** b	**10.** j
3. i	**7.** e	**11.** a
4. d	**8.** f	

KEY TERMS

1. **Emotional regulation** is the ability to control when and how emotions are expressed.

2. **Effortful control** is the ability to regulate one's actions and emotions.

3. According to Erikson, the crisis of early childhood is **initiative versus guilt**. In this crisis, young children eagerly take on new skills and activities and feel guilty when they do not succeed at them.

4. **Self-concept** refers to people's understanding of who they are.

5. **Intrinsic motivation** is the internal goals or drives to accomplish something for the joy of doing it.

6. **Extrinsic motivation** is the need for rewards from outside, such as material possessions.

7. **Imaginary friends** are make-believe friends, common among children between 3 and 7 years of age.

8. **Psychopathology** is an illness or disorder of the mind.

9. Young children who have **externalizing problems** have trouble regulating emotions and uncontrollably lash out at other people or things.

10. Children who have **internalizing problems** tend to be fearful and withdrawn as a consequence of their tendencies to keep their emotions bottled up inside themselves.

11. **Rough-and-tumble play** is physical play that often mimics aggression but involves no intent to harm.

12. In **sociodramatic play,** children act out roles and themes in stories of their own creation, allowing them to rehearse social roles, practice regulating their emotions, test their ability to convince others of their ideas, and develop a self-concept in a nonthreatening context.

13. **Authoritarian parenting** is Baumrind's term for a style of child rearing in which the parents show little affection or nurturance for their children, maturity demands are high, and parent–child communication is low.

    Memory aid: Someone who is an authoritarian demands unquestioning obedience and acts in a dictatorial way.

14. **Permissive parenting** is Baumrind's term for a style of child rearing in which the parents make few demands on their children, yet are nurturant and accepting and communicate well with their children.

15. **Authoritative parenting** is Baumrind's term for a style of child rearing in which the parents set limits and enforce rules but are willing to listen to the child's ideas and are flexible.

    Memory aid: Authoritative parents act as authorities do on a subject—by discussing and explaining why certain family rules are in place.

16. **Neglectful/uninvolved parenting** is Baumrind's term for an approach to child rearing in which the parents are indifferent toward their children.

17. **Sex differences** are biological differences between females and males.

18. **Gender differences** are cultural differences in the roles and behavior of males and females.

19. In psychoanalytic theory, the **phallic stage** is the third stage of psychosexual development, in which the penis becomes the focus of concern and pleasure.

20. According to Freud, boys in the phallic stage of psychosexual development develop a collection of feelings, known as the **Oedipus complex**, that center on sexual attraction to the mother and resentment of the father.

21. In psychoanalytic theory, the **superego** is the judgmental part of personality that internalizes the moral standards of the parents.

22. Girls in Freud's phallic stage may develop a collection of feelings, known as the **Electra complex**, that center on sexual attraction to the father and resentment of the mother.

23. In Freud's theory, **identification** is a means of defending one's self-concept by taking on the behaviors and attitudes of another person.

24. In cognitive theory, **gender schema** is the child's understanding of sex differences.

25. **Empathy** is a person's understanding of other people's feelings and concerns.

26. **Antipathy** is a person's feelings of dislike or even hatred for another person.

27. **Prosocial behavior** is feelings and actions that are helpful and kind but without any obvious benefit.

28. **Antisocial behavior** is feelings and actions that are deliberately hurtful or destructive to another person.

29. **Instrumental aggression** is hurtful behavior that is intended to get or keep a possession or privilege that another person has.

30. **Reactive aggression** is impulsive retaliation for some intentional or accidental act, verbal or physical, by another person.

    Memory aid: Instrumental aggression is behavior that is *instrumental* in allowing a child to retain a favorite toy. Reactive aggression is a *reaction* to another child's behavior.

31. **Relational aggression** involves insults and other nonphysical acts aimed at harming the social connection between the victim and other people.

32. An unprovoked, repeated physical or verbal attack on another person is an example of **bullying aggression**.

33. **Psychological control** is a form of discipline that involves threatening to withdraw love and support from a child.

34. A **time-out** is a form of discipline in which a child is required to stop all activity and sit quietly apart from other people for a few minutes.

Middle Childhood: Biosocial Development

Chapter Overview

This chapter introduces middle childhood, the years from 6 to 11. Changes in physical size and shape are described, and the problems of obesity and asthma are addressed.

The discussion then turns to the continuing development of intellectual skills during the school years, culminating in an evaluation of intelligence testing.

A final section examines the experiences of children with special needs, such as children with attention-deficit/hyperactivity disorder, those with learning disabilities, and children with autistic spectrum disorders. The causes of and treatments for these problems are discussed, with emphasis placed on insights arising from the developmental psychopathology perspective. This perspective makes it clear that the manifestations of any special childhood problem will change as the child grows older and that treatment must also consider the social context.

What Will You Know?

The text chapter should be studied one section at a time. Before you read, preview each section by skimming it, noting headings and boldface items. Then read the sections, one at a time, keeping these questions in mind.

1. What would happen if more parents let their children "go out and play"?
2. Should the epidemic of childhood obesity be blamed on parents, schools, or policies?
3. Why are IQ tests not used as often as they were a few decades ago?
4. How helpful are diagnosis, special education, and medication for children with special needs?

Chapter Review

When you have finished reading the chapter, work through the material that follows to review it. Completing the sentences and answering the questions will enable you to answer the "What Have You Learned?" questions at the end of the text chapter. Scattered throughout the Chapter Review are Study Tips, which explain how best to learn a difficult concept, and Think About It discussions and Applications, which help you to know how well you understand the material. Check your understanding of the material by consulting the answers at the end of the chapter. Do not continue with the next section until you understand each answer. If you need to, review or reread the appropriate section in the textbook before continuing.

A Healthy Time

1. Compared with biosocial development during other periods of the life span, biosocial development during this time, known as

   _____ _____ , is _____ (relatively smooth/ often fraught with problems). For example, disease and death during these years are _____ (common/rare).

2. Children grow at a _____ (faster/slower) rate during middle childhood than they did earlier.

Describe several other features of physical development during middle childhood.

3. Death during middle childhood has been reduced dramatically because of _____ . Another improvement in medical care involves _____ care.

State two important strategies for preventing many adult health problems in children.

State some of the benefits and hazards of childhood sports.

4. Especially for low-income children, participating in structured sports activities correlates with improved _____ achievement, less _____ , and development of _____ .

APPLICATIONS:

5. Jethro plays on a Little League baseball team and enjoys casual sports with his schoolfriends. Jethro will
   a. enjoy better overall health.
   b. learn to appreciate fair play.
   c. exhibit improved problem-solving abilities.
   d. accomplish all of these things.

6. Summarizing physical development during middle childhood, Professor Wilson notes each of the following except that
   a. it is the healthiest period of the life span.
   b. mortal injuries are unusual during this time.
   c. most fatal childhood diseases occur during middle childhood.
   d. growth is slower than during early childhood.

Health Problems in Middle Childhood

7. Every physical and psychological characteristic affects and is affected by the _____ context.

8. The number that expresses the relationship of height to weight is the _____ _____ _____ . Children are said to be overweight when their body mass index is above the _____ (what number?) percentile of the growth chart for their age. Childhood obesity is defined as having a BMI above the _____ (what number?) percentile.

9. Overweight children are more likely to have _____ , high _____ _____ , and elevated levels of bad _____ . As weight increases, on average, school achievement and self-esteem _____ (increase/decrease), and _____ increases.

10. (A View from Science) People who inherit a gene allele called _____ are more likely to be obese and suffer from diabetes.

11. (A View from Science) Three factors are relevant to obesity: genes, ,_____ _____ and _____ _____ that determine the quality of school lunches.

State several parenting practices that protect against childhood obesity.

12. A chronic inflammatory disorder of the airways is called _____ . This disorder is _____ (more common/less common) today than in the past.

13. The causes or triggers of asthma include _____ , not getting the infections and childhood diseases that would strengthen their _____ systems, and exposure to _____ such as pet hair. According to the _____ hypothesis, asthma is more prevalent

today because contemporary children are
_____ from viruses and bacteria.

14. The use of injections and inhalers to treat
asthma is an example of _____
prevention. The best approach to treating
childhood diseases is _____
_____ , which in the case of
asthma includes proper _____
of homes and schools, decreased
_____ , eradication
of cockroaches, and safe outdoor
_____ _____ .

THINK ABOUT IT To help you differentiate
and remember the various middle childhood
experiences that protect against or promote adult
health problems, make a list that describes your
own experiences during middle childhood. For
example, did your parents promote regular exercise?
Excessive television watching?

APPLICATIONS:

15. Because 11-year-old Wayne is obese, he runs a
greater risk of developing
a. heart problems.
b. diabetes.
c. psychological problems.
d. all of these problems.

16. Harold weighs about 20 pounds more than his
friend Jay. During school recess, Jay can usually be found playing soccer with his classmates,
while Harold sits on the sidelines by himself.
Harold's rejection is likely due to his
a. being physically different.
b. being dyslexic.
c. intimidation of his schoolmates.
d. being hyperactive.

17. Concluding her presentation on "Asthma During
Middle Childhood," Amanda mentions each of
the following except that
a. asthma is much more common today than 20
years ago.
b. genetic vulnerability is rarely a factor in a
child's susceptibility to developing asthma.
c. the incidence of asthma continues to
increase.
d. carpeted floors, airtight windows, and less
outdoor play increase the risk of asthma
attacks.

Brain Development

18. Advances in brain development during
early childhood enable emerging
_____ regulation and
_____ _____
_____ . Left–right coordination
also emerges as the _____
_____ strengthens connections
between the brain's two _____ .
The executive functions of the brain also begin
developing, along with maturation of the
_____ _____ ,
which enables control over various
_____ .

19. The length of time it takes a person to
respond to a particular stimulus is called
_____ _____ .

20. Two other advances in brain function at this
time include the ability to pay special heed to
one source of information among many, called
_____ _____ ,
and the _____ of thoughts and
actions that are repeated in sequence.

21. The potential to master a specific skill or to
learn a certain body of knowledge is a person's
_____ . The most commonly
used tests to measure this potential are
_____ _____ .
In the original version of the most commonly
used test of this type, a person's score was
calculated as a _____ (the child's
_____ _____
divided by the child's _____
_____ and multiplied by 100 to
determine his or her _____).

22. Tests that are designed to measure what a child
has learned are called _____
tests.

23. The average IQ scores of nations have
_____ (increased/decreased), a
phenomenon called the _____
_____ .

24. Many critics of IQ testing contend that we have
_____ _____ .

Robert Sternberg believes that there are three distinct types of intelligence:

_____ , _____ ,

and _____ .

25. Howard Gardner describes _____ (how many?) distinct intelligences. His theory has been influential in _____ , especially as it applies to children.

26. Another criticism of IQ testing is that every test reflects the _____ of the people who create, administer, and take it.

27. Neuroscientists agree that brain development _____ (depends/does not depend) on a person's specific experiences, that brain development _____ (continues/does not continue) throughout life, and that children with disorders _____ (do not/often do) have unusual brain patterns.

THINK ABOUT IT The board of directors for a new private school is considering the pros and cons of using IQ testing to admit and place students. Help them out by listing the major advantages and disadvantages of IQ testing as identified by developmental psychologists.

APPLICATIONS:

28. Angela was born in 1984. In 1992, she scored 125 on an intelligence test. Using the original formula, what was Angela's mental age when she took the test? _____

29. Of the following individuals, who is likely to have the longest reaction time?
    a. a 7 year old   c. an 11 year old
    b. a 9 year old   d. a 60 year old

30. Brain scans showed that Malcolm's prefrontal cortex and left inferior frontal gyrus were active while he tried to understand irony. This indicates that he had not yet achieved _____ this ability.
    a. selective attention related to
    b. automization of
    c. a high enough IQ for
    d. the coordination needed for

31. Professor Allenby teaches in a public school in a large city. Following the views of Howard Gardner and Robert Sternberg , the professor is most critical of traditional aptitude and achievement tests because they
    a. inadvertently reflect certain nonacademic competencies.
    b. do not reflect knowledge of cultural ideas.
    c. measure only a limited set of abilities.
    d. underestimate the intellectual potential of disadvantaged children.

Children with Special Needs

32. The field of study that is concerned with childhood psychological disorders is

    _____ _____ .

    This perspective has provided several lessons that apply to all children. Four of these are that _____ is normal, disability _____ (changes/ does not change) over time, adulthood may be

    _____ _____

    _____ , and diagnosis and

    treatment reflect the _____

    _____ .

33. Many disorders can be mitigated if diagnosed long before _____ and if treatment begins early. The problem is that

    _____ _____ is

    more difficult the younger a child is.

34. Disorders often occur together (that is, are _____). The principle that one cause can have many final manifestations is _____ . The principle that one developmental manifestation may have many causes is _____ .

35. A condition that manifests itself in a difficulty in concentrating for more than a few moments is called _____ -

    _____ _____ .

    There _____ (is/is not) a biological marker for this disorder.

36. ADHD is comorbid with many other conditions, including _____ .

37. Rates of ADHD in most other nations are
_____ (lower/higher) than in
the United States. Treatment for this disorder
involves three approaches:

a) _____

b) _____

c) _____

38. The most common drug for treating children
with ADHD is _____ . However,
younger children are taking at least 20 other
_____ drugs for depression,
anxiety, developmental delay, ASD, and
other conditions. Most _____
(professionals/parents) are convinced that
medication helps schoolchildren with emotional
problems, but most _____
(professionals/parents) are less sure.

39. Children who have difficulty acquiring a
particular skill that others acquire easily
are said to have a _____
_____ _____.
These deficits usually _____
(do/do not) result in lifelong impediments.

40. A disability in reading is called
_____ . A disability in math is
called _____ .

41. The most severe disturbance of early childhood
is _____ _____
_____ , which is used to
describe children who have difficulty with social
communication and interaction.

42. In autistic spectrum disorder, deficiencies appear
in two areas: problems in _____ ,
and restricted and repetitive patterns of
_____ .

43. Children who have autistic symptoms but
are unusually intelligent in some area and
have close-to-normal speech are said to be
_____-_____ .

44. Most children with autistic spectrum disorder
show signs in early _____ .
One such sign is _____ . Late
onset of ASD occurs with _____
_____ , in which a newborn girl
seems fine, but her brain develops more slowly
than normal.

45. Today, _____ (more/fewer)
children have autistic spectrum disorder than in
the past. This may be the result of an increase in
the _____ of the disorder, or an
increase in the disorder's _____ .

46. In response to a 1975 act requiring that
children with special needs be taught in the
_____ _____
_____ , the strategy of not
separating special-needs children into special
classes, called _____ ,
emerged. Some schools have developed a
_____ _____ , in
which such children spend part of each day with
a teaching specialist. In the most recent approach,
called _____ , learning-disabled
children receive targeted help within the setting
of a regular classroom.

47. Most recently, according to the strategy called
_____ _____
_____ , all children in early
grades in the United States who are below
average in _____ are given
some special intervention. If professionals
find a child has special needs, they discuss an
_____ _____
_____ with the parents, to
specify educational goals for the child.

STUDY TIP Complete the chart on the next page
as a way of organizing your understanding of the
differences among children with special needs.

Category	Characteristics	Suggested Treatment
Attention-deficit/ hyperactivity disorder		
Specific learning disorder		
Autistic spectrum disorder		
"High-functioning" ASD		

APPLICATIONS:

48. Children who are unusually _____ may also have special needs. In the practice called _____ , children are taught with others of the same _____ age. This practice is _____ (common/rare) today.

49. Children who are unusually _____ are _____ thinkers and may also need special education.

50. Dr. Rutter, who believes that knowledge about normal development can be applied to the study and treatment of psychological disorders, evidently is working from the _____ _____ perspective.

51. Ten-year-old Clarence is quick-tempered, easily frustrated, and is often disruptive in the classroom. Clarence may be suffering from _____ .

52. In determining whether her 8-year-old student has a learning disability, the teacher looks primarily for
    a. poor performance in all subject areas.
    b. the exclusion of other explanations.
    c. a family history of the learning disability.
    d. an inability to communicate.

53. Although 9-year-old Carl has severely impaired social skills, his intelligence and speech are normal. Carl is evidently displaying symptoms of "_____-_____" _____ .

54. Jennifer displays inadequate social skills and is extremely self-absorbed. It is likely that she suffers from _____ _____ .

55. Danny has been diagnosed as having attention-deficit/hyperactivity disorder. Every day, his parents make sure that he takes the proper dose of Ritalin. His parents should
    a. continue this behavior until Danny is an adult.
    b. try different medications when Danny seems to be reverting to his normal overactive behavior.
    c. also make sure that they and Danny's teachers receive training.
    d. not worry about Danny's condition; he will outgrow it.

Progress Test 1

Multiple-Choice Questions

Circle your answers to the following questions and check them with the answers at the end of the chapter. If your answer is incorrect, read the explanation for why it is incorrect and then consult the text.

1. As children move into middle childhood
    a. the rate of accidental death increases.
    b. sexual urges intensify.
    c. the rate of weight gain increases.
    d. biological growth slows and steadies.

2. Ongoing maturation of which brain area contributes most to left–right coordination?
    a. corpus callosum   c. brainstem
    b. prefrontal cortex   d. temporal lobe

3. The ability to filter out distractions and concentrate on relevant details is called
   a. automatization.   c. selective attention.
   b. reaction time.   d. inclusion.

4. Dyslexia is a specific learning disorder that affects the ability to
   a. do math.   c. write.
   b. read.   d. speak.

5. The developmental psychopathology perspective is characterized by its
   a. contextual approach.
   b. emphasis on the unchanging nature of developmental disorders.
   c. emphasis on cognitive development.
   d. concern with all of these considerations.

6. The time—usually measured in fractions of a second—it takes for a person to respond to a particular stimulus is called
   a. the interstimulus interval.
   b. reaction time.
   c. the stimulus–response interval.
   d. response latency.

7. The underlying problem in attention-deficit/ hyperactivity disorder appears to be
   a. low overall intelligence.
   b. a neurological difficulty in paying attention.
   c. a learning disability in a specific academic skill.
   d. the existence of a conduct disorder.

8. Healthy 6 year olds tend to have
   a. the lowest body mass index of any age group.
   b. the highest body mass index of any age group.
   c. more short-term illnesses than any other age group.
   d. fewer short-term illnesses than any other age group.

9. Children who have an autistic spectrum disorder have severe deficiencies in
   a. social responses.
   b. language development.
   c. play.
   d. all of these abilities.

10. Although asthma has genetic origins, several environmental factors contribute to its onset, including
    a. urbanization.
    b. airtight windows.
    c. dogs and cats living inside the house.
    d. all of these factors.

11. Psychoactive drugs are most effective in treating attention-deficit/hyperactivity disorder when they are administered
    a. before the diagnosis becomes certain.
    b. for several years after the basic problem has abated.
    c. as part of the labeling process.
    d. by trained parents and teachers.

12. Tests that measure a child's potential to learn a new subject are called _____ tests.
    a. aptitude   c. vocational
    b. achievement   d. intelligence

13. In the earliest aptitude tests, a child's score was calculated by dividing the child's _____ age by his or her _____ age to find the _____ quotient.
    a. mental; chronological; intelligence
    b. chronological; mental; intelligence
    c. intelligence; chronological; mental
    d. intelligence; mental; chronological

14. Selective attention refers to the ability to
    a. choose which of many stimuli to concentrate on.
    b. control emotional outbursts.
    c. persist at a task.
    d. perform a familiar action without much conscious thought.

15. Ongoing maturation of which brain area enables schoolchildren to analyze the potential consequences of their actions more effectively?
    a. corpus callosum   c. brain stem
    b. prefrontal cortex   d. temporal lobe

True or False Items

Write T (true) or F (false) on the line in front of each statement.

_____ 1. The rate of growth in school-age children continues at a rapid pace.

_____ 2. Genes and hereditary differences in taste preferences are the most important factors in promoting childhood obesity.

_____ 3. Childhood obesity increases the risk for serious health problems in adulthood.

_____ 4. The quick reaction time that is crucial in some sports can be readily achieved with practice.

_____ 5. The intellectual performance of children with "high-functioning" ASD is poor in all areas.

_____ 6. The incidence of children with autistic characteristics is decreasing.

_____ 7. Despite the efforts of teachers and parents, most children with specific learning disorder can expect their disabilities to persist and even worsen as they enter adulthood.

_____ 8. Stressful living conditions are an important consideration in diagnosing a learning disability.

_____ 9. Stimulant medication often helps children with ADHD to learn.

_____ 10. Mainstreaming along with use of a resource room is the most effective educational method for children with special needs.

Progress Test 2

Progress Test 2 should be completed during a final chapter review. Answer the following questions after you thoroughly understand the correct answers for the Chapter Review and Progress Test 1.

Multiple-Choice Questions

1. During the years from 7 to 11, the average child
   a. develops stronger muscles.
   b. grows at a rapid rate.
   c. has decreased lung capacity.
   d. is more likely to become obese than at any other period in the life span.

2. Comorbid refers to the presence of
   a. two or more unrelated disease conditions in the same person.
   b. abnormal neurons in the prefrontal cortex.
   c. developmental delays in physical development.
   d. any of several disorders characterized by inadequate social skills.

3. A specific learning disorder that becomes apparent when a child experiences unusual difficulty in learning to read is:
   a. dyslexia.   c. ADHD.
   b. autim spectrum disorder. d. dycalculia.

4. Marked delays in particular areas of learning are collectively referred to as
   a. specific learning disorder.
   b. attention-deficit/hyperactivity disorder.
   c. hyperactivity.
   d. dyslexia.

5. Aptitude and achievement testing are controversial in part because
   a. most tests are unreliable with respect to the individual scores they yield.
   b. a child's intellectual potential often changes over time.
   c. they often fail to identify serious learning problems.
   d. of all of these reasons.

6. The most effective form of help for children with ADHD is
   a. stimulant medication.
   b. psychotherapy.
   c. training parents and teachers.
   d. tranquilizing medication.

7. A key factor in reaction time is
   a. whether the child is male or female.
   b. brain maturation.
   c. whether the stimulus to be reacted to is an auditory or visual one.
   d. all of these conditions.

8. One of the first noticeable symptoms of autism spectrum disorder is usually
   a. a difficulty with reading.
   b. abnormal social responsiveness.
   c. hyperactivity.
   d. unpredictable.

9. Which of the following is true of children with a diagnosed learning disability?
   a. They often feel inadequate, ashamed, and stupid.
   b. They often have a specific physical handicap, such as hearing loss.
   c. They often lack basic educational experiences.
   d. All of these conditions are true.

10. Most important in the automatization of children's thoughts and actions is
    a. the continuing myelination of neurons.
    b. diet.
    c. activity level.
    d. all of these factors.

11. Which approach to education may best help children with special needs in terms of both skill remediation and social interaction with other children?
    a. mainstreaming
    b. special education
    c. response to intervention
    d. resource rooms

12. "High-functioning" ASD is a disorder in which
    a. body weight fluctuates dramatically over short periods of time.
    b. verbal skills seem normal, but social perceptions and skills are abnormal.

c. an autistic child is extremely aggressive.
d. a child of normal intelligence has difficulty mastering a specific cognitive skill.

13. Which of the following is NOT evidence of ADHD?
    a. inattentiveness   c. impulsivity
    b. poor language skills d. overreactivity

14. Tests that measure what a child has already learned are called _____ tests.
    a. aptitude   c. achievement
    b. vocational   d. intelligence

15. Which of the following is NOT a type of intelligence identified in Robert Sternberg's theory?
    a. academic   c. achievement
    b. practical   d. creative

Matching Items

Match each term or concept with its corresponding description or definition.

Terms or Concepts

_____ 1. dyslexia

_____ 2. automatization

_____ 3. "high-functioning" ASD

_____ 4. attention-deficit/hyperactivity disorder

_____ 5. asthma

_____ 6. Flynn effect

_____ 7. autism spectrum disorder

_____ 8. developmental psychopathology

_____ 9. response to intervention

_____ 10. specific learning disorder

_____ 11. mainstreaming

_____ 12. bipolar disorder

_____ 13. dyscalculia

Descriptions or Definitions

a. set of symptoms in which a child has impaired social skills despite having normal speech and intelligence

b. the rise in IQ score averages that has occurred in many nations

c. strategy in which all children who are below average in achievement receive an intervention

d. process by which thoughts and actions become routine and no longer require much thought

e. system in which children with special needs are taught in general education classrooms

f. disorder characterized by self-absorption

g. chronic inflammation of the airways

h. behavior problem involving difficulty in concentrating, as well as excitability and impulsivity

i. applies insights from studies of normal development to the study of childhood disorders

j. an unexpected difficulty with one or more academic skills

k. difficulty in reading

l. condition involving extreme mood swings

m. difficulty in math

Key Terms

Using your own words, write a brief definition or explanation of each of the following terms on a separate piece of paper.

1. middle childhood
2. childhood overweight
3. childhood obesity
4. asthma
5. reaction time
6. selective attention
7. automatization
8. aptitude
9. IQ test
10. achievement test
11. Flynn effect
12. multiple intelligences
13. developmental psychopathology
14. comorbid
15. multifinality
16. equifinality
17. attention-deficit/hyperactivity disorder (ADHD)
18. specific learning disorder (learning disability)
19. dyslexia
20. dyscalculia
21. autistic spectrum disorder
22. least restrictive environment (LRE)
23. response to intervention
24. individual education plan (IEP)

ANSWERS

CHAPTER REVIEW

1. middle childhood; relatively smooth; rare
2. slower

During middle childhood, muscles become stronger and heart and lung strength and capacity expand.

3. immunization; oral

Parents must be diligent in providing regular preventive care, and children must develop the habit of taking care of their health.

The benefits of sports include better overall health, less obesity, an appreciation for cooperation and fair play, improved problem-solving ability, and respect for teammates and opponents of many ethnicities and nationalities. The hazards may include loss of self-esteem as a result of criticism, injuries, reinforcement of existing prejudices, increased stress, and time taken away from learning academic skills.

4. academic; delinquency; friendships
5. **d.** is the answer. Participation in sports during middle childhood helps children develop not only biologically but also cognitively and socially.
6. **c.** is the answer. Just the opposite is true.
7. social
8. body mass index (BMI); 85th; 95th
9. asthma; blood pressure; cholesterol; decrease; loneliness
10. FTO
11. family eating habits; government policies

Obesity is rare if infants are breast-fed, if preschoolers rarely watch TV or drink soda, and if school-age children exercise.

12. asthma; more common
13. genes; immune; allergens; hygiene; overprotected
14. tertiary; primary prevention; ventilation; pollution; play areas
15. **d.** is the answer.
16. **a.** is the answer. Obese children are no more likely to be dyslexic, physically intimidating, or hyperactive than other children.
17. **b.** is the answer. Genes typically *do* play a role in a child's susceptibility to asthma.
18. emotional; theory of mind; corpus callosum; hemispheres; prefrontal cortex; impulses
19. reaction time
20. selective attention; automatization
21. aptitude; IQ tests; quotient; mental age; chronological age; IQ
22. achievement
23. increased; Flynn Effect
24. multiple intelligences; academic; creative; practical
25. nine; education
26. culture
27. depends; continues; often do

Think About It: See text pages 320–323 for a discussion of the pros and cons of IQ testing.

28. 10 years old. At the time she took the test, Angela's chronological age was 8. Knowing that her IQ was 125, we can solve the equation to yield a mental age of 10 ($125 = x/8$).
29. **d.** is the answer. Although reaction time decreases for a time as we age, it slowly lengthens in adulthood.
30. **b.** is the answer. Genetic variability has not changed in recent decades.
31. **c.** is the answer. Both Sternberg and Gardner believe that there are multiple intelligences rather

than the narrowly defined abilities measured by traditional aptitude and achievement tests.

32. developmental psychopathology; abnormality; changes; better or worse; social context

33. adolescence; accurate diagnosis

34. comorbid; multifinality; equifinality

35. attention-deficit disorder; is not

36. sleep deprivation, allergic reactions, and other psychological disorders

37. lower;
   a) counseling and training for family and child
   b) showing teachers how to help children
   c) medication

38. Ritalin; psychoactive; professionals; parents

39. specific learning disorder; do not

40. dyslexia; dyscalculia

41. autistic spectrum disorder

42. social interaction and the social use of language; behavior, interests, and activities

43. high-functioning

44. infancy; lack of the social smile; Rett syndrome

45. more; incidence; diagnosis

46. least restrictive environment (LRE); mainstreaming; resource room; inclusion

47. response to intervention; achievement; individual education plan (IEP)

Attention-deficit/hyperactivity disorder: difficulty concentrating plus being inattentive, impulsive, and overactive; medication, psychotherapy, and special training for parents and teachers.

Specific learning disorder (learning disability), such as dyslexia: marked delay in learning a particular skill that comes easily to others; learning disabilities do not result in lifelong impediments because most people learn how to work around them.

Autism spectrum disorder: woefully inadequate social skills, including difficulty seeing things from another person's perspective; and restricted, repetitive patterns of behavior, interests, or activities; some children never speak. Early training focuses on each of the specific deficiencies. Some programs emphasize language, others focus on play, and others stress attachment. All autistic spectrum disorders involve these treatments, varying only in the degree of help needed.

"High-functioning" ASD: deficient social understanding, but unusually talented in some specialized area.

48. gifted; acceleration; mental; rare

49. creative; divergent

50. developmental psychopathology

51. ADHD. Children with ADHD are inattentive, impulsive, and overactive.

52. **b.** is the answer.

53. "High-functioning" ASD, because the person tends to have normal or above-average intelligence, especially in a particular skill.

54. autism spectrum disorder

55. **c.** is the answer. Medication alone cannot ameliorate all the problems of ADHD.

PROGRESS TEST 1

Multiple-Choice Questions

1. **d.** is the answer.
2. **a.** is the answer.
3. **c.** is the answer.

   a. Automatization is the process in which repetition of a sequence of thoughts and actions makes the sequence routine.

   b. Reaction time is the length of time it takes to respond to a stimulus.

   d. Inclusion is an approach in which children with special needs are educated in regular classrooms along with all the other children.

4. **b.** is the answer.

   a. This is called dyscalculia.

   c. & d. The text does not give labels for learning disabilities in writing or speaking.

5. **a.** is the answer.

   b. & c. Because of its contextual approach, developmental psychopathology emphasizes *all* domains of development. Also, it points out that behaviors change over time.

6. **b.** is the answer.
7. **b.** is the answer.
8. **a.** is the answer.
9. **d.** is the answer.
10. **d.** is the answer.
11. **d.** is the answer.
12. **a.** is the answer.

   b. Achievement tests measure what has already been learned.

   c. Vocational tests, which, as their name implies, measure what a person has learned about a particular trade, are achievement tests.

   d. Intelligence tests measure general aptitude, rather than aptitude for a specific subject.

13. **a.** is the answer.

14. **a.** is the answer.

   b. This is emotional regulation.

   d. This is automatization.

15. **b.** is the answer.

   a. Maturation of the corpus callosum contributes to left–right coordination.

   c. & d. These brain areas, which were not discussed in this chapter, play important roles in regulating sleep–waking cycles (brain stem) and hearing and language abilities (temporal lobe).

True or False Items

1. F   The rate of growth slows down during middle childhood.
2. F   Environmental factors are more important in promoting obesity during middle childhood.
3. T
4. F   Reaction time depends on brain maturation and is not readily affected by practice.
5. F   Children with "high-functioning" ASD show isolated areas of remarkable skill.
6. F   Just the opposite is true, possibly because of better diagnoses.
7. F   Some children find ways to compensate for their deficiencies, and others are taught effective strategies for learning.
8. F   Stressful living conditions must be excluded before diagnosing a learning disability.
9. T
10. F   Mainstreaming did not meet all children's educational needs.

PROGRESS TEST 2

Multiple-Choice Questions

1. **a.** is the answer.

   b. & c. During this period, children's growth slows down, and they experience increased lung capacity.

   d. Although childhood obesity is a common problem, the text does not indicate that a person is more likely to become obese at this age than at any other.

2. **a.** is the answer.
3. **a.** is the answer.

   b. & c. d. These disorders do not manifest themselves in a particular academic skill but instead appear in psychological processes that affect learning in general.

   d. This is a learning disability in math.

4. **a.** is the answer.

   b. & c. ADHD is a disorder that usually does not manifest itself in specific subject areas. Hyperactivity is a facet of this disorder.

   d. Dyslexia is a learning disability in reading.

5. **b.** is the answer.
6. **a.** is the answer.
7. **b.** is the answer.
8. **b.** is the answer.
9. **a.** is the answer.
10. **a.** is the answer.
11. **c.** is the answer.

   a. Many general education teachers are unable to cope with the special needs of some children.

   b. & d. These approaches undermined the social integration of children with special needs.

12. **b.** is the answer.
13. **b.** is the answer.
14. **c.** is the answer.
15. **c.** is the answer.

Matching Items

1. k	5. g	9. c	13. m
2. d	6. b	10. j	
3. a	7. f	11. e	
4. h	8. i	12. l	

KEY TERMS

1. **Middle childhood** is the period from early childhood to adolescence, roughly ages 6 to 11.
2. **Childhood overweight** is said to occur when a child's body mass index (BMI) falls above the 85th percentile for children of that age.
3. **Childhood obesity** occurs when a child's body mass index (BMI) falls above the 95th percentile for children of that age.
4. **Asthma** is a chronic disorder in which the airways are inflamed, making breathing difficult.
5. **Reaction time** is the length of time it takes a person to respond to a stimulus, either physically or cognitively.
6. **Selective attention** is the ability to concentrate on one stimulus while ignoring others.
7. **Automatization** is the process by which thoughts and actions that are repeated often enough to become routine no longer require much conscious thought.
8. **Aptitude** is the potential to master a specific skill or learn a certain body of knowledge.

9. **IQ tests** are aptitude tests, which were originally designed to yield a measure of intelligence and originally calculated as mental age divided by chronological age, multiplied by 100.

10. **Achievement tests** measure what a child has already learned in a particular academic subject or subjects.

11. The **Flynn effect** refers to the rise in average IQ scores that has occurred over the decades in many nations.

12. **Multiple intelligences** is the idea that human intelligence is comprised of many varied abilities rather than a single, all-encompassing one.

13. **Developmental psychopathology** is a field that applies the insights into typical development to understand and remediate developmental disorders, and vice versa.

14. **Comorbid** refers to the presence of two or more unrelated disease conditions at the same time in the same person.

15. In developmental psychopathology, the principle of **multifinality** is that one cause can have many final outcomes.

16. In developmental psychopathology, the principle of **equifinality** is that one symptom can have many causes.

17. **Attention-deficit/hyperactivity disorder (ADHD)** is a behavior problem in which the individual has great difficulty concentrating and is often inattentive, impulsive, and overactive.

18. **Specific learning disorder (learning disability)** is a marked delay in a particular area of learning that is not attributable to overall intellectual slowness, a physical disability, or an unusually stressful home environment.

19. **Dyslexia** is a learning disability in reading.

20. **Dyscalculia** is a learning disability in math.

21. **Autistic spectrum disorder** is any of several disorders characterized by deficient social skills, impaired communication, and unusual play.

22. A **least restrictive environment (LRE)** is a legally required school setting that offers special-needs children as much freedom as possible to benefit from the instruction available to other children.

23. **Response to intervention** is an educational strategy in which all children in early grades who are below average in achievement are given some special intervention.

24. An **individual education plan (IEP)** is a legal document that specifies a set of educational goals for a child with special needs.

Middle Childhood: Cognitive Development

CHAPTER

Chapter Overview

Chapter 12 examines the development of cognitive abilities in children from ages 7 to 11. The first section discusses the views of Piaget and Vygotsky regarding cognitive development, which involves the child's growing ability to use logic and reasoning (as emphasized by Piaget) and to benefit from social interactions with skilled mentors (as emphasized by Vygotsky). It also explores information-processing theory, which focuses on changes in the child's processing speed and capacity, control processes, knowledge base, and metacognition.

The second section looks at language development during middle childhood. During this time, children develop a more analytic understanding of words and show a marked improvement in their language skills. This section also discusses the problems of children who speak a minority language.

The third section covers educational and environmental conditions that are conducive to learning by schoolchildren throughout the world.

What Will You Know?

The text chapter should be studied one section at a time. Before you read, preview each section by skimming it, noting headings and boldface items. Then read the sections, one at a time, keeping these questions in mind.

1. Does cognition improve naturally with age, or is teaching crucial to its development?
2. Do children learn best from experiences or from explicit instruction?
3. Why do children use slang, curse words, and bad grammar?
4. What type of school is best during middle childhood?

Chapter Review

When you have finished reading the chapter, work through the material that follows to review it. Completing the sentences and answering the questions will enable you to answer the "What Have You Learned?" questions at the end of the text chapter. Scattered throughout the Chapter Review are Study Tips, which explain how best to learn a difficult concept, and Think About It discussions and Applications, which help you to know how well you understand the material. Check your understanding of the material by consulting the answers at the end of the chapter. Do not continue with the next section until you understand each answer. If you need to, review or reread the appropriate section in the textbook before continuing.

Building on Theory

1. According to Piaget, school-age children are in the stage of _____ _____ _____ .

2. The concept that objects can be organized into categories according to some common property is _____ .

3. The knowledge that things can be arranged in a logical series is called _____ .

4. Although other research has found more _____ (continuity/discontinuity) in number skills, it nevertheless has supported Piaget's finding that what develops at this time is the ability to use _____ _____ more _____ , _____ , and _____ than younger children can.

159

5. Unlike Piaget, Vygotsky believed that in the child's _____

_____ _____

_____ , instruction by

_____ is crucial to cognitive development. In his view, formal education _____ (is/is not) the only context for learning.

6. Vygotsky's emphasis on the _____ context contrasts with Piaget's more _____ approach.

7. Educators' and psychologists' understanding of how children learn is based on the framework that was laid down by _____ and embellished by _____ .

8. The idea that the advances in thinking that accompany middle childhood occur because of basic changes in how children take in, store, and process data is central to the

_____-_____

theory.

9. Incoming stimulus information is held for a split second in _____

_____ , after which most of it is lost.

10. Meaningful material is transferred into

_____ _____ ,

which was formerly called

_____-_____

_____ . This part of memory handles mental activity that is _____ . Improvement in this type of memory occurs in two areas: the

_____ _____ ,

which stores sounds, and the

_____-_____

_____ , which stores sights.

11. The part of memory that stores information for days, months, or years is _____-

_____ _____ .

Crucial in this component of the system is not only storage of the material but also its

_____ .

12. Memory ability improves during middle childhood in part because of the child's expanded

_____ _____ .

13. The knowledge base also depends on _____ , current _____ , and personal _____ .

14. The mechanisms of the information-processing system that regulate the analysis and flow of information are the _____ _____ . These include

_____ _____ ,

_____ , and

_____ _____ .

15. The ability to evaluate a cognitive task to determine what to do—and to monitor and adjust one's performance—is called

_____ .

16. Because control processes organize, prioritize, and direct mental operations, they are also called _____ processes.

17. (A View from Science) Control processes develop spontaneously with _____ , but they are also taught, either _____ through instruction or through _____ learning.

STUDY TIP To help solidify your understanding of children's cognitive advances in middle childhood, try to find real-life situations. If you have a sister, brother, nephew, or niece who is about 7 years old, examine a few pages from one of their elementary school math workbooks. Look for examples of how children are tested on the concepts of identity, reversibility, reciprocity, and other logical constructs.

APPLICATIONS:

18. Which of the following statements is the clearest indication that the child has grasped the principle of reversibility?
    a. "See, the lemonade is the same in both our glasses; even though your glass is taller than mine, it's narrower."
    b. "Even though your dog looks funny, I know it's still a dog."
    c. "I have one sister and no brothers. My parents have two children."
    d. "I don't cheat because I don't want to be punished."

19. Dr. Larsen believes that the cognitive advances of middle childhood occur because of basic changes in children's thinking speed, knowledge base, and memory retrieval skills. Dr. Larsen evidently is working from the _____-_____ perspective.

20. Mei-Chin is able to sort her Legos into groups according to size. Clearly, she has an understanding of the principle of _____.

21. Lana is 4 years old and her brother Roger is 7. The fact that Roger remembers what their mother just told them about playing in the street while Lana is more interested in the children playing across the street is due to improvements in Roger's _____ _____.

22. For the first time, 7-year-old Nathan can remember his telephone number. This is probably the result of
    a. maturation of the sensory register.
    b. increased capacity of working memory.
    c. increased capacity of long-term memory.
    d. improved speed of processing.

23. Nine-year-old Rachel has made great strides in her ability to evaluate and monitor her learning and mastery of specific tasks. In other words, Rachel has shown great improvement in her _____.

24. Andy, who is 7 years old, spends many hours playing with Ronny, a friend who lives down the street. Vygotsky would say that this _____ _____ is important to Andy's cognitive development.

Language

25. During middle childhood, some children learn as many as _____ new words a day. Unlike the vocabulary explosion of early childhood, this language growth is distinguished by _____ and _____ . At this time, children also become much better able to understand _____ , _____ , and _____ .

26. Children are able to change from proper speech, or a _____ _____ , to a colloquial form, or _____ _____ , with their peers.

27. Children in the United States who have low proficiency in English are called _____ .

28. Decades of research throughout the world have found a strong correlation between academic achievement and _____ _____ . This connection is revealed by the fact that children from _____-_____ families are least likely to succeed in school. Their difficulty is generally in the area of _____ and includes having smaller _____ and using simpler _____ and _____ sentences.

29. Two factors that have been shown to be causal are limited early exposure to _____ , and teachers' and parents' _____ .

Teaching and Learning

30. Throughout history, children have been given new responsibility and instruction at about age _____ . Today, about _____ percent of children this age attend school.

31. National differences in curriculum content _____ (are/are not) notable.

32. Every nation creates its own _____ _____ , the unofficial rules and priorities that influence every aspect of school learning.

33. The international approach to objective assessment of fourth-grade children's achievement in reading is the _____ .

34. Science and math achievement is tested in the _____ .

35. Cross-cultural research reveals that U.S. teachers present math at a lower level with more _____ but less _____ to other learning. In contrast, teachers in Japan work more _____ to build children's knowledge.

36. In the United States, the _____ _____ _____ _____ Act is a federal law that mandates annual standardized achievement tests for public-school children.

37. The _____ is a federal project that measures achievement in reading, mathematics, and other subjects over time.

38. The approach to bilingual education in which the child's instruction occurs entirely in the second language is called _____ . In _____ _____ programs, teachers instruct children in both their native language and English.

39. In ESL, or _____ programs, children must master the basics of English before joining regular classes with other children.

40. A public school with its own set of standards and, often, private funding, is called a _____ _____ .

41. Schools funded by tuition, endowments, and church sponsors are called _____ _____ .

42. Through the use of _____ , parents in some school districts are able to choose which school their children will attend.

43. Education in which children are taught at home is called _____ _____ . The major problem with this approach is _____ (academic/social).

THINK ABOUT IT Imagine that you've been given total control over the educational experiences of a group of 7-year-old children, including microsystem factors and macrosystem factors. What factors will you focus on to promote bilingualism in your group?

For example, you might suggest putting English-speaking students in a class with non-English-speaking students so they could help each other out.

APPLICATIONS:

44. Seven-year-old Kyra has just moved to the United States from Colombia and knows very little English. Her school believes that she will best learn English if classes are in both Spanish, her native language, and English. This strategy is referred to as _____ _____ .

45. After moving to a new country, Arlene's parents are struck by the greater tendency of math teachers in their new homeland to work collaboratively and to emphasize social interaction in the learning process. To which country have these parents probably moved?
    a. the United States   c. Japan
    b. Germany   d. Australia

46. During the school board meeting, a knowledgeable parent proclaimed that the board's position on achievement testing and class size was an example of the district's "hidden curriculum." The parent was referring to
    a. the unofficial and unstated educational priorities of the school district.
    b. the political agendas of individual members of the school board.
    c. the legal mandates for testing and class size established by the state board of education.
    d. the federally sponsored measure of children's achievement in reading, math, and other subjects.

47. Four-year-old Tasha, who is learning to read by sounding out the letters of words, evidently is being taught using the _____ approach. Tabatha, on the other hand, is learning by talking and listening, reading and writing. She is being taught using the _____-_____ approach.

Progress Test 1

Multiple-Choice Questions

Circle your answers to the following questions and check them with the answers at the end of the chapter. If your answer is incorrect, read the explanation for why it is incorrect and then consult the text.

1. According to Piaget, the stage of cognitive development in which a person understands specific logical ideas and can apply them to concrete problems is called
   a. preoperational thought.
   b. operational thought.
   c. concrete operational thought.
   d. formal operational thought.

2. Low-SES children usually have poorer linguistic skills than high-SES children, primarily because they
   a. hear less language at home, and adult expectations for their learning are low.
   b. are less intelligent.
   c. attend schools with poor teachers.
   d. are too easily distracted.

3. The knowledge that things can be arranged in a sequence is called
   a. seriation.
   b. reversibility.
   c. classification.
   d. automatization.

4. Information-processing theorists contend that major advances in cognitive development occur during the school years because
   a. the child's mind becomes more like a computer as he or she matures.
   b. children become better able to process and analyze information.
   c. most mental activities become automatic by the time a child is about 13 years old.
   d. the major improvements in reasoning that occur during the school years involve increased long-term memory capacity.

5. Cross-cultural research on children's cognition reveals
   a. the same patterns of development worldwide.
   b. significant variations from country to country.
   c. that children's understanding of classification is unrelated to social interaction.
   d. that children's understanding of reversibility is unrelated to social interaction.

6. During middle childhood, children
   a. understand classification.
   b. demonstrate conservation.
   c. develop transitive inference.
   d. do all of these things.

7. The term for the ability to monitor and adjust one's cognitive performance—to think about thinking—is
   a. pragmatics.
   b. information processing.
   c. selective attention.
   d. metacognition.

8. Long-term memory is _____ permanent and _____ limited than working memory.
   a. more; less
   b. less; more
   c. more; more
   d. less; less

9. Passed in 2001, the federal law that mandates annual standardized achievement tests for public school children is the
   a. Reading First Act.
   b. National Assessment of Educational Progress.
   c. No Child Left Behind Act.
   d. Trends in Math and Science Study.

10. Which theorist believed that cultures (tools, customs, and people) teach children best?
    a. Piaget
    b. Vygotsky
    c. Skinner
    d. Chomsky

11. Which aspect of memory is most likely to change during the school years?
    a. sensory memory
    b. long-term memory
    c. the speed and efficiency of working memory
    d. All of these aspects change.

12. Eight-year-old Cho, who recently emigrated from Myanmar, attends a school in Canada in which all subjects are taught in English. Cho's school is using which strategy to teach English-language learners?
    a. bilingual education
    b. hidden curriculum
    c. immersion
    d. ESL

13. Many American children attend charter schools. These are
    a. private schools.
    b. schools that offer instruction in their first language and in English.
    c. public schools that set their own standards.
    d. schools that do not fit into an existing school district.

14. Which theorist emphasized the critical role of maturation in cognitive development?
    a. Piaget
    b. Vygotsky
    c. Skinner
    d. Chomsky

15. Of the following, which was NOT identified as an important factor in the difference between success and failure in second-language learning?
    a. national policies
    b. family ethnotheories
    c. socioeconomic status
    d. the difficulty of the language

True or False Items

Write T (true) or F (false) on the line in front of each statement.

_____ 1. A major objection to Piaget's theory is that he underestimated the influence of context, instruction, and culture.

_____ 2. Immersion is the best strategy for teaching English-language learners.

_____ 3. Vygotsky emphasized the child's own logical thinking.

_____ 4. Working memory improves steadily and significantly every year from about age 4 to age 15.

_____ 5. Children become better at controlling their thinking as the prefrontal cortex matures.

_____ 6. Culture affects only what children learn, not how they learn.

_____ 7. Socioeconomic status does not affect bilingualism.

_____ 8. Most information that comes into the sensory memory is lost or discarded.

_____ 9. Information-processing theorists believe that advances in the thinking of school-age children occur primarily because of changes in long-term memory.

_____ 10. Compared with children in the United States, children in East Asia are more likely to excel on measures of reading, math, and science.

_____ 11. Charter schools are regulated by the same standards as the public schools in a given school district.

Progress Test 2

Progress Test 2 should be completed during a final chapter review. Answer the following questions after you thoroughly understand the correct answers for the Chapter Review and Progress Test 1.

Multiple-Choice Questions

1. The first component of the information-processing system is
   a. sensory memory.
   b. working memory.
   c. long-term memory.
   d. control process.

2. Research regarding Piaget's theory has found that
   a. cognitive development seems to be considerably less affected by sociocultural factors than Piaget's descriptions imply.
   b. the movement to a new level of thinking is much more erratic than Piaget predicted.
   c. there is no dramatic shift in the thinking of children when they reach the age of 5.
   d. all of these statements are true.

3. The major problem with home schooling is
   a. that many parents are not conscientious teachers.
   b. home-schooled children consistently score lower than other children on achievement tests.
   c. children have no interaction with classmates.
   d. the use of out-of-date materials.

4. When psychologists look at the ability of children to receive, store, and organize information, they are examining cognitive development from a view based on
   a. the observations of Piaget.
   b. information processing.
   c. behaviorism.
   d. the idea that the key to thinking is the sensory register.

5. The National Assessment of Educational Progress (NAEP)
   a. measures achievement in reading, mathematics, and other subjects over time.
   b. federally mandates annual achievement testing for public school children.
   c. established a five-year cycle of international trend studies in reading ability.
   d. provides states with funding for early reading instruction.

6. The logical operations of concrete operational thought are particularly important to an understanding of the elementary-school subject of
   a. spelling.
   c. math.
   b. reading.
   d. social studies.

7. Which of the following is especially helpful in making it easier to master new information in a specific subject?
   a. a large sensory register
   b. a large knowledge base
   c. unlimited long-term memory
   d. working memory

8. Language "codes" include variations in
   a. pronunciation.
   b. gestures.
   c. vocabulary.
   d. all of these aspects.

9. When we refer to a child's improved memory capacity, we are referring to
   a. the child's ability to selectively attend to more than one thought.
   b. the amount of information the child is able to hold in working memory.
   c. the size of the child's knowledge base.
   d. all of these things.

10. Retaining information in memory is called
    a. retrieval.
    b. storage.
    c. automatization.
    d. metacognition.

11. Which of the following terms does NOT belong with the others?
    a. selective attention
    b. metacognition
    c. emotional regulation
    d. knowledge base

12. Which aspect of the information-processing system assumes an executive role in regulating the analysis and transfer of information?
    a. sensory register
    b. working memory
    c. long-term memory
    d. control processes

13. Which of the following is the primary international test of reading ability?
    a. TIMSS
    c. NCLB
    b. PIRLS
    d. NAEP

14. Low-SES children tend to have lower linguistic skills because
    a. they hear less language at home.
    b. adult expectations for their learning are low.
    c. they hear less language and home and adults expect less for their learning.
    d. they have fewer social interactions than do higher-SES children.

15. Juan attends a school that offers instruction in both English and Spanish. This strategy for teaching English-language learners is called
    a. bilingual schooling.
    b. immersion.
    c. heritage language instruction.
    d. ESL.

Matching Items

Match each term or concept with its corresponding description or definition.

Terms or Concepts

_____ 1. working memory

_____ 2. reversibility

_____ 3. classification

_____ 4. charter

_____ 5. information processing

_____ 6. control processes

_____ 7. retrieval

_____ 8. storage

_____ 9. metacognition

_____ 10. total immersion

_____ 11. concrete operational thought

_____ 12. voucher

_____ 13. seriation

Descriptions or Definitions

a. mechanism for regulating the analysis and flow of information within the information-processing system

b. the idea that a transformation process can be undone to restore the original conditions

c. public school with its own set of standards

d. developmental perspective that conceives of cognitive development as the result of changes in the processing and analysis of information

e. Piaget's term for the ability to reason logically about direct experiences

f. an educational technique in which instruction occurs entirely in the second language

g. accessing previously learned information

h. holding information in memory

i. the logical principle that things can be organized into groups

j. area where current, conscious mental activity occurs

k. the ability to evaluate a cognitive task and to monitor one's performance on it

l. permission to choose the school your child will attend

m. the concept that things can be arranged in a logical series

Key Terms

Using your own words, write a brief definition or explanation of each of the following terms on a separate piece of paper.

1. concrete operational thought
2. classification
3. seriation
4. sensory memory
5. working memory
6. long-term memory
7. knowledge base
8. control processes
9. metacognition
10. ELLs (English Language Learners)
11. hidden curriculum
12. Trends in Math and Science Study (TIMSS)
13. Progress in International Reading Literacy Study (PIRLS)
14. No Child Left Behind Act

15. National Assessment of Educational Progress (NAEP)
16. immersion
17. bilingual schooling
18. ESL (English as a second language)
19. charter school
20. private school
21. voucher
22. home schooling

ANSWERS

CHAPTER REVIEW

1. concrete operational thought
2. classification
3. seriation
4. continuity; mental categories; flexibly; inductively; simultaneously

5. zone of proximal development; others; is not

6. sociocultural; maturational

7. Piaget; Vygotsky

8. information-processing

9. sensory memory (the sensory register)

10. working memory; short-term memory; conscious; phonological loop; visual–spatial sketchpad

11. long-term memory; retrieval

12. knowledge base

13. experience; opportunity; motivation

14. control processes; selective attention; metacognition; emotional regulation

15. metacognition

16. executive

17. age; explicitly; discovery

18. **a.** is the answer. Reversibility is the logical principle that something that has been changed (such as the height of lemonade poured from one glass into another) can be returned to its original shape by reversing the process of change (pouring the liquid back into the other glass).

19. information-processing

20. classification. This is the process of organizing things into groups according to some common property.

21. control processes. The control processes, which include selective attention, metacognition, and emotional regulation, are the executives of the information-processing system. They regulate the analysis and flow of information.

22. **b.** is the answer. The capacity of working memory increases during middle childhood.

23. metacognition. Metacognition has been referred to as "thinking about thinking."

24. social interaction. Vygotsky believed that peers and teachers provide the bridge between the child's developmental potential and the needed skills and knowledge, via guided participation.

25. 20; logic; flexibility; metaphors; jokes; puns

26. formal code; informal code

27. ELLs (English Language Learners)

28. socioeconomic status; low-income; language; vocabularies; grammar; shorter

29. words; expectations

30. 7; 95

31. are

32. hidden curriculum

33. Progress in International Reading Literacy Study (PIRLS)

34. Trends in Math and Science Study (TIMSS)

35. definitions; connection; collaboratively

36. No Child Left Behind

37. National Assessment of Educational Progress

38. immersion; bilingual education

39. English as a second language

40. charter school

41. private schools

42. vouchers

43. home schooling; social

44. bilingual schooling

45. **c.** is the answer.

46. **a.** is the answer.

47. phonics; whole-word

PROGRESS TEST 1

Multiple-Choice Questions

1. **c.** is the answer.
   a. Preoperational thought is "pre-logical" thinking.
   b. There is no such stage in Piaget's theory.
   d. Formal operational thought extends logical reasoning to abstract problems.

2. **a.** is the answer.

3. **a.** is the answer.
   b. This is the concept that a thing that has been changed can returned to its original state.
   c. This is the organization of things into groups.
   d. This is the process by which familiar mental activities become routine and automatic.

4. **b.** is the answer.
   a. Information-processing theorists use the mind–computer metaphor at every age.
   c. Although increasing automatization is an important aspect of development, the information-processing perspective does not suggest that most mental activities become automatic by age 13.
   d. Most of the important changes in reasoning that occur during the school years are due to the improved processing capacity of the person's *working memory.*

5. **a.** is the answer.

6. **d.** is the answer.

7. **d.** is the answer.
   a. Pragmatics refers to the practical use of language to communicate with others.

b. The information-processing perspective views the mind as being like a computer.

c. This is the ability to screen out distractions in order to focus on important information.

8. **a.** is the answer.

9. **c.** is the answer.

10. **b.** is the answer.

   a. Piaget emphasized the importance of maturation in cognitive development.

   c. & d. Skinner and Chomsky each developed a theory of language development.

11. **c.** is the answer. During middle childhood, speed of processing increases and automatization improves, thus improving the efficiency of working memory.

12. **c.** is the answer.

   a. In bilingual education, instruction occurs in both languages.

   b. Hidden curriculum is not a method of instruction.

   d. ESL children are taught intensively in English for a few months to prepare them for regular classes. It is not clear that Cho received this type of preparatory instruction.

13. **c.** is the answer.

14. **a.** is the answer.

15. **d.** is the answer.

True or False Items

1. T
2. F   No single approach to teaching a second language is best for all children in all contexts.
3. F   This is true of Piaget.
4. T
5. T
6. F   Culture affects not only what children learn but also how they learn.
7. F   The likelihood of parents, school, or culture encouraging bilingualism in children depends on the family's socioeconomic status.
8. T
9. F   They believe that the changes are due to basic changes in control processes.
10. T
11. F   Charter schools set their own standards.

PROGRESS TEST 2

Multiple-Choice Questions

1. **a.** is the answer.
2. **b.** is the answer.
3. **c.** is the answer.
4. **b.** is the answer.
5. **a.** is the answer.
6. **c.** is the answer.
7. **b.** is the answer.

   a. The sensory register briefly stores incoming sensations. Its capacity does not change with maturation.

   c. & d. Working memory and long-term memory are important in all forms of learning. Unlike a broad knowledge base in a specific area, however, these memory processes do not selectively make it easier to learn more in a specific area.

8. **d.** is the answer.

9. **b.** is the answer.

10. **b.** is the answer.

   a. This is the *accessing* of already learned information.

   c. Automatization is the process by which well-learned activities become routine and automatic.

   d. This is the ability to evaluate a task and to monitor and adjust one's performance on it.

11. **d.** is the answer.

   a., b., & c. Each of these is a control process.

12. **d.** is the answer.

   a. The sensory register stores incoming information for a split second.

   b. Working memory is the part of memory that handles current, conscious mental activity.

   c. Long-term memory stores information for days, months, or years.

13. **b.** is the answer.

14. **c.** is the answer.

15. **a.** is the answer.

Matching Items

1. j	5. d	9. k	13. m
2. b	6. a	10. f	
3. i	7. g	11. e	
4. c	8. h	12. l	

KEY TERMS

1. During Piaget's stage of **concrete operational thought,** school-age children can think logically about direct experiences and perceptions but are not able to reason abstractly.

2. **Classification** is the logical principle that things can be organized into groups according to some common property.

3. **Seriation** is the concept that things can be arranged in a logical sequence.

4. **Sensory memory** is the first component of the information-processing system that stores incoming stimuli for a split second, after which it is passed into working memory, or discarded as unimportant; also called the *sensory register*.

5. **Working memory** is the component of the information-processing system that handles current, conscious mental activity; formerly called *short-term memory*.

6. **Long-term memory** is the component of the information-processing system that stores unlimited amounts of information for days, months, or years.

7. The **knowledge base** is a broad body of knowledge in a particular subject area that has been learned, making it easier to learn new information in that area.

8. **Control processes** (including selective attention, metacognition, and emotional regulation) regulate the analysis and flow of information within the information-processing system.

9. **Metacognition** is the ability to evaluate a cognitive task to determine what to do and to monitor and adjust one's performance on that task.

10. **ELLs (English Language Learners)** are U.S. children whose proficiency in English is low.

11. The **hidden curriculum** is the unofficial, unstated, or implicit rules and priorities that influence the academic curriculum and every other aspect of school learning.

12. The **TIMSS (Trends in Math and Science Study)** is an international assessment of the math and science skills of fourth- and eighth-graders.

13. **Progress in International Reading Literacy Study (PIRLS),** inaugurated in 2001, is a five-year cycle of trend studies of reading ability of fourth-graders around the world.

14. The **No Child Left Behind Act** is a controversial law, enacted in 2001, that uses multiple assessments and achievement standards to try to improve public education in the United States.

15. The **National Assessment of Educational Progress (NAEP)** is an ongoing and nationally representative measure of U.S. children's achievement in reading, mathematics, and other subjects.

16. **Immersion** is an approach to bilingual education in which the child's instruction occurs entirely in the new language.

17. **Bilingual schooling** is a strategy in which school subjects are taught in both the learner's original language and the second (majority) language.

18. **ESL (English as a second language)** is an approach to bilingual education in which children are taught separately, and exclusively in English, to prepare them for attending regular classes.

19. A **charter school** is a public school with its own set of standards that is funded by the state or local district in which it is located.

20. A **private school** is a non-public school funded by tuition and/or endowments and nonprofit sponsors.

21. A **voucher** gives parents permission to choose which school their child will attend, with some or all of the cost of that child's education borne by the local government.

22. **Home schooling** is education in which children are taught at home, usually by their parents.

Middle Childhood: Psychosocial Development

Chapter Overview

This chapter brings to a close the unit on middle childhood. We have seen that from ages 6 to 11, the child becomes stronger and more competent, mastering the biosocial and cognitive abilities that are important in his or her culture. Psychosocial accomplishments are equally impressive.

The first section explores the growing social competence of children, as described by Erikson and Freud. The section continues with a discussion of the growth of social awareness and self-understanding and closes with a discussion of the ways in which children cope with stressful situations.

The next section explores the ways in which families influence children, including the experience of living in single-parent, extended, and blended families. Although no particular family structure guarantees optimal child development, income, harmony, and stability are important factors in the quality of family functioning.

Children's interactions with peers and others in their ever-widening social world are the subject of the third section. Because middle childhood is also a time of expanding moral reasoning, the final section examines Kohlberg's stage theory of moral development, as well as current evaluations of his theory. Although the peer group often is a supportive, positive influence on children, some children are rejected by their peers or become the victims of bullying.

What Will You Know?

The text chapter should be studied one section at a time. Before you read, preview each section by skimming it, noting headings and boldface items. Then read the sections, one at a time, keeping these questions in mind.

1. What helps some children thrive in difficult family or neighborhood conditions?

2. Should parents marry, risking divorce, or not marry and thus avoid divorce?

3. What can be done to stop a bully?

4. When would children lie to adults to protect a friend?

Chapter Review

When you have finished reading the chapter, work through the material that follows to review it. Completing the sentences and answering the questions will enable you to answer the "What Have You Learned?" questions at the end of the text chapter. Scattered throughout the Chapter Review are Study Tips, which explain how best to learn a difficult concept, and Think About It discussions and Applications, which help you to know how well you understand the material. Check your understanding of the material by consulting the answers at the end of the chapter. Do not continue with the next section until you understand each answer. If you need to, review or reread the appropriate section in the textbook before continuing.

The Nature of the Child

1. According to Erikson, the crisis of middle childhood is _____

   _____ _____ .

2. Freud describes middle childhood as the period of _____ , when emotional drives are _____ and unconscious sexual conflicts are _____ .

3. As their self-understanding sharpens, children gradually become _____ (more/less) self-critical, and their self-esteem _____ (rises/dips). One reason is that they more often evaluate themselves through

   _____ _____ .

4. Self-esteem that is unrealistically high may reduce the child's _____ _____ , thus lowering _____ and increasing _____ . However, the same may occur if _____ is unrealistically low. Self-esteem _____ (is/is not) universally valued; many cultures expect children to be _____ .

5. Some children are better able to adapt within the context of adversity; that is, they seem to be more _____ . This trait is a _____ process that represents a _____ adaptation to stress.

6. Difficult daily _____ may build up stress in children.

7. A key aspect of resilience is the child's _____ of a family situation. When children feel responsible for whatever happens in their family, the problem called _____ has occurred. Also, the child's ability to develop _____ , _____ , and _____ is important.

8. Children are less affected by influences that arise from being in the same environment, called _____ environment, than by the different experiences of two siblings. These latter influences are called _____ environment.

9. Psychopathology, happiness, and sexual orientation arise primarily from _____ and _____ environment.

_____

STUDY TIP To consolidate your understanding of how stress can affect children during middle childhood, write a paragraph describing a hypothetical child who remains resilient despite experiencing chronic daily stress. Be sure to describe various protective factors such as social support that promote this child's resistance.

_____

APPLICATIONS:

10. Dr. Ferris believes that skill mastery is particularly important because children develop views of themselves as either competent or incompetent in skills valued by their culture. Dr. Ferris is evidently working from the perspective of

_____ .

11. The Australian saying that "tall poppies" are cut down underscores the fact that
    a. older children often ignore their parents and teachers.
    b. culture influences standards of social comparison.
    c. middle childhood is a time of emotional latency.
    d. personal friendships become even more important in middle childhood.

12. Concluding her presentation on resilient children, Brenda notes that
    a. children who are truly resilient are resilient in all situations.
    b. resilience is merely the absence of pathology.
    c. resilience is a stable trait that becomes apparent very early in life.
    d. resilience is a dynamic process that represents a positive adaptation to significant adversity or stress.

13. Shen's parents have separated. Since then, his grades have dropped, he's moody, and he spends most of his time alone in his room. Research regarding the factors that contribute to problems such as Shen's found the strongest correlation between children's peace of mind and
    a. marital discord.
    b. income.
    c. illness in the family.
    d. feelings of self-blame and vulnerability.

14. Of the following children, who is likely to have the lowest overall self-esteem?
    a. Karen, age 5   c. Carl, age 9
    b. David, age 7   d. Cindy, age 10

15. Ten-year-old Benjamin is less optimistic and self-confident than his 5-year-old sister. This may be explained in part by the tendency of older children to
    a. evaluate their abilities by comparing them with their own competencies a year or two earlier.
    b. evaluate their competencies by comparing them with those of others.
    c. be less realistic about their own abilities.
    d. be overly confident about their abilities.

Families and Children

16. No human trait is entirely _____ or entirely _____ .

17. The legal and genetic connections among related people living in the same household are referred to as _____ _____ .

18. Family function refers to how well the family _____ .

19. A functional family nurtures school-age children by providing basic material _____ , encouraging _____ , fostering the development of _____ , nurturing peer _____ , and ensuring _____ and _____ .

20. (text and Table 13.2) Family structure is defined as the _____ . Identify each of the following family structures:

    a. _____ A family that includes three or more biologically related generations, including parents and children.

    b. _____ A family that consists of the father, the mother, and their biological children.

    c. _____ A family that consists of one parent with his or her biological children.

    d. _____ In some nations, a family that consists of one man, several wives, and their children.

    e. _____ A family that consists of one or more nonbiological children whom adults have legally taken to raise as their own.

    f. _____ A family that consists of a parent, his or her biological children, and his or her spouse, who is not biologically related to the children.

    g. _____ A family that consists of one or two grandparents and their grandchildren.

    h. _____ A family that consists of a same-sex couple and the biological or adopted children of one or both partners.

21. Although the _____ family is still the most common, more than _____ (what percentage?) of all school-age children live in _____-_____ households.

22. In polygamous families, income per child _____ (increases/decreases), as does _____ , especially for girls.

Give several reasons for the benefits of the nuclear family structure.

23. A crucial factor in good family function is the formation of a _____ _____ , whereby mother and father support each other. Shared parenting decreases the risk of child _____ .

24. Adoptive parents, same-sex parents, and stepfamilies _____ (can function well/do not function well) for children. The most common form of foster care is the _____-_____ family, in which grandparents provide full-time care without parents present.

25. Another factor that has a crucial impact on children is the _____ that characterizes family interaction. Children are particularly harmed when adults fight about _____ _____ .

26. (A View from Science) The main reason children are harmed by divorce is the _____ that can result.

27. Family income _____ (correlates/does not correlate) with both structure and function. Economic distress _____ family functioning.

According to the _____-_____model, economic hardship in a family increases _____ . In high-income families, children may have problems because of parental pressure to _____ .

APPLICATION:

28. Kyle and Jessica are as different as two siblings can be, despite growing up in the same nuclear family structure. In explaining these differences, a developmentalist is likely to point to
    a. shared environmental influences.
    b. nonshared environmental influences.
    c. genetic differences and shared environmental influences.
    d. genetic differences and nonshared environmental influences.

The Peer Group

29. Getting along with _____ is especially important during middle childhood. Compared with younger children, school-age children are _____ (more/less) deeply affected by others' acceptance or rejection.

30. Peers create their own _____ _____ , which includes the particular rules and rituals that are passed down from slightly older to younger children and that _____ (mirror/do not necessarily mirror) the values of adults.

31. _____ (In some parts of the world/Throughout the world), the culture of children encourages _____ from adults.

32. The culture of children includes not only fashions and gestures but also _____ and _____ .

33. Having a personal friend is _____ (more/less) important to children than acceptance by the peer group.

34. Friendships during middle childhood become more _____ and _____ . As a result, older children _____ (change/ do not change) friends as often and find it

_____ (easier/harder) to make new friends.

35. Gender differences persist in activities: Girls _____ more, whereas boys _____ .

36. Middle schoolers tend to choose best friends whose _____ , _____ , and _____ are similar to their own.

37. Two factors that affect what makes a child well liked or not are _____ and _____ .

38. Children who are not really rejected but not picked as friends are _____ . Children who are actively rejected tend to be either _____-_____ or _____-_____ .

Briefly explain why rejected children are disliked.

39. Bullying is defined as _____ efforts to inflict harm on a weaker person. A key aspect in the definition of bullying is that harmful attacks are _____ . Three types of bullying are _____ , _____ , and _____ . A particularly devastating form of bullying uses electronic means to harm another, and so is called _____ .

40. Most bullies usually _____ (have/do not have) friends who admire them, and they are socially _____ but without _____ .

41. Victims of bullying are often _____-rejected children. Less often, _____-rejected children become _____-_____ .

42. Boys who are bullies are often above average in _____ , whereas girl bullies are often _____-_____ . Boys who are bullies typically use _____ aggression, whereas girls use _____ aggression.

43. The origins of bullying may lie in a _____ _____ or a _____ predisposition and are then strengthened by _____ _____ , a stressful _____ life, ineffective _____ , hostile _____ , and other problems that intensify _____ impulses. _____ are also influential; children in groups that approve of _____ bullying may be influenced more by group members than by their own beliefs.

44. Increasing students' awareness of bullying and instituting a zero-tolerance school policy for fighting are _____ (effective/ineffective) strategies in stopping bullying.

45. Research studies have found that school climate as a _____ needs to change in order to prevent bullying.

APPLICATIONS:

46. Concluding her presentation on bullying, Olivia notes that bullying may be the result of
   a. an inborn brain abnormality.
   b. insecure attachment.
   c. the presence of hostile siblings.
   d. any of these factors.

47. Ten-year-old Ramón, who is disliked by many of his peers because of his antagonistic, confrontational nature, would probably be labeled as _____-_____ .

48. In discussing friendship, 9-year-old Melissa, in contrast to a younger child, will
   a. deny that friends are important.
   b. have a larger circle of friends.
   c. stress the importance of loyalty and similar interests.
   d. be less choosy about whom she calls a friend.

49. Eight-year-old Henry is unpopular because he is a very timid and anxious child. Developmentalists would classify Henry as _____-_____ .

50. Of the following children, who is most likely to become a bully?
   a. Karen, who is taller than average
   b. David, who is above average in verbal assertiveness
   c. Carl, who is insecure and lonely
   d. Cindy, who was insecurely attached

51. I am an 8-year-old who frequently is bullied at school. If I am like most victims of bullies, I am probably
   a. obese.
   b. unattractive.
   c. a child who speaks with an accent.
   d. anxious and insecure.

Children's Moral Values

52. The theorist who has extensively studied moral development by presenting people with stories that pose ethical dilemmas is _____ . According to his theory, the three levels of moral reasoning are _____ , _____ , and _____ .

53. (Table 13.3) In preconventional reasoning, emphasis is on getting _____ and avoiding _____ . "Might makes right" describes stage _____ (one/two), whereas "look out for number one" describes stage _____ (one/two).

54. (Table 13.3) In conventional reasoning, emphasis is on _____ _____ , such as being a dutiful citizen, in stage _____ (three/four), or on winning approval from others, in stage _____ (three/four).

55. (Table 13.3) In postconventional reasoning, emphasis is on _____ _____ , such as _____-_____ (stage five) and _____-_____ (stage six).

56. One criticism of Kohlberg's theory is that
    it does not take _____ or
    _____ differences into account.

APPLICATION:

57. During a neighborhood game of baseball, Sam
    insists that Bobby cannot take another swing at
    the bat following his third strike because "that's
    the rule." Sam is evidently thinking about this
    issue at Kohlberg's _____
    stage of moral reasoning.

Progress Test 1

Multiple-Choice Questions

Circle your answers to the following questions
and check them with the answers at the end of
the chapter. If your answer is incorrect, read the
explanation for why it is incorrect and then consult
the text.

1. Between 9 and 11 years of age, children are likely
   to demonstrate moral reasoning at which of
   Kohlberg's stages?
   a. preconventional
   b. conventional
   c. postconventional
   d. It is impossible to predict based only on a
      child's age.

2. Which of the following is NOT among the highest
   values of middle childhood?
   a. protect your friends
   b. don't tell adults what really goes on
   c. try not to be too different from other children
   d. don't depend on others

3. The best strategy for helping children who are
   at risk of developing serious psychological
   problems because of multiple stresses would be
   to
   a. obtain assistance from a psychiatrist.
   b. increase the child's competencies or social
      supports.
   c. change the household situation.
   d. reduce the peer group's influence.

4. The culture of children refers to
   a. the specific habits, styles, and values that
      reflect the rules and rituals of children.
   b. a child's tendency to assess abilities by
      measuring them against those of peers.

   c. children's ability to understand social
      interactions.
   d. all of these factors.

5. Girls who are bullies are often above average
   in _____ , whereas boys
   who are bullies are often above average in

   _____ .

   a. size; verbal assertiveness
   b. verbal assertiveness; size
   c. intelligence; aggressiveness
   d. aggressiveness; intelligence

6. A family that consists of two parents, at least one
   with biological children from a previous union,
   and any children the two adults have together is
   called a(n) _____ family.
   a. extended
   b. polygamous
   c. nuclear
   d. blended

7. Compared with average or popular children,
   rejected children tend to be
   a. brighter and more competitive.
   b. affluent and "stuck-up."
   c. economically disadvantaged.
   d. socially immature.

8. School-age children advance in their awareness of
   classmates' opinions and accomplishments. These
   abilities are best described as advances in their
   a. social comparison.
   b. social cognition.
   c. metacognition.
   d. pragmatic intelligence.

9. Resilience is characterized by all but which of the
   following characteristics?
   a. Resilience is a dynamic trait that varies with
      the situation.
   b. Resilience represents a positive adaptation to
      stress.
   c. Resilience involves passive endurance.
   d. Resilience is the capacity to develop optimally
      despite significant adversity.

10. With their expanding social world and
    developing cognition, children may be stressed
    by a variety of disturbing problems. Which of the
    following is NOT a means by which children can
    overcome these problems?
    a. school success
    b. healthy diet
    c. religious faith
    d. after-school achievements

11. Erikson's crisis of the school years is that of
   a. industry versus inferiority.
   b. acceptance versus rejection.
   c. initiative versus guilt.
   d. male versus female.

12. Bully-victims are typically children who would be categorized as
   a. aggressive-rejected.
   b. withdrawn-rejected.
   c. isolated-rejected.
   d. immature-rejected.

13. Bullying during middle childhood
   a. occurs only in certain cultures.
   b. is more common in rural schools than in urban schools.
   c. seems to be universal.
   d. is rarely a major problem because other children usually intervene to prevent it from getting out of hand.

14. During middle childhood, children become _____ selective about their friends, and their friendship groups become _____ .
   a. less; larger
   b. less; smaller
   c. more; larger
   d. more; smaller

15. Erikson's crisis of industry versus inferiority corresponds to which of Freud's psychosexual stages?
   a. genital stage
   b. oral stage
   c. anal stage
   d. period of latency

True or False Items

Write T (true) or F (false) on the line in front of each statement.

_____ 1. As they evaluate themselves according to increasingly complex self-theories, school-age children typically experience a rise in self-esteem.

_____ 2. During middle childhood, acceptance by the peer group is valued more than having a close friend.

_____ 3. Children from low-income homes often experience more stress.

_____ 4. Bullies and their victims are usually of the same gender.

_____ 5. Children who are labeled *resilient* demonstrate an ability to adapt positively in all situations.

_____ 6. The primary advantage of the stepparent structure is financial.

_____ 7. Withdrawn-rejected and aggressive-rejected children both have problems regulating their emotions.

_____ 8. Most aggressive-rejected children clearly interpret other people's words and behavior.

_____ 9. School-age children are less able than younger children to cope with chronic stresses.

_____ 10. Children's ability to cope with stress may depend as much on their appraisal of events as on the objective nature of the actual events.

_____ 11. Friendship circles become wider as children grow older.

Progress Test 2

Progress Test 2 should be completed during a final chapter review. Answer the following questions after you thoroughly understand the correct answers for the Chapter Review and Progress Test 1.

Multiple-Choice Questions

1. Children who are categorized as _____ are particularly vulnerable to bullying.
   a. aggressive-rejected
   b. passive-aggressive
   c. withdrawn-rejected
   d. passive-rejected

2. Environmental influences on children's traits that result from contact with different teachers and peer groups are classified as
   a. shared influences.
   b. nonshared influences.
   c. epigenetic influences.
   d. nuclear influences.

3. Compared with parents in other family structures, married parents tend to be
   a. wealthier.
   b. better educated.
   c. healthier.
   d. all of these things.

4. More than half of all school-age children live in
   a. one-parent families.
   b. blended families.
   c. extended families.
   d. nuclear families.

5. Typically, children in middle childhood experience a decrease in self-esteem as a result of
   a. a wavering self-theory.
   b. increased awareness of personal shortcomings and failures.
   c. a lack of emotional regulation.
   d. difficulties with members of the opposite sex.

6. A 10-year-old's sense of self-esteem is most strongly influenced by his or her
   a. peers.
   b. siblings.
   c. mother.
   d. father.

7. Which of the following most accurately describes how friendships change during the school years?
   a. Friendships become more casual and less intense.
   b. Older children demand less of their friends.
   c. Older children change friends more often.
   d. Close friendships increasingly involve members of the same sex, ethnicity, and socioeconomic status.

8. Which of the following is an accurate statement about school-age bullies?
   a. They are socially perceptive but not empathic.
   b. They usually have a few admiring friends.
   c. They are adept at being aggressive.
   d. All of these statements are accurate.

9. One effective intervention to prevent bullying in the school is to
   a. change the culture through community-wide and classroom education.
   b. target one victimized child at a time.
   c. target each bully as an individual.
   d. focus on improving the academic skills of all children in the school.

10. Which of the following most accurately describes the relationship between family income and child development?
    a. Adequate family income allows children to own whatever possessions help them to feel accepted.
    b. Because parents need not argue about money, household wealth provides harmony and stability.
    c. The basic family functions are enhanced by adequate family income.
    d. Family income is not correlated with child development.

11. Two factors that most often help the child cope well with stress are social support and
    a. social comparison.
    b. religious faith.
    c. remedial education.
    d. referral to mental health professionals.

12. An 8-year-old child who measures her achievements by measuring them against those of her friends is engaging in social
    a. cognition.
    b. comparison.
    c. reinforcement.
    d. modeling.

13. In Kohlberg's theory, moral reasoning that is based on seeking rewards and avoiding punishment is called
    a. universal
    b. postconventional
    c. preconventional
    d. conventional

14. According to Freud, the period between ages 6 and 11 when a child's sexual drives are relatively quiet is the
    a. phallic stage.
    b. genital stage.
    c. period of latency.
    d. period of industry versus inferiority.

15. Children who are forced to cope with one serious ongoing stress (for example, poverty or large family size) are
    a. more likely to develop serious psychiatric problems.
    b. no more likely to develop problems.
    c. more likely to develop intense, destructive friendships.
    d. less likely to be accepted by their peer group.

Matching Items

Match each term or concept with its corresponding description or definition.

Terms or Concepts

_____ **1.** relational bullying

_____ **2.** nuclear family

_____ **3.** social comparison

_____ **4.** provocative victim

_____ **5.** foster family

_____ **6.** aggressive-rejected

_____ **7.** withdrawn-rejected

_____ **8.** physical bullying

_____ **9.** effortful control

_____ **10.** blended family

_____ **11.** extended family

Descriptions or Definitions

a. another term for a bully-victim

b. adults living with their children from previous marriages as well as their own biological children

c. a father, a mother, and the biological children they have together

d. used by boy bullies

e. children who are disliked because of their confrontational nature

f. evaluating one's abilities by measuring them against those of other children

g. three or more generations of biologically related individuals living together

h. children who are disliked because of timid, anxious behavior

i. used by girl bullies

j. a family in which one or more children are temporarily cared for by an adult individual or couple to whom they are not biologically related

k. the ability to regulate one's emotions

Key Terms

Using your own words, write a brief definition or explanation of each of the following terms on a separate piece of paper.

1. industry vs. inferiority
2. latency
3. social comparison
4. resilience
5. family structure
6. family function
7. nuclear family
8. single-parent family
9. extended family
10. polygamous family
11. child culture
12. aggressive-rejected
13. withdrawn-rejected
14. bullying
15. bully-victim
16. preconventional moral reasoning
17. conventional moral reasoning
18. postconventional moral reasoning

ANSWERS

CHAPTER REVIEW

1. industry versus inferiority
2. latency; quiet; submerged
3. more; dips; social comparison
4. effortful control; achievement; aggression; self-esteem; is not; modest
5. resilient; dynamic; positive
6. hassles
7. interpretation; parentification; friends; skills; activities
8. shared; nonshared
9. genes; nonshared
10. Erik Erikson's theory of development. The question describes what is, for Erikson, the crisis of middle childhood: industry versus inferiority.
11. **b.** is the answer.
12. **d.** is the answer.
13. **d.** is the answer. More important than marital discord, income, or illness is the child's interpretation of the situation. If the child blames himself or herself for the problems, psychic and academic problems are more likely to occur.

14. **d.** is the answer. Self-esteem decreases throughout middle childhood.

15. **b.** is the answer. Social comparison becomes important for these children as they evaluate their competencies.

16. genetic; environmental

17. family structure

18. works to meet the needs of its members

19. necessities; learning; self-respect; relationships; harmony; stability

20. genetic and legal relationships among related people living in the same household

    a. extended family

    b. nuclear family

    c. single-parent family

    d. polygamous family

    e. adoptive family

    f. stepparent family

    g. grandparents alone

    h. two same-sex parents

21. nuclear; 31 percent; single-parent

22. decreases; education

Parents in a nuclear family tend to be wealthier, better educated, and healthier than other parents. Shared parenting decreases the risk of maltreatment.

23. parental alliance; maltreatment

24. can function well; skipped-generation

25. conflict; child rearing

26. lack of stability

27. correlates; decreases; family-stress; stress; excel

28. **d.** is the answer. Even within the same family, siblings experience nonshared environments.

29. peers; more

30. child culture; do not necessarily mirror

31. Throughout the world; independence

32. values; rituals

33. more

34. intense; intimate; do not change; harder

35. converse; play more active games

36. interests; values; backgrounds

37. culture; cohort

38. neglected; aggressive-rejected; withdrawn-rejected

Aggressive-rejected children are disliked because of their antagonistic and confrontational behavior, while withdrawn-rejected children are timid, withdrawn,

and anxious. Both types often misinterpret social situations, lack emotional regulation, and are likely to be mistreated at home.

39. systematic; repeated; physical; verbal; relational; cyberbullying

40. have; perceptive; empathy

41. withdrawn; aggressive; bully-victims

42. size; sharp-tongued; physical; verbal

43. brain abnormality; genetic; insecure attachment; home; discipline; siblings; aggressive; Peers; relational

44. ineffective

45. whole

46. **d.** is the answer.

47. aggressive-rejected. Children such as Ramón tend to misread social situations and lack emotional regulation.

48. **c.** is the answer. In middle childhood, friendship becomes more selective and intimate, and children choose each other because of similar interests, values, and backgrounds.

49. withdrawn-rejected. Withdrawn-rejected children are most likely to become bully-victims. Like aggressive-rejected children, they tend to misread social situations and lack emotional regulation.

50. **b.** is the answer. Verbal bullying is one of the three major types of bullying (physical and relational are the other two types of bullying).

51. **d.** is the answer. Surprisingly, children who are different because of obesity or looks, for example, are not necessarily singled out for bullying.

52. Lawrence Kohlberg; preconventional; conventional; postconventional

53. rewards; punishments; 1; 2

54. social rules; 4; 3

55. moral principles; social contracts; universal ethical principles

56. cultural; gender

57. conventional. During Stage Four, law and order, being a proper citizen means obeying the rules set down by society.

PROGRESS TEST 1

Multiple-Choice Questions

1. **b.** is the answer.

2. **d.** is the answer.

3. **b.** is the answer.

4. **a.** is the answer.

b. This is social comparison.

c. This is social cognition.

5. **b.** is the answer.

6. **d.** is the answer.

a. In an extended family, children live with grandparents or other relatives.

b. In a polygamous family, one man has several wives.

c. A nuclear family has two parents and their biological children.

7. **d.** is the answer.

8. **b.** is the answer.

a. Social comparison is the tendency to assess one's abilities by measuring them against those of others, especially those of one's peers.

c. Metacognition, which is not discussed in this chapter, is the ability to monitor and adjust one's cognitive processes.

d. This term was not discussed in the chapter.

9. **b.** is the answer. Resilience involves positive adaptation to stress.

10. **b.** is the answer.

11. **a.** is the answer.

12. **a.** is the answer.

b. Withdrawn-rejected children are often the victims of bullies, but rarely are bullies themselves.

c. & d. There are no such categories.

13. **c.** is the answer.

d. In fact, children rarely intervene, unless a best friend is involved.

14. **d.** is the answer.

15. **d.** is the answer.

True or False Items

1. F   In fact, just the opposite is true.

2. F   In fact, just the opposite is true.

3. T

4. T

5. F   A given child is not resilient in all situations.

6. T

7. T

8. F   Just the opposite is true: They tend to misinterpret other people's words and behavior.

9. F   Because of the coping strategies that many school-age children develop, they are better able than younger children to cope with stress.

10. T

11. F   Friendship circles become narrower because friendships become more intense and intimate.

PROGRESS TEST 2

Multiple-Choice Questions

1. **c.** is the answer.

a. These are usually bullies.

b. & d. These are not subcategories of rejected children.

2. **b.** is the answer.

a. Shared influences are those that occur because children are raised by the same parents in the same home, although children raised in the same home do not necessarily share the same home environment.

c. & d. There are no such influences.

3. **d.** is the answer.

4. **d.** is the answer.

5. **b.** is the answer.

a. This tends to promote, rather than reduce, self-esteem.

c. Emotional regulation improves during middle childhood.

d. This issue becomes more important during adolescence.

6. **a.** is the answer.

7. **d.** is the answer.

a., b., & c. In fact, just the opposite is true of friendship during middle childhood.

8. **d.** is the answer.

9. **a.** is the answer.

10. **c.** is the answer.

11. **b.** is the answer.

12. **b.** is the answer.

13. **d.** is the answer.

14. **c.** is the answer.

15. **b.** is the answer.

c. & d. The text did not discuss how stress influences friendship or peer acceptance.

Matching Items

1. i	5. j	9. k
2. c	6. e	10. b
3. f	7. h	11. g
4. a	8. d	

KEY TERMS

1. According to Erikson, the crisis of middle childhood is **industry versus inferiority,** in which children try to master many skills and develop views of themselves as either competent and industrious or incompetent and inferior.

2. In Freud's theory, middle childhood is a period of **latency,** during which emotional drives are quieter and unconscious sexual conflicts are submerged.

3. **Social comparison** is the tendency to assess one's abilities, achievements, social status, and other attributes by measuring them against those of others, especially those of one's peers.

4. **Resilience** is the capacity to adapt positively despite adversity and to overcome serious stress.

5. **Family structure** refers to the legal and genetic relationships among relatives in the same household.

6. **Family function** refers to the ways families work to meet the needs of its members, which for children is meeting their basic material needs, encouraging them to learn, helping them to develop self-respect, nurturing friendships, and fostering harmony and stability.

7. A **nuclear family** consists of two parents and their mutual biological offspring under age 18.

8. A **single-parent family** consists of one parent and his or her biological children under age 18.

9. An **extended family** consists of three or more generations living in one household.

10. A **polygamous family** consists of one man with several wives, each bearing his children.

11. Child culture refers to the specific habits, styles, and values that reflect the rules and rituals of children.

12. **Aggressive-rejected** children are rejected by the peer group because of their antagonistic, confrontational behavior.

13. **Withdrawn-rejected** children are shunned by the peer group because of their timid, withdrawn, and anxious behavior.

14. **Bullying** is the repeated, systematic effort to inflict harm through physical, verbal, or social attacks on a weaker person.

15. A **bully-victim** is a bully who has also been a victim of bullying; also called *provocative victim.*

16. **Preconventional moral reasoning** is Kohlberg's first level of moral reasoning, emphasizing rewards and punishments.

17. **Conventional moral reasoning** is Kohlberg's second level of moral reasoning, emphasizing social rules.

18. **Postconventional moral reasoning** is Kohlberg's third level of moral reasoning, emphasizing moral principles.

14 CHAPTER

Adolescence: Biosocial Development

Chapter Overview

Between the ages of 11 and 18, young people cross the great divide between childhood and adulthood. This crossing encompasses all three domains of development—biosocial, cognitive, and psychosocial. Chapter 14 focuses on the dramatic changes that occur in the biosocial domain, beginning with puberty and the growth spurt. The biosocial metamorphosis of the adolescent is discussed in detail, with emphasis on factors that affect the age of puberty, growth, brain development, and sexual maturation.

In discussing the adolescent's sexual maturation, the text describes the problems that may result from this newfound sexuality.

What Will You Know?

The text chapter should be studied one section at a time. Before you read, preview each section by skimming it, noting headings and boldface items. Then read the sections, one at a time, keeping these questions in mind.

1. Since puberty begins anytime from age 8 to 14, how can onset be predicted for a particular child?
2. Why do some teenagers starve themselves and others overeat?
3. Since adolescent sexual impulses are powerful and inevitable, why is there so much variation in rates of teen pregnancy and STIs?

Chapter Review

When you have finished reading the chapter, work through the material that follows to review it. Completing the sentences and answering the questions will enable you to answer the "What Have You Learned?" questions at the end of the text

chapter. Scattered throughout the Chapter Review are Study Tips, which explain how best to learn a difficult concept, and Think About It discussions and Applications, which help you to know how well you understand the material. Check your understanding of the material by consulting the answers at the end of the chapter. Do not continue with the next section until you understand each answer. If you need to, review or reread the appropriate section in the textbook before continuing.

Puberty Begins

1. The period of rapid physical growth and sexual maturation that ends childhood and brings the young person to adult size, shape, and sexual potential is called _____ .
The physical changes of puberty typically are complete _____ (how long?) after puberty begins. Although puberty begins at various ages, the _____ is almost always the same.

2. The average girl experiences her first menstrual period, called _____ , at age _____ .

3. The average boy experiences his first ejaculation of seminal fluid, called _____ , at age _____ .

4. Puberty begins when biochemical signals from the _____ trigger hormone production in the _____ _____ , which in turn triggers increased hormone production by the _____ _____ .
This route is called the _____ .

5. Another route, called the _____ _____ , affects the body's entire shape and functioning. The hormone _____ causes the gonads, the _____ in males and the _____ in females, to dramatically increase their production of sex hormones, especially _____ in girls and _____ in boys.

6. Emotional extremes and sexual urges _____ (usually do/do not usually) increase during adolescence. This is due in part to the increasingly high levels of hormones such as _____ , a type of estrogen, and _____ , a type of androgen.

7. Not only are brain and body affected by hormones, but _____ is as well. In addition, thoughts and emotions _____ hormonal changes.

8. The natural rhythms of every living creature, called _____ , are altered by puberty because hormones cause a "phase delay" in _____–_____ patterns. Day–night cycles of biological activity that occur approximately every 24 hours are called _____ _____ . Individuals who are naturally more alert in the evening than in the morning possess the trait called _____ . This is more common in _____ (males/females).

9. Normal children begin to notice pubertal changes between the ages of _____ and _____ . Two-thirds of the variation in the age of puberty is caused by _____ . Girls are about _____ (how many?) years ahead of boys in height.

10. The amount of _____ _____ affects the onset of puberty. Urban areas with the highest rates of childhood obesity also have the _____ (earliest/latest) ages of puberty. This is particularly true for _____ (boys/girls).

11. The _____ _____ refers to the long-term upward or downward direction of a statistical measurement. An example is the earlier growth of children over the last two centuries as _____ and _____ have improved. This trend _____ (continues/has stopped) in developed nations. Puberty that begins before age 8 is called _____ _____ .

12. One hormone that has been implicated in the onset of puberty is _____ , which stimulates the appetite.

13. Another influence on the age of puberty is _____ .

14. Research suggests that family stress may _____ (accelerate/delay) the onset of puberty.

15. Stress may cause production of the hormones that cause _____ . Support for this hypothesis comes from a study showing that early puberty correlated with _____ .

16. (A View from Science) An evolutionary explanation of the relationship between stress and puberty is that ancestral females growing up in stressful environments may have increased their _____ _____ by accelerating physical maturation.

17. For girls, _____ (early/late) maturation may be especially troublesome.

Describe several common problems and developmental hazards experienced by early-maturing girls.

18. For boys, _____ (early/late/ both early and late) maturation may be difficult. _____ (Early/Late) maturing boys are more _____ , _____–_____ ,

and alcohol-abusing. _____
(Early/Late) maturing boys tend to be more
anxious, depressed, and afraid of sex.

_____

STUDY TIP To consolidate your understanding of
the major physical changes that accompany puberty,
list, in order, the major physical changes of puberty.

19. Girls: _____

_____

Boys: _____

_____

_____

APPLICATIONS:

20. I am the hormone that causes the gonads to
dramatically increase their production of sex
hormones. I am _____ .

21. Which of the following students is likely to be
the most popular in a sixth-grade class?
   a. Vicki, the most sexually mature girl in the
      class
   b. Sandra, the tallest girl in the class
   c. Brad, who is at the top of the class scholasti-
      cally
   d. Dan, the tallest boy in the class

22. Regarding the effects of early and late maturation on boys and girls, which of the following is
NOT true?
   a. Late-maturing boys are more likely to rebel
      against laws.
   b. Early puberty that leads to romantic relation-
      ships often leads to stress and depression
      among both girls and boys.
   c. Early-maturing girls may be drawn into
      involvement with older boys.
   d. Late puberty is often difficult for boys.

23. Monica is 16 years old. Her parents are divorced
and she lives with her mother in a city. It is most
likely that she will experience puberty
_____ than other teens, perhaps
as a result of _____ .
   a. earlier; greater stress
   b. later; greater stress
   c. earlier; poor nutrition
   d. later; poor nutrition

24. I am the sex hormone that is secreted in greater
amounts by females than males. I am

_____ .

25. Of the following teenagers, those most likely to
be distressed about their physical development
are
   a. late-maturing girls.
   b. early-maturing girls.
   c. early-maturing boys.
   d. girls or boys who masturbate.

Growth and Nutrition

26. A major _____ spurt occurs
in late childhood and early adolescence,
during which growth proceeds from the
_____ (core/extremities)
to the _____ (core/
extremities). At the same time, children begin to
_____ (gain/lose) weight at a
relatively rapid rate.

27. The amount of weight gain an individual
experiences depends on several factors, including

_____ , _____ ,

_____ , _____ ,

and _____ .

28. During the growth spurt, a greater percentage of
fat is retained by _____ (males/
females).

29. About a year after the height and weight changes
occur, a period of _____
increase occurs, causing the pudginess and
clumsiness of an earlier age to disappear. In
boys, this increase is particularly notable in the

_____ .

30. Internal organs also grow during puberty. The
_____ increase in size and
capacity, the _____ doubles
in size, pulse rate _____
(increases/decreases), and blood pressure
_____ (increases/decreases).
These changes increase the adolescent's physical

_____ .

31. During puberty, one organ system, the
_____ system, decreases in size,
making teenagers _____ (more/
less) susceptible to respiratory ailments.

32. Most teenagers _____ (do/
do not) consume the recommended daily dose
of iron, calcium, zinc, and other minerals.
There is a direct link between deficient diets
and the availability of _____
_____ in schools. Also,
_____-_____
establishments cluster around high schools.

33. Another reason for dietary deficiencies
is concern about _____
_____ , defined as a person's
idea of how _____ .

34. In an attempt to improve body image, many girls
_____ _____
or take _____
_____ , and many boys take
_____ .

35. The disorder characterized by self-starvation is
_____ _____ .
This disorder is suspected when a person's
_____ _____
_____ is _____
(what number?) or lower, or if the person loses
more than _____ (what percent?)
of body weight within a month or two.

36. A more common eating disorder is
_____ _____ ,
which is diagnosed when young adults
_____ compulsively,
and then _____ through
vomiting or laxatives. A new disorder called
_____ _____
_____ is indicated when
the sufferer does not _____
but feels out of control, distressed, and
_____ .

THINK ABOUT IT To underscore the prevalence of
nutritional deficiencies during adolescence, evaluate
your own dietary consumption of iron, calcium, and
zinc for a few days. How do your results compare
with recommended minimum levels of consumption
for these minerals?

APPLICATION:
37. Thirteen-year-old Kristin is more likely to
   a. drink too much milk.
   b. eat more than five servings of fruit per day.
   c. choose expensive foods over inexpensive
      ones.
   d. be iron deficient.

THINK ABOUT IT At the beginning of puberty,
many young people want to know whether they will
be short or tall, like one of their parents, or closer
in height to their grandparents. The answer is that
their full adult height will probably fall somewhere
in between that of their parents. One frequently
used rule of thumb is to add the heights of both
parents, divide by two, then add 3 inches for a boy
or subtract 3 inches for a girl. The result is said to be
correct within 2 inches about 95 percent of the time.
How well does this formula work in your case?

Brain Development

38. Different parts of the brain grow at
_____ (the same/different)
rates. The emotional control center, called the
_____ _____ ,
matures _____ (before/after) the
_____ _____ ,
where planning, _____
regulation, and _____ control
occur.

39. Early puberty _____ (increases/
decreases/has no effect on) emotional surges.
This is because the _____
of puberty directly target the brain's
_____ . The emotional control
areas of the brain are not fully developed until
_____ .

40. The benefits of adolescent brain development
include increased _____ and
slower _____ , which make
reactions much faster. The growth of neural
_____ in the brain also enhances
_____ development.

Sexual Maturation

41. Changes in _____
_____ _____
involve the sex organs that are directly involved

in reproduction. By the end of puberty, reproduction _____ (is/is still not) possible.

42. Sexual features other than those associated with reproduction are referred to as

_____ _____

_____ .

Describe the major pubertal changes in the secondary sex characteristics of both sexes.

43. Although sex hormones trigger thoughts about sexual intimacy, sexual behavior among teens reflects _____ ,

_____ , and

_____ more than biology.

44. Sex has become less problematic among adolescents, as seen from the following: teen _____ overall have decreased, the use of _____ has risen, and the teen _____ rate has decreased.

45. A major developmental risk for sexually active adolescent girls is _____ . If the girl is under 16, she is at increased risk of many complications, including _____ . Babies born to young parents have higher rates of

_____ , _____ ,

and _____ problems lifelong.

46. Any sexual activity between a juvenile and an older person is considered _____

_____ _____ .

This is more common in _____

_____ than at any other time.

47. _____ (Girls/Boys) are particularly vulnerable to child sexual abuse.

48. Worldwide, sexually active teens have higher rates of diseases caused by sexual contact, called

_____ _____

_____ , than any other age group.

49. The most frequently reported STI is

_____ . Another STI, called

_____ _____ ,

has no immediate consequences but later increases a female's risk of _____

_____ and death.

APPLICATIONS:

50. Calvin, the class braggart, boasts that because his beard has begun to grow, he is more virile than his male classmates. Jacob informs him that
    a. the tendency to grow facial and body hair has nothing to do with virility.
    b. beard growth is determined by heredity.
    c. girls also develop some facial hair and more noticeable hair on their arms and legs, so it is clearly not a sign of masculinity.
    d. all of these statements are true.

51. Eleven-year-old Linda, who has just begun to experience the first signs of puberty, laments, "When will the agony of puberty be over?" You tell her that the major events of puberty typically end about _____ after the first visible signs appear.

Progress Test 1

Multiple-Choice Questions

Circle your answers to the following questions and check them with the answers at the end of the chapter. If your answer is incorrect, read the explanation for why it is incorrect and then consult the text.

1. Which of the following most accurately describes the sequence of pubertal development in girls?
   a. breasts and pubic hair; growth spurt in which fat is deposited on hips and buttocks; first menstrual period; ovulation
   b. growth spurt; breasts and pubic hair; first menstrual period; ovulation
   c. first menstrual period; breasts and pubic hair; growth spurt; ovulation
   d. breasts and pubic hair; growth spurt; ovulation; first menstrual period

2. Although both sexes grow rapidly during adolescence, boys typically gain more than girls in their
   a. muscle strength.   c. internal organ growth.
   b. body fat.   d. lymphoid system.

3. For girls, the first readily observable sign of the onset of puberty is
   a. the onset of breast growth.
   b. the appearance of facial, body, and pubic hair.
   c. a change in the shape of the eyes.
   d. a lengthening of the torso.

4. More than any other group in the population, adolescent girls are likely to have
   a. asthma.
   b. acne.
   c. anemia.
   d. testosterone deficiency.

5. The HPA axis is the
   a. route followed by many hormones to regulate stress, growth, sleep, and appetite.
   b. pair of sex glands in humans.
   c. cascade of sex hormones in females and males.
   d. area of the brain that regulates the pituitary gland.

6. For males, the secondary sex characteristic that usually occurs last is
   a. breast enlargement.
   b. the appearance of facial hair.
   c. growth of the testes.
   d. the final growth of pubic hair.

7. For girls, the specific event that is taken to indicate fertility is _____; for boys, it is _____ .
   a. the growth of breast buds; voice deepening
   b. menarche; spermarche
   c. hip widening; the testosterone surge
   d. the growth spurt; pubic hair

8. The most significant hormonal changes of puberty include an increase of _____ in _____ and an increase of _____ in _____ .
   a. estrogen; boys; estradiol; girls
   b. estradiol; boys; testosterone; girls
   c. androgen; girls; estradiol; boys
   d. estradiol; girls; testosterone; boys

9. A child who is malnourished will likely
   a. begin menarche at a younger-than-average age.
   b. begin menarche later than the normal age range.
   c. never experience menarche.
   d. never experience spermarche.

10. Dr. Ramirez suspects Jennifer may be suffering from anorexia nervosa because her BMI is
    a. lower than 18.   c. higher than 25.
    b. lower than 25.   d. higher than 30.

11. Today, adolescence tends to begin _____ and end _____ .
    a. later biologically; later sociologically
    b. earlier biologically; later sociologically
    c. later sociologically; earlier biologically
    d. earlier sociologically; later biologically

12. Early physical growth and sexual maturation
    a. tend to be equally difficult for girls and boys.
    b. tend to be more difficult for boys than for girls.
    c. tend to be more difficult for girls than for boys.
    d. are easier for both girls and boys than late maturation.

13. Pubertal changes in growth and maturation typically are complete how long after puberty begins?
    a. one to two years
    b. two to three years
    c. four years
    d. The variation is too great to generalize.

14. The hypothalamus–pituitary–adrenal axis triggers
    a. puberty.
    b. the growth spurt.
    c. the development of sexual characteristics.
    d. all of these events.

15. One reason adolescents like intensity, excitement, and risk taking is that
    a. the limbic system matures faster than the prefrontal cortex.
    b. the prefrontal cortex matures faster than the limbic system.
    c. brain maturation is synchronous.
    d. puberty is occurring at a younger age today than in the past.

True or False Items

Write T (true) or F (false) on the line in front of each statement.

_____ 1. The secular trend is as strong today as ever.

_____ 2. During puberty, hormonal bursts lead to quick emotional extremes.

_____ 3. The first indicator of reproductive potential in males is menarche.

_____ 4. Lung capacity, heart size, and blood pressure increase significantly during adolescence.

_____ 5. Puberty generally begins sometime between ages 8 and 14.

_____ 6. Girls are about two years ahead of boys in height as well as sexually and hormonally.

_____ 7. During the growth spurt, peak height usually precedes peak weight.

_____ 8. Only adolescent girls suffer from anemia.

_____ 9. Early-maturing girls tend to have lower self-esteem.

_____ 10. Both the sequence and timing of pubertal events vary greatly from one young person to another.

Progress Test 2

Progress Test 2 should be completed during a final chapter review. Answer the following questions after you thoroughly understand the correct answers for the Chapter Review and Progress Test 1.

Multiple-Choice Questions

1. Which of the following is the correct sequence of pubertal events in boys?
   a. growth spurt, pubic hair, facial hair, first ejaculation, pubic hair, deepening of voice
   b. pubic hair, first ejaculation, growth spurt, deepening of voice, facial hair, pubic hair
   c. deepening of voice, pubic hair, growth spurt, facial hair, first ejaculation, pubic hair
   d. pubic hair, growth spurt, facial hair, deepening of voice, pubic hair, first ejaculation

2. Which of the following statements about adolescent physical development is NOT true?
   a. Hands and feet generally lengthen before arms and legs.
   b. Facial features usually grow before the head itself reaches adult size and shape.
   c. Oil, sweat, and odor glands become more active.
   d. The lymphoid system increases slightly in size, and the heart increases by nearly half.

3. In puberty, a hormone that increases markedly in girls (and only somewhat in boys) is
   a. estradiol.
   b. testosterone.
   c. androgen.
   d. menarche.

4. Nutritional deficiencies in adolescence are frequently the result of
   a. eating red meat.
   b. poor eating habits.
   c. menstruation.
   d. excessive exercise.

5. In females, puberty is typically marked by a(n)
   a. significant widening of the shoulders.
   b. significant widening of the hips.
   c. enlargement of the torso and upper chest.
   d. decrease in the size of the eyes and nose.

6. Nonreproductive sexual characteristics, such as the deepening of the voice and the development of breasts, are called
   a. gender-typed traits.
   b. primary sex characteristics.
   c. secondary sex characteristics.
   d. pubertal prototypes.

7. Puberty is initiated when hormones are released from the _____ , then from the _____ gland, and then from the adrenal glands and the _____ .
   a. hypothalamus; pituitary; gonads
   b. pituitary; gonads; hypothalamus
   c. gonads; pituitary; hypothalamus
   d. pituitary; hypothalamus; gonads

8. If a girl under age 15 becomes pregnant, she is at greater risk for
   a. a low-birthweight baby.
   b. high blood pressure.
   c. stillbirth.
   d. all of these conditions.

9. During adolescence, reactions become faster partly as a result of the brain's
   a. increased myelination and reduced inhibition.
   b. increased myelination and increased inhibition.
   c. decreased myelination and reduced inhibition.
   d. decreased myelination and increased inhibition.

10. The HPG axis is the
    a. route followed by many hormones to affect the body's shape and functioning.
    b. pair of sex glands in humans.
    c. cascade of sex hormones in females and males.
    d. area of the brain that regulates the pituitary gland.

11. An example of the secular trend is the
    a. complex link between pubertal hormones and emotions.
    b. effect of chronic stress on pubertal hormones.
    c. earlier growth of children due to improved nutrition and medical care.
    d. effect of malnutrition on the onset of puberty.

12. Puberty is *most accurately* defined as the period
    a. of rapid physical growth that occurs during adolescence.
    b. during which sexual maturation is attained.
    c. of rapid physical growth and sexual maturation that ends childhood.
    d. during which adolescents establish identities separate from their parents.

13. Which of the following does NOT typically occur during puberty?
    a. The lungs increase in size and capacity.
    b. The heart's size and rate of beating increase.
    c. Blood pressure increases.
    d. The lymphoid system decreases in size.

14. Teenagers' susceptibility to respiratory ailments typically _____ during adolescence, due to a(n) _____ in the size of the lymphoid system.
    a. increases; increase
    b. increases; decrease
    c. decreases; increase
    d. decreases; decrease

Matching Items

Match each term or concept with its corresponding description or definition.

Terms or Concepts

_____ 1. puberty
_____ 2. gonadotropin-releasing hormone (GnRH)
_____ 3. testosterone
_____ 4. estradiol
_____ 5. growth spurt
_____ 6. primary sex characteristics
_____ 7. menarche
_____ 8. spermarche
_____ 9. secondary sex characteristics
_____ 10. body image
_____ 11. anorexia nervosa
_____ 12. bulimia nervosa

Descriptions or Definitions

a. onset of menstruation
b. period of rapid physical growth and sexual maturation that ends childhood
c. an affliction characterized by self-starvation
d. hormone that causes the gonads to enlarge and increase their production of sex hormones
e. hormone that increases dramatically in girls during puberty
f. first sign is increased bone length
g. attitude toward one's physical appearance
h. an affliction characterized by binge–purge eating
i. the sex organs involved in reproduction
j. first ejaculation containing sperm
k. hormone that increases dramatically in boys during puberty
l. physical characteristics not involved in reproduction

Key Terms

Using your own words, write a brief definition or explanation of each of the following terms on a separate piece of paper.

1. puberty
2. menarche
3. spermarche
4. hormone
5. pituitary
6. adrenal glands
7. HPA axis
8. gonads

9. HPG axis

10. estradiol

11. testosterone

12. circadian rhythm

13. secular trend

14. leptin

15. growth spurt

16. body image

17. anorexia nervosa

18. bulimia nervosa

19. primary sex characteristics

20. secondary sex characteristics

21. child sexual abuse

22. sexually transmitted infections (STIs)

ANSWERS

CHAPTER REVIEW

1. puberty; four years; sequence

2. menarche; 12 years, 8 months

3. spermarche; (just under) 13

4. hypothalamus; pituitary gland; adrenal glands; HPA axis

5. HPG axis; GnRH (gonadotropin-releasing hormone); testes; ovaries; estradiol; testosterone

6. usually do; estradiol; testosterone

7. behavior; cause

8. biorhythms; sleep–wake; circadian rhythms; eveningness; males

9. 8; 13; genes; two

10. body fat; earliest; girls

11. secular trend; nutrition; medicine; has stopped; precocious puberty

12. leptin

13. stress

14. accelerate

15. puberty; harsh parenting in early childhood

16. reproductive success

17. early

Early-maturing girls may be teased about their developing breasts. They tend to have older boyfriends, which may lead to drug and alcohol use; they have lower self-esteem, more depression, and poorer body image than their classmates do; they exercise less; they engage in sexual activity, which may result in teenage parenthood; and they have a greater risk of violent victimization.

18. both early and late; Early; aggressive; law-breaking; Late

19. Girls: onset of breast growth, initial pubic hair, peak growth spurt, widening of the hips, first menstrual period, first ovulation, voice lowers, visible facial hair, completion of pubic-hair growth, and final breast development

    Boys: increased production of testosterone, growth of the testes and scrotum, initial pubic hair, growth of the penis, first ejaculation of seminal fluid, peak height spurt, peak muscle and organ growth, voice deepening, visible facial hair, and completion of pubic-hair growth

20. GnRH

21. d. is the answer. Early-maturing boys benefit more than early-maturing girls or late-maturing boys.

22. a. is the answer. Late-maturing boys tend to be more anxious, depressed, and afraid of sex.

23. a. is the answer. Surprisingly, stress often results in an earlier onset of puberty.

24. estradiol

25. b. is the answer. Early-maturing girls tend to have lower self-esteem, more depression, and poorer body image than late-maturing girls.

26. growth; extremities; core; gain

27. gender; heredity; diet; exercise; hormones

28. females

29. muscle; arms

30. lungs; heart; decreases; increases; endurance

31. lymphoid; less

32. do not; vending machines; fast-food

33. body image; his or her body looks

34. eat erratically; diet pills; steroids

35. anorexia nervosa; body mass index; 18; 10

36. bulimia nervosa; overeat; purge; binge eating disorder; purge; depressed

37. d. is the answer. Many teenage girls, and some boys, suffer from anemia (iron deficiency).

38. different; limbic system; before; prefrontal cortex; emotional; impulse

39. increases; hormones; amygdala; adulthood

40. myelination; inhibition; synapses; moral

41. primary sex characteristics; is

42. secondary sex characteristics

Males grow taller than females and become wider at the shoulders than at the hips. Females become wider at the hips, and their breasts begin to develop. Many boys experience some temporary breast enlargement.

43. gender; culture; cohort

44. births; contraception; abortion
45. pregnancy; spontaneous abortion, high blood pressure, stillbirth, preterm birth, and a low-birthweight baby; medical; educational; social
46. child sexual abuse; early puberty
47. Girls
48. sexually transmitted infections
49. Chlamydia; human papillomavirus (HPV); uterine cancer
50. **a.** is the answer.
51. 4 years

PROGRESS TEST 1

Multiple-Choice Questions

1. **a.** is the answer.
2. **a.** is the answer.

    b. Girls gain more body fat than boys do.

    c. & d. The text does not indicate that these are different for boys and girls.

3. **a.** is the answer.
4. **c.** is the answer. This is because each menstrual period depletes some iron from the body.
5. **a.** is the answer.

    b. This describes the gonads.

    c. These include estradiol and testosterone.

    d. This is the hypothalamus.

6. **d.** is the answer.
7. **b.** is the answer.
8. **d.** is the answer.
9. **b.** is the answer.
10. **a.** is the answer.

    b. This is a healthy BMI.

    c. & d. These BMIs are associated with being overweight.

11. **b.** is the answer.
12. **c.** is the answer.
13. **c.** is the answer.
14. **d.** is the answer.
15. **a.** is the answer.

    c. Brain maturation is asynchronous.

    d. This may be true, but it doesn't explain why adolescents have always liked intensity and excitement.

True or False Items

1. F   The secular trend has stopped in developed nations.
2. T
3. F   The first indicator of reproductive potential in males is ejaculation of seminal fluid containing sperm (spermarche). Menarche (the first menstrual period) is the first indication of reproductive potential in females.
4. T
5. T
6. F   Hormonally and sexually, girls are ahead by only a few months.
7. F   During the growth spurt, peak weight usually precedes peak height.
8. F   Boys also suffer from anemia, especially if they engage in physical labor or competitive sports.
9. T
10. F   Although there is great variation in the timing of pubertal events, the sequence is very similar for all young people.

PROGRESS TEST 2

Multiple-Choice Questions

1. **b.** is the answer.
2. **d.** is the answer. During adolescence, the lymphoid system *decreases* in size and the heart *doubles* in size.
3. **a.** is the answer.

    b. Testosterone increases markedly in boys.

    c. Testosterone is the best known of the androgens (the general category of male hormones).

    d. Menarche is the first menstrual period.

4. **b.** is the answer.
5. **b.** is the answer.

    a. The shoulders of males tend to widen during puberty.

    c. The torso typically lengthens during puberty.

    d. The eyes and nose *increase* in size during puberty.

6. **c.** is the answer.

    a. Although not a term used in the textbook, a gender-typed trait is one that is typical of one sex but not the other.

    b. Primary sex characteristics are those involving the reproductive organs.

d. This is not a term used by developmental psychologists.

7. **a.** is the answer.

8. **d.** is the answer.

9. **a.** is the answer.

10. **a.** is the answer.

b. The gonads are the sex glands.

c. & d. Hormones and brain areas are involved in the HPG axis, which describes the route taken by the hormones.

11. **c.** is the answer.

12. **c.** is the answer.

13. **b.** is the answer. Although the size of the heart increases during puberty, heart rate *decreases*.

14. **d.** is the answer.

Matching Items

1. b	5. f	9. l
2. d	6. i	10. g
3. k	7. a	11. c
4. e	8. j	12. h

KEY TERMS

1. **Puberty** is the period of rapid physical growth and sexual maturation that ends childhood and brings the young person to adult size, shape, and sexual potential.

2. **Menarche,** which refers to the first menstrual period, signals that the adolescent girl has begun ovulation.

3. **Spermarche,** which refers to the first ejaculation of sperm, signals sperm production in adolescent boys.

4. A **hormone** is an organic chemical substance produced by one body tissue that travels via the bloodstream to another to affect some physiological function.

5. The **pituitary** is a gland in the brain that responds to a biochemical signal from the hypothalamus by producing hormones that regulate growth and control other glands.

6. The **adrenal glands** are two glands, located above the kidneys, that secrete epinephrine and norepinephrine, hormones that prepare the body to deal with stress.

7. The **HPA (hypothalamus–pituitary–adrenal) axis** is the route followed by many hormones to trigger puberty and to regulate responses to stress, growth, and other bodily changes.

8. The **gonads** are the paired sex glands in humans—the ovaries in females and the testes, or testicles, in males.

9. The **HPG (hypothalamus–pituitary–gonads) axis** is the route followed by many hormones to affect the body's shape and functioning.

10. **Estradiol** is a sex hormone that is secreted in much greater amounts by females than by males; considered the chief estrogen.

11. **Testosterone** is a sex hormone that is secreted much more by males than by females; considered the best-known androgen.

12. A **circadian rhythm** is a natural day–night cycle of biological activity, such as sleep, that occurs approximately every 24 hours.

13. The **secular trend** is the long-term upward or downward direction of a certain set of statistical measurements. For example, it is the tendency toward earlier and larger growth that has occurred among adolescents over the past two centuries.

14. **Leptin** is a hormone that affects appetite and is believed to affect the onset of puberty.

15. The **growth spurt,** which is the relatively sudden and rapid physical growth of every part of the body, is one of the many observable signs of puberty.

16. **Body image** is a person's concept of his or her body's appearance.

17. **Anorexia nervosa** is an eating disorder characterized by self-starvation.

18. **Bulimia nervosa** is an eating disorder characterized by binge eating and subsequent purging.

19. During puberty, changes in the **primary sex characteristics** involve those sex organs that are directly involved in reproduction.

20. During puberty, changes in the **secondary sex characteristics** involve parts of the body that are not directly involved in reproduction but that signify sexual maturity.

21. **Child sexual abuse** is any erotic activity that arouses an adult and excites, shames, or confuses a child—even if the abuse does not involve genital contact.

22. **Sexually transmitted infections (STIs),** such as syphilis, gonorrhea, genital herpes, chlamydia, and HIV, are those that are spread by sexual contact.

Adolescence: Cognitive Development

Chapter Overview

Chapter 15 describes the cognitive advances and limitations of adolescence. With the attainment of formal operational thought, the developing person becomes able to think in an adult way, that is, to be logical, to think in terms of possibilities, and to reason scientifically and abstractly. This advanced logic is counterbalanced by the increasing power of intuitive thinking.

Even those who reach the stage of formal operational thought spend much of their time thinking at less advanced levels. The discussion of adolescent egocentrism supports this generalization in showing that adolescents have difficulty thinking rationally about themselves and their immediate experiences. Adolescent egocentrism makes them see themselves as psychologically unique and more socially significant than they really are.

The last section of the chapter explores teaching and learning in middle school and high school. As adolescents enter secondary school, their grades often suffer and their level of participation decreases. The rigid behavioral demands and intensified competition of most secondary schools do not, unfortunately, provide a supportive learning environment for adolescents.

What Will You Know?

The text chapter should be studied one section at a time. Before you read, preview each section by skimming it, noting headings and boldface items. Then read the sections, one at a time, keeping these questions in mind.

1. Why do most young adolescents think everyone else is focused on them?

2. Why don't adolescents use their new cognitive ability to think logically?

3. How do computers and cell phones affect adolescent learning?

4. Which adolescents (age and background) in which schools (size and type) are likely to feel lost and ignored?

Chapter Review

When you have finished reading the chapter, work through the material that follows to review it. Completing the sentences and answering the questions will enable you to answer the "What Have You Learned?" questions at the end of the text chapter. Scattered throughout the Chapter Review are Study Tips, which explain how best to learn a difficult concept, and Think About It discussions and Applications, which help you to know how well you understand the material. Check your understanding of the material by consulting the answers at the end of the chapter. Do not continue with the next section until you understand each answer. If you need to, review or reread the appropriate section in the textbook before continuing.

Logic and Self

1. The characteristic of adolescent thinking that leads young people to think only about themselves is called adolescent

   _____ .

2. The adolescent's belief that he or she is unique is called the _____

   _____ . An adolescent's tendency to feel that he or she is somehow immune to the consequences of dangerous or illegal behavior is expressed in the _____

   _____ . Research studies have found that some adolescents do not feel

   _____ .

3. Adolescents, who believe that they are under constant scrutiny from nearly everyone, create for themselves an _____ _____ .

4. On the positive side, young adolescents who feel psychologically invincible tend to be _____ and _____ .

5. Piaget's term for the fourth stage of cognitive development is _____ _____ thought. Adolescent thinking _____ (is/is not) limited by concrete experiences.

6. Piaget devised a number of famous tasks to demonstrate that formal operational adolescents imagine all possible _____. of a problem's solution in order to draw the appropriate _____ .

Briefly describe how children reason differently about the "balance beam" problem at ages 3 to 5, 7, 10, and 13 or 14.

7. The kind of thinking in which adolescents consider unproven possibilities that are logical but not necessarily real is called _____ thought.

8. Adolescents become more capable of _____ reasoning—that is, they can begin with an abstract idea or _____ and then use _____ to draw specific _____ . This type of reasoning is a hallmark of formal operational thought.

9. This kind of reasoning contrasts with reasoning that progresses from specifics to reach a general conclusion, called _____ reasoning. One research study found that older

adolescents, who think _____ , reason that racism is a(n) _____ (society-wide/individual) problem.

10. The belief that if time, effort, or money has already been invested in something, then more time, effort, or money should be invested is called the _____ _____ _____ .

11. In another common fallacy, people ignore information about the frequency of a phenomenon; this is called _____ _____ _____ .

The prevalence of these fallacies makes it apparent that formal operational thinking _____ (does/does not) come to everyone at a certain developmental stage.

Two Modes of Thinking

12. The fact that adolescents can use _____-_____ reasoning does not necessarily mean that they do use it.

13. Researchers believe that the adult brain has two distinct pathways; this is called the _____-_____ model.

14. The first mode of thinking, which begins with a prior _____ , is called _____ . The second mode, Piaget's formal hypothetical-deductive reasoning, is called _____ thought.

15. Intuitive thinking generally is _____ and _____ , and it leads adolescents to make risky decisions. With maturity, though, adolescents are neither paralyzed by too much _____ nor plummeted into danger via _____ .

16. Most adolescents _____ (feel/do not feel) that religious belief is important in daily life. Adolescents' religious beliefs tend to be _____ and _____ , not analytic. Most

children and adolescents _____ (do/do not) adhere to their parents' beliefs.

17. Because the brain's _____ system is activated by puberty, but the

_____ _____

matures more gradually, it is understandable why adolescents are swayed by their

_____ instead of

_____ .

STUDY TIP To consolidate your understanding of how the types of thinking that are typical of the adolescent differ from one another, consider the following problem and, using each type of cognition, come up with one or more examples of how an adolescent might reason about the situation. To get you started, the first example has been completed for you.

Problem: Returning to campus following spring break, you hear an odd noise coming from under the hood of your car. You are running late, and the noise seems to be getting louder.

18.

Type of Thinking	Examples
Egocentrism	"Why do these catastrophes always happen to me and not to someone else?" (personal fable)
Hypothetical-Deductive	
Intuitive Thought	
Analytic Thought	

APPLICATIONS:

19. An experimenter hides a ball in her hand and says, "The ball in my hand is either red or it is not red." Most preadolescent children say
    a. the statement is true.
    b. the statement is false.
    c. they cannot tell if the statement is true or false.
    d. they do not understand what the experimenter means.

20. Fourteen-year-old Monica is very idealistic and often develops crushes on people she doesn't even know. This reflects her newly developed cognitive ability to
    a. deal simultaneously with two sides of an issue.
    b. take another person's viewpoint.
    c. imagine possible worlds and people.
    d. see herself as others see her.

21. Which of the following is the best example of the sunk cost fallacy?
    a. Adriana imagines that she is destined for a life of fame and fortune.
    b. Ben makes up stories about his experiences to impress his friends.
    c. Kalil continues to work on his old clunker of a car after hours of unsuccessful efforts to get it to run.
    d. Julio believes that every girl he meets is attracted to him.

22. Which of the following is the best example of the adolescent's ability to think hypothetically?
    a. Twelve-year-old Stanley feels that people are always watching him.
    b. Fourteen-year-old Mindy engages in many risky behaviors, reasoning that "nothing bad will happen to me."
    c. Fifteen-year-old Philip feels that no one understands his problems.
    d. Thirteen-year-old Josh delights in finding logical flaws in virtually everything his teachers and parents say.

23. Frustrated because of the dating curfew her parents have set, Melinda exclaims, "You just don't know how it feels to be in love!" Melinda's thinking demonstrates
    a. the invincibility fable.
    b. the personal fable.
    c. the imaginary audience.
    d. hypothetical thinking.

24. Compared with her 13-year-old brother, 17-year-old Yolanda is likely to
    a. be more critical about herself.
    b. be more egocentric.
    c. have less confidence in her abilities.
    d. be more capable of reasoning hypothetically.

25. Nathan's fear that his friends will ridicule him because of a pimple that has appeared on his nose reflects a preoccupation with an

    _____ _____ .

26. The reasoning behind the conclusion, "If it waddles like a duck and quacks like a duck, then it must be a duck," is called

    _____ _____ .

27. Which of the following is an example of deductive reasoning?
    a. Alonza is too lazy to look up an unfamiliar word he encounters while reading.
    b. Brittany loves to reason from clues to figure out "whodunit" crime mysteries.
    c. Morgan, who has enjoyed unscrambling anagrams for years, prefers to follow his hunches rather than systematically evaluate letter combinations.
    d. When taking multiple-choice tests, Trevor carefully considers every possible answer before choosing one.

Digital Natives

28. The "digital divide" that once separated _____ from _____ and _____ from _____ is _____ (growing/shrinking).

29. The only significant digital divide now is

    _____ .

30. Potential dangers of the use of computers include encouraging rapid shifts of _____ , multitasking without _____ , and _____ learning instead of invisible analysis. One research study found

that the heaviest users of video games got _____ (higher/lower) school grades and had _____ (more/fewer) physical fights than did average users.

31. Other dangers include sexual predators; _____ , which occurs when one person spreads online insults and rumors about someone else; and _____ , or sending sexual photographs. Another potentially destructive side of the Internet is that it allows adolescents to connect with others who share their _____ and _____ obsessions.

Teaching and Learning

32. The period after primary education and before _____ education is called _____ education. With puberty coming _____ (earlier/later) than in years past, many intermediate _____ schools have been established to educate children in grades 6, 7, and 8.

33. Many developmentalists believe that the weakest link in the educational sequence is _____ (primary schools/middle schools/high schools/college). During the middle school years, academic achievement often _____ (slows down/speeds up). In addition, behavioral problems become _____ (more/less) common. Most developmentalists think that this occurs more because of the _____ _____ of middle schools than because of the _____ _____ of puberty. One hypothesis is that middle schools cause this problem by undercutting _____-_____ _____ .

34. Most middle school students seek _____ approval in ways that _____ disapprove. Signs of this include increased _____ and greater importance placed on _____ and _____ .

35. According to the _____ approach to intelligence, ability is innate and fixed at birth. Students who believe in this approach cope with academic stress by _____ _____ . Students who believe in the _____ approach to intelligence believe they can master whatever they seek to learn. Consequently, they are more likely to _____ . This type of effort exemplifies intrinsic, or _____ , motivation.

36. The first year of a new school is _____ , and ongoing minor stresses can become overwhelming, causing _____ if they are repeated day after day.

37. Minority students who experience _____ _____ feel anxiety because they believe that others judge them in stereotyped ways.

38. Signs of middle school stress include _____ , _____ behavior, and _____ _____ of school.

39. By high school, curriculum and teaching style are often quite _____ , _____ , _____ , and _____ .

40. Another feature of the high school environment is _____-_____ testing, so called because the consequences of failing are so severe. The effects of this type of testing _____ (are/are not) in dispute. High school graduation rates are _____ (increasing/decreasing). The concern is that those who do not graduate are _____ about education.

41. A crucial question for every adolescent is what _____ he or she hopes to have as an adult.

42. An international test designed to measure problem solving and practical cognition needed in adult life is the _____ .

43. Adolescents are more likely to be engaged with school if the school is _____

(small/large). Also, adolescents who are active in school _____ _____ are more likely to be engaged. Another way to encourage engagement is to reduce _____ . Although school violence is _____ (increasing/decreasing), fear of violence is _____ (increasing/decreasing).

THINK ABOUT IT During adolescence, formal operational thought—including scientific reasoning, logical construction of arguments, and critical thinking—becomes possible. Consider the kinds of multiple-choice and essay questions you have been given as a student. Which kind of question typically gives you the most trouble? Does this type of question require thinking at the formal operational level?

APPLICATIONS:

44. Summarizing her presentation on the mismatch between the needs of adolescents and the traditional structure of their schools, Megan notes that
    a. most high schools feature intensified competition.
    b. the curriculum of most high schools emphasizes formal operational thinking.
    c. the academic standards of most schools do not reflect adolescents' needs.
    d. all of these statements are true.

45. Malcolm, a middle schooler who lately is very sensitive to the criticism of others, feels significantly less motivated and capable than when he was in elementary school. Malcolm probably
    a. is experiencing a sense of vulnerability that is common in adolescents.
    b. is a lower-track student.
    c. is a student in a school that emphasizes rigid routines.
    d. has all of these characteristics.

46. Concluding her presentation on academic achievement during adolescence, LaToya notes that the "low ebb" of learning is the
    a. last year of primary education.
    b. first year of tertiary education.
    c. first year of middle school.
    d. last year of middle school.

Progress Test 1

Multiple-Choice Questions

Circle your answers to the following questions and check them with the answers at the end of the chapter. If your answer is incorrect, read the explanation for why it is incorrect and then consult the text.

1. Many psychologists consider the distinguishing feature of adolescent thought to be the ability to think in terms of
   a. moral issues.
   b. concrete operations.
   c. possibility, not just reality.
   d. logical principles.

2. Piaget's last stage of cognitive development is
   a. formal operational thought.
   b. concrete operational thought.
   c. universal ethical principles.
   d. symbolic thought.

3. The sunk cost fallacy is the mistaken assumption that
   a. because one has already spent time on something, one should spend more.
   b. analytical thinking works in all situations.
   c. intuitive thinking is generally best.
   d. emotional thinking is sometimes better.

4. The adolescent who takes risks and feels immune to the laws of mortality is showing evidence of the
   a. invincibility fable.
   b. personal fable.
   c. imaginary audience.
   d. death instinct.

5. Imaginary audiences and invincibility fables are expressions of adolescent
   a. morality.
   b. thinking games.
   c. decision making.
   d. egocentrism.

6. The typical adolescent
   a. is tough-minded.
   b. is indifferent to public opinion.
   c. is self-absorbed and hypersensitive to criticism.
   d. has all of these characteristics.

7. When adolescents enter middle school, many
   a. experience a drop in their academic performance.
   b. show increased behavioral problems.
   c. lose connections to teachers.
   d. experience all of these things.

8. The psychologist who first described adolescent egocentrism is
   a. Jean Piaget.
   b. David Elkind.
   c. Lev Vygotsky.
   d. Noam Chomsky.

9. Thinking that begins with a general premise and then draws logical conclusions from it is called
   a. inductive reasoning.
   b. deductive reasoning.
   c. intuitive thinking.
   d. hypothetical reasoning.

10. Serious reflection on important issues is a wrenching process for many adolescents because of their newfound ability to reason
    a. inductively.
    b. deductively.
    c. hypothetically.
    d. symbolically.

11. Hypothetical-deductive thinking is to contextualized thinking as
    a. rational analysis is to intuitive thought.
    b. intuitive thought is to rational analysis.
    c. experiential thinking is to intuitive reasoning.
    d. intuitive thinking is to analytical reasoning.

12. Many adolescents seem to believe that *their* lovemaking will not lead to pregnancy. This belief is an expression of the
    a. sunk cost fallacy.
    b. invincibility fable.
    c. imaginary audience.
    d. "game of thinking."

13. Current high school education in the United States does not seem to meet the needs of the sizable number of students who
    a. are primarily auditory learners.
    b. are qualified to take advanced placement (AP) courses.
    c. do not go on to college.
    d. enjoy high-stakes testing

14. One problem with many high schools is that the formal curriculum ignores the fact that adolescents thrive on
    a. formal operational thinking.
    b. intellectual challenges that require social interaction.
    c. inductive reasoning.
    d. deductive reasoning.

15. A research study investigating teenage religion found that
    a. most adolescents did not feel close to God.
    b. most adolescents identified with the same tradition as their parents.
    c. few respondents claimed that their beliefs were important to their daily life.
    d. faith was generally not viewed as a personal tool to be used in times of difficulty.

True or False Items

Write T (true) or F (false) on the line in front of each statement.

_____ 1. The appropriateness of the typical high school's high-stakes testing environment has been questioned.

_____ 1. The appropriateness of the typical high school's high-stakes testing environment has been questioned.

_____ 2. Adolescents tend to consider faith a personal tool to be used in times of difficulty.

_____ 3. Adolescents' egos sometimes seem to overwhelm logic.

_____ 4. When high-stakes tests are a requisite for graduation, there is a potential consequence of discouraging students' interest in education.

_____ 5. Adolescents often create an imaginary audience as they envision how others will react to their appearance and behavior.

_____ 6. Thinking reaches heightened self-consciousness at puberty.

_____ 7. Adolescent egocentrism is always irrational.

_____ 8. Inductive reasoning is a hallmark of formal operational thought.

_____ 9. Academic achievement often slows down during the middle school years.

_____ 10. The brain has two distinct processing networks.

_____ 11. Students who believe in the entity approach to intelligence pay more attention and work harder than students who believe in the incremental approach.

Progress Test 2

Progress Test 2 should be completed during a final chapter review. Answer the following questions after you thoroughly understand the correct answers for the Chapter Review and Progress Test 1.

Multiple-Choice Questions

1. Adolescents who fall prey to the invincibility fable may be more likely to
   a. engage in risky behaviors.
   b. suffer from depression.
   c. have low self-esteem.
   d. drop out of school.

2. Thinking that extrapolates from a specific experience to form a general premise is called
   a. inductive reasoning.
   b. deductive reasoning.
   c. intuitive thinking.
   d. hypothetical reasoning.

3. Education during grades 7 through 12 is generally called
   a. primary education
   b. secondary education
   c. tertiary education.
   d. analytical education.

4. When young people overestimate their significance to others, they are displaying
   a. concrete operational thought.
   b. adolescent egocentrism.
   c. a lack of cognitive growth.
   d. immoral development.

5. The imaginary audience refers to adolescents imagining that
   a. they are immune to the dangers of risky behaviors.
   b. they are always being scrutinized by others.
   c. their own lives are unique, heroic, or even legendary.
   d. the world revolves around their actions.

6. The typical high school environment
   a. limits social interaction.
   b. does not meet the cognitive needs of the typical adolescent.
   c. emphasizes formal operational thought.
   d. is described by all of these conditions.

7. As compared with elementary schools, most middle schools exhibit all of the following, except
   a. a more flexible approach to education.
   b. intensified competition.
   c. inappropriate academic standards.
   d. less individualized attention.

8. Which of the following is true regarding intuitive thinking?
   a. It does not advance significantly in most people until adulthood.
   b. It is slower than formal operational thinking.
   c. It is quicker and more passionate than formal operational thinking.
   d. It often deteriorates during early adolescence.

9. Which of the following most accurately expresses how the typical adolescent feels about religion?
   a. Most adolescents consider themselves to be religious.
   b. Most adolescent do not consider themselves to be religious.
   c. Adolescent girls are more religious than adolescent boys.
   d. Adolescent boys are more religious than adolescent girls.

10. Analytic thinking is to _____ thinking as emotional force is to _____ thinking.
    a. intuitive; egocentric
    b. egocentric; intuitive
    c. formal; intuitive
    d. intuitive; formal

11. One of the hallmarks of formal operational thought is
    a. egocentrism.
    b. deductive reasoning.
    c. symbolic thinking.
    d. all of these types of thinking.

12. Analytic thinking and intuitive thinking
    a. both use the same neural pathways in the brain.
    b. are really the same type of information processing.
    c. both improve during adolescence.
    d. are characterized by all of these conditions.

13. In the United States, the greatest divide between Internet users and nonusers is now
    a. gender.
    b. age.
    c. ethnicity.
    d. income.

14. Which of the following is NOT true regarding cyberbullying?
    a. It is experienced by fewer than 1 percent of secondary school students.
    b. Those most likely to be involved are already bully-victims.
    c. Relational bullying in particular accelerates with cyberbullying.
    d. The shame of cyberbullying is magnified by the imaginary audience.

Matching Items

Match each term or concept with its corresponding description or definition.

Terms or Concepts

_____ **1.** invincibility fable

_____ **2.** imaginary audience

_____ **3.** high-stakes testing

_____ **4.** hypothetical thought

_____ **5.** deductive reasoning

_____ **6.** inductive reasoning

_____ **7.** formal operational thought

_____ **8.** sunk cost fallacy

_____ **9.** dual-process model

_____ **10.** adolescent egocentrism

_____ **11.** base rate neglect

_____ **12.** PISA

_____ **13.** incremental approach

_____ **14.** entity approach

Descriptions or Definitions

a. the tendency of adolescents to focus on themselves to the exclusion of others

b. belief that intelligence is unrelated to effort

c. mistaken belief that if a person has already spent time or money on something, he or she should continue to do so

d. reasoning about propositions that may or may not reflect reality

e. the idea that there are two thinking networks in the brain

f. belief that intelligence is increased by effort

g. the last stage of cognitive development, according to Piaget

h. test that measures practical problem-solving skills

i. thinking that moves from a specific experience to a general premise

j. an evaluation that is critical in determining success or failure

k. faulty reasoning that ignores the actual frequency of some behavior

l. the idea held by many adolescents that others are intensely interested in them, especially in their appearance and behavior

m. thinking that moves from premise to conclusion

n. the tendency of adolescents to feel immune to the consequences of dangerous behavior

Key Terms

Using your own words, write a brief definition or explanation of each of the following terms on a separate piece of paper.

1. adolescent egocentrism
2. personal fable
3. invincibility fable
4. imaginary audience
5. formal operational thought
6. hypothetical thought
7. deductive reasoning
8. inductive reasoning
9. sunk cost fallacy
10. base rate neglect
11. dual-process model
12. intuitive thought
13. analytic thought
14. cyberbullying
15. secondary education
16. middle school
17. entity approach to intelligence
18. incremental approach to intelligence
19. high-stakes test
20. PISA (Programme for International Student Assessment)

ANSWERS

CHAPTER REVIEW

1. egocentrism
2. personal fable; invincibility fable; invincible
3. imaginary audience
4. resilient; less likely to be depressed
5. formal operational; is not
6. determinants; conclusions

Three- to five-year-olds have no understanding of how to solve the problem. By age 7, children understand balancing the weights but don't know that distance from the center is also a factor. By age 10, they understand the concepts but use trial and error, not logic. By ages 13 or 14, they are able to solve the problem.

7. hypothetical
8. deductive; premise; logic; conclusions
9. inductive; deductively; society-wide
10. sunk cost fallacy
11. base rate neglect; does not
12. hypothetical-deductive
13. dual-process
14. belief, assumption, or general rule; intuitive (or contextualized or experiential); analytic
15. quick; powerful; analysis; intuition
16. feel; egocentric; intuitive; do
17. limbic; prefrontal cortex; intuition; logic
18. Possible answers follow.

Type of Thinking	Examples
Egocentrism	"Why do these catastrophes always happen to me and not to someone else?" (personal fable)
Hypothetical-Deductive	"I think there's a gremlin in my car and he's letting me know he's there" (thinking about possibilities that may not be real)
Intuitive Thought	"Last time this happened my car broke down. What am I going to do?" (experiential)
Analytic Thought	"I need to get my car to a mechanic as soon as possible."(logical thought)

19. **c.** is the answer. Although this statement is logically verifiable, preadolescents who lack formal operational thought cannot prove or disprove it.

20. **c.** is the answer. Monica now has the ability to use hypothetical-deductive reasoning.
21. **c.** is the answer. **a.** is an example of a personal fable. The behaviors described in **b.** and **d.** are more indicative of a preoccupation with the imaginary audience.
22. **d.** is the answer. Hypothetical reasoning involves thinking about possibilities. **a.** is an example of the imaginary audience. **b.** is an example of the invincibility fable. **c.** is an example of adolescent egocentrism.
23. **b.** is the answer. The personal fable is the adolescent's belief that his or her feelings and thoughts are unique.
24. **d.** is the answer. Adolescents become less critical of themselves and less egocentric as they mature and as the prefrontal cortex matures.
25. imaginary audience.
26. inductive reasoning. This is reasoning that moves from the specific to reach a general conclusion.
27. **b.** is the answer. Solving mysteries is an example of deductive reasoning.
28. boys; girls; rich; poor; shrinking
29. age
30. attention; reflection; visual; lower; more
31. cyberbullying; sexting; prejudices; self-destructive
32. tertiary; secondary; earlier; middle
33. middle schools; slows down; more; organizational structure; biological stresses; student–teacher relationships
34. peer; adults; bullying; appearance; status symbols
35. entity; avoiding effort; incremental; pay attention, participate in class, study, and complete their homework; mastery
36. stressful; pathology
37. stereotype threat
38. absenteeism; externalizing; dropping out
39. analytic; abstract; hypothetical; logical
40. high-stakes; are; increasing; discouraged
41. job
42. PISA (Programme for International Student Assessment)
43. small; extracurricular activities; harassment; decreasing; increasing
44. **d.** is the answer.
45. **a.** is the answer. Middle school is a time when

academic achievement slows down. Also, adolescents become more self-conscious socially because they are confronted by many new classmates.

46. **c.** is the answer. Some psychologists have proposed that this occurs because students lose close connection to teachers in overly large classes.

PROGRESS TEST 1

Multiple-Choice Questions

1. **c.** is the answer.

   a. Although moral reasoning becomes much deeper during adolescence, it is not limited to this stage of development.

   b. & d. Concrete operational thought, which *is* logical, is the distinguishing feature of childhood thinking.

2. **a.** is the answer.

   b. In Piaget's theory, this stage precedes formal operational thought.

   c. & d. These are not stages in Piaget's theory.

3. **a.** is the answer.

4. **a.** is the answer.

   b. This concept refers to adolescents' tendency to imagine their own lives as unique, heroic, or even legendary.

   c. This refers to adolescents' tendency to fantasize about how others will react to their appearance and behavior.

   d. This is a concept in Freud's theory.

5. **d.** is the answer. These thought processes are manifestations of adolescents' tendency to see themselves as being much more central and important to the social scene than they really are.

6. **c.** is the answer.

7. **d.** is the answer.

8. **b.** is the answer.

9. **b.** is the answer.

   a. Inductive reasoning moves from specific facts to a general conclusion.

   c. By its very nature, intuitive thinking does not move logically either from a general conclusion to specific facts or from specific facts to a general conclusion.

   d. Hypothetical reasoning involves thinking about possibilities rather than facts.

10. **c.** is the answer.

11. **a.** is the answer.

    c. Contextualized thinking is both experiential *and* intuitive.

12. **b.** is the answer.

    a. The sunk cost fallacy is the mistaken belief that, because one has invested time and effort in something, one should continue doing so.

    c. This refers to adolescents' tendency to fantasize about how others will react to their appearance and behavior.

    d. This concept was not discussed in the text.

13. **c.** is the answer.

14. **b.** is the answer.

    a., c., & d. Adolescents are more likely to thrive on *intuitive* thinking.

15. **b.** is the answer.

True or False Items

1. T
2. T
3. T
4. T
5. T
6. T
7. F   Adolescents *do* judge each other.
8. F   Deductive reasoning is a hallmark of formal operational thought.
9. T
10. T
11. F   Just the opposite is true.

PROGRESS TEST 2

Multiple-Choice Questions

1. **a.** is the answer.

   b., c., & d. The invincibility fable leads some teens to believe that they are immune to the dangers of risky behaviors; it is not necessarily linked to depression, low self-esteem, or the likelihood that an individual will drop out of school.

2. **a.** is the answer.

   b. Deductive reasoning begins with a general premise and then draws logical conclusions from it.

c. By its very nature, intuitive thinking does not move logically either from a general conclusion to specific facts or from specific facts to a general conclusion.

d. Hypothetical reasoning involves thinking about possibilities rather than facts.

3. **b.** is the answer.

4. **b.** is the answer.

5. **b.** is the answer.

a. This describes the invincibility fable.

c. This describes the personal fable.

d. This describes adolescent egocentrism in general.

6. **d.** is the answer.

7. **a.** is the answer.

8. **c.** is the answer.

9. **a.** is the answer.

10. **c.** is the answer.

11. **b.** is the answer.

12. **c.** is the answer.

13. **b.** is the answer.

14. **a.** is the answer.

Matching Items

1. n	**5.** m	**9.** e	**13.** f
2. l	**6.** i	**10.** a	**14.** b
3. j	**7.** g	**11.** k	
4. d	**8.** c	**12.** h	

KEY TERMS

1. **Adolescent egocentrism** refers to the tendency of young people (ages 10 to 13) to focus on themselves to the exclusion of others.

2. The **personal fable,** an aspect of adolescent egocentrism, refers to an adolescent's belief that his or her thoughts, feelings, and experiences are unique.

3. The **invincibility fable** is the adolescent's egocentric conviction that he or she is immune to the dangers of risky behaviors.

4. Adolescents often create an **imaginary audience** for themselves because they assume that others are as intensely interested in them as they themselves are.

5. In Piaget's theory, the last stage of cognitive development, which arises from a combination of maturation and experience, is called **formal operational thought.** A hallmark of formal operational thinking is more systematic logic and the ability to understand and systematically manipulate abstract ideas.

6. **Hypothetical thought** involves reasoning about propositions and possibilities that may not reflect reality.

7. **Deductive reasoning** is thinking that moves from the general to the specific, or from a premise to a logical conclusion; also called *top-down reasoning.*

8. **Inductive reasoning** is thinking that moves from one or more specific experiences or facts to a general conclusion; also called *bottom-up reasoning.*

9. The **sunk cost fallacy** is the mistaken belief that, because one has already invested unrecoverable money, time, or effort in an endeavor, one should continue doing so in an effort to reach the desired goal.

10. **Base rate neglect** is a faulty form of emotional decision making that ignores the actual frequency of a behavior or characteristic.

11. The **dual-process model** is the idea that there are two thinking networks in the human brain, one for emotional and one for analytical processing of stimuli.

12. **Intuitive thought** is that which arises from a hunch or emotion, often triggered by past experiences and cultural assumptions.

13. **Analytic thought** is logical thinking that arises from rational analysis and the systematic evaluation of consequences and possibilities.

14. **Cyberbullying** occurs when one person spreads insults or rumors about someone else by means of e-mails, text messages, or cell phone videos.

15. **Secondary education** is education that follows primary education and precedes tertiary education, usually occurring from about age 12 to 18.

16. **Middle school** refers to a school for children in grades between elementary school and high school.

17. The **entity approach to intelligence** views ability as innate, fixed at birth, and unrelated to effort.

18. The **incremental approach to intelligence** holds that intelligence is directly related to effort.

19. **High-stakes tests** are exams and other forms of evaluation that are critical in determining a person's success or failure.

20. The **PISA (Programme for International Student Assessment)** is an international test taken by 15-year-olds in 50 nations that measures practical problem-solving and cognition in daily life.

Adolescence: Psychosocial Development

Chapter Overview

Chapter 16 focuses on the adolescent's psychosocial development. The first section explores the paths that lead to the formation of identity, which is required for the attainment of adult status and maturity. The next two sections examine the influences of family and friends on adolescent psychosocial development, including the development of romantic relationships and sexual activity. Depression and suicide are then explored. The special problems posed by adolescent lawbreaking and drug use and abuse are discussed, and suggestions for alleviating or treating these problems are given. The chapter concludes with the message that with the help of family and friends, most adolescents make it through the teen years unscathed.

What Will You Know?

The text chapter should be studied one section at a time. Before you read, preview each section by skimming it, noting headings and boldface items. Then read the sections, one at a time, keeping these questions in mind.

1. Why do some teenagers seem to markedly change their appearance, their behavior, and their goals from one year to the next?

2. When teenagers disagree with their parents on every issue, is it time for the parents to give up, become stricter, or do something else?

3. Does knowing about sex make it more likely that a teenager will be sexually active?

4. Is delinquency a temporary phase or a sign that a person is likely to commit serious crimes in adulthood?

5. Since most adolescents try alcohol, why do laws forbid it?

Chapter Review

When you have finished reading the chapter, work through the material that follows to review it. Completing the sentences and answering the questions will enable you to answer the "What Have You Learned?" questions at the end of the text chapter. Scattered throughout the Chapter Review are Study Tips, which explain how best to learn a difficult concept, and Think About It discussions and Applications, which help you to know how well you understand the material. Check your understanding of the material by consulting the answers at the end of the chapter. Do not continue with the next section until you understand each answer. If you need to, review or reread the appropriate section in the textbook before continuing.

Identity

1. The momentous changes that occur during the teen years challenge adolescents to find their own

    _____ .

2. According to Erikson, the challenge of

    adolescence is _____

    _____ _____

    _____ .

3. The ultimate goal of adolescence is to establish a new identity that involves both rejection and acceptance of childhood values; this is called

    _____ _____ .

4. The young person who lacks a commitment to goals or values and is apathetic about defining his or her identity is experiencing

    _____ _____ .

5. The young person who prematurely accepts earlier roles and parental values without

exploring alternatives or truly forging a
unique identity is experiencing identity

_____ .

6. A time-out period during which a young person
experiments with different identities, postponing
important choices, is called an identity
_____ . An obvious institutional
example of this in North America is attending
_____ .

7. Erikson described four aspects of identity:

_____ , _____ ,

_____ , and

_____ .

8. Most adolescents _____
(follow/do not follow) the religious and political
traditions of their parents.

9. Vocational identity _____
(is/is not) relevant today for two
reasons: _____ and
_____

10. Adolescents who work more than
_____ (how many?) hours a
week during the school year tend to quit school
and hate their jobs when they become adults.

11. Although adolescence was once a time for
_____ _____ , in
terms of sexual identity this is no longer true.

12. Today, a person's identification as either male
or female is called _____
_____ . Gender identity usually
begins with the person's _____
_____ and leads to assumption
of a _____ _____ .

STUDY TIP To keep the differences among the
identity statuses of role confusion, foreclosure, and
moratorium straight, remember that role confusion
is a state in which adolescents seem unfocused
and unconcerned about their future. Foreclosure
and moratorium represent different strategies for
dealing with this state of confusion. You may find it
helpful to think of how foreclosure is used in financial
circumstances. Economic foreclosure occurs when
someone who has borrowed money, typically to
purchase a home, defaults on the loan. To foreclose
is to deprive the borrower of the right to ownership.
Similarly, adolescents who have foreclosed on their
identities have deprived themselves of the healthy

practice of thoughtfully questioning and trying out
different possible identities before settling on one.
In contrast, a moratorium is a time-out during which
adolescents postpone their final identity, often
by attending college or engaging in other socially
acceptable activities that allow them to make a more
mature decision.

APPLICATIONS:

13. From childhood, Sharon thought she wanted
to follow in her mother's footsteps and be a
homemaker. Now, at age 40 with a home and
family, she admits to herself that what she really
wanted to be was a medical researcher. Erik
Erikson would probably say that Sharon
   a. experienced role confusion when she was a child.
   b. experienced identity foreclosure at an early age.
   c. never progressed beyond the obvious identity diffusion she experienced as a child.
   d. took a moratorium from identity formation.

14. Jennifer has a well-defined religious identity. This
means that
   a. she self-identifies as a religious person.
   b. she follows her parents' practice of worshiping regularly.
   c. as a Muslim, she may wear a headscarf.
   d. she does all of these things.

15. Compared with adolescents in her parents' and
grandparents' generations, 12-year-old Raisel is
likely to
   a. have an easier time achieving her own unique identity.
   b. have a more difficult time forging her identity.
   c. prematurely foreclose on her identity.
   d. have a shorter span of time in which to forge her identity.

Relationships with Adults

16. Adolescence is often characterized as
a time of waning adult influence; this
_____ (is/is not) necessarily true.

17. Parent–adolescent conflict peaks during
_____ _____
and is particularly notable with
_____ (mothers/fathers) and
their _____ (sons/daughters).

18. Parent–adolescent conflict often involves
_____ , which refers to repeated,
petty arguments about daily habits.

19. By age 18, increased _____ maturity and reduced _____ bring some renewed appreciation for parents.

20. There _____ (are/are not) cultural differences in parent–adolescent relationships. Some cultures value _____ above all else and avoid conflict. Thus, the very idea of adolescent rebellion may be a _____ construction in Western culture.

21. Four other elements of parent–teen relationships that have been heavily researched include _____ , _____ , _____ , and _____ .

22. In terms of family control, a powerful deterrent to drugs and risky sex is _____ _____ . Too much interference, however, may contribute to adolescent _____ .

23. (A View from Science) A longitudinal study of African American families in rural Georgia found that family training that encouraged youth to postpone _____ _____ , _____ _____ , and _____ had helped, especially for youth who inherited the short_____ of one _____ .

24. An important aspect of healthy development is supportive relationships with _____ adults.

APPLICATIONS:

25. Bill's parents insist on knowing the whereabouts and activities of their son at all times. Clearly, they are very good at _____ _____ .

26. First-time parents Norma and Norman are worried that, during adolescence, their healthy parental influence will be undone as their children are encouraged by peers to become sexually promiscuous, drug-addicted, or delinquent. Their wise neighbor, who is a developmental psychologist, tells them that
   a. peers are constructive as often as they are destructive.
   b. research suggests that peers provide a negative influence in every major task of adolescence.
   c. only through authoritarian parenting can parents give children the skills they need to resist peer pressure.
   d. unless their children show early signs of learning difficulties or antisocial behavior, parental monitoring is unnecessary.

Peer Power

27. Social pressure to conform to peer activities is called _____ _____ . This pressure is _____ as often as it is _____ . Destructive peer support is called _____ _____ .

28. Two helpful concepts in understanding the influence of peers are _____ , meaning that peers _____ one another; and _____ , referring to the fact that peers encourage one another to do things that _____ .

Briefly outline the four-stage progression of heterosexual involvement.

29. Culture _____ (affects/does not affect) the _____ and _____ of these stages, but the basic _____ seems to be based on _____ . In modern developed nations, each stage typically lasts several years.

30. Norms for sexual activity _____ (vary/do not vary) from nation to nation.

31. The direction of a person's erotic desires is called

    _____ _____ .

    The number of early adolescents who do not identify with their biological sex seems to be

    _____ (increasing/decreasing). Some of these may be diagnosed with

    _____-_____

    _____ . Variations in sexual

    relations reflect _____ ,

    _____ , and the words used in surveys.

32. Sex information comes from various sources:

    the _____ , parents, and

    _____ . Developmentalists agree

    that high schools _____ (should/ should not) teach sex education and that sex

    also should be part of _____–

    _____ conversations.

33. Sex education _____ (varies/ does not vary) from nation to nation. The timing and content of sex education in the United States

    _____ (varies/does not vary) by state and community.

34. Research shows that sex education programs

    generally _____ (are/are

    not) successful in delaying the age at which adolescents become sexually active. Research on the value of abstinence-only programs indicates

    that they _____ (do/do not)

    make a difference in teen sexual activity.

THINK ABOUT IT To help you understand the role of the peer group during adolescence, think about your own social experiences as a teenager. Did you hang out in loosely associated groups of girls and boys before gradually joining together? Did you double- or triple-date to avoid the awkwardness of being alone with someone you "liked"? Did you have a best friend of the same gender with whom you shared details of your sexual experiences to confirm that they were normal?

APPLICATION:

35. Padma's parents are concerned because their 14-year-old daughter has formed an early romantic relationship with a boy. You tell them

    a. not to worry, because boys are more likely to say they have a girlfriend than vice versa.

    b. not to worry; many teenage romances do not include sexual intercourse.

    c. most romantic relationships last throughout high school.

    d. they should do everything they can to break up the relationship.

Sadness and Anger

36. About _____ (how many?) percent of youth experience problem emotions. Most of these problems are

    _____ , meaning several occur together.

37. From late childhood through adolescence, people

    generally feel _____ (more/less) confident.

38. Self-esteem is generally lower in

    _____ (girls/boys) and higher

    in _____ (girls/boys), lower

    among _____ Americans and

    higher among _____ Americans.

    Besides the effects of parents and peers, one factor in an individual's level of self-esteem may

    be the adolescents' own _____

    propensity. The belief that family members should make sacrifices for one another is called

    _____ .

39. Clinical depression _____ (increases/decreases) at puberty, especially

    among_____ (boys/girls). One explanation is that talking about and mentally replaying past experiences, which is called

    _____ , is more common among

    _____ (boys/girls).

40. Thinking about committing suicide, called

    _____ _____ , is

    _____ (common/relatively rare) among high school students.

41. Most suicide attempts in adolescence

    _____ (do/do not) result

    in death. A deliberate act of self-destruction that does not result in death is called a

    _____ .

42. Adolescents are _____ (more/ less) likely to kill themselves than adults are. Although depression and parasuicide are

more common among _____
(males/females), completed suicide is higher for
_____ (males/females) in every
nation except China.

43. When a town or school sentimentalizes
the "tragic end" of a teen suicide, the
publicity can trigger _____
_____ .

44. Since 1990, rates of adolescent suicide
have _____ (risen/fallen),
especially among _____-
_____ teenagers.

45. Psychologists influenced by the
_____ perspective believe that
adolescent rebellion and defiance are normal.

46. In terms of the frequency of arrests,
_____ (only a few/virtually all)
adolescents break the law at least once before age
20.

47. Developmentalists have found that it
_____ (is/is not) currently
possible to distinguish children who actually
will become career criminals. Two clusters
of factors, one from childhood (primarily
_____-based) and one from
adolescence (primarily _____),
predict delinquency.

List several of the childhood factors that correlate
with delinquency.

48. Experts find it useful to distinguish
_____-_____
offenders, whose criminal activity stops
by age 21, from _____-
_____-_____
offenders, who become career criminals.

APPLICATIONS:

49. Carl is a typical 16-year-old who has no special
problems. It is likely that Carl has
   a. contemplated suicide.
   b. engaged in some minor illegal act.
   c. struggled with "who he is."
   d. engaged in all of these behaviors.

50. Statistically, who of the following is most likely to
commit suicide?
   a. Elena, a 16-year-old female
   b. Yan, a 45-year-old male
   c. James, a 16-year-old male
   d. Alison, a 45-year-old female

51. Coming home from work, Rashid hears a radio
announcement warning parents to be alert for
possible cluster suicide signs in their teenage
children. What might have precipitated such an
announcement?
   a. government statistics that suicide is on the
   rise
   b. the highly publicized suicide of a teen from a
   school in town
   c. the recent crash of an airliner, killing all on
   board
   d. any of these events

Drug Use and Abuse

52. Most teenagers _____ (try/
do not try) psychoactive drugs. Between 10 and
25 years of age, both the _____
and _____ of drug use increase.
The one exception to this trend is for the use of
_____ .

53. Drug use _____ (varies/does not
markedly vary) from nation to nation.

54. In the United States, use of most drugs has
_____ (increased/decreased)
since 1976.

55. Adolescent _____ (boys/girls)
use more drugs, and use them more often,
than _____ (boys/girls) do.
_____ drugs are used more by
boys and _____ drugs by more
girls.

56. Drug abuse is defined as using a drug in a
manner that is _____ . When
the absence of a drug in a person's system
causes physiological or psychological craving,
_____ is apparent.

57. Heavy use of alcohol impairs _____ and _____ by damaging the brain's _____ and _____ .

58. An important factor in drug use is

_____ _____ ,

which is the idea that each generation forgets what the previous generation learned.

Progress Test 1

Multiple-Choice Questions

Circle your answers to the following questions and check them with the answers at the end of the chapter. If your answer is incorrect, read the explanation for why it is incorrect and then consult the text.

1. According to Erikson, the primary task of adolescence is that of establishing
   a. basic trust.
   b. an identity.
   c. intimacy.
   d. integrity.

2. According to developmentalists who study identity formation, foreclosure involves
   a. accepting an identity prematurely, without exploration.
   b. taking time off from school, work, and other commitments.
   c. opposing parental values.
   d. failing to commit oneself to a vocational goal.

3. What percent of adolescents experience depression, anger, or other emotional troubles?
   a. less than 5
   b. 10
   c. 20
   d. 30

4. The main sources of social support for most young people who are establishing independence from their parents are
   a. older adolescents of the opposite sex.
   b. older siblings.
   c. teachers.
   d. peer groups.

5. Which of the following correlates with depression during adolescence?
   a. decreasing parental control
   b. decreasing parental monitoring
   c. overly restrictive and controlling parenting
   d. absence of parental monitoring

6. In a crime-ridden neighborhood, parents can protect their adolescents by keeping close watch over activities, friends, and so on. This practice is called
   a. a moratorium.
   b. foreclosure.
   c. peer screening.
   d. parental monitoring.

7. Conflict between adolescent girls and their mothers is most likely to involve
   a. bickering over hair, neatness, and other daily habits.
   b. political, religious, and moral issues.
   c. peer relationships and friendships.
   d. relationships with boys.

8. Destructive peer support in which one adolescent shows another how to rebel against authority is called
   a. peer pressure.
   b. deviancy training.
   c. peer selection.
   d. peer facilitation.

9. In our society, obvious examples of institutionalized moratoria on identity formation are
   a. the Boy Scouts and the Girl Scouts.
   b. college and the military.
   c. marriage and divorce.
   d. bar mitzvahs and baptisms.

10. In a Disney movie, two high school students encourage each other to participate in the school musical. This type of peer influence is called
    a. peer pressure.
    b. deviancy training.
    c. selection.
    d. peer facilitation.

11. Jill, who has cut herself and engaged in other self-destructive acts, is receiving treatment for these acts of
    a. suicidal ideation.
    b. foreclosure.
    c. parasuicide.
    d. rumination.

12. Thirteen-year-old Adam, who has never doubted his faith, identifies himself as an orthodox member of a particular religious group. A developmentalist would probably say that Adam's religious identity is
    a. achieved.
    b. foreclosed.
    c. in moratorium.
    d. oppositional in nature.

13. The early predictors of life-course-persistent offenders include all of the following except
    a. short attention span.
    b. hyperactivity.
    c. high intelligence.
    d. inadequate emotional regulation.

14. Regarding gender differences in self-destructive acts, the rate of parasuicide is _____ and the rate of suicide is _____ .
    a. higher in males; higher in females
    b. higher in females; higher in males
    c. the same in males and females; higher in males
    d. the same in males and females; higher in females

15. Conflict between parents and adolescent offspring is
    a. most likely to involve fathers and their early-maturing offspring.
    b. more frequent in single-parent homes.
    c. more likely between daughters and their mothers.
    d. likely in all of these situations.

True or False Items

Write T (true) or F (false) on the line in front of each statement.

_____ 1. Identity achievement before age 18 is elusive.

_____ 2. Most adolescents have political views and educational values that are markedly different from those of their parents.

_____ 3. Peer pressure is inherently destructive to the adolescent seeking an identity.

_____ 4. For most adolescents, group socializing and dating precede the establishment of true intimacy with one member of the opposite sex.

_____ 5. Worldwide, virtually every adolescent breaks the law at least once before age 20.

_____ 6. Abstinence-only sex education has led to decreased rates of adolescent sex.

_____ 7. Because of their tendency to ruminate, girls are more likely than boys to be clinically depressed.

_____ 8. In finding themselves, teens try to find a consistent identity.

_____ 9. From ages 6 to 18, children feel more confident.

_____ 10. Serious, distressing thoughts about killing oneself are most common at about age 15.

Progress Test 2

Progress Test 2 should be completed during a final chapter review. Answer the following questions after you thoroughly understand the correct answers for the Chapter Review and Progress Test 1.

Multiple-Choice Questions

1. Which of the following is not one of the arenas of identity formation in Erik Erikson's theory?
   a. religious   c. political
   b. sexual   d. social

2. Which of the following is true of gender identity?
   a. It is a person's self-definition as male or female.
   b. It always leads to sexual orientation.
   c. It is a person's biological male/female characteristics.
   d. It is established at birth.

3. Rodesia repeatedly thinks and talks about past experiences to the extent that her doctor believes it is contributing to her depression. Rodesia's behavior is an example of
   a. role confusion.   c. parasuicide.
   b. deviancy training. d. rumination.

4. Ray endured severe child abuse, has difficulty controlling his emotions, and exhibits symptoms of autism spectrum disorder. These factors would suggest that Ray is at high risk of
   a. becoming an adolescent-limited offender.
   b. becoming a life-course-persistent offender.
   c. developing an antisocial personality.
   d. foreclosing his identity prematurely.

5. Thinking about committing suicide is called
   a. cluster suicide.   c. suicidal ideation.
   b. parasuicide.   d. rumination.

6. One reason rates of teenage pregnancy in most European nations are lower than those in the United States is that most European schools
   a. have no sex education as part of the curriculum.
   b. delay sex education until middle school.
   c. delay sex education until high school.
   d. begin sex education in elementary school.

7. The adolescent experiencing role confusion is typically
   a. very apathetic.
   b. experimenting with alternative identities without trying to settle on any one.
   c. willing to accept parental values wholesale, without exploring alternatives.
   d. one who rebels against all forms of authority.

8. The term that refers to whether a person is attracted to others of the same sex, the opposite sex, or both sexes is
   a. gender identity.   c. sexual identity.
   b. gender role.   d. sexual orientation.

9. Of the following individuals, who is likely to experience low self-esteem?
   a. Kanye, a 15-year-old Hispanic American
   b. Doris, a 17-year-old African American
   c. Emily, a 14-year-old Asian American
   d. Danny, a 16-year-old European American

10. Which of the following is the most common problem behavior among adolescents?
    a. pregnancy
    b. daily use of illegal drugs
    c. minor lawbreaking
    d. attempts at suicide

11. A time-out period during which a young person experiments with different identities, postponing important choices, is called
    a. foreclosure.
    b. rumination.
    c. identity diffusion.
    d. a moratorium.

12. Heavy use of alcohol impairs memory and self-control by damaging the brain's
    a. hypothalamus and thalamus.
    b. occipital lobe and reticular formation.
    c. hippocampus and prefrontal cortex.
    d. temporal lobe and parietal lobe.

13. Which of the following is NOT true regarding the rate of clinical depression among adolescents?
    a. At puberty the rate more than doubles.
    b. It affects a higher proportion of teenage boys than girls.
    c. Genetic vulnerability is a predictor of teenage depression.
    d. The adolescent's school setting is a factor.

14. Parent–teen conflict tends to center on issues related to
    a. politics and religion.
    b. education.
    c. vacations.
    d. daily details, such as musical tastes.

15. Suicidal ideation is
    a. not as common among high school students as it was in the past.
    b. more common among males than among females.
    c. more common among females than among males.
    d. more common among high-achieving students.

Matching Items

Match each term or concept with its corresponding description or definition.

Terms or Concepts

_____ 1. identity achievement
_____ 2. foreclosure
_____ 3. comorbid
_____ 4. role confusion
_____ 5. moratorium
_____ 6. peer selection
_____ 7. peer pressure
_____ 8. parental monitoring
_____ 9. parasuicide
_____ 10. cluster suicide
_____ 11. generational forgetting
_____ 12. familism

Descriptions or Definitions

a. premature identity formation
b. a group of suicides that occur in the same community, school, or time period
c. the adolescent has few commitments to goals or values
d. process by which adolescents choose their friends based on shared interests
e. self-destructive act that does not result in death
f. each generation relearns what the previous generation learned
g. a time-out period during which adolescents experiment with alternative identities
h. the adolescent establishes his or her own goals and values
i. encouragement to conform with one's friends in behavior, dress, and attitude
j. two or more problems occurring together
k. awareness of where children are and what they are doing
l. the belief that family members should sacrifice to help one another

Key Terms

Using your own words, write a brief definition or explanation of each of the following terms on a separate piece of paper.

1. identity versus role confusion
2. identity achievement
3. role confusion
4. foreclosure
5. moratorium
6. gender identity
7. parental monitoring
8. peer pressure
9. deviancy training
10. sexual orientation
11. familism
12. clinical depression
13. rumination
14. suicidal ideation
15. parasuicide
16. cluster suicides
17. adolescent-limited offender
18. life-course-persistent offender
19. generational forgetting

ANSWERS

Chapter Review

1. identity
2. identity versus role confusion
3. identity achievement
4. role confusion (identity or role diffusion)
5. foreclosure
6. moratorium; college
7. religion; gender (sex); politics; vocation
8. follow
9. is not; the number of careers now available; the fact that at age 18 a person is not yet ready to choose a lifetime career
10. 20
11. gender intensification
12. gender identity; biological sex; gender role
13. **b.** is the answer. Apparently, Sharon never explored alternatives or truly forged a unique personal identity.
14. **d.** is the answer.
15. **b.** is the answer.
16. is not
17. early adolescence; mothers; daughters

18. bickering

19. emotional; egocentrism

20. are; harmony; social

21. communication; support; connectedness; control

22. parental monitoring; depression

23. alcohol use; marijuana use; sex; allele; gene

24. non-parent or unrelated

25. parental monitoring

26. **a.** is the answer. Developmentalists recommend authoritative, rather than authoritarian, parenting. And, parental monitoring is important for all adolescents.

27. peer pressure; constructive; destructive; deviancy training

28. selection; choose; facilitation; none of them would do alone

The progression begins with groups of same-sex friends. Next, a loose, public association of a girls' group and a boys' group forms. Then, a small, mixed-sex group forms from the more advanced members of the crowd. Finally, more intimate couples peel off.

29. affects; timing; manifestations; sequence; biology

30. vary

31. sexual orientation; increasing; gender-identity disorder; culture; cohort

32. media; peers; should; parent–child

33. varies; varies

34. are; do not

35. **b.** is the answer. Girls are more likely to say they have a boyfriend than vice versa (**a.**). **c.** is not true; most teen romantic relationships last about a year. And, there's nothing to indicate that the daughter's boyfriend is a negative influence (**d.**). The relationship may actually be healthy for their daughter, so they shouldn't arbitrarily break it up.

36. 20; comorbid

37. less

38. girls; boys; Asian; African; neurological; familism

39. increases; girls; rumination; girls

40. suicidal ideation; common

41. do not; parasuicide

42. less; females; males

43. cluster suicides

44. fallen; high-SES

45. psychoanalytic (Freudian)

46. virtually all

47. is; brain; contextual

Among the brain-based factors are short attention span, being the victim of severe child abuse, hyperactivity, inadequate emotional regulation, maternal cigarette smoking, slow language development, low intelligence, early and severe malnutrition, and autistic tendencies. Psychosocial factors include having deviant friends; having few connections to school; living in a crowded, violent, unstable neighborhood; not having a job; using drugs and alcohol; and having close relatives (especially older siblings) in jail.

48. adolescent-limited; life-course-persistent

49. **d.** is the answer.

50. **c.** is the answer. Males are more likely to commit suicide, although parasuicide is more common among females. Suicide rates are higher among older adults than among adolescents.

51. **b.** is the answer. Cluster suicides occur when the suicide of a local teen leads others to attempt suicide.

52. try; incidence; prevalence; inhalants

53. varies

54. decreased

55. boys; girls; Steroid; diet

56. harmful; addiction

57. self-control; memory; hippocampus; prefrontal cortex

58. generational forgetting

PROGRESS TEST 1

Multiple-Choice Questions

1. **b.** is the answer.

    a. According to Erikson, this is the crisis of infancy.

    c. & d. In Erikson's theory, these crises occur later in life.

2. **a.** is the answer.

    b. This describes an identity moratorium.

    c. This describes an oppositional, negative identity.

    d. This describes role confusion (identity diffusion).

3. **c.** is the answer.

4. **d.** is the answer.

5. **c.** is the answer.

6. **d.** is the answer.

    a. A moratorium is a time-out during which adolescents experiment with different identities.

b. Foreclosure refers to the premature establishment of identity.

c. Peer screening is an aspect of parental monitoring, but it was not specifically discussed in the text.

7. **a.** is the answer.

8. **b.** is the answer.

9. **b.** is the answer.

10. **d.** is the answer.

11. **c.** is the answer.

12. **b.** is the answer. Foreclosed members of a religious group have, like Adam, never really doubted.

a. Because there is no evidence that Adam has asked the "hard questions" regarding his religious beliefs, a developmentalist would probably say that his religious identity is not achieved.

c. Adam clearly does have a religious identity.

d. There is no evidence that Adam's religious identity was formed in opposition to expectations.

13. **c.** is the answer. Life-course-persistent offenders tend to have low intelligence.

14. **b.** is the answer.

15. **c.** is the answer.

a. In fact, parent–child conflict is more likely to involve mothers and their daughters.

b. The text did not compare the rate of conflict in two-parent and single-parent homes.

True or False Items

1. T

2. F   Parent–teen conflicts center on day-to-day details, not on politics or educational issues.

3. F   The opposite is just as likely to be true.

4. T

5. T

6. F   Researchers found no significant difference in rates of adolescent sex after abstinence-only sex education.

7. T

8. T

9. F   Just the opposite is true.

10. T

PROGRESS TEST 2

Multiple-Choice Questions

1. **d.** is the answer.

2. **a.** is the answer.

3. **d.** is the answer.

4. **b.** is the answer.

5. **c.** is the answer.

6. **d.** is the answer.

7. **a.** is the answer.

b. This describes an adolescent undergoing an identity moratorium.

c. This describes identity foreclosure.

d. This describes an adolescent who is adopting an oppositional, negative identity.

8. **d.** is the answer.

9. **c.** is the answer. Self-esteem is, on average, lower in girls and higher in boys, lower in Asian Americans and higher in African Americans, lower in younger adolescents and higher in older adolescents.

10. **c.** is the answer.

11. **d.** is the answer.

a. Identity foreclosure occurs when the adolescent prematurely adopts an identity, without fully exploring alternatives.

b. Rumination involves repeatedly thinking and talking about past experiences to the extent of contributing to depression.

c. Identity diffusion occurs when the adolescent is apathetic and has few commitments to goals or values.

12. **c.** is the answer.

13. **b.** is the answer.

14. **d.** is the answer.

a., b., & c. In fact, on these issues parents and teenagers tend to show substantial *agreement*.

15. **c.** is the answer.

Matching Items

1. h	5. g	9. e
2. a	6. d	10. b
3. j	7. i	11. f
4. c	8. k	12. l

KEY TERMS

1. Erikson's term for the psychosocial crisis of adolescence, **identity versus role confusion,** refers to adolescents' need to combine their self-understanding and social roles into a coherent identity.

2. In Erikson's theory, **identity achievement** occurs when adolescents attain their new identities by establishing their own goals and values and abandoning some of those set by their parents and culture and accepting others.

3. Adolescents who experience **role confusion,** according to Erikson, lack a commitment to goals or values and are often apathetic about trying to find an identity; sometimes called *identity or role diffusion.*

4. In **foreclosure,** according to Erikson, the adolescent forms an identity prematurely, accepting parents' or society's roles and values wholesale.

5. According to Erikson, in the process of finding a mature identity, many young people seem to declare an identity **moratorium,** a socially acceptable time-out during which they experiment with alternative identities without trying to settle on any one.

6. **Gender identity** is a person's self-identification of being female or male.

7. **Parental monitoring** is parents' ongoing awareness about where their children are, what they are doing, and with whom.

8. **Peer pressure** refers to the social pressure to conform with one's friends in behavior, dress, and attitude. It may be positive or negative in its effects.

9. **Deviancy training** is destructive peer support in which one person shows another how to rebel against authority or social norms.

10. **Sexual orientation** refers to a person's sexual and romantic attraction toward a person of the other sex, the same sex, or both sexes.

11. **Familism** is the belief that family members should sacrifice to care for one another.

12. **Clinical depression** describes the syndrome in which feelings of hopelessness, lethargy, and worthlessness last in a person for two weeks or longer.

13. **Rumination** is repeatedly thinking and talking about past experiences to the extent of contributing to depression.

14. **Suicidal ideation** refers to thinking about committing suicide, usually with some serious emotional and intellectual or cognitive overtones.

15. **Parasuicide** is any deliberate self-harm that does not result in death.

16. **Cluster suicides** are several suicides committed by members of a group within a brief period of time.

17. An **adolescent-limited offender** is a juvenile delinquent whose criminal activity stops by age 21.

18. A **life-course-persistent offender** is an adolescent lawbreaker who later becomes a career criminal.

19. **Generational forgetting** is the tendency of each new generation to forget what the previous generation learned.

Emerging Adulthood: Biosocial Development

Chapter Overview

In this chapter we encounter the developing person in the prime of life. Emerging adulthood is the best time for hard physical labor—because strength is at a peak—and for reproduction—because overall health is good and fertility is high. However, with the attainment of full maturity, a new aspect of physical development comes into play—that is, decline. Chapter 17 takes a look at how people perceive changes that occur as the body ages as well as how decisions they make regarding lifestyle affect the course of their overall development.

The chapter begins with a description of the growth, strength, and health of the individual during emerging adulthood, as well as changes in the efficiency of the body's systems. Sexual-reproductive health, a matter of great concern to young adults, is also discussed, with particular attention paid to trends in sexual responsiveness during adulthood and sexually transmitted infections.

Although physical well-being increases during emerging adulthood, so does the rate of psychopathology. The second section discusses how the stresses of this period of life combine with genetic vulnerability in some individuals to trigger the development of mood disorders, anxiety disorders, or schizophrenia.

The final section of the chapter addresses the importance of good health habits, including regular exercise, good nourishment, and avoiding risky behaviors, such as drug abuse. The section concludes with a discussion of how social norms can reduce risk taking and improve health habits in this age group.

What Will You Know?

The text chapter should be studied one section at a time. Before you read, preview each section by skimming it, noting headings and boldface items. Then read the sections, one at a time, keeping these questions in mind.

1. Why do emerging adults want sex but not marriage?
2. Why are emerging adults unlikely to go to doctors for checkups?
3. Why would anyone risk his or her life unnecessarily?
4. How can drug abuse among college students be reduced?

Chapter Review

When you have finished reading the chapter, work through the material that follows to review it. Completing the sentences and answering the questions will enable you to answer the "What Have You Learned?" questions at the end of the text chapter. Scattered throughout the Chapter Review are Study Tips, which explain how best to learn a difficult concept, and Think About It discussions and Applications, which help you to know how well you understand the material. Check your understanding of the material by consulting the answers at the end of the chapter. Do not continue with the next section until you understand each answer. If you need to, review or reread the appropriate section in the textbook before continuing.

Growth and Strength

1. The beginning of young adulthood is the best time for _____ and _____ .

2. Girls usually reach their maximum height by age _____ , and boys by age _____ .

3. Growth in _____ and increases in _____ continue into the 20s.

4. Physical strength _____ (increases/decreases) during the 20s.

5. Every body system functions optimally at
   the beginning of _____ .
   This is true of the _____ ,

   _____ , _____ ,

   and _____-
   _____ systems.

6. The average emerging adult sees a health
   professional _____ (how
   many times?) a year, compared with about
   _____ annual medical visits for
   those aged 75 or older.

7. Many diagnostic tests, including

   _____ , _____ ,

   and _____ are not recommended
   until age 40, or later.

8. When overall growth stops,
   _____ , or aging, begins.

9. Many of the body's functions serve to maintain
   _____ ; that is, they keep
   physiological functioning in a state of balance.
   A related process is _____ , which
   represents the body's dynamic adjustment over
   longer time periods. Over time, a person who
   overeats, starves, or otherwise adversely affects
   health day after day is said to have an increased

   _____ _____ .

10. The older a person is, the _____
    (less time/longer) it takes for these adjustments
    to occur. This is one reason emerging adults are
    less likely to _____ than older
    adults.

11. The other major reason young adults
    rarely experience serious illness is

    _____ _____ ,

    which is defined as _____ .

12. The muscles of the body _____
    (do/do not) have the equivalent of an organ
    reserve. Maximum strength potential typically
    begins to decline by age _____ .

13. The average maximum heart rate
    _____ (declines/remains
    stable/increases) with age. Resting heart rate
    _____ (declines/remains stable/
    increases) with age.

Briefly explain why most of the age-related biological
changes that occur during the first decades of
adulthood are of little consequence to the individual.

14. Attractiveness in _____ ,
    _____ , and
    _____ correlate with
    _____ _____ and
    _____ _____ .

15. At every stage of life, _____
    protects against serious illness.

State some of the health benefits of exercise.

16. Formerly active adults often quit exercising as the
    demands of _____ ,
    _____ , and
    _____ increase. People
    tend to exercise more if they are part of a
    _____ network that exercises
    and live in a _____ that provides
    convenient exercise facilities.

17. At every stage of life, _____
    affects development.

18. For body weight, there is a homeostatic

    _____ _____

    that is affected by _____ ,

    _____ , _____ ,

    _____ , and

    _____ .

19. To measure whether a person is too fat or too thin, clinicians calculate his or her

    _____ _____

    _____ , defined as the ratio of

    _____ (in kilograms) divided by

    _____ (in meters squared).

20. A BMI above _____ is considered overweight; _____ or more is considered obese. A BMI below

    _____ is a symptom of anorexia.

APPLICATIONS:

21. I reduce blood pressure, strengthen the heart and lungs, and make depression less likely. What am I?
    a. a healthy diet
    b. a low-stress lifestyle
    c. an optimistic temperament
    d. exercise

22. Sheila dieted for several weeks until she lost 10 pounds. Upon returning to a normal diet, she is horrified to find that she has gained some of the weight back. It is likely that Sheila's weight gain was caused by
    a. overconsumption of high-fat foods.
    b. too little exercise in her daily routine.
    c. her homeostatic mechanism returning to her natural set point.
    d. a low body set point.

23. Dr. Ramirez suspects Jennifer may be suffering from anorexia because her BMI is
    a. lower than 18.
    b. 23.
    c. higher than 25.
    d. higher than 30.

24. Lucretia, who has a BMI of 24, has been trying unsuccessfully to lose 10 pounds. It is likely that her difficulty is due to the fact that
    a. she has a glandular disorder.
    b. she suffers from bulimia nervosa.
    c. her natural weight set point is higher than she would like.
    d. her obesity is accompanied by a very low metabolic rate.

25. Responding to a question from a reporter, one of the authors of the CARDIA study notes that a key finding of the study was that
    a. the least fit participants were four times more likely to develop diabetes and high blood pressure 15 years later.
    b. half of those who were obese as children became normal-weight young adults.

c. young adults eat more fast food than those of other ages.
d. people with BMIs under 20 have shorter life expectancies.

THINK ABOUT IT Emerging adulthood is the time when health habits lay the foundation for years to come. Is your lifestyle a healthy one? Which of your habits promote a healthy adulthood? Which habits do you need to change?

Sexual Activity

Briefly describe sexual activity and the health of the sexual-reproductive system in emerging adulthood.

26. Most emerging adults today

    _____ (condone/do not condone) premarital sex. Most sexually active adults have _____ (one steady partner/multiple partners) at a time. This pattern of sexual activity is called _____

    _____ .

27. One consequence of sexual patterns among today's young adults is that the incidence of

    _____ _____

    _____ is high among people younger than 26.

28. The best way to prevent STIs is

_____ _____ .

29. Most people in the United States believe
that the primary purpose of sex is to

_____ _____ . This attitude is especially

common among _____ (women/

men). About one-fourth of all people in the

United States believe that the primary purpose

of sex is _____ . This attitude

is more common among _____

(women/men) and _____

(younger/older) adults. The remainder

believe that the primary purpose of sex is

_____ . This attitude is more

common among _____ (women/

men).

_____

THINK ABOUT IT The Visualizing Development chart
on page 494 gives estimates of the average age at
which today's cohort of emerging adults graduate
from college, obtain steady employment, marry,
and achieve other developmental milestones. If you
are between 18 and 25, how do these estimates fit
with your own developmental plan? If you are older,
how do the estimates compare with your own life
experiences?

APPLICATIONS:

30. When we are hot, we perspire in order to give
off body heat. This is an example of the way our
body functions maintain

   a. senescence.   c. set point.
   b. homeostasis.   d. BMI.

31. Due to a decline in organ reserve, 28-year-old
Brenda

   a. has a higher resting heart rate than she did
      when she was younger.
   b. needs longer to recover from strenuous exer-
      cise than she did when she was younger.
   c. has a higher maximum heart rate than her
      younger sister.
   d. has all of these conditions.

32. Janine has decided to write her term paper on
the brain's regulation of homeostatic processes.
Her research should focus on the

   a. cortex.   c. amygdala.
   b. hippocampus.   d. pituitary.

33. Summarizing her presentation on sexual attitudes among emerging adults, Carla notes that
most

   a. believe that physical relationships need not
      involve emotional connections.
   b. condone premarital sex.
   c. no longer believe that marriage is a desirable
      commitment.
   d. believe the primary purpose of sex is repro-
      duction.

34. Elderly Mr. Wilson believes that young adults
today have too many sexual partners. Fueling his
belief is the fact that

   a. sexually transmitted infections were almost
      unknown in his day.
   b. half of all emerging adults in the United
      States have had at least one sexually trans-
      mitted infection.
   c. most sexually active adults have several part-
      ners at a time.
   d. all of these statements are true.

Psychopathology

35. Unlike _____ health,
which peaks during the years of emerging
adulthood, _____ health does
not peak for all adults at this age. Except
for _____ , emerging adults
experience more of every diagnosed disorder, or

_____ _____ ,

than any older group.

36. According to the _____ –

_____ _____ ,

psychopathology is the result of

_____ interacting with an

underlying _____ that may be

_____ , _____ ,

or _____ in origin.

37. Before age 30, approximately

_____ percent of U.S.

residents suffer from a mood disorder, such as

_____ , _____

_____ , or _____

_____ .

38. The most common mood disorder is

_____ _____ ,
defined as the loss of interest in nearly all
activities lasting for _____ (how
long?) or more. This disorder may be rooted in
biochemical imbalances in _____
and _____ , which may be
activated by the social problems of emerging
adulthood.

39. Another major problem is _____
disorders, which are suffered by
_____ (what proportion?)
of young adults in the United States. These
disorders include _____-
_____ _____
_____ , _____-
_____ _____ ,
and _____ _____ .

40. Anxiety disorders are affected by every aspect of
the _____ context. A common
anxiety disorder that keeps some young adults
away from college is _____
_____ . In Japan, a new
disorder called *hikikomori* is related to
anxiety about the _____ and
_____ pressures of high school
and college.

41. Schizophrenia is experienced by about
_____ percent of all
adults. This disorder is partly the result of
_____ , and partly the result of
vulnerabilities such as _____
when the brain is developing and
extensive _____ pressure.
Symptoms of this disorder typically begin in
_____ .

APPLICATIONS:

42. Professor Ryan begins class by asking, "Which
disorder is a leading cause of lifelong impairment?" The correct answer is
   a. post-traumatic stress disorder.
   b. obsessive-compulsive disorder.
   c. schizophrenia.
   d. depression.

43. Twenty-three-year-old Yoko's anxiety about
college has caused her to withdraw from most
activities and stay in her room almost all the
time. Yoko's problem would likely be diagnosed
as
   a. depression.
   b. *hikikomori.*
   c. a phobia.
   d. obsessive-compulsive disorder.

Taking Risks

44. Many emerging adults are attracted to
recreational activities and occupations that
include competitive _____
_____ , such as motocross.

45. Drug abuse is defined as using a drug in a
manner that is _____ . When
the absence of a drug in a person's system
causes physiological or psychological craving,
_____ _____
is apparent. These destructive behaviors are
more common among _____
_____ than among their peers
who _____ .

46. Standards for typical behaviors within a given
society are called _____
_____ .

Briefly explain the social norms approach to reducing
risky behavior.

APPLICATION:

47. Michael is a college freshman who enjoys weekend "booze parties." He has just learned that a
survey regarding drinking on campus found that
most of his classmates avoid binge drinking.
Michael is most likely to
   a. continue drinking on the weekends.
   b. follow this social norm.
   c. increase his drinking to prove he's not like
   everyone else.
   d. become more secretive about his drinking.

Progress Test 1

Multiple-Choice Questions

Circle your answers to the following questions and check them with the answers at the end of the chapter. If your answer is incorrect, read the explanation for why it is incorrect and then consult the text.

1. Senescence refers to
   a. a loss of efficiency in the body's regulatory systems.
   b. age-related gradual physical decline.
   c. decreased physical strength.
   d. vulnerability to disease.

2. When do noticeable increases in height stop?
   a. at about the same age in men and women
   b. at an earlier age in women than in men
   c. at an earlier age in men than in women
   d. There is such diversity in physiological development that it is impossible to generalize regarding this issue.

3. A difference between men and women during early adulthood is that men have
   a. a higher percentage of body fat.
   b. lower metabolism.
   c. proportionately more muscle.
   d. greater organ reserve.

4. The majority of young adults rate their own health as
   a. very good or excellent.
   b. average or fair.
   c. poor.
   d. worse than it was during adolescence.

5. The automatic adjustment of the body's systems to keep physiological functions in a state of equilibrium, even during heavy exertion, is called
   a. organ reserve.   c. stress.
   b. homeostasis.   d. muscle capacity.

6. During emerging adulthood
   a. age signifies cognitive norms and abilities.
   b. age is a more imperfect guide to development than it was during childhood.
   c. social roles become more rigidly determined.
   d. cohort has little effect on behavior.

7. The age of first marriage in the United States today is
   a. about 26 for women and 27 for men.
   b. about 23 for women and 25 for men.

   c. significantly earlier than it was in the middle of the twentieth century.
   d. has not changed significantly since the middle of the twentieth century.

8. Which of the following is true of every body system?
   a. They all function optimally at the beginning of adulthood.
   b. They all begin to decline at the beginning of adulthood.
   c. They all undergo dramatic changes.
   d. They all begin to show the effects of early lifestyle choices.

9. The decrease in physical strength that occurs over the years of adulthood
   a. occurs more rapidly in the arm and upper torso than in the legs.
   b. occurs more rapidly in the back and leg muscles than in the arm.
   c. occurs at the same rate throughout the body.
   d. varies from individual to individual.

10. Body mass index is calculated as
    a. height divided by weight.
    b. weight divided by height squared.
    c. the percentage of total weight that is fat.
    d. the percentage of total weight that is muscle.

11. Diagnostic tests such as mammograms and colonoscopy are not recommended until age
    a. 25   c. 40
    b. 30   d. 50

12. A 50-year-old can expect to retain what percentage of the muscle reserve he or she had at age 20?
    a. 25   c. 75
    b. 50   d. 90

13. The most common mood disorder is
    a. mania.
    b. bipolar disorder
    c. major depression
    d. obsessive-compulsive disorder

14. Social norms
    a. are standards of behavior within a given society or culture.
    b. are particularly strong for emerging adults.
    c. change over time.
    d. have all of these characteristics.

15. Which of the following was NOT suggested as a reason for the high rate of drug use and abuse in emerging adulthood?
   a. Young adults spend time with friends who use drugs.
   b. Young adults are trying to imitate their parents' behavior.
   c. Young adults may use drugs as a way of relieving social anxiety.
   d. The college culture seems to encourage drug use.

True or False Items

Write T (true) or F (false) on the line in front of each statement.

_____ 1. At least until middle age, declines in homeostasis and organ reserve are usually unnoticed.

_____ 2. Few adults actually use all the muscle capacity that they could develop during young adulthood.

_____ 3. Most young adults avoid doctors unless they are injured or pregnant.

_____ 4. Extreme sports such as motocross have existed since the 1950s.

_____ 5. The use of illegal drugs peaks from ages 18 to 25.

_____ 6. The process of aging begins as soon as full growth is reached.

_____ 7. The rate of psychological disorders decreases during emerging adulthood.

_____ 8. Death from eating disorders is more likely in the 20s than in the teens.

_____ 9. Normal weight is somewhere between 20 and 25 BMI.

_____ 10. Most sexually active young adults have several sexual partners at a time.

Progress Test 2

Progress Test 2 should be completed during a final chapter review. Answer the following questions after you thoroughly understand the correct answers for the Chapter Review and Progress Test 1.

Multiple-Choice Questions

1. The early 20s are the peak years for
   a. hard physical work.
   b. problem-free reproduction.
   c. athletic performance.
   d. all of these things.

2. Serial monogamy refers to the practice among sexually active adults of
   a. having more than one partner at a time.
   b. having one steady partner at a time.
   c. engaging in premarital sex.
   d. engaging in extramarital sex.

3. The process of aging, or senescence, begins
   a. after retirement.
   b. during adolescence.
   c. at birth.
   d. as soon as full growth is reached

4. Maximum strength potential typically begins to decline by age:
   a. 25.
   b. 40.
   c. 55.
   d. 65.

5. Normally, the average resting heart rate for both men and women
   a. declines noticeably during the 30s.
   b. declines much faster than does the average maximum heart rate.
   c. reaches a peak at about age 30.
   d. remains stable until late adulthood.

6. During emerging adulthood, people follow patterns of development and behavior that vary by
   a. age.
   b. culture.
   c. cohort.
   d. all of these factors.

7. During emerging adulthood, many age differences in behavior and development
   a. result more from social factors than from biological ones.
   b. result more from biological factors than from social ones.
   c. are unpredictable.
   d. reflect developmental patterns that were established early in childhood.

8. Most people in the United States believe that the main purpose of sex is
   a. reproduction.
   b. to strengthen pair bonding.
   c. recreation.
   d. different for women than for men.

9. A loss of interest or pleasure in most activities that lasts for two weeks or more is likely to be diagnosed as
   a. social phobia.
   b. anxiety disorder.
   c. obsessive-compulsive disorder.
   d. major depression.

10. The disorder characterized by disorganized thoughts, delusions, and hallucinations is
   a. post-traumatic stress disorder.
   b. anxiety disorder.
   c. schizophrenia.
   d. obsessive-compulsive disorder.

11. Which of the following terms does not belong with the others?
   a. *hikikomori*
   b. PTSD
   c. panic attacks
   d. major depression

12. The social norms approach refers to
   a. the particular settings of an individual's various homeostatic processes.
   b. an approach to prevention that increases young adults' awareness of social norms for risky behaviors.
   c. the ratio between a person's weight and height.

   d. the average age at which certain behaviors and events occur

13. Professor Whelan believes that schizophrenia and other disorders are caused by the interaction of stress and an underlying biological, psychosocial, or sociocultural predisposition. This belief is the basis of which model?
   a. diathesis–stress
   b. *hikikomori*
   c. social norms
   d. homeostasis

14. Rates of drug abuse, except when it involves alcohol use and cigarette smoking, often fall
   a. during adolescence.
   b. in the early 50s.
   c. over the years of adulthood.
   d. during late adulthood.

15. The body's dynamic adjustment to exercise, diet, and other factors that affect overall physiology over time is called
   a. senescence.
   b. allostasis.
   c. homeostasis.
   d. delay discounting.

Matching Items

Match each definition or description with its corresponding term.

Terms

_____ 1. senescence
_____ 2. homeostasis
_____ 3. organ reserve
_____ 4. set point
_____ 5. allostatic load
_____ 6. drug abuse
_____ 7. body mass index
_____ 8. drug addiction
_____ 9. anorexia nervosa
_____ 10. obesity
_____ 11. extreme sports

Definitions or Descriptions

a. using a drug to the extent of impairing one's well-being
b. physiological adjustment that may result in a long-term health risk
c. recreation that includes apparent risk of injury or death
d. extra capacity for responding to stressful events
e. a state of physiological equilibrium
f. a BMI above 30
g. age-related decline
h. the ratio of a person's weight divided by his or her height
i. a BMI below 18
j. the body weight that a person's homeostatic processes strive to maintain
k. a condition in which the absence of a drug triggers withdrawal symptoms

Key Terms

Using your own words, write a brief definition or explanation of each of the following terms on a separate piece of paper.

1. emerging adulthood
2. senescence
3. organ reserve
4. homeostasis
5. allostasis
6. set point
7. body mass index (BMI)
8. diathesis–stress model
9. *hikikomori*
10. extreme sports
11. drug abuse
12. drug addiction
13. social norms approach

ANSWERS

CHAPTER REVIEW

1. hard physical work; safe reproduction
2. 16; 18
3. muscle; fat
4. increases
5. adulthood; digestive; respiratory; circulatory; sexual-reproductive
6. once; 10
7. PSA; mammograms; colonoscopy
8. senescence
9. homeostasis; allostasis; allostatic load
10. longer; get sick, fatigued, or obese
11. organ reserve; the extra capacity that each organ has for coping with stress or physiological extremes
12. do; 25
13. declines; remains stable

The declines of aging primarily affect our organ reserve. In the course of normal daily life, adults seldom have to call on this capacity, so the deficits in organ reserve generally go unnoticed.

14. face; body; clothing; better jobs; higher pay
15. exercise

Exercise reduces blood pressure, strengthens the heart and lungs, and makes depression, osteoporosis, heart disease, arthritis, and some cancers less likely.

16. marriage; parenthood; career; social; community
17. diet (nutrition)
18. set point; genes; diet; age; hormones; exercise
19. body mass index (BMI); weight; height
20. 25; 30; 18
21. **d.** is the answer.
22. **c.** is the answer.
23. **a.** is the answer.

    b. This is a healthy BMI.

    c. & d. These BMIs are associated with being overweight or obese.
24. **c.** is the answer.

    a. & d. There is no evidence that Lucretia has a glandular disorder or is obese. In fact, a BMI of 24 is well within the normal weight range.

    b. There is no evidence that Lucretia is bingeing and purging.
25. **a.** is the answer.

Responses will vary.

The sexual-reproductive system is at its strongest during emerging adulthood. Young adults have a strong sex drive; fertility is greater and miscarriage is less common; orgasm is more frequent; and testosterone is higher in both men and women.

26. condone; one steady partner; serial monogamy
27. sexually transmitted infections (STIs)
28. lifelong monogamy
29. strengthen pair bonding; women; reproduction; women; older; recreation; men
30. **b.** is the answer.

    a. This is age-related gradual physical decline.

    c. This refers to the weight that an individual's homeostatic processes strive to maintain.

    d. This is a measure of weight.
31. **b.** is the answer.

    a. Resting heart rate remains stable throughout adulthood.

    c. Maximum heart rate declines with age.
32. **d.** is the answer.
33. **b.** is the answer.

    a. & c. Most emerging adults believe that sexual activity should involve an emotional connection and that marriage is a desirable commitment.

    d. Most believe that the primary purpose of sex is to strengthen pair bonding.
34. **b.** is the answer.

    a. STIs have been part of life since the beginning of time.

c. Most sexually active adults have one steady partner at a time.

35. physical; psychological; dementia; mental illness

36. diathesis–stress model; stress; predisposition; biological; psychosocial; sociocultural

37. 8; mania; bipolar disorder; major depression

38. major depression; two weeks; neurotransmitters; hormones

39. anxiety; one-fourth; post-traumatic stress disorder; obsessive-compulsive disorder; panic attacks

40. cultural; social phobia; social; academic

41. 1; genes; malnutrition; social; adolescence

42. **d.** is the answer.

43. **b.** is the answer.

44. extreme sports

45. harmful to the user's physical, cognitive, or psychosocial well-being; drug addiction; college students; are not in college

46. social norms

The social norms approach uses survey responses to make emerging adults more aware of actual social norms for risky behaviors.

47. **b.** is the answer.

PROGRESS TEST 1

Multiple-Choice Questions

1. **b.** is the answer.

   a., c., & d. Each of these is a specific example of the more general process of senescence.

2. **b.** is the answer.

3. **c.** is the answer.

   a. & b. These are true of women.

   d. Men and women do not differ in this characteristic.

4. **a.** is the answer.

5. **b.** is the answer.

   a. This is the extra capacity that each organ of the body has for responding to unusually stressful events or conditions that demand intense or prolonged effort.

   c. Stress, which is not defined in this chapter, refers to events or situations that tax the body's resources.

   d. This simply refers to a muscle's potential for work.

6. **b.** is the answer.

   c. & d. Just the opposite are true.

7. **a.** is the answer.

   c. & d. The age of first marriage is significantly later today than it was in the middle of the twentieth century.

8. **a.** is the answer.

   d. These effects generally do not appear until later in life. Moreover, it is not until early adulthood that most individuals begin making such choices.

9. **b.** is the answer.

10. **b.** is the answer.

11. **c.** is the answer.

12. **d.** is the answer.

13. **c.** is the answer.

   d. This is an anxiety disorder, not a mood disorder.

14. **d.** is the answer.

15. **b.** is the answer. In fact, just the opposite is true. Young adults may use drugs to express independence from their parents.

True or False Items

1. T

2. T

3. T

4. F   Extreme sports did not exist before emerging adulthood was identified.

5. T

6. T

7. F   Generally, well-being increases during emerging adulthood, but so does the rate of psychological disorders.

8. T

9. T

10. F   Most sexually active adults have one steady partner at a time.

PROGRESS TEST 2

Multiple-Choice Questions

1. **d.** is the answer.

2. **b.** is the answer.

3. **d.** is the answer.

4. **a.** is the answer.

5. **d.** is the answer.

6. **d.** is the answer.

7. **a.** is the answer.

8. **b.** is the answer.

9. **d.** is the answer.

   a. Social phobia is a fear of talking to people.

   b. Depression is a mood disorder.

   c. Obsessive-compulsive disorder is an anxiety disorder.

10. **c.** is the answer.

    a., b., & d. Post-traumatic stress disorder and obsessive-compulsive disorder are anxiety disorders and do not have these symptoms.

11. **d.** is the answer. Major depression is a mood disorder; the other disorders are all anxiety disorders.

12. **b.** is the answer.

    c. This is the body mass index.

13. **a.** is the answer.

14. **c.** is the answer.

15. **b.** is the answer.

Matching Items

1. g	5. b	9. i
2. e	6. a	10. f
3. d	7. h	11. c
4. j	8. k	

KEY TERMS

1. **Emerging adulthood** is the period of life between the ages of 18 and 25.

2. **Senescence** is age-related gradual physical decline throughout the body.

3. **Organ reserve** is the extra capacity of each body organ for responding to unusually stressful events or conditions that demand intense or prolonged effort.

4. **Homeostasis** refers to the process by which body functions are automatically adjusted to keep our physiological functioning in a state of balance.

5. **Allostasis** is the body's longer-term physiological adjustment to activity, and whatever a person eats, breathes, and so forth.

6. **Set point** is the specific body weight that a person's homeostatic processes strive to maintain.

7. The **body mass index (BMI)** is the ratio of a person's weight in kilograms divided by his or her height in meters squared.

8. The **diathesis–stress model** is the view that mental disorders are caused by the interaction of a genetic vulnerability with stressful environmental factors and life events.

9. *Hikikomori* is a Japanese word meaning "pull away," referring to a common anxiety disorder in Japan in which emerging adults refuse to leave their rooms for months or even years at a time.

10. **Extreme sports** are forms of recreation that include apparent risk of injury or death and are attractive and thrilling as a result.

11. **Drug abuse** is drug use to the extent of impairing the user's biological or psychological health.

12. **Drug addiction** is evident in a person when the absence of a drug in his or her body produces the drive to ingest more of the drug.

13. The **social norms approach** to reducing risky behaviors uses survey data regarding the prevalence of risky behaviors to make emerging adults more aware of social norms within their peer group.

Emerging Adulthood: Cognitive Development

Chapter Overview

During the course of adulthood, there are many shifts in cognitive development—in the speed and efficiency with which we process information, in the focus and depth of our cognitive processes, perhaps in the quality, or wisdom, of our thinking. Developmental psychologists use three different approaches in explaining these shifts, with each approach providing insights into the nature of adult cognition. This chapter takes a stage approach, describing age-related changes in an attempt to uncover patterns.

The chapter begins by describing how adult thinking differs from adolescent thinking. The experiences and challenges of adulthood result in a new, postformal thought, evidenced by practical, flexible, and dialectical thinking—the dynamic, in-the-world cognitive style that adults typically use to solve the problems of daily life.

The second section explores how the events of early adulthood can affect moral and religious development. Of particular interest are Fowler's six stages in the development of faith.

The third section examines the effect of the college experience on cognitive growth; findings here indicate that years of education correlate with virtually every measure of cognition as thinking becomes progressively more flexible and tolerant.

What Will You Know?

The text chapter should be studied one section at a time. Before you read, preview each section by skimming it, noting headings and boldface items. Then read the sections, one at a time, keeping these questions in mind.

1. How is adults' thinking about problems different from that of adolescents?

2. Is there evidence that adults are more moral than adolescents?

3. What nation has the highest proportion of young adults who graduate from college?

4. How does college affect a person's thinking processes?

Chapter Review

When you have finished reading the chapter, work through the material that follows to review it. Completing the sentences and answering the questions will enable you to answer the "What Have You Learned?" questions at the end of the text chapter. Scattered throughout the Chapter Review are Study Tips, which explain how best to learn a difficult concept, and Think About It discussions and Applications, which help you to know how well you understand the material. Check your understanding of the material by consulting the answers at the end of the chapter. Do not continue with the next section until you understand each answer. If you need to, review or reread the appropriate section in the textbook before continuing.

1. Developmentalists have used three approaches to explain cognitive development: the _____ approach, the _____ approach, and the _____-_____ approach. In this chapter, Kathleen Berger emphasizes the _____ approach.

Postformal Thought

2. Compared with adolescent thinking, adult thinking is more _____ , _____ , and _____ .

3. Reasoning that is adapted to the subjective real-life contexts to which it is applied is called _____ _____ . It is characterized by problem _____ , not just problem _____ . Emerging adults struggle with the problem of planning ahead, or _____ _____ .

4. The logical error in which people undervalue, or ignore, future consequences in favor of more immediate gratification is called _____ _____ . Psychoactive drugs such as _____ and _____ make this error _____ (more/less) likely.

5. Scholars _____ (agree/ do not agree) that there are stages of adult cognition. Several studies have found that adults _____ (do/do not) think in ways that adolescents _____ (do/ do not). One study found that although logical skills stay steady after emerging adulthood, _____ _____ continues to advance.

6. Developmentalists distinguish between _____ thinking, which arises from the _____ experiences and _____ of an individual, and _____ thinking, which follows abstract _____ .

7. The difference between adolescent and young adult reasoning is particularly apparent for reasoning requiring the integration of _____ and _____ .

8. In contrast to adolescent inflexibility regarding personal experiences, adults are more likely to demonstrate _____ _____ when suggesting solutions to real-life problems. One of the hallmarks of postformal thought is the ability to find _____ _____ to practical problems.

9. This cognitive ability is crucial to countering _____ . Researchers have found that adults have become _____ (more/less) prejudiced about race. When the mere possibility of being negatively stereotyped arouses emotions that disrupt cognition, _____ _____ has occurred.

10. Stereotype threat can make _____ and _____ doubt their intellectual ability. As a result, they may become _____ in academic contexts and perform below their _____ . Research studies have shown that intellectual performance among students increases if they _____ the concept that intelligence is plastic and can be changed.

11. Some theorists consider _____ _____ the most advanced form of cognition. This thinking recognizes that every idea, or _____ , implies an opposing idea, or _____ ; these are then forged into a(n) _____ of the two. This type of thinking fosters the view that life-span change is multidirectional, ongoing, and often surprising—that is, a _____ dialectical process. This type of thinking is more often found in _____ -aged people than in _____ adults.

12. Some researchers believe that some _____ encourage flexible, dialectical reasoning more than others. According to this view, ancient _____ philosophy has led Europeans to use _____ _____ , whereas _____ and _____ have led Asians to think more _____ .

THINK ABOUT IT In what ways do you use postformal thinking as a college student, employee, roommate, or any other adult roles that you fill?

APPLICATIONS:

13. Concluding her comparison of postformal thinking with Piaget's cognitive stages, Lynn notes that
    a. postformal thinking is characterized by "problem finding."
    b. formal operational thinking is characterized by "problem solving."
    c. intuitive, postformal thinking is used when logical reasoning is too cumbersome.
    d. all of these statements are true.

14. Which of the following is an example of responding to a stereotype threat?
    a. Because Jessie's older sister teases her for not being as good as she is at math, Jessie protects her self-concept by devaluing math.
    b. Feeling angered that others may think him less capable because of his ethnicity, Liam becomes flustered when trying to solve a problem in front of the class.
    c. Dave writes a scathing criticism of an obviously racist comment made by a local politician.
    d. As an elderly adult, Kathy takes pride in displaying her quick wit and intelligence to others.

15. Dr. Polaski studies how thinking during adulthood is at a different level than that of adolescence. Evidently, Dr. Polaski follows the _____ approach to the study of development.
    a. stage
    b. psychometric
    c. cognitive
    d. information-processing

16. When she was younger, May-Ling believed that "Honesty is always the best policy." She now realizes that although honesty is desirable, it is not always the best policy. May-Ling's current thinking is an example of _____ thought.
    a. formal
    b. dialectical
    c. mythic-literal
    d. conjunctive

17. Research demonstrates that which of the following is effective in reducing stereotype threat among college students?
    a. creating educational environments among students who have gender in common
    b. creating educational environments among students who have race in common
    c. interventions that help students internalize the concept that intelligence can change
    d. All of these conditions are effective in reducing stereotype threat.

18. In concluding his paper on postformal thinking, Stanley notes that
    a. postformal thinking is not the same kind of universal, age-related stage that Piaget described for earlier cognitive growth.
    b. very few adults attain this highest stage of reasoning.
    c. most everyday problems require sensitivity to subjective feelings and therefore do not foster postformal thinking.
    d. all of these statements are true.

Morals and Religion

19. According to many researchers, moral reasoning and religious beliefs are affected by adult _____ , _____ , and _____ . Research by one expert indicates that one catalyst for propelling young adults from a lower moral stage to a higher one is _____ .

20. Carol Gilligan believes that in matters of moral reasoning , _____ (males/females) tend to be more concerned with the question of rights and justice, whereas _____ (males/females) are more concerned with personal relationships. In her view, women are raised to develop a morality of _____ , while men are taught to develop a morality of _____ . Other research _____ (does/does not) support Gilligan's description of gender differences in morality. Other factors, such as education, specific dilemmas, and _____ , correlate more strongly with morality.

21. Other moral issues that contemporary adults are likely to confront arise from increasing _____ and advanced _____ , including satellite videos, international music, and the _____ .

22. The current approach to research on moral reasoning is based on a series of questions about moral reasoning called the _____ _____ _____ . In general, scores on this test increase with _____ .

23. The theorist who has outlined six stages in the development of faith is _____ .

24. In the space below, identify and briefly describe each stage in the development of faith.

    Stage 1: _____

    _____

    Stage 2: _____

    _____

    Stage 3: _____

    _____

    Stage 4: _____

    _____

    Stage 5: _____

    _____

    Stage 6: _____

    _____

25. Although Fowler's stage theory of faith _____ (is/is not) totally accepted, the idea that religion plays an important role in human development _____ (is/is not).

26. Emerging adults are _____ (more/less) likely than older or younger people to attend religious services and to pray.

_____

THINK ABOUT IT The more years of higher education and life experience a person has, the deeper and more dialectical that person's reasoning becomes. Give a specific example of how your thinking about an issue today is deeper than it was when you were younger, or before you started college.

_____

APPLICATIONS:

27. Carol Gilligan's research suggests that the individual who is most likely to allow the context of personal relationships to wholly determine moral decisions is a
    a. 20-year-old man.
    b. 20-year-old woman.
    c. 40-year-old man.
    d. Gilligan does not deal with gender differences in moral thinking.

28. Jack's uncle believes strongly in God but recognizes that other, equally moral people do not. The openness of his faith places him in which of Fowler's stages?
    a. universalizing faith
    b. conjunctive faith
    c. individual-reflective faith
    d. mythic-literal faith

29. In Fowler's theory, at the highest stages of faith development, people incorporate into their lives a powerful vision of compassion for others. This stage is called
    a. conjunctive faith.
    b. individual-reflective faith.
    c. synthetic-conventional faith.
    d. universalizing faith.

Cognitive Growth and Higher Education

30. Compared with other adults, college graduates tend to be _____ and _____ . In terms of health behaviors, college graduates smoke _____ (more/less), eat _____ (better/worse), exercise _____ (more/less), and live _____ (longer/shorter) lives. They are also more likely to be spouses, homeowners, and _____ .

Briefly outline the year-by-year progression in how the thinking of college students becomes more flexible and tolerant.

31. William Perry found that the thinking of students, over the course of their college careers, progressed through _____ levels of complexity.

32. Research has shown that the more years of higher education a person has, the deeper and more _____ that person's reasoning is likely to become.

33. Worldwide, the number of students who receive higher education _____ (has increased/has not increased) since the first half of the twentieth century. The idea that college education can benefit everyone is _____ . The United States _____ (is/is no longer) the leader in this trend.

34. Collegiate populations have become _____ (more/less) diverse in recent years. College majors also are changing, with fewer students concentrating on the _____ _____ and more on _____ and the _____ . The structure of higher education also _____ (has changed/remains the same).

35. A class in which students watch videos of lectures before attending class, with class time then used for discussion, is called a _____ class. A _____ _____ _____ _____ is a course offered totally online and at very low cost.

APPLICATIONS:

36. (Table 18.1) In his scheme of cognitive and ethical development, Perry describes a position in which the college student says, "I see I'm going to have to make my own decisions in an uncertain world with no one to tell me I'm right." This position marks the culmination of a phase of
   a. either/or dualism.
   b. modified dualism.
   c. relativism.
   d. commitments in relativism.

37. Research suggests that a college sophomore or junior is most likely to have reached a phase in which he or she
   a. believes that there are clear and perfect truths to be discovered.
   b. questions personal and social values, and even the idea of truth itself.
   c. rejects opposing ideas in the interest of finding one right answer.
   d. accepts a simplistic either/or dualism.

38. Who would be the most likely to agree with the statement, "College can be a powerful stimulus to cognitive growth"?
   a. Kohlberg   c. Fowler
   b. Piaget   d. Perry

39. Spike is in his third year at a private, religious liberal arts college, while his brother Lee is in his third year at a public, secular community college. In terms of their cognitive growth, what is the most likely outcome?
   a. Spike will more rapidly develop complex critical thinking skills.
   b. Lee will develop greater self-confidence in his abilities because he is studying from the secure base of his home and family.
   c. All other things being equal, Spike and Lee will develop quite similarly.
   d. It is impossible to predict.

40. In concluding her presentation on "The College Student of Today," Coretta states that
   a. "The number of students in higher education has increased significantly in virtually every country worldwide."
   b. "There are more low-income and ethnic-minority students today than ever before."
   c. "There are more women and minority instructors than ever before."
   d. all of these statements are true.

41. Which of the following would be most helpful to know about a person in predicting whether that individual will go to college and graduate?
   a. age
   b. educational background
   c. household income
   d. Cognitive development is unpredictable from any of these factors.

Progress Test 1

Multiple-Choice Questions

Circle your answers to the following questions and check them with the answers at the end of the chapter. If your answer is incorrect, read the explanation for why it is incorrect and then consult the text.

1. Differences in the reasoning maturity of adolescents and young adults are most likely to be apparent when
   a. low-SES and high-SES groups are compared.
   b. ethnic-minority adolescents and adults are compared.
   c. ethnic-majority adolescents and adults are compared.
   d. emotionally charged issues are involved.

2. Which of the following is NOT one of the major approaches to the study of adult cognition described in the text?
   a. the information-processing approach
   b. the stage approach
   c. the systems approach
   d. the psychometric approach

3. Compared with adolescent thinking, adult thinking tends to be
   a. more flexible.
   b. more practical.
   c. more dialectical.
   d. all of these things.

4. A hallmark of mature adult thought is
   a. the ability to engage in dialectical thinking.
   b. the reconciliation of both objective and subjective approaches to real-life problems.
   c. the adoption of conjunctive faith.
   d. all of these factors.

5. According to James Fowler, the experience of college often is a springboard to
   a. intuitive-projective faith
   b. mythic-literal faith
   c. individual-reflective faith
   d. synthetic-conventional faith

6. Which approach to adult cognitive development focuses on life-span changes in the efficiency of encoding, storage, and retrieval?
   a. stage
   b. information-processing
   c. psychometric
   d. dialectical

7. Postformal thinking is most useful for solving _____ problems.
   a. science
   b. mathematics
   c. everyday
   d. abstract, logical

8. The term for the kind of thinking that involves the consideration of both poles of an idea and their reconciliation, or synthesis, in a new idea is
   a. subjective thinking.
   b. postformal thought.
   c. adaptive reasoning.
   d. dialectical thinking.

9. Thesis is to antithesis as _____ is to _____ .
   a. a new idea; an opposing idea
   b. abstract; concrete

   c. concrete; abstract
   d. provisional; absolute

10. Which of the following adjectives best describe(s) cognitive development during adulthood?
    a. multidirectional and dynamic
    b. linear
    c. steady
    d. tumultuous

11. Which of the following most accurately describes postformal thought?
    a. subjective thinking that arises from the personal experiences and perceptions of the individual
    b. objective reasoning that follows abstract, impersonal logic
    c. a form of logic that combines subjectivity and objectivity
    d. thinking that is rigid, inflexible, and fails to recognize the existence of other potentially valid views

12. The Defining Issues Test is a
    a. standardized test that measures postformal thinking.
    b. projective test that assesses dialectical reasoning.
    c. series of questions about moral dilemmas.
    d. test that assesses the impact of life events on cognitive growth and moral reasoning.

13. According to Carol Gilligan
    a. in matters of moral reasoning, females tend to be more concerned with the question of rights and justice.
    b. in matters of moral reasoning, males tend to put human needs above principles of justice.
    c. moral reasoning advances during adulthood in response to the more complex moral dilemmas that life poses.
    d. all of these statements are true.

14. Colleges today have become
    a. larger.
    b. more career oriented.
    c. diverse.
    d. all of these things.

15. Research has revealed that a typical outcome of college education is that students become
    a. very liberal politically.
    b. less committed to any particular values.
    c. more committed to a particular value.
    d. less open-minded.

True or False Items

Write T (true) or F (false) on the line in front of each statement.

_____ 1. Only 9 percent of low-income students have a bachelor's degree by age 24.

_____ 2. Most people are usually aware of their stereotypes.

_____ 3. After their early 20s, most adults are mature enough to know to drink alcohol in moderation.

_____ 4. Because they recognize the changing and subjective nature of beliefs and values, dialectical thinkers avoid making personal or intellectual commitments.

_____ 5. The process of moral thinking improves with age.

_____ 6. In developed nations in 2010, almost one in two emerging adults earned a degree.

_____ 7. Postformal thought is less absolute and less abstract than formal thought.

_____ 8. Mythic-literal faith, like other "lower" stages in the development of faith, is not generally found past adolescence.

_____ 9. Students who internalize that intelligence is plastic are less likely to experience stereotype threat.

_____ 10. Moral values are powerfully affected by circumstances.

_____ 11. Delay discounting occurs at every age.

Progress Test 2

Progress Test 2 should be completed during a final chapter review. Answer the following questions after you thoroughly understand the correct answers for the Chapter Review and Progress Test 1.

Multiple-Choice Questions

1. Which approach to adult cognitive development emphasizes the analysis of components of intelligence?
   a. postformal
   b. psychometric
   c. information-processing
   d. all of these approaches

2. Which approach to adult cognitive development "picks up where Piaget left off"?
   a. psychometric
   b. information-processing
   c. postformal
   d. dialectical

3. As adult thinking becomes more focused on occupational and interpersonal demands, it also becomes less inclined toward
   a. inflexibility.
   b. dialectical thought.
   c. adaptive thought.
   d. all of these ways of thinking.

4. The result of dialectical thinking is a view that
   a. one's self is an unchanging constant.
   b. life-span change is dynamic.
   c. "everything is relative."
   d. all of these statements are true.

5. The existence of a fifth, postformal stage of cognitive development during adulthood
   a. is recognized by most developmentalists.
   b. has very little empirical support.
   c. remains controversial among developmental researchers.
   d. is widely accepted in women, but not in men.

6. Formal operational thinking is most useful for solving problems that
   a. involve logical relationships or theoretical possibilities.
   b. require integrative skills.
   c. involve the synthesis of diverse issues.
   d. require seeing perspectives other than one's own.

7. College seems to make people more accepting of other people's attitudes because it
   a. boosts self-esteem.
   b. promotes recognition of many perspectives.
   c. promotes extroversion.
   d. does all of these things.

8. The goal of dialectical thinking is forging a(n) _____ from opposing poles of an idea.
   a. thesis   c. synthesis
   b. antithesis   d. hypothesis

9. Formal operational thinking is to postformal thinking as _____ is to

   _____ .

   a. psychometric; information-processing
   b. adolescence; adulthood
   c. thesis; antithesis
   d. self-esteem; extroversion

10. According to James Fowler, which type of faith is typical of middle childhood?

    a. intuitive-projective
    b. mythic-literal
    c. synthetic-conventional
    d. individual-reflective

11. According to James Fowler, individual-reflective faith is marked by

    a. a willingness to accept contradictions.
    b. a burning need to enunciate universal values.
    c. a literal, wholehearted belief in myths and symbols.
    d. the beginnings of independent questioning of teachers and other figures of authority.

12. Moral principles that judge right and wrong in absolute terms constitute a

    a. morality of care.
    b. morality of justice.
    c. morality of compassion.
    d. morality of truth.

13. According to James Fowler, the simplest stage of faith is the stage of

    a. universalizing faith.
    b. intuitive-projective faith.
    c. mythic-literal faith.
    d. conventional faith.

14. Many of the problems of adult life are characterized by ambiguity, partial truths, and extenuating circumstances, and therefore are often best solved using _____ thinking.

    a. formal
    b. reintegrative
    c. postformal
    d. executive

15. A classic study by Perry showed that the thinking of students in college progresses through how many levels of complexity?

    a. 6   c. 12
    b. 9   d. 15

Matching Items

Match each term or concept with its corresponding description or definition.

Terms or Concepts

_____   1. delay discounting
_____   2. Defining Issues Test
_____   3. dialectical thought
_____   4. subjective thought
_____   5. objective thought
_____   6. thesis
_____   7. antithesis
_____   8. synthesis
_____   9. morality of care
_____   10. morality of justice
_____   11. postformal thought
_____   12. massification
_____   13. MOOC

Descriptions or Definitions

a. a statement that contradicts another
b. the final stage of dialectical thinking
c. undervaluing future consequences
d. a statement of belief
e. thinking best suited to solving real-world problems
f. giving human needs and relationships highest priority
g. the idea that college education benefits everyone
h. a for-credit course offered online
i. used to assess moral reasoning
j. emphasis is placed on distinguishing right from wrong
k. considering both poles of an idea simultaneously
l. thinking based on personal experiences and perceptions
m. thinking that follows impersonal logic

Key Terms

Using your own words, write a brief definition or explanation of each of the following terms on a separate piece of paper.

1. postformal thought
2. delay discounting
3. subjective thought
4. objective thought
5. stereotype threat
6. dialectical thought
7. thesis
8. antithesis
9. synthesis
10. morality of care
11. morality of justice
12. Defining Issues Test
13. massification
14. massive open online course (MOOC)

ANSWERS

CHAPTER REVIEW

1. stage; psychometric; information-processing; stage
2. practical; flexible; dialectical
3. postformal thought; finding; solving; time management
4. delay discounting; alcohol; marijuana; more
5. do not agree; do; do not; social understanding
6. subjective; personal; perceptions; objective; logic
7. emotion; logic
8. cognitive flexibility (or flexible problem solving); multiple solutions
9. stereotypes; less; stereotype threat
10. women; minorities; anxious; potential; internalize
11. dialectical thought; thesis; antithesis; synthesis; dynamic; middle; emerging
12. cultures; Greek; analytic logic; Confucianism; Taoism; dialectically
13. **d.** is the answer.
14. **b.** is the answer.
15. **a.** is the answer.

    b. This approach analyzes components of intelligence such as those measured by IQ tests.

    c. Each of these approaches is cognitive in nature.

    d. This approach studies the encoding, storage, and retrieval of information throughout life.

16. **b.** is the answer. May-Ling has formed a synthesis between the thesis that honesty is the best policy and its antithesis.

    a. This is an example of postformal rather than formal thinking.

    c. & d. These are stages in the development of faith as proposed by James Fowler.

17. **d.** is the answer.
18. **a.** is the answer.

    b. Because postformal thinking is typical of adult thought, this is untrue.

    c. It is exactly this sort of problem that *fosters* postformal thinking.

19. responsibilities; experiences; education; college
20. males; females; care; justice; does not; culture
21. globalization; communication; Internet
22. Defining Issues Test; age
23. James Fowler
24. Intuitive-projective faith is magical, illogical, filled with fantasy, and typical of children ages 3 to 7.

    Mythic-literal faith, which is typical of middle childhood, is characterized by taking the myths and stories of religion literally.

    Synthetic-conventional faith is a nonintellectual acceptance of cultural or religious values in the context of interpersonal relationships.

    Individual-reflective faith is characterized by intellectual detachment from the values of culture and the approval of significant others.

    Conjunctive faith incorporates both powerful unconscious ideas and rational, conscious values.

    Universalizing faith is characterized by a powerful vision of universal compassion, justice, and love that leads people to put their own personal welfare aside in an effort to serve these values.

25. is not; is
26. less
27. **b.** is the answer.

    a. & c. According to Gilligan, males tend to be more concerned with human rights and justice than with human needs and personal relationships, which are more the concern of females.

    d. Just the opposite is true of Gilligan's research.

28. **b.** is the answer.
29. **d.** is the answer.
30. healthier; wealthier; less; better; more; longer; parents of healthy children

First-year students often believe that there are clear and perfect truths to be found. This phase is followed by a wholesale questioning of personal and social values. Finally, after considering opposite ideas, students become committed to certain values, at the same time realizing the need to remain open-minded.

31. nine
32. dialectical
33. has increased; massification; is no longer
34. more; liberal arts; business; professions; has changed
35. flipped; massive open online course (MOOC)
36. c. is the answer.
37. b. is the answer.

a. First-year college students are more likely to believe this is so.

c. & d. Over the course of their college careers, students become less likely to do either of these.

38. d. is the answer.
39. c. is the answer.
40. d. is the answer.
41. c. is the answer.

PROGRESS TEST 1

Multiple-Choice Questions

1. d. is the answer.

a., b., & c. Socioeconomic status and ethnicity do not predict reasoning maturity.

2. c. is the answer.
3. d. is the answer
4. b. is the answer.
5. c. is the answer.
6. b. is the answer.

a. This approach emphasizes the emergence of a new stage of thinking that builds on the skills of formal operational thinking.

c. This approach analyzes the measurable components of intelligence.

d. This is a type of thinking rather than an approach to the study of cognitive development.

7. c. is the answer.

a., b., & d. Because of its more analytical nature, formal thinking is most useful for solving these types of problems.

8. d. is the answer.

a. Thinking that is subjective relies on personal reflection rather than objective observation.

b. Although dialectical thinking is characteristic of postformal thought, this question refers specifically to dialectical thinking.

c. Adaptive reasoning, which also is characteristic of postformal thought, goes beyond mere logic in solving problems to also explore real-life complexities and contextual circumstances.

9. a. is the answer.
10. a. is the answer.

b. & c. Comparatively speaking, linear and steady are more descriptive of childhood and adolescent cognitive development.

11. c. is the answer.
12. d. is the answer.
13. c. is the answer.

a. In Gilligan's theory, this is more true of males than females.

b. In Gilligan's theory, this is more true of females than males.

14. d. is the answer.
15. c. is the answer. Although they become more committed, they realize they need to remain open-minded.

True or False Items

1. T
2. F People are often unaware of their stereotypes.
3. T
4. F Dialectical thinkers recognize the need to make commitments to values even though these values will change over time.
5. T
6. T
7. T
8. F Many adults remain in the "lower" stages of faith, which, like "higher" stages, allow for attaining strength and wholeness.
9. T
10. T
11. T

PROGRESS TEST 2

Multiple-Choice Questions

1. b. is the answer.

a. This approach emphasizes the possible emergence in adulthood of new stages of thinking that build on the skills of earlier stages.

c. This approach studies the encoding, storage, and retrieval of information throughout life.

2. c. is the answer.

3. **a.** is the answer.

    b. & c. During adulthood, thinking typically becomes more dialectical and adaptive.

4. **b.** is the answer.

    a. & c. On the contrary, a dialectic view recognizes the limitations of extreme relativism and that one's self evolves continuously.

5. **c.** is the answer.

6. **a.** is the answer.

    b., c., & d. Postformal thought is most useful for solving problems such as these.

7. **b.** is the answer.

    a. & c. The impact of college on self-esteem and extroversion were not discussed. Moreover, it is unclear how such an impact would make a person more accepting of others.

8. **c.** is the answer.

    a. A thesis is a new idea.

    b. An antithesis is an idea that opposes a particular thesis.

    d. Hypotheses, which are testable predictions about behavior, are not an aspect of dialectical thinking.

9. **b.** is the answer.

10. **b.** is the answer.

    a. Intuitive-projective faith is typical of children ages 3 to 7.

    c. & d. Synthetic-conventional faith and individual-reflective faith are more typical of adulthood.

11. **d.** is the answer.

    a. This describes conjunctive faith.

    b. This describes universalizing faith.

    c. This describes mythic-literal faith.

12. **b.** is the answer.

13. **b.** is the answer.

14. **c.** is the answer.

    a. Formal thinking is best suited to solving problems that require logic and analytical thinking.

    b. & d. These terms are not discussed in the text.

15. **b.** is the answer.

Matching Items

1. c	5. m	9. f	13. h
2. i	6. d	10. j	
3. k	7. a	11. e	
4. l	8. b	12. g	

KEY TERMS

1. Proposed by some developmentalists as a fifth stage of cognitive development, **postformal thought** is suited to solving real-world problems and is more practical, more flexible, and more dialectical than adolescent thought.

2. **Delay discounting** is a logical error in which people undervalue, or ignore, future consequences in favor of more immediate gratification.

3. **Subjective thought** is thinking that arises from our personal experiences and perceptions.

4. **Objective thought** is thinking that follows abstract, impersonal logic.

5. **Stereotype threat** is the possibility that one's appearance or behavior may be misread to confirm another person's oversimplified, prejudiced attitude.

6. **Dialectical thought** is the most advanced cognitive process that involves considering both poles of an idea (thesis and antithesis) simultaneously and then forging them into a synthesis.

7. The first stage of dialectical thinking, a **thesis** is a proposition or statement of belief.

8. A statement that contradicts the thesis, an **antithesis** is the second stage of dialectical thinking.

9. The final stage of dialectical thinking, the **synthesis** reconciles thesis and antithesis into a new, more comprehensive level of truth.

10. According to Carol Gilligan, women are raised to develop a **morality of care;** they give human needs and relationships highest priority.

11. According to Carol Gilligan, men are raised to develop a **morality of justice;** their emphasis is on distinguishing right from wrong.

12. The **Defining Issues Test (DIT)** is a series of questions developed by James Rest about moral dilemmas used to assess moral reasoning.

13. **Massification** is the idea that higher (college) education could benefit everyone.

14. A **massive open online course (MOOC)** is a for-credit course offered online, and typically for very low tuition.

Emerging Adulthood: Psychosocial Development

Chapter Overview

Biologically mature and no longer bound by parental authority, the emerging adult typically is now free to choose a particular path of development. Today, the options are incredibly varied. Not surprisingly, then, the hallmark of psychosocial development during emerging adulthood is diversity. Nevertheless, developmentalists have identified several themes or patterns that help us understand the course of development between the ages of 20 and 40.

The chapter begins with a discussion of the continuing identity crisis during emerging adulthood, as young people seek to find their own unique path. Ethnic identity is difficult to achieve for children of immigrants trying to reconcile their parents' background with their new social context.

The next section of the chapter addresses the need for intimacy in adulthood, focusing on the development of friendship and love. Intimacy needs are universal, but vary by culture and cohort.

The final section of the chapter discusses emerging adults and their parents. Although parental support is typical everywhere, being too dependent on parents presents complications for emerging adults.

What Will You Know?

The text chapter should be studied one section at a time. Before you read, preview each section by skimming it, noting headings and boldface items. Then read the sections, one at a time, keeping these questions in mind.

1. What typically happens to a shy child's temperament when he or she grows up?
2. Does cohabitation before marriage make a marriage happier?
3. In cases of spouse abuse, is it better for partners to be counseled or to separate?

4. Why do some emerging adults live with their parents?

Chapter Review

When you have finished reading the chapter, work through the material that follows to review it. Completing the sentences and answering the questions will enable you to answer the "What Have You Learned?" questions at the end of the text chapter. Scattered throughout the Chapter Review are Study Tips, which explain how best to learn a difficult concept, and Think About It discussions and Applications, which help you to know how well you understand the material. Check your understanding of the material by consulting the answers at the end of the chapter. Do not continue with the next section until you understand each answer. If you need to, review or reread the appropriate section in the textbook before continuing.

Continuity and Change

1. Norms that set the "best" ages for certain life events represent the developmental timetable called the _____ _____ . It is important to remember that _____ and _____ are evident throughout life.

2. The identity crisis sometimes causes _____ , _____ , or _____ . A more mature response to the crisis would probably be to seek a _____ .

3. Examples of moratoria include _____ .

4. In the United States and Canada, about _____ (what proportion?) of emerging adults are of African, Asian, Native American, or Latino heritage. Most of them _____ (identify/do not identify) with specific ethnic groups.

5. Identity achievement _____ (is/is not) particularly difficult for immigrants. Briefly explain why this is so. _____

_____

6. Today, achieving vocational identity is _____ (easier/more difficult) than ever.

7. Today, between the ages of 18 and 27 the average U.S. worker has held _____ (how many?) jobs.

8. Although continuity and change _____ (are/are not) evident in personality in emerging adulthood, personality endures _____ . However, personality is not _____ .

9. Research studies generally show that transitions such as entering college or getting a job are accompanied by _____ (increased/decreased) well-being.

10. Shifts toward positive development are especially apparent among emerging adults who, as children, displayed extreme _____ or marked _____ . These findings demonstrate _____ in development.

11. Genes and _____ that make people more susceptible to environmental influences are called _____ .

STUDY TIP To consolidate your understanding of continuity and change during emerging adulthood, write a paragraph describing a typical young adult who is uncertain about his or her career goals. Be sure to describe various moratoria on identity achievement that your person may have taken advantage of.

APPLICATION:

12. Which of the following would be the worst advice for a young adult entering the job market today?
   a. Seek education that fosters a variety of general abilities and human relations skills.
   b. Expect that educational requirements for work will shift every few years.
   c. To avoid diluting your skills, concentrate your education on preparing for one specific job.
   d. Be flexible and willing to adjust to the varied pacing and timing of today's jobs.

Intimacy

13. In Erikson's theory, the identity crisis of adolescence is followed in emerging adulthood by the crisis of _____

_____ _____ .

The same need is expressed by other theorists as

_____ , _____ ,

_____ , _____ ,

_____ , _____ ,

or _____ .

The most recent theory notes that an important aspect of close human connections is

"_____-_____ ."

14. To defend against stress and provide joy, _____ are particularly important. Briefly state why this is so.

15. People tend to make more friends during the period of _____ _____ than at any other time.

16. Gender differences in friendship _____ (are/are not) especially apparent during adulthood. In general, men's friendships are based on _____ _____and _____ , whereas friendships between women tend to be more _____ and

_____ .

17. Research finds that _____ (women/men) demand less from their friendships than do _____ (women/men), and thus have more friends.

18. Cross-sex friendships are _____ (more/less) common today than in the past.

19. Humans _____ (find it difficult/ do not find it difficult) to sustain more than one sexual or romantic relationship at a time.

20. Robert Sternberg has argued that love has three distinct components: _____ , _____ , and _____ .

21. Sternberg believes that the relative absence or presence of these components gives rise to _____ (how many?) different forms of love.

22. For both men and women, _____ seems to fade, but _____ increases when children are born. This is why most sexually active adults avoid pregnancy unless they believe their partner is a _____ mate.

23. Commitment takes time. It is strengthened by _____ _____ , and it is affected by _____ .

24. When commitment is added to passion and intimacy, the result is _____ love.

25. Sexual encounters between two people in which neither _____ nor _____ are expected are called _____ . The desire for this type of arrangement may be stronger in young _____ than in young _____ .

26. One potential problem with technology in matchmaking is _____ _____ , which occurs when people perceive _____ .

27. Increasingly common among young adults in many countries is the living pattern called _____ , in which two unrelated adults live together in a committed sexual relationship. This living pattern _____ (varies/does not vary)

from nation to nation. In the United States it _____ (is the norm/is not the norm).

28. (Opposing Perspectives) Cohabitation _____ (does/does not) seem to prevent problems that might arise after a wedding. Particularly problematic is _____ , which occurs when couples live together, then break up, then come back together. Such relationships have high rates of _____ and _____ _____ .

29. Worldwide, couples today marry _____ (earlier/later) than earlier cohorts did.

30. In about one-third of the world's families, marriage _____ (is/is not) based on romantic love. In another third of families, _____ _____ is required. In the newest pattern, young people socialize, _____ , and marry when they are financially and emotionally able to be independent.

List some factors that lead to improvement in marriage over time.

31. Marriage between people who are similar in age, SES, ethnicity, and the like is called _____ . Marriage that is outside the group is called _____ .

32. Research by John Gottman demonstrates that _____ in marriage is less predictive of _____ than _____ because the latter closes down _____ . This finding is _____ (widely supported/ controversial). The destructive pattern called _____ / _____ interaction is common in ailing marriages.

33. There are numerous causes of domestic violence, including _____ .

34. One form of domestic abuse,

_____ _____

_____ , entails outbursts of

fighting, with both partners sometimes becoming

involved, which is brought on more by the

situation than by the individuals' personalities.

35. The second type of abuse, _____

_____ , occurs when one partner,

almost always the _____ , uses

a range of methods to punish and degrade the

other.

APPLICATIONS:

36. Professor Samuels believes that people enlarge
their understanding, resources, and experiences
through their intimate friends. This idea is called
   a. interdependence.   c. communion.
   b. affiliation.   d. self-expansion.

37. Marie notes that her parents have been married
for 25 years, even though each seems somewhat unfulfilled in terms of their relationship. Her
friends had a similar relationship and divorced
after five years. Given the research on what
makes a marriage work how might Marie explain
the differences?
   a. "My parents are just much more patient with
      and understanding of each other."
   b. "Couples today expect more of each other."
   c. "My parents feel that they must stay together
      for financial reasons."
   d. "I can't understand what keeps my parents
      together."

38. Rwanda and Rodney have been dating for about
a month. Their relationship is most likely characterized by
   a. strong feelings of commitment.
   b. consummate love.
   c. physical intimacy and feelings of closeness.
   d. all of these conditions.

39. I am 25 years old. It is most likely that I
   a. am married.
   b. am divorced.
   c. have never been married.
   d. am divorced and remarried.

40. Arthur and Mabel have been married for five
years. According to Sternberg, if their relationship is a satisfying one, which of the following
best describes their relationship?
   a. They are strongly committed to each other.
   b. They are passionately in love.
   c. They are in the throes of establishing
      intimacy.

   d. They are beginning to wonder why the pas-
      sion has left their relationship.

41. Philip and Phyllis have an ailing relationship.
After dinner, Philip says, "We need to talk about
this." In reply, Phyllis says, "I'm too busy." This
pattern of interaction is called
   a. passive-aggressive.
   b. demand/withdraw.
   c. heterogamy.
   d. social homogamy.

42. Your sister, who is about to marry, seeks your
advice on what makes a happy marriage. You
should mention that all but which one of the following factors contribute to marital happiness?
   a. cohabitation before marriage
   b. the degree to which a couple is homogamous
      or heterogamous
   c. the degree of marital equity
   d. whether identity needs have been met before
      marriage

Emerging Adults and Their Parents

43. Members of families have _____

lives, meaning that experiences and needs of

members at one stage are affected by those at

other stages.

44. Although emerging adults strive for

independence, family support in the form

of _____ aid and gifts of

time are important. Family dependence

_____ (varies/does not vary)

between Western nations and developing nations.

45. One downside to parental support is that it may

impede _____ in emerging

adults. Parents who hover over their emerging

adult child are called _____

parents.

Progress Test 1

Multiple-Choice Questions

Circle your answers to the following questions
and check them with the answers at the end of
the chapter. If your answer is incorrect, read the
explanation for why it is incorrect and then consult
the text.

1. According to Erik Erikson, the first basic task of
adulthood is to establish
   a. a residence apart from parents.
   b. intimacy with others.

c. generativity through work or parenthood.

d. a career commitment.

2. Most developmental psychologists believe that identity

a. takes longer to achieve than in the past.

b. is usually achieved during adolescence.

c. is harder for women to achieve than for men.

d. is no longer a useful concept in developmental science.

3. If asked to explain the high failure rate of marriages between young adults, Erik Erikson would most likely say that

a. achievement goals are often more important than intimacy in emerging adulthood.

b. intimacy is difficult to establish until identity is formed.

c. divorce has almost become an expected stage in development.

d. young adults today have higher expectations of marriage than did previous cohorts.

4. Which of the following is true of emerging adults who are of African, Asian, Native American, or Latino heritage?

a. Their ethnic pride generally correlates with social adjustment.

b. Their ethnic identity does not change throughout the life span.

c. They easily reconcile their parents' background with their new social context.

d. They tend to identify with very specific ethnic groups.

5. To determine ways to lower the high rate of divorce, Dr. Wilson is conducting research on marital satisfaction and the factors that contribute to it. Which of the following would he consider to be important factors?

a. homogamy

b. maturity

c. financial security

d. All of these factors contribute to marital satisfaction.

6. According to Erikson, the failure to achieve intimacy during emerging adulthood is most likely to result in

a. generativity.   c. role diffusion.

b. stagnation.   d. isolation.

7. Friendships are important for emerging adults because

a. friendship ties are voluntary.

b. they defend against stress.

c. they are likely to postpone marriage.

d. of all of these reasons.

8. According to research by John Gottman, _____ in marriage is less predictive of separation than

_____ .

a. conflict; disgust

b. disgust; conflict

c. anger; depression

d. depression; anger

9. According to Robert Sternberg, consummate love emerges

a. as a direct response to passion.

b. as a direct response to physical intimacy.

c. when commitment is added to passion and intimacy.

d. during the early years of parenthood.

10. An arrangement in which two unrelated, unmarried adults live together in a romantic partnership is called

a. cross-sex friendship.

b. a passive-congenial pattern.

c. cohabitation.

d. affiliation.

11. Differences in religious customs or rituals are most likely to arise in a

a. homogamous couple.

b. heterogamous couple.

c. cohabiting couple.

d. very young married couple.

12. Between ages 18 and 25, the average worker in the United States has how many jobs?

a. one   c. five

b. two   d. six

13. Homogamy is to heterogamy as

a. marriage outside the group is to marriage within the group.

b. marriage within the group is to marriage outside the group.

c. companionate love is to passionate love.

d. passionate love is to companionate love.

14. The situation in which one partner in a romantic relationship wants to discuss an issue and the other refuses is called

a. intimate terrorism.

b. demand/withdraw interaction.

c. heterogamy.

d. homogamy.

15. During which period of life do people tend to make the most friends?

    a. early childhood
    b. adolescence
    c. emerging adulthood
    d. adulthood

True or False Items

Write T (true) or F (false) on the line in front of each statement.

    1. According to Erikson, the adult experiences a crisis of intimacy versus isolation after achieving identity.

    2. Intimate partner violence is common only in certain countries.

    3. According to Sternberg, early in a relationship, companionate love is at its highest.

    4. Cross-sex friendships are rarer today than in the past.

    5. Cohabitation solves all the problems that might arise after marriage.

    6. Most successful couples learn to compromise.

    7. Throughout the world, marriage is generally based on romantic love.

    8. Because of the complexity of the high-tech work world, most young adults can expect to remain at the same job throughout their careers.

    9. Domestic violence is more common among cohabiting couples than among married couples.

    10. According to some research, lust and affection arise from different parts of the brain.

Progress Test 2

Progress Test 2 should be completed during a final chapter review. Answer the following questions after you thoroughly understand the correct answers for the Chapter Review and Progress Test 1.

Multiple-Choice Questions

1. Emerging adults are more likely to avoid serious risks to their health and safety if they had

    a. parents who remain married.
    b. excellent teachers.
    c. a wealthy upbringing.
    d. close relationships with their parents.

2. The key difference between situational couple violence and intimate terrorism is

    a. the presence of mental illness in the violent partner in intimate terrorism.
    b. the violent control of one partner by the other in intimate terrorism.
    c. the presence of children in intimate terrorism.
    d. the cyclical nature of situational couple violence.

3. Kwame and Kendra both enjoy dancing, going to the movies, and working out. Developmentalists would say their marriage is characterized by

    a. heterogamy.
    b. companionate attachment.
    c. social homogamy.
    d. romantic attachment.

4. A hookup is best defined as

    a. a homogamous sexual relationship.
    b. a heterogamous sexual relationship.
    c. a sexual relationship involving neither intimacy nor commitment.
    d. a form of serial cohabitation.

5. The Western ideal of love is best described in Sternberg's theory as

    a. romantic.   **c.** companionate.
    b. fatuous.   **d.** consummate.

6. Which of the following is NOT true today regarding marriage?

    a. Most couples in the United States cohabit during emerging adulthood.
    b. Couples are marrying earlier.
    c. Arranged marriage is practiced in one-third of all nations.
    d. In North America and Europe, more than half of those age 18 to 25 have never married.

7. Whereas men's friendships tend to be based on _____ , friendships between women tend to be based on

_____ .

    a. shared confidences; shared interests
    b. cooperation; competition
    c. shared interests; shared confidences
    d. finding support for personal problems; discussion of practical issues

8. According to Robert Sternberg, the three dimensions of love are

    a. passion, intimacy, and consummate love.
    b. physical intimacy, emotional intimacy, and consummate love.
    c. passion, commitment, and consummate love.
    d. passion, intimacy, and commitment.

9. Research on cohabitation suggests that
   a. there is little variation in why couples cohabit.
   b. emerging adults in the United States, Canada, and England cohabit at higher rates than those in Japan, Ireland, and Italy.
   c. adults who cohabit tend to be older and wealthier than married people.
   d. cohabitation leads to a stronger marriage.

10. A homogamous marriage is best defined as a marriage between
    a. people who are physically similar to each other.
    b. people of similar social backgrounds.
    c. people of dissimilar socioeconomic backgrounds.
    d. two caring people of the same sex.

11. Compared with married adults, cohabiting adults tend to
    a. be older.
    b. be wealthier.
    c. be less likely to end the relationship.
    d. have the same problems that might arise after a wedding.

12. Today, male–female friendships
    a. are more common than in the past.
    b. are not usually preludes to romance.
    c. can last a lifetime.
    d. are characterized by all of these conditions.

13. The culturally preferred timetable for getting married, having children, and other key life events is called the
    a. social network.
    b. social clock.
    c. moratorium.
    d. normative dial.

14. Having many possibilities or options in purchasing a product
    a. leads to a quicker decision.
    b. leads to a faulty decision.
    c. leads to a better decision.
    d. may create choice overload.

15. Our friendships are more intimate, emotional, and tend to share secrets. Who are we?
    a. women   c. adolescents
    b. men   d. emerging adults

Matching Items

Match each definition or description with its corresponding term.

Terms

_____ 1. choice overload
_____ 2. cohabitation
_____ 3. intimate terrorism
_____ 4. heterogamy
_____ 5. hookup
_____ 6. social exchange theory
_____ 7. social homogamy
_____ 8. demand/withdraw
_____ 9. homogamy
_____ 10. situational couple violence
_____ 11. plasticity gene

Definitions or Descriptions

a. abusive relationship that leads to battered-wife syndrome
b. one partner in a romantic relationship wants to discuss an issue while the other does not
c. the similarity with which a couple regards leisure interests and role preferences
d. a marriage between people with dissimilar interests and backgrounds
e. making a choice is difficult because there are so many possibilities
f. predicts success in marriages in which each partner contributes something useful to the other
g. arrangement in which two unrelated, unmarried adults live together in a romantic partnership
h. sexual encounter between two people in which neither intimacy nor commitment are expected
i. a marriage between people with similar interests and backgrounds
j. abusive relationship that tends to improve with time
k. an allele that makes a person more susceptible to certain experiences

Key Terms

Using your own words, write a brief definition or explanation of each of the following terms on a separate piece of paper.

1. social clock

2. plasticity genes

3. intimacy versus isolation

4. hookup

5. choice overload

6. cohabitation

7. homogamy

8. heterogamy

9. demand/withdraw interaction

10. situational couple violence

11. intimate terrorism

12. linked lives

13. helicopter parents

ANSWERS

CHAPTER REVIEW

1. social clock; continuity; change

2. confusion; diffusion; foreclosure; moratorium

3. college, military service, religious mission work, apprenticeships, and internships

4. half; identify

5. is; Achieving identity is difficult for immigrants because it means reconciling their parents' background with their new social context.

6. more difficult

7. six

8. are; lifelong; static

9. increased

10. shyness; aggression; plasticity

11. alleles; plasticity genes

12. c. is the answer.

    a., b., & d. These would all be good pieces of advice for new workers today.

13. intimacy versus isolation; affiliation; affection; interdependence; communion; belonging; love; self-expansion

14. friends

Friends choose each other, often for the very qualities that make them good sources of emotional support. They provide advice, companionship, information, and sympathy. They are also a source of self-esteem.

15. emerging adulthood

16. are; shared activities; interests; intimate; emotional

17. men; women

18. more

19. find it difficult

20. passion; intimacy; commitment

21. seven

22. passion; commitment; lifelong

23. social forces; culture

24. consummate

25. intimacy; commitment; hookups; men; women

26. choice overload; too many choices

27. cohabitation; varies; is the norm

28. does not; churning; verbal; physical abuse

29. later

30. is not; parental blessing; fall in love

Among the factors that lead to improvement are good communication, financial security, growing maturity, and the end of addiction or illness.

31. homogamy; heterogamy

32. conflict; separation; disgust; intimacy; controversial; demand/withdraw

33. youth, poverty, personality (such as poor impulse control), mental illness, and drug and alcohol addiction

34. situational couple violence

35. intimate terrorism; male

36. d. is the answer.

37. b. is the answer.

38. c. is the answer.

    a. & b. These feelings emerge more gradually in relationships.

39. c. is the answer.

40. a. is the answer.

41. b. is the answer.

42. a. is the answer. Cohabitation before marriage does not strengthen the relationship.

43. linked

44. financial; varies

45. independence; helicopter

PROGRESS TEST 1

Multiple-Choice Questions

1. b. is the answer.

2. a. is the answer.

   c. Identity formation is equally challenging for women and men.

3. b. is the answer.

   a. In Erikson's theory, the crisis of intimacy precedes the need to be productive through work.

   c. & d. Although these items are true, Erikson's theory does not address these issues.

4. d. is the answer.

5. d. is the answer.

6. d. is the answer.

   a. Generativity is a characteristic of the crisis following the intimacy crisis.

   b. Stagnation occurs when generativity needs are not met.

   c. Erikson's theory does not address this issue.

7. d. is the answer.

8. b. is the answer.

9. c. is the answer.

   d. Sternberg's theory is not concerned with the stages of parenthood.

10. c. is the answer.

11. b. is the answer.

   a. By definition, homogamous couples share values, background, and the like.

   c. & d. These may or may not be true, depending on the extent to which such a couple is homogamous.

12. d. is the answer.

13. b. is the answer.

14. b. is the answer.

   a. Intimate terrorism is a violent form of partner abuse.

   c. Heterogamy refers to marriage between people who are dissimilar in attitudes, SES, interests, ethnicity, and the like.

   d. Homogamy refers to marriage between people who are similar in attitudes, SES, interests, ethnicity, and the like.

15. c. is the answer.

True or False Items

1. T

2. F Intimate partner violence is common worldwide.

3. F This comes only with time.

4. F Just the reverse is true.

5. F Cohabitation does *not* solve the problems of marriage.

6. T

7. F In about one-third of all nations, marriages are arranged by parents. In another third, parental blessing is required.

8. F Most young adults should learn basic skills so that they have the flexibility to move into different jobs.

9. T

10. T

PROGRESS TEST 2

Multiple-Choice Questions

1. d. is the answer.

2. b. is the answer.

3. c. is the answer.

4. c. is the answer.

5. d. is the answer.

6. b. is the answer.

7. c. is the answer.

8. d. is the answer.

   a., b., & c. According to Sternberg, consummate love emerges when commitment is added to passion and intimacy.

9. b. is the answer.

   a. Slightly more than half of all women age 25 to 40 in the United States cohabit before their first marriage.

   c. In fact, a large study of adults found that cohabitants were much *less* happy and healthy than married people.

   d. No such finding was reported in the text.

10. b. is the answer.

   a. & d. These characteristics do not pertain to homogamy.

   c. This describes a heterogamous marriage.

11. d. is the answer.

12. d. is the answer.

13. b. is the answer.

14. **d.** is the answer.

15. **a.** is the answer.

Matching Items

1. e	5. h	9. i
2. g	6. f	10. j
3. a	7. c	11. k
4. d	8. b	

KEY TERMS

1. The **social clock** is a timetable for certain life events that is based on social norms.

2. **Plasticity genes** are genes and alleles that do not determine behavior, but make a person more or less susceptible to environmental events.

3. According to Erik Erikson, the first crisis of adulthood is **intimacy versus isolation,** which involves the need to share one's personal life with someone else or risk profound loneliness and isolation.

4. A **hookup** is a sexual encounter between two people in which neither intimacy nor commitment is expected.

5. **Choice overload** occurs when having so many possibilities makes choosing one difficult.

6. Increasingly common among emerging adults in all industrialized countries is the living pattern called **cohabitation,** in which two unrelated, unmarried adults live together in a committed sexual relationship.

7. **Homogamy** refers to marriage between people who are similar in attitudes, goals, socioeconomic status, interests, ethnicity, religion, and the like.

8. **Heterogamy** refers to marriage between people who are dissimilar in attitudes, interests, SES, religion, ethnic background, and goals.

9. A **demand/withdraw interaction** occurs when one partner in a romantic relationship wants to address an issue and the other refuses, resulting in opposite reactions.

10. **Situational couple violence** is a form of abuse in which both partners in a couple fight and yet are caring and affectionate. It is brought on more by the situation than the deep personality problems of the individuals.

11. **Intimate terrorism** is the form of partner abuse in which the abuser (usually a male) uses violent methods of accelerating intensity to isolate, degrade, and punish the victim (usually a female).

12. Members of a family have **linked lives** in that the success, health, and well-being of each family member are connected to those of other members, including those of another generation.

13. **Helicopter parents** are parents who hover over their emerging adult children, ready to provide help if a problem arises.

20

Adulthood: Biosocial Development

Chapter Overview

This chapter deals with biosocial development during the years from 25 to 65. The first section describes changes in appearance and in the functioning of the sense organs and the brain, noting the potential impact of these changes. The next section discusses the changes in the sexual-reproductive system that occur during middle adulthood. This is followed in the next section with a discussion of the health habits of adults, focusing on drug abuse, overeating, and inactivity. The final section discusses the latest ways in which variations in health are measured to reflect quality of living as well as traditional measures of illness and death rates.

What Will You Know?

The text chapter should be studied one section at a time. Before you read, preview each section by skimming it, noting headings and boldface items. Then read the sections, one at a time, keeping these questions in mind.

1. When does a person start to show his or her age?
2. Which of the senses declines before age 65?
3. Should a woman bear children before age 30, 40, or 50?
4. How can a person be vitally healthy *and* severely disabled?

Chapter Review

When you have finished reading the chapter, work through the material that follows to review it. Completing the sentences and answering the questions will enable you to answer the "What Have You Learned?" questions at the end of the text chapter. Scattered throughout the Chapter Review are Study Tips, which explain how best to learn a difficult concept, and Think About It discussions and

Applications, which help you to know how well you understand the material. Check your understanding of the material by consulting the answers at the end of the chapter. Do not continue with the next section until you understand each answer. If you need to, review or reread the appropriate section in the textbook before continuing.

Senescence

1. The gradual physical decline that occurs with age is called _____ .

2. Two invisible aspects of aging that predict heart disease are increases in _____ and in _____ _____ . Three physiological aspects of the body that protect aging adults are _____ _____ , _____ , and _____ .

3. With age, neurons in the brain fire more _____ (slowly/rapidly). In addition, by middle adulthood there are fewer _____ and _____ . These changes contribute to a lengthening of _____ _____ , and _____ becomes more difficult, _____ takes longer, and complex _____-_____ tasks may become impossible.

4. Less than _____ (what percent?) of people under age 65 experience significant brain loss with age. For those who do, the cause usually is _____

   _____ , _____

   _____ , _____ ,

   or _____ .

5. Some of the normal changes in appearance that occur during middle adulthood include changes in hair, which _____ , and changes in skin, which _____ .

6. The "middle-age spread" causes an increase in

   _____ _____ .

   In addition, the _____ weaken and pockets of fat settle on the _____ . By late middle age, bones lose _____ , making the _____ shrink and causing a decrease in _____ .

7. The aging of the body is most evident in sports that require _____ ,

   _____ , and _____ .

8. After age 20, the lens of the eye gradually becomes _____ . This contributes to _____ , or difficulty seeing close objects. Difficulty seeing objects at a distance is called _____ .

9. The loss of hearing associated with senescence is called _____ . This often does not become apparent until after age

   _____ .

10. Speech-related hearing losses are first apparent for _____ - (high/low) frequency sounds.

STUDY TIP To consolidate your understanding of the physical changes that accompany normal aging during adulthood, write a paragraph describing changes in appearance and the functioning of brain and body systems experienced by a typical adult in his or her 30s, 40s, 50s, and beyond.

APPLICATION:

11. Josef has enjoyed playing football with friends during most of his adult life. He has just turned 45 and notices that he no longer tackles with the same force he had 10 years ago. This is probably because
    a. his reaction time has slowed.
    b. his Type II muscle fibers have decreased substantially.
    c. his stomach muscles have weakened.
    d. of all of these reasons.

The Sexual-Reproductive System

12. With age, sexual _____ is slower and _____ becomes reduced. Most people _____ (are/are not) sexually active throughout adulthood.

13. Infertility is defined as _____ . Fertility peaks during _____ . From a biological perspective, women should try to conceive before age _____ and men before age _____ .

14. Overall in the United States, about _____ percent of all couples are infertile. A common reason for male infertility is a low _____ _____ . Female infertility may be the result of _____ _____ disease.

15. The collective name for the various methods of medical intervention to restore fertility is

    _____ _____

    _____ .

16. At an average age of _____ , a woman reaches _____ , as ovulation and menstruation stop and the production of _____ ,

    _____ , and

    _____ drops considerably. This condition may occur prematurely if a woman has her uterus removed surgically through a

    _____ .

17. The psychological consequences of menopause are _____ (variable/not variable). European and North American cultures' perceptions of this aspect of menopause _____ (have/have not) changed over time.

18. Over the past two or three decades, many women used _____

_____ _____ to reduce post-menopausal symptoms.

19. Long-term use of HRT beyond menopause has been shown to increase the risk of

_____ _____ ,

_____ , and

_____ _____ and has no proven effects on _____ . However, it _____ (does/ does not) reduce hot flashes and decrease

_____ .

20. Although some experts believe men undergo _____ , most believe that physiologically, men _____ (do/ do not) experience anything like menopause.

APPLICATIONS:

21. Fifty-five-year-old Dewey is concerned because sexual stimulation seems to take longer and needs to be more direct than earlier in his life. As a friend, you should tell him
    a. "You should see a therapist. It is not normal."
    b. "See a doctor if your 'sexual prowess' doesn't improve soon. You may have some underlying physical problem."
    c. "Don't worry. This is normal for middle-aged men."
    d. "You're too old to have sex, so just give it up."

22. Female fertility may be affected by
    a. obesity.
    b. pelvic inflammatory disease.
    c. smoking.
    d. all of these things.

Health Habits and Age

23. Rates of drug abuse _____ (increase/decrease) sharply by age 40.

24. In North America today, _____ (fewer/more) people begin smoking than in the past. Today, twice as many women die from _____ cancer as from cancer of the breast, uterus, or ovary combined. Variations in smoking rates from nation to nation, and from one cohort to another, demonstrate that

smoking is affected by _____

_____ , laws, and advertisements.

25. Some studies find that adults who drink moderately may live longer, possibly because alcohol increases the blood's supply of

_____-_____

_____ , the "good" cholesterol, and reduces _____-

_____ _____ , the "bad" cholesterol. It also lowers

_____ _____

and _____ . However, even moderate alcohol consumption poses a health risk if it leads to _____ ,

_____ , or other destructive habits.

List some of the health hazards of excessive alcohol use.

26. Between emerging adulthood and late adulthood, a person's metabolism _____ (decreases/increases) by about a third, which means that middle-aged people need to eat _____ (more/less) simply to maintain their weight.

27. In the United States, on average, adults gain _____ (how many?) pounds per year because they consume too many

_____-_____

_____ and engage in too little _____ . The United States is the world leader in _____ and

_____ .

28. Overweight, defined as _____ , is present in _____ (what proportion?) of all adults in the United States. Obesity is defined as _____ .

29. In the United States, about _____ of adults are obese.

30. Current explanations for the trends in overweight and obesity focus on _____ , on _____ , on the _____ of meals, and on _____ .

31. The typical family in the United States consumes more _____ and _____ and less _____ than people in other parts of the world.

State some of the health benefits of exercise.

32. (A View From Science) The steps in breaking a habit are _____ , _____ , _____ , _____ , and _____ . Our resolve in breaking bad health habits and maintaining good ones may fade when we face _____ . This phenomenon is called _____ .

APPLICATIONS:

33. Maureen is British and Maria is Italian. Based on averages, which of the following is most likely true of the two women?
    a. Maria is less obese than Maureen.
    b. Maureen is less obese than Maria.
    c. Both women are equally obese.
    d. Both women are thin.

34. Forty-five-year-old Val is the same weight she has been since college and continues to eat the same types and amounts of food she has always eaten. To maintain her weight through middle age, Val should
    a. continue to eat the same amounts and types of foods.
    b. reduce her caloric intake.
    c. eat more foods high in LDL.
    d. reduce her intake of foods high in HDL.

35. Jack, who is approaching adulthood, wants to know which health habits have the greatest influence on physical well-being. You point to
    a. tobacco and alcohol use.

    b. overeating.
    c. exercise.
    d. all of these habits.

Measuring Health

36. Perhaps the most solid indicator of health of given age groups is the rate of _____ , or death. This rate is often _____-adjusted to take into account the higher death rate among the very old. By this measure, the country with the lowest rate is _____ , and the country with the highest rate is _____ .

37. A more comprehensive measure of health is _____ , defined as _____ of all kinds.

38. To truly portray quality of life, we need to measure _____ , which refers to a person's inability to perform basic activities, and _____ , which refers to how healthy and energetic a person feels.

39. In terms of quality of life, _____ is probably the most important measure of health.

40. The concept of _____-_____ _____ _____ indicates how many years of full vitality are lost as a result of a particular disease or disability. The reciprocal of this statistic is known as _____-_____ _____ _____ .

41. Individuals who are relatively well-educated and financially secure tend to live _____ (shorter/longer) lives and have _____ (more/fewer) chronic illnesses or disabilities.

42. In every way, human development is harmed by low _____ .

STUDY TIP To consolidate your understanding of socioeconomic status and other variables in healthy aging, write a paragraph explaining why low SES does not inevitably lead to poor health.

APPLICATIONS:

43. Which of the following would entail the greatest loss of QALYs?
    a. a 70-year-old man dies in an automobile accident
    b. a 20-year-old woman is permanently disabled and unable to work following an automobile accident
    c. a 50-year-old man is forced to switch jobs after a skiing accident
    d. It is impossible to determine from the information given.

44. Fifty-year-old Beth has a college degree and a good job and lives near Seattle, Washington. Compared with her sister, who dropped out of high school and is struggling to survive on a dairy farm in rural Wisconsin, Beth is most likely to
    a. live longer.
    b. have fewer chronic illnesses.
    c. have fewer disabilities.
    d. do or have all of these things.

45. Kirk wants to move to the part of the world that has the lowest annual mortality. You tell him to buy a ticket to
    a. Germany.
    b. Canada.
    c. France.
    d. Japan.

46. Morbidity is to mortality as _____ is to _____ .
    a. disease; death
    b. death; disease
    c. inability to perform normal daily activities; disease
    d. disease; subjective feeling of being healthy

Progress Test 1

Multiple-Choice Questions

Circle your answers to the following questions and check them with the answers at the end of the chapter. If your answer is incorrect, read the explanation for why it is incorrect and then consult the text.

1. During the years from 25 to 65, the average adult
    a. becomes proportionally slimmer.
    b. gains about 5 pounds per year.
    c. gains about 10 pounds per year.
    d. is more likely to have pockets of fat settle on various parts of the body.

2. Senescence refers to
    a. the average age at which menopause begins.
    b. the average age at which andropause begins.
    c. age-related physical decline.
    d. premature dementia.

3. Age-related deficits in speech-related hearing are most noticeable for
    a. high-frequency sounds.
    b. low-frequency sounds.
    c. mid-range-frequency sounds.
    d. rapid conversation.

4. Regarding age-related changes in vision, most older adults are
    a. nearsighted.
    b. farsighted.
    c. nearsighted and farsighted.
    d. neither nearsighted nor farsighted.

5. As we age
    a. neurons fire more slowly.
    b. the size of the brain is reduced.
    c. there are fewer synapses.
    d. each of these conditions exists.

6. At midlife, individuals who _____ tend to live longer and have fewer chronic illnesses or disabilities.
    a. are relatively well educated
    b. are financially secure
    c. live in richer nations
    d. are or do all of these things

7. The term that refers to diseases of all kinds is
    a. mortality.
    b. morbidity.
    c. disability.
    d. vitality.

8. On average, women reach menopause at age
    a. 39.
    b. 42.
    c. 46.
    d. 51.

9. DALYs is a measure of
    a. the quality of a person's life.
    b. the impact of disability on the quality of a person's life.
    c. how healthy and energetic a person feels.
    d. long-term difficulty in performing normal activities.

10. Infertility is defined as
    a. being unable to conceive a child at any age.
    b. being unable to conceive a child after age 40.
    c. being unable to conceive a child after age 50.
    d. being unable to conceive a child after at least a year of trying.

11. Mortality is usually expressed as
    a. the number of deaths each year per 1,000 individuals in a particular population.
    b. the total number of deaths per year in a given population.
    c. the average age of death among the members of a given population.
    d. the percentage of people of a given age who are still living.

12. The concept that indicates how many years of full physical, intellectual, and social health are lost to a particular physical disease or disability is
    a. vitality.
    b. disability.
    c. morbidity.
    d. quality-adjusted life years.

13. Because his BMI is 42, Melvin is considered
    a. morbidly obese.
    b. of normal body weight.
    c. overweight.
    d. obese.

14. Two invisible aspects of aging that predict heart disease are
    a. increases in blood pressure and in LDL cholesterol.
    b. increases in blood pressure and in HDL cholesterol.
    c. decreases in bone density and immunity.
    d. decreases in organ reserve and maximum heart rate.

15. What percentage of people under age 65 experience significant brain loss with age?
    a. less than 1 percent
    b. 3 percent
    c. 5 percent
    d. 10 percent

True or False Items

Write T (true) or F (false) on the line in front of each statement.

_____ 1. Europe is the world leader of the obesity and diabetes epidemics.

_____ 2. During adulthood, back muscles, connecting tissues, and bones lose density.

_____ 3. Approximately half of all adults in the United States are obese.

_____ 4. Moderate users of alcohol are more likely than teetotalers to have heart attacks.

_____ 5. Those who exercise regularly have lower rates of serious illness than do sedentary people.

_____ 6. Rates of drug abuse increase markedly by age 30 in every nation.

_____ 7. During middle adulthood, sexual responses slow down.

_____ 8. Senescence refers specifically to the psychological changes that accompany menopause.

_____ 9. Despite popular reference to it, there is no "male menopause."

_____ 10. The psychological consequences of menopause vary more than the physiological ones.

Progress Test 2

Progress Test 2 should be completed during a final chapter review. Answer the following questions after you thoroughly understand the correct answers for the Chapter Review and Progress Test 1.

Multiple-Choice Questions

1. The first visible age-related changes are seen in the
   a. hair.
   b. muscles.
   c. teeth.
   d. skin.

2. Of the following, which is the most costly to society?
   a. disability
   b. morbidity
   c. mortality
   d. acute illness

3. Diabetes and obesity are most prevalent in which of the following countries?
   a. Mexico
   b. France
   c. Canada
   d. the United States

4. Problems that correlate with loss of brain cells in adulthood include
   a. drug abuse.
   b. viruses.
   c. poor circulation.
   d. all of these problems.

5. Which of the following is NOT true regarding infertility?
   a. About one-third of the time the problem can be traced to the man.
   b. About one-third of the time the problem can be traced to the woman.
   c. Age is the determining factor for both men and women.
   d. Low sperm count and pelvic inflammatory disease are common causes of infertility.

6. Menopause is caused by a sharp decrease in the production of
   a. sex hormones.
   b. neurons.
   c. synapses.
   d. all of these things.

7. To be a true index of health, morbidity rates must be refined in terms of which of the following health measure(s)?
   a. mortality rate
   b. disability and mortality rates
   c. vitality
   d. disability and vitality

8. The term "male menopause" was probably coined to refer to
   a. the sudden dip in testosterone that sometimes occurs in men who have been sexually inactive.
   b. age-related declines in fertility among men.
   c. men suffering from erectile dysfunction.
   d. age-related declines in testosterone levels in middle-aged men.

9. Which of the following is NOT true regarding hormone replacement therapy (HRT)?
   a. Long-term use (10 years or more) increases the risk of heart disease, stroke, and breast cancer.
   b. HRT reduces hot flashes and decreases osteoporosis.
   c. HRT has no proven effects on dementia.
   d. For most women, the benefits of HRT outweigh the risks.

10. The leading cause of cancer deaths in North America is
    a. lung cancer.
    b. breast cancer.
    c. prostate cancer.
    d. skin cancer.

11. Which of the following was NOT cited as a possible reason for the high incidence of overweight among children and adults?
    a. genes
    b. diet
    c. culture
    d. glandular problems

12. Which of the following is NOT true regarding alcohol consumption?
    a. Alcohol decreases the blood's supply of high-density lipoprotein.
    b. Drinking alcohol in moderation can be beneficial.
    c. Alcohol is a major cause of injury and disease worldwide.
    d. Alcohol abuse contributes to osteoporosis.

13. The highest rates of obesity are found during
    a. adolescence.
    b. early adulthood.
    c. middle adulthood.
    d. late adulthood.

14. Which of the following is true of sexual expressiveness in adulthood?
    a. Menopause impairs a woman's sexual relationship.
    b. Men's frequency of ejaculation increases until approximately age 55.
    c. Signs of arousal in a woman are as obvious as they were at age 20.
    d. The levels of sex hormones gradually diminish and responses slow down.

15. A BMI over 30
    a. is less harmful among people of African American, Latino, or Asian American ethnicity.
    b. is less harmful among European Americans.
    c. is less harmful to women than men.
    d. is always harmful.

Matching Items

Match each definition or description with its
corresponding term.

Terms

_____ **1.** mortality
_____ **2.** morbidity
_____ **3.** vitality
_____ **4.** menopause
_____ **5.** andropause
_____ **6.** ART
_____ **7.** HRT
_____ **8.** osteoporosis
_____ **9.** disability
_____ **10.** quality-adjusted life years
_____ **11.** infertility

Definitions or Descriptions

a. disease of all kinds
b. collective term for infertility treatments
c. often prescribed to treat the symptoms of
   menopause
d. a condition of fragile bones
e. death; as a measure of health, it usually refers
   to the number of deaths each year per thousand
   individuals
f. the cessation of ovulation and menstruation
g. more important to quality of life than any other
   measure of health
h. male menopause
i. the inability to perform normal activities
j. number of years of full vitality lost because of
   disease or disability
k. being unable to conceive after at least a year of
   trying

Key Terms

Using your own words, write a brief definition or
explanation of each of the following terms on a
separate piece of paper.

1. senescence
2. presbycusis
3. infertility
4. menopause
5. hormone replacement therapy (HRT)
6. andropause
7. mortality
8. morbidity
9. disability
10. disability-adjusted life years (DALYs)
11. vitality
12. quality-adjusted life years (QALYs)

ANSWERS

CHAPTER REVIEW

1. senescence
2. hypertension (high blood pressure); LDL
   cholesterol; organ reserve; homeostasis; allostasis
3. slowly; neurons; synapses; reaction time;
   multitasking; processing; working-memory
4. 1; drug abuse; poor circulation; viruses; genes
5. turns gray and thins; becomes thinner, less
   flexible, dryer, rougher, less regular in color, and
   more wrinkled
6. waist circumference; muscles; abdomen, upper
   arms, buttocks, and chin; density; vertebrae;
   height
7. strength; agility; speed
8. thicker; farsightedness; nearsightedness
9. presbycusis; 60
10. high
11. d. is the answer.
12. responsiveness; fertility; are
13. being unable to conceived after trying for at least
    a year; late adolescence; 25; 30
14. 12; sperm count; pelvic inflammatory
15. assisted reproductive technology (ART)
16. 51; menopause; estrogen; progesterone;
    testosterone; hysterectomy
17. variable; have
18. hormone replacement therapy (HRT)
19. heart disease, stroke, and breast cancer; dementia;
    does; osteoporosis
20. andropause; do not
21. c. is the answer.

22. **d.** is the answer.

23. decrease

24. fewer; lung; social norms

25. high-density lipoprotein (HDL); low-density lipoprotein (LDL); blood pressure; glucose; smoking; overeating

Heavy drinking is the main cause of liver disease; it also destroys brain cells; contributes to osteoporosis; decreases fertility; is a risk factor for many forms of cancer; and accompanies many suicides, homicides, and accidents.

26. decreases; less

27. 1 to 2; high-calorie foods; activity; obesity; diabetes

28. a BMI above 25; two-thirds; a BMI of 30 or more

29. one-third

30. genes; diet; context; inactivity

31. meat; fat; fiber

Exercise reduces blood pressure; strengthens the heart and lungs; and makes depression, osteoporosis, heart disease, arthritis, and some cancers less likely.

32. denial; awareness; planning; implementation; maintenance; stress; attention myopia

33. **a.** is the answer.

34. **b.** is the answer.

    a. As Val ages, her metabolism will slow down, so she should reduce her caloric intake.

    c. & d. Just the opposite is true. She should decrease her intake of foods high in LDL and increase her intake of foods high in HDL.

35. **d.** is the answer.

36. mortality; age; Japan; Sierra Leone

37. morbidity; disease

38. disability; vitality

39. vitality

40. quality-adjusted life years (QALYs); disability-adjusted life years (DALYs)

41. longer; fewer

42. SES

43. **b.** is the answer. Being permanently disabled and unable to work, the 20-year-old woman clearly has lost more years of vitality than either an elderly man, who statistically would be expected to die soon anyway (**a.**), or a middle-aged man who is simply forced to change jobs following an accident (**c.**).

44. **d.** is the answer. People who are relatively well-educated, financially secure, and live in or near cities tend to receive all of these benefits.

45. **d.** is the answer.

46. **a.** is the answer.

    b. This answer would be correct if the statement was "Mortality is to morbidity."

    c. This answer would be correct if the statement was "Disability is to morbidity."

    d. This answer would be correct if the statement was "Morbidity is to vitality."

PROGRESS TEST 1

Multiple-Choice Questions

1. **d.** is the answer.

    b. & c. Weight gain varies substantially from person to person.

2. **c.** is the answer.

3. **a.** is the answer.

4. **c.** is the answer.

5. **d.** is the answer.

6. **d.** is the answer.

7. **b.** is the answer.

    a. This is the overall death rate.

    c. This refers to a person's inability to perform normal activities of daily living.

    d. This refers to how physically, intellectually, and socially healthy an individual feels.

8. **d.** is the answer.

9. **b.** is the answer.

    a. This refers to QALYs.

    c. This refers to vitality.

    d. This refers to the disability itself.

10. **d.** is the answer.

11. **a.** is the answer.

12. **d.** is the answer.

    a. Vitality is a measure of how healthy and energetic a person feels.

    b. Disability measures only the inability to perform basic activities.

    c. Morbidity refers only to the rate of disease.

13. **a.** is the answer.

14. **a.** is the answer.

15. **a.** is the answer.

True or False Items

1. F   The United States is the world leader of the obesity and diabetes epidemics.

2. T

3. F   Approximately two of every three are overweight, and half of those are obese.

4. F   Moderate use of alcohol is associated with reduced risk of heart attacks.

5. T

6. F   Rates actually decrease.

7. T

8. F   Senescence is the gradual physical decline that occurs with age.

9. T

10. T

PROGRESS TEST 2

Multiple-Choice Questions

1. **d.** is the answer.

2. **a.** is the answer. When a person is disabled, society not only loses an active contributor but may also need to provide special care.

3. **d.** is the answer.

4. **d.** is the answer.

5. **c.** is the answer. Age is one factor, but not the determining one.

6. **a.** is the answer.

7. **d.** is the answer.

8. **a.** is the answer.

    b. Most men continue to produce sperm throughout adulthood and are, therefore, theoretically fertile indefinitely.

    c. This disorder was not discussed.

    d. For men, there is no sudden drop in hormone levels during middle adulthood.

9. **d.** is the answer.

10. **a.** is the answer.

11. **d.** is the answer.

12. **a.** is the answer. Alcohol increases the blood's supply of HDL, which is one possible reason that adults who drink in moderation may live longer than "teetotalers."

13. **c.** is the answer.

14. **d.** is the answer.

15. **d.** is the answer.

Matching Items

1. e	5. h	9. i
2. a	6. b	10. j
3. g	7. c	11. k
4. f	8. d	

KEY TERMS

1. **Senescence** refers to the gradual physical decline that accompanies aging.

2. **Presbycusis** is the significant loss of hearing associated with aging.

3. **Infertility** is the inability to conceive a child after trying for at least one year.

4. At **menopause,** which usually occurs around age 50, ovulation and menstruation stop and the production of the hormones estrogen, progesterone, and testosterone drops.

5. **Hormone replacement therapy (HRT)** is intended to help relieve menopausal symptoms; it involves taking hormones (in pills, patches, or injections) to compensate for hormone reduction.

6. **Andropause,** or male menopause, refers to a drop in testosterone levels in older men, which normally results in reduced sexual desire, muscle mass, and erections.

7. **Mortality** means death. As a measure of health, it usually refers to the number of deaths each year per 1,000 members of a given population.

8. **Morbidity** means disease. As a measure of health, it refers to the rate of diseases of all kinds in a given population, which can be sudden and severe (acute) or extend over a long time period (chronic).

9. **Disability** refers to a person's inability to perform normal activities of daily life because of a physical, mental, or emotional condition.

10. **Disability-adjusted life years (DALYs),** the reciprocal of QALYs, is a measure of the reduced quality of life caused by disability.

11. **Vitality** refers to how healthy and energetic—physically, intellectually, and socially—an individual actually feels.

12. **Quality-adjusted life years (QALYs)** is the concept that indicates how many years of full vitality an individual loses due to a particular disease or disability.

Adulthood: Cognitive Development

Chapter Overview

The way psychologists conceptualize intelligence has changed considerably in recent years. Chapter 21 begins by examining the different methods of measuring intelligence (psychometrics), which may lead to different conclusions regarding increases or decreases in intelligence over the life span.

The next section examines the contemporary view of intelligence, which emphasizes its multidimensional nature. Most experts now believe that there are several distinct intelligences rather than a single general entity. This section focuses on two proposals, one that posits two abilities and the other that advocates three.

The final section first focuses on the tendency of adults to select certain aspects of their lives to focus on as they age. In doing so, they optimize development in those areas and compensate for declines in others. Each person's cognitive development occurs in a unique context influenced by variations in genes, life experiences, and cohort effects. The section then discusses the cognitive expertise that often comes with experience, pointing out the ways in which expert thinking differs from that of the novice. Expert thinking is more specialized, flexible, and intuitive and is guided by more and better problem-solving strategies. The chapter concludes with a brief discussion of the recent shift in society in which family skills have become more highly valued when performed by both women and men.

What Will You Know?

The text chapter should be studied one section at a time. Before you read, preview each section by skimming it, noting headings and boldface items. Then read the sections, one at a time, keeping these questions in mind.

1. Why does each generation think it is smarter than earlier generations?
2. Why does each older generation think it knows more than younger generations?
3. What aspects of thinking improve during the years of adulthood?
4. Is everyone an expert at something?

Chapter Review

When you have finished reading the chapter, work through the material that follows to review it. Completing the sentences and answering the questions will enable you to answer the "What Have You Learned?" questions at the end of the text chapter. Scattered throughout the Chapter Review are Study Tips, which explain how best to learn a difficult concept, and Think About It discussions and Applications, which help you to know how well you understand the material. Check your understanding of the material by consulting the answers at the end of the chapter. Do not continue with the next section until you understand each answer. If you need to, review or reread the appropriate section in the textbook before continuing.

What Is Intelligence?

1. Measuring psychological characteristics such as intelligence is taking a _____ approach to research.

2. Historically, psychologists have thought of intelligence as _____ (a single entity/several distinct abilities).

3. A leading theoretician, _____ , argued that there is such a thing as general intelligence, which he called _____ .

4. For the first half of the twentieth century, psychologists were convinced that intelligence peaks during _____ and then gradually declines. During the 1950s, Nancy Bayley and Melita Oden found that on several tests of concept mastery, the scores of gifted individuals _____ (increased/ decreased/remained unchanged) between ages 20 and 50.

5. Follow-up research by Bayley demonstrated a general _____ (increase/ decrease) in intellectual functioning from childhood through young adulthood. This developmental trend was true on tests of

_____ , _____ ,

and _____ .

6. Bayley's study is an example of a _____ (cross-sectional/ longitudinal) research design. Earlier studies relied on _____ (cross-sectional/ longitudinal) research designs.

Briefly explain why cross-sectional research can sometimes yield a misleading picture of adult development.

7. Throughout the world, studies have shown a general trend toward _____ (increasing/decreasing) average IQ over successive generations. This trend is called the.

_____ _____ .

8. Cite three reasons that longitudinal findings may be misleading.

   a. _____

   b. _____

   c. _____

9. One of the first researchers to recognize the problems of cross-sectional and longitudinal studies of intelligence was _____ .

10. Schaie developed a new research technique combining cross-sectional and longitudinal approaches, called _____-

_____ research.

Briefly explain this type of research design.

11. Using this design, Schaie found that on five

_____ _____

_____ , most people improved throughout most of adulthood. The results of his research are known collectively as the

_____ _____

_____ .

APPLICATIONS:

12. Professor Iglesias is a psychometrician. This means that she specializes in the
    a. study of intelligence.
    b. study of cognitive development.
    c. measurement of psychological characteristics, especially intelligence.
    d. measurement of age-related psychopathologies.

13. A psychologist has found that the mathematical ability of adults born in the 1920s is significantly different from that of those born in the 1950s. She suspects that this difference is a reflection of the different educational emphases of the two historical periods. This is an example of
    a. longitudinal research.
    b. sequential research.
    c. a cohort effect.
    d. all of these factors.

14. A contemporary developmental psychologist is most likely to DISAGREE with the statement that
    a. many people show increases in intelligence during middle adulthood.
    b. for many behaviors, the responses of older adults are slower than those of younger adults.
    c. intelligence peaks during adolescence and declines thereafter.
    d. intelligence is multidimensional and multidirectional.

15. Regarding their accuracy in measuring adult intellectual decline, cross-sectional research is to longitudinal research as _____ is to _____ .
  a. underestimate; overestimate
  b. overestimate; underestimate
  c. accurate; inaccurate
  d. inaccurate; accurate

16. Dr. Hatfield wants to analyze the possible effects of retesting, cohort differences, and aging on adult changes in intelligence. Which research method should she use?
  a. cross-sectional c. cross-sequential
  b. longitudinal d. case study

17. During World War I, psychologists were convinced that intelligence peaks during
  a. late childhood.
  b. adolescence.
  c. emerging adulthood.
  d. middle adulthood.

Components of Intelligence: Many and Varied

18. In the 1960s, researchers _____ and _____ differentiated two aspects of intelligence, which they called _____ and _____ intelligence.

19. As its name implies, _____ intelligence is flexible reasoning used to draw inferences and understand relations between concepts. This type of intelligence is also made up of basic mental abilities, including _____ _____ , _____ , and _____ _____ _____ .

20. The accumulation of facts, information, and knowledge that comes with education and experience with a particular culture is referred to as _____ intelligence.

21. During adulthood, _____ intelligence declines markedly, primarily because everything slows down with age. However, if a person's intelligence is simply measured by one _____ score, this decline is temporarily disguised by a(n) _____ (increase/decrease) in _____ intelligence.

22. The theorist who has proposed that intelligence is composed of three fundamental aspects is _____ . The _____ aspect consists of the mental processes that foster academic proficiency by making efficient learning, remembering, and thinking possible. This type of thinking is particularly valued at _____ _____ (what stage of life?).

23. The _____ aspect enables the person to be flexible and innovative when dealing with new situations. This type of thinking is always _____ rather than _____ , meaning that such thinkers frequently find _____ solutions to problems rather than relying on the one that has always been considered correct.

24. The _____ aspect concerns the ability to adapt to the contextual demands of a given situation. This type of thinking is particularly useful for managing the conflicting personalities in a _____ or _____ .

25. Practical intelligence _____ (is/is not) related to traditional intelligence as measured by IQ tests.

26. The value placed on different dimensions of intellectual ability _____ (varies/does not vary) from culture to culture _____ (and/but not) from one stage of life to another.

27. Another factor in the value placed on different dimensions of intellectual ability is the _____ context.

STUDY TIP Students often find it difficult to distinguish between fluid intelligence and crystallized intelligence. Fluid intelligence is the capacity to think, learn, and solve problems, while crystallized intelligence refers to specific, acquired knowledge. To keep the two separate, it may help you to think of the meanings of the words crystal and crystallized. A "crystal" is a solid form, and to crystallize means "to cause to take a definite form," as in "she tried to crystallize her thoughts."

APPLICATIONS:

28. In Sternberg's theory, which aspect of intelligence is most similar to the abilities comprising fluid intelligence?
    a. analytic
    b. creative
    c. practical
    d. None of these is part of Sternberg's theory.

29. Sharetta knows more about her field of specialization now at age 45 than she did at age 35. This increase is most likely due to
    a. an increase in crystallized intelligence.
    b. an increase in fluid intelligence.
    c. increases in both fluid and crystallized intelligence.
    d. a cohort difference.

30. Joseph has remained associated with interesting and creative people throughout his life. In contrast, James has become increasingly isolated as he has aged. Given these lifestyle differences, which aspect of intelligence will be most affected in Joseph and James?
    a. fluid intelligence
    b. crystallized intelligence
    c. overall IQ
    d. It is impossible to predict how their intelligence will be affected.

31. When Merle retired from teaching, he had great difficulty adjusting to the changes in his lifestyle. Robert Sternberg would probably say that Merle was somewhat lacking in which aspect of his intelligence?
    a. analytic   c. fluid
    b. creative   d. plasticity

32. Compared with her 20-year-old daughter, 40-year-old Lynda is likely to perform better on measures of what type of intelligence?
    a. fluid
    b. practical
    c. analytic
    d. none of these types of intelligence

Selective Gains and Losses

33. A stressor is defined as _____
    _____ .

34. Coping with a stressor by ignoring, forgetting, or hiding it is called _____
    _____ . In _____-
    _____ coping, people try to cope with stress by tackling the problem directly. In
    _____-_____
    coping, people cope with stress by trying to change

their emotions. Generally speaking, women may be more _____-focused than men, as their bodies produce the hormone _____ that triggers
_____-_____-
_____ behaviors.

35. The gradual accumulation of stressors over a long period of time is called _____ .

36. The process of turning to one's faith as a means of coping with a stressor is called
    _____ _____ .

37. When challenges are successfully met, the body's damaging responses to stressors _____ (are/are not necessarily) averted.

38. Researchers such as Paul and Margaret Baltes have found that people devise alternative strategies to compensate for age-related declines in ability. The Balteses call this
    _____ _____
    _____ _____ .

39. Some developmentalists believe that as we age, we develop specialized competencies, or _____ , in activities that are important to us.

40. There are several differences between experts and novices. First, novices tend to rely more on _____ (formal/informal) procedures and rules to guide them, whereas experts rely more on their _____ _____ and the immediate _____ to guide them. This makes the actions of experts more _____ and less _____ .

41. Second, many elements of expert performance become _____ , almost instinctive, which enables experts to process information more quickly and efficiently. This type of thinking is called _____ _____ .

42. A third difference is that experts have more and better _____ for accomplishing a particular task.

43. A final difference is that experts are more _____ .

44. In developing their abilities, experts point to the importance of _____ , usually at least several hours a day for _____ (how long?) before their full potential is achieved. This highlights the importance of _____ in the development of expertise.

45. Research studies indicate that the benefits of expertise are quite _____ (general/specific) and that practice and specialization_____ (can/cannot) always overcome the effects of age.

46. Historically, research on expertise has focused on occupations that once had more _____ (male/female) than _____ (male/female) workers. Today, more women _____ (are/ are not) working in occupations traditionally reserved for men. In addition, domestic and caregiving tasks that were once considered _____ _____ have gained new respect and are considered _____ when performed by both women and men.

STUDY TIP To consolidate your understanding of automatic processing, flexibility, and other aspects of expertise, think about your own highly developed skills. How is your thinking about whatever you are an expert in different from ordinary thinking? What changed as your expertise developed?

APPLICATION:

47. Compared with novice chess players, chess experts most likely
   a. have superior long-term memory.
   b. have superior short-term memory.
   c. are very disciplined in their play, sticking closely to formal rules for responding to certain moves their opponents might make.
   d. are quite flexible in their play, relying on their years of practice and accumulated experience.

Progress Test 1

Multiple-Choice Questions

Circle your answers to the following questions and check them with the answers at the end of

the chapter. If your answer is incorrect, read the explanation for why it is incorrect and then consult the text.

1. Most of the evidence for an age-related decline in intelligence came from
   a. cross-sectional research.
   b. longitudinal research.
   c. cross-sequential research.
   d. random sampling.

2. The major flaw in cross-sectional research is the virtual impossibility of
   a. selecting subjects who are similar in every aspect except age.
   b. tracking all subjects over a number of years.
   c. finding volunteers with high IQs.
   d. testing concept mastery.

3. Because of the limitations of other research methods, K. Warner Schaie developed a new research design based on
   a. observer–participant methods.
   b. in-depth questionnaires.
   c. personal interviews.
   d. both cross-sectional and longitudinal methods.

4. Why don't traditional intelligence tests reveal age-related cognitive declines during adulthood?
   a. They measure only fluid intelligence.
   b. They measure only crystallized intelligence.
   c. They separate verbal and nonverbal IQ scores, obscuring these declines.
   d. They yield a single IQ score, allowing adulthood increases in crystallized intelligence to mask these declines.

5. Which of the following is most likely to DECREASE with age?
   a. vocabulary
   b. accumulated facts
   c. working memory
   d. practical intelligence

6. The basic mental abilities that go into learning and understanding any subject have been classified as
   a. crystallized intelligence.
   b. plastic intelligence.
   c. fluid intelligence.
   d. rote memory.

7. Some psychologists contend that intelligence consists of fluid intelligence, which _____ during adulthood, and crystallized intelligence, which _____ .
   a. remains stable; declines
   b. declines; remains stable
   c. increases; declines
   d. declines; increases

8. Charles Spearman argued for the existence of a single general intelligence factor, which he referred to as
   a. *g.*
   b. practical intelligence.
   c. analytic intelligence.
   d. creative intelligence.

9. The Flynn effect refers to
   a. the trend toward increasing average IQ.
   b. age-related declines in fluid intelligence.
   c. ethnic differences in average IQ scores.
   d. the impact of practice on expertise.

10. The shift from conscious, deliberate processing of information to a more unconscious, effortless performance requires
    a. automatic responding.
    b. subliminal execution.
    c. plasticity.
    d. encoding.

11. Concerning expertise, which of the following is true?
    a. In performing tasks, experts tend to be more set in their ways, preferring to use strategies that have worked in the past.
    b. The reasoning of experts is usually more formal, disciplined, and stereotypic than that of the novice.
    c. In performing tasks, experts tend to be more flexible and to enjoy experimentation more than novices do.
    d. Experts often have difficulty adjusting to situations that are exceptions to the rule.

12. Compared with his sister, Melvin is more likely to respond to stress
    a. in a problem-focused manner.
    b. in an emotion-focused manner.
    c. in a tend-and-befriend manner.
    d. with lower arousal of his sympathetic nervous system.

13. Which of the following describes the results of Nancy Bayley's follow-up study of members of the Berkeley study?
    a. Most subjects reached a plateau in intellectual functioning at age 21.
    b. The typical person at age 36 improved on 2 of 10 subtests of adult intelligence scales: picture completion and arithmetic.
    c. The typical person at age 36 was still improving on the most important subtests of the intelligence scale.
    d. No conclusions could be reached because the sample of subjects was not representative.

14. Which of the following is NOT one of the general conclusions of research about intellectual changes during adulthood?
    a. In general, most intellectual abilities increase or remain stable throughout early and middle adulthood until the 60s.
    b. Cohort differences have a powerful influence on intellectual differences in adulthood.
    c. Intellectual functioning is affected by educational background.
    d. Intelligence becomes less specialized with increasing age.

15. The psychologist who has proposed that intelligence is composed of analytic, creative, and practical aspects is
    a. Charles Spearman.   c. Robert Sternberg.
    b. Paul Baltes.   d. K. Warner Schaie.

True or False Items

Write T (true) or F (false) on the line in front of each statement.

_____ 1. Age impairs processing speed and short-term memory.

_____ 2. A person's IQ is unaffected by school achievement.

_____ 3. To date, cross-sectional research has shown a gradual increase in intellectual ability.

_____ 4. Longitudinal research usually shows that intelligence in most abilities increases throughout early and middle adulthood.

_____ 5. By age 60, most people decline in even the most basic cognitive abilities.

_____ 6. IQ scores have shown a steady upward drift over most of the twentieth century.

_____ 7. All people reach an intellectual peak in adolescence.

_____ 8. Historically, most psychologists have considered intelligence to be comprised of several distinct abilities.

_____ 9. Today, most researchers studying cognitive abilities believe that intelligence is multidimensional.

_____ 10. Compared with novices, experts tend to be more intuitive and less stereotyped in their work performance.

Progress Test 2

Progress Test 2 should be completed during a final chapter review. Answer the following questions after you thoroughly understand the correct answers for the Chapter Review and Progress Test 1.

Multiple-Choice Questions

1. The debate over the status of adult intelligence focuses on the question of its inevitable decline and on
   a. pharmacological deterrents to that decline.
   b. the accompanying decline in moral reasoning.
   c. its possible continuing growth.
   d. the validity of longitudinal versus personal-observation research.

2. Which of the following generational differences emerged in Schaie's studies of intelligence?
   a. Recent cohorts of young adults were better at math than those who were young in previous decades.
   b. Recent cohorts of young adults were better at reasoning ability, but worse at math, than those who were young in previous decades.
   c. Recent cohorts of young adults were better at all intellectual abilities than those who were young in previous decades.
   d. Recent cohorts of young adults were worse at all intellectual abilities than those who were young in previous decades.

3. The accumulation of facts that comes about with education and experience has been classified as
   a. crystallized intelligence.
   b. plastic intelligence.
   c. fluid intelligence.
   d. rote memory.

4. According to the text, the current view of intelligence recognizes all of the following characteristics EXCEPT
   a. multidimensionality.
   b. plasticity.
   c. interindividual variation.
   d. _g_.

5. Thinking that is more intuitive, flexible, specialized, and automatic is characteristic of
   a. fluid intelligence.
   b. crystallized intelligence.
   c. expertise.
   d. plasticity.

6. IQ scores increased over the twentieth century in part because
   a. more recent tests focus more on fluid intelligence than on crystallized intelligence.
   b. more recent tests focus more on crystallized intelligence than on fluid intelligence.
   c. later cohorts have had more education.
   d. later tests were made less difficult.

7. Which of the following is NOT true regarding family skills?
   a. They were undervalued skills in earlier generations.
   b. They were once considered the primary responsibility of women.
   c. They are now recognized and valued as expert work by both women and men.
   d. A "maternal instinct" is innate to every mother.

8. At the present stage of research in adult cognition, which of the following statements has the most research support?
   a. Intellectual abilities inevitably decline from adolescence onward.
   b. Each person's cognitive development occurs in a unique context influenced by variations in genes, life experiences, and cohort effects.
   c. Some 90 percent of adults tested in cross-sectional studies show no decline in intellectual abilities until age 40.
   d. Intelligence becomes crystallized for most adults between ages 32 and 41.

9. Research on expertise indicates that during adulthood, intelligence
   a. increases in most primary mental abilities.
   b. increases in specific areas of interest to the person.
   c. increases only in those areas associated with the individual's career.
   d. shows a uniform decline in all areas.

10. Research indicates that during adulthood declines occur in
   a. crystallized intelligence.
   b. fluid intelligence.
   c. both crystallized and fluid intelligence.
   d. neither crystallized nor fluid intelligence.

11. Fluid intelligence is based on all of the following EXCEPT
    a. working memory.
    b. abstract analysis.
    c. speed of thinking.
    d. general knowledge.

12. In recent years, researchers are more likely than before to consider intelligence as
    a. a single entity.
    b. primarily determined by heredity.
    c. entirely the product of learning.
    d. made up of several abilities.

13. Which of the following is a drawback of longitudinal studies of intelligence?
    a. They are especially prone to the distortion of cohort effects.
    b. People who are retested may show improved performance as a result of practice.

c. The biases of the experimenter are more likely to distort the results than is true of other research methods.
d. All of these are drawbacks.

14. To a developmentalist, an *expert* is a person who
    a. is extraordinarily gifted at a particular task.
    b. is significantly better at a task than people who have not put time and effort into performing that task.
    c. scores at the 90th percentile or better on a test of achievement.
    d. is or does none of these things.

15. One reason for the variety in patterns in adult intelligence is that during adulthood
    a. intelligence is fairly stable in some areas.
    b. intelligence increases in some areas.
    c. intelligence decreases in some areas.
    d. people develop specialized competencies in activities that are personally meaningful.

Matching Items

Match each definition or description with its corresponding term.

Terms

_____ 1. fluid intelligence
_____ 2. crystallized intelligence
_____ 3. analytic intelligence
_____ 4. selective optimization with compensation
_____ 5. general intelligence
_____ 6. creative intelligence
_____ 7. practical intelligence
_____ 8. Seattle Longitudinal Study
_____ 9. cognitive artifacts
_____ 10. Flynn effect
_____ 11. avoidant coping
_____ 12. problem-focused coping
_____ 13. weathering

Definitions or Descriptions

a. intellectual skills used in everyday problem solving
b. Spearman's idea that intelligence is one basic trait, underlying all cognitive abilities
c. all the mental abilities that foster academic proficiency
d. first study of adult intelligence that used a cross-sequential research design
e. flexible reasoning used to draw inferences
f. the capacity for flexible and innovative thinking
g. the tendency of adults to optimize certain aspects of their lives in order to offset declines in other areas
h. the accumulation of facts, information, and knowledge
i. trend toward increasing average IQ
j. intellectual tools passed from one generation to the next
k. thinking that doesn't require deliberate, conscious effort
l. the gradual accumulation of stressors over time
m. coping with a stressor by ignoring it
n. coping with a stressor by tackling its problems head on

Key Terms

Using your own words, write a brief definition or explanation of each of the following terms on a separate piece of paper.

1. general intelligence (*g*)
2. Seattle Longitudinal Study
3. fluid intelligence
4. crystallized intelligence
5. analytic intelligence
6. creative intelligence
7. practical intelligence
8. cognitive artifacts
9. stressor
10. avoidant coping
11. problem-focused coping
12. emotion-focused coping
13. weathering
14. religious coping
15. selective optimization with compensation
16. expertise
17. automatic processing

ANSWERS

CHAPTER REVIEW

1. psychometric
2. a single entity
3. Charles Spearman; *g*
4. adolescence; increased
5. increase; vocabulary; comprehension; information
6. longitudinal; cross-sectional

Cross-sectional research may be misleading because each cohort has its own unique history of life experiences and because in each generation, academic intelligence increases as a result of improved education and health.

7. increasing; Flynn effect
8. **a.** People who are retested several times may improve their performance simply as a result of practice.

    b. Because people may drop out of lengthy longitudinal studies, the remaining subjects may be a self-selected sample.

    c. Longitudinal research takes a long time.
9. K. Warner Schaie
10. cross-sequential

In this approach, each time the original group of subjects is retested, a new group is added and tested at each age interval.

11. primary mental abilities; Seattle Longitudinal Study
12. **c.** is the answer.
13. **c.** is the answer.

    a. & b. From the information given, it is impossible to determine which research method the psychologist used.
14. **c.** is the answer.
15. **b.** is the answer.

    c. & d. Both cross-sectional and longitudinal research are potentially misleading.
16. **c.** is the answer.

    a. & b. Schaie developed the cross-sequential research method to overcome the drawbacks of the cross-sectional and longitudinal methods, which were susceptible to cohort and retesting effects, respectively.

    d. A case study focuses on a single subject and therefore could provide no information on cohort effects.
17. **a.** is the answer.
18. Raymond Cattell; John Horn; fluid; crystallized
19. fluid; abstract analysis; working (short-term) memory; speed of thinking
20. crystallized
21. fluid; IQ; increase; crystallized
22. Robert Sternberg; analytic; emerging adulthood
23. creative; divergent; convergent; unusual (unexpected, imaginative)
24. practical; family; organization
25. is not
26. varies; and
27. historical
28. **a.** is the answer. This aspect consists of mental processes fostering academic proficiency by making efficient learning, remembering, and thinking possible.

    b. This aspect enables the person to accommodate successfully to changes in the environment.

c. This aspect concerns the extent to which intellectual functions are applied to situations that are familiar or novel in a person's history.

29. **a.** is the answer.

    b. & c. According to the research, fluid intelligence declines markedly during adulthood.

    d. Cohort effects refer to generational differences in life experiences.

30. **b.** is the answer. Because the maintenance of crystallized intelligence depends partly on how it is used, the consequences of remaining socially involved or of being socially isolated become increasingly apparent in adulthood.

31. **b.** is the answer. Creative intelligence enables the person to accommodate successfully to changes in the environment, such as those accompanying retirement.

    a. This aspect of intelligence consists of mental processes that foster efficient learning, remembering, and thinking.

    c. Fluid intelligence is not an aspect of Sternberg's theory. Moreover, it refers to basic mental abilities such as short-term memory.

    d. Plasticity refers to the flexible nature of intelligence; it is not an aspect of Sternberg's theory.

32. **b.** is the answer.

33. any situation, event, experience, or other stimulus that causes a person to feel stressed

34. avoidant coping; problem-focused; emotion-focused; emotion; oxytocin; tend-and-befriend

35. weathering

36. religious coping

37. are

38. selective optimization with compensation

39. expertise; selective expert

40. formal; past experiences; context; intuitive; stereotypic

41. automatic; automatic processing

42. strategies

43. flexible (or creative)

44. practice; 10 years; motivation

45. specific; cannot

46. male; female; are; women's work; important

47. **d.** is the answer.

a. & b. The text does not suggest that experts have special memory abilities.

c. This describes the performance of novices rather than experts.

PROGRESS TEST 1

Multiple-Choice Questions

1. **a.** is the answer.

   b. Although results from this type of research may also be misleading, longitudinal studies often demonstrate age-related *increases* in intelligence.

   c. Cross-sequential research is the technique devised by K. Warner Schaie that combines the strengths of the cross-sectional and longitudinal methods.

   d. Random sampling refers to the selection of subjects for a research study.

2. **a.** is the answer.

   b. This is a problem in longitudinal research.

   c. & d. Neither of these is particularly troublesome in cross-sectional research.

3. **d.** is the answer.

   a., b., & c. Cross-sequential research as described in this chapter is based on *objective* intelligence testing.

4. **d.** is the answer.

   a. & b. Traditional IQ tests measure both fluid and crystallized intelligence.

5. **c.** is the answer.

   a., b., & d. These often increase with age.

6. **c.** is the answer.

   a. Crystallized intelligence is the accumulation of facts and knowledge that comes with education and experience.

   b. Although intelligence is characterized by plasticity, "plastic intelligence" is not discussed as a specific type of intelligence.

   d. Rote memory is memory that is based on the conscious repetition of to-be-remembered information.

7. **d.** is the answer.

8. **a.** is the answer.

   b. Practical intelligence refers to the intellectual skills used in everyday problem solving and is identified in Sternberg's theory.

c. & d. These are two other aspects of intelligence identified in Sternberg's theory.

9. **a.** is the answer.

10. **a.** is the answer.

b. This was not discussed in the chapter.

c. Plasticity refers to the flexible nature of intelligence.

d. Encoding refers to the placing of information into memory.

11. **c.** is the answer.

a., b., & d. These are more typical of *novices* than experts.

12. **a.** is the answer.

13. **c.** is the answer.

b. The text does not indicate that they improved on those tests.

d. No such criticism was made of Bayley's study.

14. **d.** is the answer. In fact, intelligence often becomes *more* specialized with age.

15. **c.** is the answer.

a. Charles Spearman proposed the existence of an underlying general intelligence, which he called *g*.

b. Paul Baltes coined the term selective optimization with compensation.

d. K. Warner Schaie was one of the first researchers to recognize the potentially distorting cohort effects on cross-sectional research.

True or False Items

1. T
2. F   Intellectual functioning as measured by IQ tests is powerfully influenced by school achievement.
3. F   Cross-sectional research shows a decline in intellectual ability.
4. T
5. F   Many adults show intellectual improvement over most of adulthood, with no decline, even by age 60.
6. T
7. F   Psychologists now agree that intelligence does *not* peak in adolescence and decline thereafter.
8. F   Historically, psychologists have conceived of intelligence as a single entity.

9. T
10. T

PROGRESS TEST 2

Multiple-Choice Questions

1. **c.** is the answer.
2. **b.** is the answer.
3. **a.** is the answer.

b. Although intelligence is characterized by plasticity, "plastic intelligence" is not discussed as a specific type of intelligence.

c. Fluid intelligence consists of the basic abilities that go into the understanding of any subject.

d. Rote memory is based on the conscious repetition of to-be-remembered information.

4. **d.** is the answer. This is Charles Spearman's term for his idea of a general intelligence, in which intelligence is a single entity.

a. Multidirectionality simply means that abilities follow different trajectories with age, as explained throughout the chapter.

b. Plasticity simply refers to the ability to change.

c. Interindividual variation is a way of saying that each person is unique.

5. **c.** is the answer.
6. **c.** is the answer.
7. **d.** is the answer.
8. **b.** is the answer.

a. There is agreement that intelligence does *not* peak during adolescence.

c. Cross-sectional research usually provides evidence of *declining* ability throughout adulthood.

d. Crystallized intelligence refers to the accumulation of knowledge with experience; intelligence does not "crystallize" at any specific age.

9. **b.** is the answer.

10. **b.** is the answer.

a., c., & d. Crystallized intelligence typically *increases* during adulthood.

11. **d.** is the answer. This is an aspect of crystallized intelligence.

12. **d.** is the answer.

a. Contemporary researchers emphasize the different aspects of intelligence.

b. & c. Contemporary researchers see intelligence as the product of both heredity and learning.

13. b. is the answer.

a. This is a drawback of cross-sectional research.

c. Longitudinal studies are no more sensitive to experimenter bias than other research methods.

14. b. is the answer.

15. d. is the answer.

Matching Items

1. e	**5.** b	**9.** j	**13.** l
2. h	**6.** f	**10.** i	
3. c	**7.** a	**11.** m	
4. g	**8.** d	**12.** n	

KEY TERMS

1. **General intelligence (g)** is Spearman's idea that intelligence is one basic trait, underlying all cognitive abilities.

2. The **Seattle Longitudinal Study** was the first study of adult intelligence that used a cross-sequential research design.

3. **Fluid intelligence** is made up of those basic mental abilities—abstract thinking, short-term memory, speed of thinking, and the like—required for understanding any subject matter.

4. **Crystallized intelligence** is the accumulation of facts, information, and knowledge that comes with education and experience.

5. In Robert Sternberg's theory, **analytic intelligence** includes all the mental processes that foster academic proficiency by making efficient learning, remembering, and thinking possible.

6. In Sternberg's theory, **creative intelligence** involves the capacity for flexible and innovative thinking.

7. According to Sternberg, **practical intelligence** involves the capacity to adapt one's behavior to the demands of the situation. This type of intelligence includes the intellectual skills used in everyday problem solving.

8. **Cognitive artifacts** are intellectual tools that are handed down from one generation to the next.

9. A **stressor** is any situation, event, experience, or other stimulus that causes a person to feel stressed.

10. In **avoidant coping**, people respond to a stressor by ignoring, forgetting, or hiding it.

11. In **problem-focused coping**, people try to solve their problems by attacking them in some way.

12. In **emotion-focused coping**, people try to change their emotions as a way of dealing with stress.

13. **Weathering** is the gradual accumulation of stressors over a long period of time, wearing down the resilience and resistance of a person.

14. **Religious coping** is the process of using one's faith as a means of coping with stress.

15. **Selective optimization with compensation** is Paul and Margaret Baltes' theory describing the tendency of adults to select certain aspects of their lives to focus on, and optimize, to compensate for declines in other areas.

16. **Expertise** refers to specialized skills and knowledge developed around a specific area of interest.

17. **Automatic processing** is thinking that occurs without deliberate, conscious thought, as in the way experts process most tasks.

Adulthood: Psychosocial Development

Chapter Overview

Chapter 22 is concerned with adulthood, which was commonly believed to be a time of crisis and transition. Today, researchers realize the fluidity of age boundaries and that good and bad events may occur at any age. The chapter begins by examining the concept of stages during adulthood, then identifies five basic clusters of personality traits that remain fairly stable throughout adulthood.

The next two sections explore changes in relationships with friends and relatives and in the marital relationship in adulthood, including gay and lesbian partners. It also depicts the effects of divorce and remarriage on family interaction.

The final section examines the importance of generativity in the individual's life during adulthood. As many women and men begin to balance their work lives with parenthood, caring for parents, and other concerns, the motivation for many adults shifts from extrinsic rewards to intrinsic ones.

What Will You Know?

The text chapter should be studied one section at a time. Before you read, preview each section by skimming it, noting headings and boldface items. Then read the sections, one at a time, keeping these questions in mind.

1. Do adults still have the personality they had as infants?
2. When is it better to divorce than to stay married?
3. When is it better to be unemployed than to have a job?

Chapter Review

When you have finished reading the chapter, work through the material that follows to review it. Completing the sentences and answering the questions will enable you to answer the "What Have You Learned?" questions at the end of the text chapter. Scattered throughout the Chapter Review are Study Tips, which explain how best to learn a difficult concept, and Think About It discussions and Applications, which help you to know how well you understand the material. Check your understanding of the material by consulting the answers at the end of the chapter. Do not continue with the next section until you understand each answer. If you need to, review or reread the appropriate section in the textbook before continuing.

Personality Development in Adulthood

1. In Erikson's theory, the identity crisis of adolescence is followed in early adulthood by the crisis of _____ _____ _____ , and then in middle age by the crisis of _____ _____ _____ .

2. The theorist who took a different view and refused to link chronological age and adult development was _____ . Instead, this theorist described _____ (how many?) stages.

3. The notion of a midlife crisis _____ (is/is not) accepted by most developmentalists as an inevitable event during middle age.

4. List and briefly describe the Big Five personality factors.

a. _____

_____

b. _____

_____

c. _____

_____

d. _____

_____

e. _____

_____

5. The stability of personality results in large part from the fact that beginning in early adulthood most people have settled into an

_____ _____ .

6. Although personality certainly begins with _____ and is manifested in the decisions that form the person's lifestyle, it may shift if the _____ shifts.

7. Of the Big Five traits, _____ and _____ tend to increase slightly with age, while _____ , _____ , and _____ tend to decrease.

8. (Opposing Perspectives) One hypothesis is that personality is shaped by _____ . If personality changes occur, they happen more often _____ (early in life/late in life/in the middle of life/early or late in life.

THINK ABOUT IT Instead of linking adult development to chronological age, Abraham Maslow described adult development in terms of a hierarchy of needs achieved in sequence. Does this approach make sense to you? Does it seem to fit your own adult development? Or does the idea of chronological stages seem a more accurate description of your life?

_____

APPLICATIONS:

9. Forty-five-year-old Ken, who has been single-mindedly climbing the career ladder, now feels that he has no more opportunity for advancement and that he has neglected his family and made many wrong decisions in charting his life's course. Ken's feelings are probably signs of
a. normal development during middle age.
b. an unsuccessful passage through early adulthood.
c. neuroticism.
d. his being in the sandwich generation.

10. It has long been assumed that, for biological reasons, I will inevitably experience a midlife crisis. I am
a. a middle-aged man.
b. a middle-aged woman.
c. either a middle-aged man or a middle-aged woman.
d. neither a. nor b.

Intimacy: Friends and Family

11. During the sixth stage of Erikson's theory of development, adults seek to _____ . This stage is called _____ versus _____ .

12. The group of people with whom we form relationships that guide us through life constitutes our _____ _____ .

13. The most supportive members of the social convoy tend to be _____ . In addition to these people, neighbors, coworkers, and other _____ _____ often have an impact on our lives.

14. The belief that all family members are affected by events and conditions that affect one another is called _____ _____ .

15. Someone who becomes accepted as part of a family to which he or she is unrelated is called _____ _____ .

THINK ABOUT IT Consequential strangers are people who are not in a person's closest friendship circle but nonetheless have an impact on their development. Who are the one or two most consequential strangers in your life? How have they affected your development?

APPLICATION:

16. Sam's neighbor of 10 years has been an important source of support for him in dealing with his divorce, change in employment, and other aspects of life. Sam's neighbor is an example of a(n)
    a. fictive kin.
    b. consequential stranger.
    c. mentor.
    d. kinkeeper

Intimacy: Romantic Partners

17. Generally, married people are somewhat
    _____ , _____ , and _____ than unmarried ones of the same age and background.

18. The long-term quality of a marriage is affected by many factors, including the _____ experiences of both spouses, _____ before marriage, and the partners' _____ .

19. The time in parents' lives when grown children leave the family home is called the _____ _____ .

20. Older couples have less _____-_____ stress, higher _____ , and more time together than younger couples.

21. Research findings on marital success and satisfaction generally _____ (apply/do not apply) to gay and lesbian partners.

22. In the United States, about _____ (what proportion?) of first marriages end in divorce. With subsequent marriages, the odds of divorce _____ (increase/decrease).

23. Divorce usually increases _____ and _____ ; remarriage brings relief. However, early happiness in a remarriage _____ (may/may not) endure.

APPLICATION:

24. Ben and Nancy have been married for 20 years. Although they are very happy, Nancy worries that with time this happiness will decrease. Research would suggest that Nancy's fear
    a. may or may not be reasonable, depending on whether she and her husband are experiencing a midlife crisis.
    b. is reasonable, because marital discord is most common in couples who have been married 10 years or more.
    c. is unfounded, because after 10 or 20 years of declining satisfaction, partnerships improve as time goes on.
    d. is probably a sign of neuroticism.

Generativity

25. According to Erikson, after intimacy comes _____ versus _____ .

26. Because of their role in maintaining the links between the generations, mature adults become the _____ . This role tends to be filled most often by _____ (women/men); with today's smaller families, however, gender equity in this role _____ (is/is not) more apparent.

27. For most adults, the chief form of generativity involves caring for _____ .

28. Proportionately, about _____ of all North American adults will become stepparents, adoptive parents, or foster parents at some point in their lives.

29. Strong bonds between parent and child are particularly hard to create when a child has already formed _____ _____ to other caregivers.

30. Because they are legally connected to their children for life, _____ (adoptive/step/foster) parents have an advantage in establishing bonds with their children.

31. Middle-aged people have been called the _____ generation because they feel pressured to fulfill the needs of both younger and older generations. This analogy _____ (is/is not) misleading.

32. Since caregiving _____ (does/ does not) have benefits as well as costs, and since grown children _____ (are/are not) usually full-time caregivers, _____ (few/most) adults are sandwiched.

33. As people age, the _____ (intrinsic/extrinsic) rewards associated with working tend to become more important than the _____ (intrinsic/extrinsic) rewards.

34. Developmentalists welcome employee diversity in _____ , _____ , and _____ . In the United States, nearly _____ (what proportion?) of the civilian labor force is female and nearly _____ is of non-European ancestry.

35. (A View from Science) Researchers have begun to explore _____- _____ that are unnoticed by workers who are members of the majority, yet seem aggressive to minority workers.

36. Job change _____ (is/is not) common after emerging adulthood.

37. State four reasons that losing a job is more devastating the older a worker is.

   a.

   b.

   c.

   d.

38. Today, nontraditional work hours are increasingly _____ (common/rare) in the workplace.

STUDY TIP To reinforce your understanding of Erikson's four stages of adulthood, write a sentence or two describing two hypothetical adults in each stage: (a) one who is successfully meeting the challenges and (b) one who is not.

• Identity versus role confusion

   (a)

   (b)

• Intimacy versus isolation

   (a)

   (b)

• Generativity versus stagnation

   (a)

   (b)

• Integrity versus despair

   (a)

   (b)

APPLICATIONS:

39. Manuel is 50 years old. Although he is financially independent, he continues to work. Which of the following was NOT mentioned as a way that work helps meet his generativity needs?
   a. It helps Manuel with his need to accumulate personal wealth.
   b. It helps him express creative energy.
   c. It helps him support the health of his family.
   d. It helps him contribute to the community.

40. The parents of Rebecca and her adult twin, Josh, have become frail and unable to care for themselves. It is likely that
   a. Rebecca and Josh will play equal roles as caregivers for their parents.
   b. Rebecca will play a larger role in caring for their parents.
   c. Josh will play a larger role in caring for their parents.
   d. If Rebecca and Josh are well educated, their parents will be placed in a professional caregiving facility.

41. Forty-five-year-old Elena has been working for the telephone company for 20 years. Because of technological advances, she has been laid off. According to the text, this job loss is devastating to her because
   a. she can't work the long hours new jobs require.
   b. she doesn't have the knowledge needed to perform available jobs.
   c. she wants to spend time with her grandchildren and all new jobs are 9 A.M. to 5 P.M.
   d. her husband planned on retiring as long as she was still bringing in a paycheck.

42. After a painful phone call with her unhappy mother, your college roommate confides her fear that she will not be able to handle the burdens of children, career, and caring for her aging parents. Your response is that

a. she's right to worry, because women who juggle these roles simultaneously almost always feel unfairly overburdened.

b. her mother's unhappiness is a warning sign that she herself may be genetically prone toward developing a midlife crisis.

c. both a. and b. are true.

d. if these roles are important to her, if her relationships are satisfying, and if the time demands are not overwhelming, filling these roles is likely to be a source of satisfaction.

Progress Test 1

Multiple-Choice Questions

Circle your answers to the following questions and check them with the answers at the end of the chapter. If your answer is incorrect, read the explanation for why it is incorrect and then consult the text.

1. The most important factor in how a person adjusts to adulthood is his or her

a. gender.
b. developmental history.
c. age.
d. race.

2. The Big Five personality factors are

a. emotional stability, openness, introversion, sociability, locus of control.
b. neuroticism, extroversion, openness, emotional stability, sensitivity.
c. extroversion, agreeableness, conscientiousness, neuroticism, openness.
d. neuroticism, gregariousness, extroversion, impulsiveness, openness.

3. Concerning the prevalence of midlife crises, which of the following statements has the GREATEST empirical support?

a. Virtually all men, and most women, experience a midlife crisis.
b. Virtually all men, and about 50 percent of women, experience a midlife crisis.
c. Women are more likely to experience a midlife crisis than are men.
d. Few contemporary developmentalists believe that the midlife crisis is a common experience.

4. Shifts in personality during adulthood often reflect

a. increased agreeableness, conscientiousness, and generativity.
b. rebellion against earlier life choices.
c. the tightening of gender roles.
d. all of these effects.

5. All his life, Bill has been a worrier, often suffering from bouts of anxiety and depression. Which personality cluster best describes these traits?

a. neuroticism
b. extroversion
c. openness
d. conscientiousness

6. Regarding the concept of the sandwich generation, most developmentalists agree that

a. middle-aged adults often are burdened by being pressed on one side by adult children and on the other by aging parents.
b. women are more likely than men to feel "sandwiched."
c. men are more likely than women to feel "sandwiched."
d. this concept is largely a myth.

7. Jan and her sister Sue have experienced similar frequent changes in careers, residences, and spouses. Jan has found these upheavals much less stressful than Sue and so is probably characterized by which of the following personality traits?

a. agreeableness
b. conscientiousness
c. openness
d. extroversion

8. In families, one member tends to function as the _____ , celebrating family achievements, keeping the family together, and staying in touch with distant relatives.

a. sandwich generation
b. nuclear bond
c. intergenerational gatekeeper
d. kinkeeper

9. According to Erikson, the failure to achieve intimacy during early adulthood is most likely to result in

a. generativity.
b. stagnation.
c. role diffusion.
d. isolation.

10. Marge plans to retire from her job as soon as she has enough money saved to do so. Marge is evidently motivated by
   a. extrinsic rewards of work.
   b. intrinsic rewards of work.
   c. familism.
   d. generativity.

11. Erikson theorized that if generativity is not attained, the adult is most likely to experience
   a. lack of advancement in his or her career.
   b. infertility or childlessness.
   c. feelings of emptiness and stagnation.
   d. feelings of profound aloneness or isolation.

12. Concerning the degree of stability of personality traits, which of the following statements has the greatest research support?
   a. There is little evidence that personality traits remain stable during adulthood.
   b. In women, but less so in men, there is notable continuity in many personality characteristics.
   c. In men, but less so in women, there is notable continuity in many personality characteristics.
   d. In both men and women, there is notable continuity in many personality characteristics.

13. People who exhibit the personality dimension of _____ tend to be outgoing, active, and assertive.
   a. extroversion
   b. agreeableness
   c. conscientiousness
   d. neuroticism

14. In the United States, about how many employees still work on the traditional work schedule of Monday to Friday, 9:00 A.M. to 5:00 P.M.?
   a. 5 percent   c. 50 percent
   b. 25 percent   d. 75 percent

15. Which of the following personality traits was NOT identified in the text as either increasing or decreasing slightly during adulthood?
   a. neuroticism
   b. introversion
   c. openness
   d. conscientiousness

True or False Items

Write T (true) or F (false) on the line in front of each statement.

_____ 1. At least 75 percent of American men experience a significant midlife crisis between ages 38 and 43.

_____ 2. Better than age as a predictor of whether a midlife crisis will occur is an individual's developmental history.

_____ 3. The Big Five personality traits remain quite stable throughout adulthood.

_____ 4. Marriage typically occurs earlier than it did in previous decades.

_____ 5. Women with children are more likely to remarry.

_____ 6. The empty nest usually brings a time for improved relationships.

_____ 7. Living arrangements are a good measure of family closeness.

_____ 8. Intergenerational relationships are becoming weaker as more adult children live apart from their parents.

_____ 9. As adults mature, personality tends to improve slightly.

_____ 10. There is no evidence that the stability of personality traits is influenced by heredity.

Progress Test 2

Progress Test 2 should be completed during a final chapter review. Answer the following questions after you thoroughly understand the correct answers for the Chapter Review and Progress Test 1.

Multiple-Choice Questions

1. An individual's social convoy is most likely to be made up of
   a. older relatives.
   b. younger relatives.
   c. people of the same gender.
   d. members of the same generation.

2. Which of the following would be a good example of an ecological niche?
   a. an extrovert marries an introvert
   b. a conscientious person cohabits with someone who is disorganized
   c. a sculptor marries a canvas artist
   d. a workaholic marries a homebody

3. For her class presentation, Christine plans to discuss the Big Five personality factors. Which of the following is NOT a factor that Christine will discuss?
   a. extroversion   c. independence
   b. openness   d. agreeableness

4. Jack doesn't plan to retire as long as his job continues to be satisfying and boosts his self-esteem. Jack is clearly motivated by
   a. extrinsic rewards of work.
   b. intrinsic rewards of work.
   c. familism.
   d. generativity.

5. Whether a person ranks high or low in each of the Big Five personality factors is determined by
   a. heredity.
   b. temperament.
   c. his or her lifestyle.
   d. the interaction of genes, culture, and early experiences.

6. Regarding the strength of the contemporary family bond, most developmentalists believe that
   a. family links are considerably weaker in the typical contemporary American family than in earlier decades.
   b. family links are considerably weaker in the typical contemporary American family than in other cultures.
   c. both a. and b. are true.
   d. despite the fact that families do not usually live together, family links are not weaker today.

7. Your brother, who became a stepparent when he married, complains that he can't seem to develop a strong bond with his 9-year-old stepchild. You tell him
   a. strong bonds between parent and child are particularly hard to create once a child is old enough to have formed attachments to other caregivers.
   b. the child is simply immature emotionally and will, with time, warm up considerably.
   c. most stepparents find that they eventually develop a deeper, more satisfying relationship with stepchildren than they had ever imagined.
   d. he should encourage the child to think of him as the child's biological father.

8. Which of the following statements explains why couples in long-term marriages are particularly likely to report an increase in marital satisfaction?
   a. Marital satisfaction is closely tied to financial security, which tends to improve throughout adulthood.
   b. When children leave the family home, the relationship between husband and wife improves.

c. The couple has more time to spend together, without the stresses of child-rearing.
   d. All of these statements are correct.

9. Which of the following are typically the most supportive members of a person's social convoy?
   a. parents
   b. children
   c. coworkers
   d. friends

10. Which of the following is NOT true concerning divorce and remarriage during adulthood?
    a. Divorce is most likely to occur within the first five years of a wedding.
    b. Women with children are less likely to remarry.
    c. Remarriages break up more often than first marriages.
    d. Remarried people report higher average levels of happiness than people in first marriages.

11. Jan has been so much a part of her best friend's life that she effectively has been "adopted" by her family. In other words, Jan has become
    a. a kinkeeper.
    b. fictive kin.
    c. part of the sandwich generation.
    d. part of the social convoy.

12. Which of the following personality traits tends to remain quite stable throughout adulthood?
    a. agreeableness
    b. neuroticism
    c. openness
    d. all of these traits

13. How often does divorce end an abusive, destructive relationship?
    a. less than 1 percent of the time
    b. in 1 out of every 10 divorces
    c. one-third of the time
    d. about half of the time

14. The idea that family members are mutually affected by events and conditions is called
    a. linked lives.
    b. kinkeeping.
    c. empty nest syndrome.
    d. gender convergence.

15. Even decades after divorce, which of these factors still tend(s) to be lower for divorced adults than for nondivorced adults?
    a. income   c. self-esteem
    b. family welfare   d. all of these

Matching Items

Match each definition or description with its corresponding term.

Terms

_____ 1. kinkeepers
_____ 2. sandwich generation
_____ 3. extroversion
_____ 4. agreeableness
_____ 5. conscientiousness
_____ 6. neuroticism
_____ 7. social convoy
_____ 8. ecological niche
_____ 9. linked lives
_____ 10. openness
_____ 11. consequential strangers
_____ 12. extrinsic reward of work
_____ 13. fictive kin
_____ 14. intrinsic reward of work

Definitions or Descriptions

a. tendency to be outgoing
b. a person who becomes accepted as part of an unrelated family
c. tendency to be organized
d. those who focus more on the family
e. people who, although not part of our social convoy, affect our lives
f. those pressured by the needs of the older and younger generations
g. tendency to be moody
h. salary and health insurance
i. a chosen lifestyle and context
j. a protective layer of social relations
k. tendency to be helpful
l. events that affect one family member also affect other family members
m. tendency to be imaginative
n. self-esteem and job satisfaction

Key Terms

Using your own words, write a brief definition or explanation of each of the following terms on a separate piece of paper.

1. midlife crisis
2. Big Five
3. ecological niche
4. intimacy versus isolation
5. social convoy
6. consequential strangers
7. linked lives
8. fictive kin
9. empty nest
10. generativity versus stagnation
11. kinkeeper
12. sandwich generation
13. extrinsic rewards of work
14. intrinsic rewards of work

ANSWERS

CHAPTER REVIEW

1. intimacy versus isolation; generativity versus stagnation

2. Abraham Maslow; five

3. is not

4. a. extroversion: outgoing, assertive

   b. agreeableness: kind, helpful

   c. conscientiousness: organized, conforming

   d. neuroticism: anxious, moody

   e. openness: imaginative, curious

5. ecological niche

6. genes; context

7. agreeableness; conscientiousness; openness; neuroticism; extroversion

8. culture; early or late in life

9. a. is the answer.

   b. & c. Ken's feelings are common in middle-aged male workers, and not necessarily indicative of neuroticism.

   d. The sandwich generation refers to middle-aged adults being squeezed by the needs of the younger and older generations.

10. d. is the answer. Researchers have found no evidence that a midlife crisis is inevitable in middle adulthood.

11. connect with others; intimacy; isolation

12. social convoy

13. friends; consequential strangers

14. linked lives

15. fictive kin

16. **b.** is the answer.

   a. Fictive kin refers to a person who becomes accepted as a part of an unrelated family.

   c. Mentors assist inexperienced workers with their on-the-job skills.

   d. Kinkeepers are people who gather family members together.

17. happier; healthier; wealthier

18. childhood; cohabitation; personalities

19. empty nest

20. child-rearing; incomes

21. apply

22. one-third; increase

23. depression; loneliness; may not

24. **c.** is the answer.

   a. Marital satisfaction can be an important buffer against midlife stress.

   d. There is no reason to believe Nancy's concern is abnormal, or neurotic.

25. generativity; stagnation

26. kinkeepers; women; is

27. children

28. one-third

29. strong attachments

30. adoptive

31. sandwich; is

32. does; are not; few

33. intrinsic; extrinsic

34. background; gender; ethnicity; one-half; one-fourth

35. micro-aggressions

36. is

37. **a.** Older workers have higher salaries, more respect, and greater expertise.

   b. Older workers may never have learned the skills required for a new job.

   c. Age discrimination may make finding a new job more difficult.

   d. Older workers find relocation more difficult.

38. common

39. **a.** is the answer.

40. **b.** is the answer. Because women tend to be kinkeepers, Rebecca is likely to play a larger role than her brother.

   d. The relationship of education to care of frail parents is not discussed in the text.

41. **b.** is the answer.

42. **d.** is the answer.

PROGRESS TEST 1

Multiple-Choice Questions

1. **b.** is the answer.

2. **c.** is the answer.

3. **d.** is the answer.

   a. & b. Recent studies have shown that the prevalence of the midlife crisis has been greatly exaggerated.

   c. The text does not suggest a gender difference in terms of the midlife crisis.

4. **a.** is the answer.

   b. This answer reflects the notion of a midlife crisis—a much rarer event than is popularly believed.

   c. Gender roles tend to loosen in middle adulthood.

5. **a.** is the answer.

   b. This is the tendency to be outgoing.

   c. This is the tendency to be imaginative and curious.

   d. This is the tendency to be organized, deliberate, and conforming.

6. **d.** is the answer.

   b. & c. Women are no more likely than men to feel burdened by the younger and older generations.

7. **c.** is the answer. Openness to new experiences might make these life experiences less threatening.

8. **d.** is the answer.

   a. This was a term used to describe adult women and men who are pressured by the needs of both the younger and older generations.

   b. & c. These terms are not used in the text.

9. **d.** is the answer.

a. Generativity is a characteristic of the crisis following the intimacy crisis.

b. Stagnation occurs when generativity needs are not met.

c. Erikson's theory does not address this issue.

10. **a.** is the answer.

11. **c.** is the answer.

a. Lack of career advancement may prevent generativity.

b. Erikson's theory does not address these issues.

d. Such feelings are related to the need for intimacy rather than generativity.

12. **d.** is the answer.

13. **a.** is the answer.

b. This is the tendency to be kind and helpful.

c. This is the tendency to be organized, deliberate, and conforming.

d. This is the tendency to be anxious, moody, and self-punishing.

14. **c.** is the answer.

15. **b.** is the answer.

True or False Items

1. F Studies have found that crises at midlife are not inevitable.

2. T

3. T

4. F Marriage is occurring later today.

5. F Women with children are less likely to remarry, but when they do, their new husbands often have children from a previous marriage also.

6. T

7. F Just the opposite is true.

8. F Intergenerational relationships are becoming stronger, not weaker, as more adult children live apart from their parents.

9. T

10. F The stability of personality is at least partly attributable to heredity.

PROGRESS TEST 2

Multiple-Choice Questions

1. **d.** is the answer.

2. **c.** is the answer.

3. **c.** is the answer.

4. **b.** is the answer.

5. **d.** is the answer.

6. **d.** is the answer.

7. **a.** is the answer.

b. Many stepchildren remain fiercely loyal to the absent parent.

c. Most stepparents actually have unrealistically high expectations of the relationship they will establish with their stepchildren.

d. Doing so would only confuse the child and, quite possibly, cause resentment and further alienation.

8. **d.** is the answer.

9. **d.** is the answer.

10. **d.** is the answer.

11. **b.** is the answer.

12. **d.** is the answer.

13. **c.** is the answer.

14. **a.** is the answer.

15. **d.** is the answer.

Matching Items

1. d   6. g   11. e
2. f   7. j   12. h
3. a   8. i   13. b
4. k   9. l   14. n
5. c   10. m

KEY TERMS

1. A once-popular myth, the **midlife crisis** is a period of unusual anxiety, radical reexamination, and sudden transformation that is widely associated with middle age but has more to do with developmental history than with chronological age.

2. The **Big Five** are clusters of personality traits that remain quite stable throughout adulthood: openness, conscientiousness, extroversion, agreeableness, and neuroticism.

3. **Ecological niche** refers to the lifestyle and social context adults settle into that are compatible with their individual personality needs and interests.

4. During **intimacy versus isolation**, the sixth stage of Erikson's theory, adults connect with other people or experience aloneness.

5. A **social convoy** is a group of people of the same generation who guide, encourage, and socialize with each other as they move through life.

6. **Consequential strangers** are neighbors, coworkers, and other people who are not in our closest social convoy but who still have an impact on our lives.

7. **Linked lives** is the idea that events or conditions that affect one family member tend to affect them all.

8. **Fictive kin** refers to a person who becomes accepted as part of an unrelated family.

9. The **empty nest** refers to the time in the lives of parents when their grown children have left the family home to pursue their own lives.

10. **Generativity versus stagnation**, the seventh stage of Erikson's theory, is based on adults' need to be productive in a caring way.

11. Because women tend to focus more on family than men do, they are the **kinkeepers**, the people who celebrate family achievements, gather the family together, and keep in touch with family members who have moved away.

12. Middle-aged adults were once commonly referred to as the **sandwich generation** because of the false belief that they are often squeezed by the needs of the younger and older generations.

13. The **extrinsic rewards** of work include salary, health insurance, pension, and other tangible benefits.

14. The **intrinsic rewards** of work include job satisfaction, self-esteem, and other intangible benefits.

Late Adulthood: Biosocial Development

Chapter Overview

Chapter 23 covers biosocial development during late adulthood, discussing the myths and reality of this final stage of the life span. In a society such as ours, which glorifies youth, there is a tendency to exaggerate the physical decline brought on by aging. In fact, the changes that occur during the later years are largely a continuation of those that began earlier in adulthood, and the vast majority of the elderly are healthy and active.

Nonetheless, the aging process is characterized by an increased incidence of impaired vision and hearing and by declines in the major body systems. These are all changes to which the individual must adjust. In addition, the incidence of life-threatening diseases becomes more common with every decade.

Several theories have been advanced to explain the aging process. The most useful of these focus on our genetic makeup and cellular malfunctions, which include declining immune function. However, environment and lifestyle factors also play a role, as is apparent from studies of those who live a long life.

What Will You Know?

The text chapter should be studied one section at a time. Before you read, preview each section by skimming it, noting headings and boldface items. Then read the sections, one at a time, keeping these questions in mind.

1. How is ageism like racism?
2. What percentage of older people are in nursing homes?
3. Can people slow down the aging process?
4. Why would anyone want to live to 100?

Chapter Review

When you have finished reading the chapter, work through the material that follows to review it. Completing the sentences and answering the questions will enable you to answer the "What Have You Learned?" questions at the end of the text chapter. Scattered throughout the Chapter Review are Study Tips, which explain how best to learn a difficult concept, and Think About It discussions and Applications, which help you to know how well you understand the material. Check your understanding of the material by consulting the answers at the end of the chapter. Do not continue with the next section until you understand each answer. If you need to, review or reread the appropriate section in the textbook before continuing.

Prejudice and Predictions

1. The prejudice that people tend to feel about older people is called _____ .
    Although this prejudice may seem harmless, it actually undermines the older person's

    _____-_____

    and may become a _____-

    _____ _____ .

2. Elderly people who fear losing their minds because they think old age inevitably leads to dementia may act in ways that undermine their

    _____ _____ .

    This is an example of _____

    _____ .

3. Prejudice aimed at aging may also lead to disease because older adults are expected to _____ less. Inactive older adults have poorer _____ ,

    _____ , and

    _____ function.

4. The day–night circadian rhythm _____ (strengthens/diminishes) with age.

5. Sometimes, younger adults automatically lapse into _____ when they talk to older adults.

Describe this form of speech.

6. (A View From Science) The cultural bias that labels older people as infirm and ill _____ (is/is not) weakening.

7. The study of the characteristics of human populations is called _____ . Today, because of changes in the proportions of the population in various age groups, we are witnessing a _____ _____ .

8. The fastest-growing age group today is the _____ , defined as people over age _____ .

9. In the past, when populations were sorted according to age, the resulting picture was a(n) _____ , with the youngest and _____ (smallest/largest) group at the bottom and the oldest and _____ (smallest/largest) group at the top.

List three reasons for this picture.

a. _____

_____

b. _____

_____

c. _____

_____

10. Today, because of _____ _____ and increased _____ , the shape of the population is becoming closer to a(n) _____ .

11. Today, fewer workers are needed to provide the food, shelter, and other goods used by the rest of the population. This is because of advances in _____ .

12. Statisticians consider the _____ _____ to be an estimate of the proportion of the population that depends on care from others.

13. Most people over age 65 _____ (are/are not) "dependent."

14. Older adults who are healthy, relatively well-off financially, and integrated into the lives of their families and society are classified as _____-_____ .

15. Older adults who suffer physical, mental, or social deficits are classified as _____-_____ .

The _____-_____ are dependent on others for almost everything; they are _____ (the majority/a small minority) of those over age 65. Age _____ (is/is not) an accurate predictor of dependency. For this reason, some gerontologists prefer to use the terms _____ aging, _____ aging, and _____ aging.

APPLICATIONS:

16. Loretta majored in psychology at the local university. Because she wanted to serve her community, she applied to a local agency to study the effects of aging on the elderly. Loretta is a
    a. developmental psychologist.
    b. behaviorist.
    c. gerontologist.
    d. demographer.

17. An 85-year-old man enjoys good health and actively participates in family and community activities. This person is best described as being
    a. ageist.
    b. young-old.
    c. old-old.
    d. a gerontologist.

18. Concluding her presentation on demographic trends in the United States, Marisa states that, "By the year 2050
  a. there will be more people age 60 and older than below age 30."
  b. there will be more people age 30 to 59 than below age 30."
  c. there will be more people below age 30 than above age 60."
  d. people over age 65 might make up 16 percent of the world's population."

Selective Optimization with Compensation

19. A key factor in how people age is how well they respond with _____ _____ _____, choosing activities they can do well as their adjustment to aging.

20. (A Case to Study) A recent study that interviewed older couples concluded that sexual activity was more a _____ _____ than a _____ event. The method used by the researchers is called _____ _____ .

21. Older adult drivers compensate for age-related sensory changes by driving _____ and avoiding driving in the _____ .

22. Older people often suffer from one of three major eye diseases. The first of these, _____, involves a thickening of the _____ of the eye. The second, _____, involves a buildup of _____ within the eye that damages the _____ _____ . The disease _____ _____ involves deterioration of the _____ .

23. Fortunately, _____ is available for every sensory loss. Many deaf people benefit from a _____ _____, a device that enables people with hearing aids to hear words and music more easily.

24. Disability advocates promote more widespread use of principles of _____ _____, which makes settings and equipment usable by everyone, whether or not they are able-bodied and sensory-acute.

25. As people age, the brain _____ down, and connections between parts _____ . The _____ of the brain also decreases at an accelerating rate after age _____ . Brain shrinkage is most evident in the_____ , especially in the _____ and _____ _____ .

Aging and Disease

26. In discussing the aging process, gerontologists distinguish between the irreversible changes that occur with time, called _____ _____ , and _____ _____, which refers to changes caused by particular _____ influences or _____ . The distinction between these categories of age-related changes _____ (is/is not) clear-cut.

27. During late adulthood, all the major body systems become _____ and less _____ . Older people take _____ (less/more) time to recover from illnesses and are _____ (less/more) likely to die of them.

28. Allostatic load is measured by 10 or more biomarkers, including _____ .

29. An illness that is sudden and severe is called a(n) _____ _____ . An illness that begins gradually and is ongoing is called a(n) _____ _____ . Heart disease is an example of a(n) _____ _____ .

30. The leading cause of death for both men and women is _____ _____ .

31. A goal of many researchers is a limiting of the time any person spends ill, that is, a(n)_____

_____ _____

_____ .

32. With age, the bones become more

_____ , losing

_____ and _____ ,

and in advanced states resulting in the condition

called _____ . This condition

results from both _____ aging

and _____ aging. Too much

_____ and _____

and too little _____ and

_____-_____

_____ contribute to the develop-

ment of fragile bones.

_____

STUDY TIP To consolidate your understanding of aging and how the young-old can optimize their later years, give several examples of primary aging during late adulthood and compensations that can help prevent disability and maintain vitality.

_____

APPLICATION:

33. Concluding her presentation on sleep patterns among older adults, Marisol notes that each of the following changes are likely EXCEPT that older adults
    a. take longer to fall asleep.
    b. wake up more often in the night.
    c. feel drowsy more often during the day.
    d. generally are not worried about changes in their sleep.

Theories of Aging

34. The oldest theory of aging is the

_____-_____-

_____ theory, which compares

the human body to a(n) _____ .

Although this theory explains some aging, it

_____ (is/is not) contradicted.

State three facts that support the wear-and-tear theory.

35. Some theorists believe that, rather than being a mistake, aging is incorporated into the

_____ of all species in a kind of

_____ _____ .

36. Another theory of aging suggests that some

occurrence in the _____ them-

selves, such as the accumulation of accidents

that occur during _____

_____ , causes aging. According

to this theory, toxic environmental agents and

minor errors in _____ accumu-

late.

37. When human cells are allowed to repli-cate outside the body, the cells stop repli-cating at a certain point, referred to as the

_____ _____ .

38. The very ends of chromosomes, called

the _____ , are much

_____ (longer/shorter) in older

cells.

39. One possible strategy for slowing the

aging process is _____

_____ . Another is the use of

drugs that increase life-extending proteins called

_____ .

APPLICATION:

40. The wear-and-tear theory might be best suited to explain
    a. the overall process of aging.
    b. the wrinkling of the skin that is characteristic of older adults.
    c. the arm and shoulder problems of a veteran baseball pitcher.
    d. the process of cell replacement by which minor cuts are healed.

The Centenarians

41. Three places famous for long-lived people are

    _____ , _____ ,

    and _____ . Because of the

    absence of _____ , some

    researchers believe the people in these regions are

    lying about their true age.

    List four characteristics shared by long-lived people
    in these regions.

    a. _____

    b. _____

    c. _____

    d. _____

    _____

    STUDY TIP Create a developmental profile of a
    hypothetical adult who has a good chance of becom-
    ing a centenarian.

    _____

42. The oldest age to which members of a spe-
    cies can live—called the _____

    _____ ,

    which in humans is approximately

    _____ years—is quite

    different from _____

    _____ _____ ,

    which is defined as _____ .

43. Life expectancy varies according to

    _____ , _____ ,

    and _____ factors that affect

    frequency of _____ in child-
    hood, adolescence, or middle age. In the United
    States today, average life expectancy at birth
    is about _____ for men and

    _____ for women.

Progress Test 1

Multiple-Choice Questions

Circle your answers to the following questions and
check them with the answers at the end of the chapter. If your answer is incorrect, read the explanation
for why it is incorrect and then consult the text.

1. Ageism is
   a. the study of aging and the aged.
   b. prejudice or discrimination against older peo-
      ple.
   c. the genetic disease that causes children to age
      prematurely.
   d. the view of aging that the body and its parts
      deteriorate with use.

2. The U.S. demographic pyramid is becoming a
   rectangle because of
   a. increasing birth rates and life spans.
   b. decreasing birth rates and life spans.
   c. decreasing birth rates and increasing life
      spans.
   d. rapid population growth.

3. Primary aging refers to the
   a. changes that are caused by illness.
   b. changes that can be reversed or prevented.
   c. irreversible changes that occur with time.
   d. changes that are caused by poor health habits.

4. Demography is the
   a. science that describes populations.
   b. study of secondary aging.
   c. multidisciplinary study of old age.
   d. study of optimal aging.

5. Which disease involves the buildup of fluid that
   damages the optic nerve?
   a. cataracts
   b. glaucoma
   c. macular degeneration
   d. myopia

6. The dependency ratio compares the number of
   people _____ to the number

   _____ .
   a. aged 15 to 64; under age 15 or over 64
   b. under age 15 or over 64; aged 15 to 64.
   c. with acute illnesses; with chronic illnesses
   d. with chronic illnesses; with acute illnesses

7. A direct result of damage to cellular DNA is
   a. errors in the reproduction of cells.
   b. an increase in the formation of free radicals.
   c. decreased efficiency of the immune system.
   d. the occurrence of a disease called progeria.

8. Which theory explains aging as due in part to mutations in the cell structure?
   a. wear and tear
   b. immune system deficiency
   c. cellular aging
   d. genetic clock

9. According to the genetic adaptation theory of a genetic clock, aging
   a. is actually directed by the genes.
   b. occurs as a result of damage to the genes.
   c. occurs as a result of hormonal abnormalities.
   d. can be reversed through environmental changes.

10. Laboratory research on the reproduction of cells cultured from humans and animals has found that
   a. cell division cannot occur outside the organism.
   b. the number of cell divisions was the same regardless of the species of the donor.
   c. the number of cell divisions was different depending on the age of the donor.
   d. under the ideal conditions of the laboratory, cell division can continue indefinitely.

11. Drugs that increase proteins called _____ may delay aging.
   a. ApoE4
   b. progeria
   c. alleles
   d. sirtuins

12. The genetic disease called _____ causes children to die in their teens of heart diseases typically found in elderly adults.
   a. SIR2
   b. Hutchinson-Gilford syndrome
   c. Type 2 diabetes
   d. osteoporosis

13. In triggering our first maturational changes and then the aging process, our genetic makeup is in effect acting as a(n)
   a. immune system.
   b. secondary ager.
   c. demographic pyramid.
   d. genetic clock.

14. With age, the immune system
   a. becomes stronger.
   b. becomes weaker.
   c. loses B cells.
   d. loses T cells.

15. Professor Wilson believes that primary aging occurs because there is no reason for "mother nature" to waste resources on adults who are no longer able to produce the next generation. Professor Wilson is evidently a proponent of
   a. wear-and-tear theory.
   b. cellular aging theory.
   c. evolutionary theory.
   d. free radical theory.

True or False Items

Write T (true) or F (false) on the line in front of each statement.

_____ 1. Most older adults are happy, healthy, and active.

_____ 2. About 25 percent of the elderly are dependent.

_____ 3. Because of demographic changes, the majority of America's elderly population is now predominantly old-old rather than young-old.

_____ 4. Gerontologists focus on distinguishing aging in terms of the quality of aging, that is, in terms of young-old versus old-old.

_____ 5. Cells never stop duplicating.

_____ 6. The immune system helps to control the effects of cellular damage.

_____ 7. The volume of the brain shrinks with age.

_____ 8. Although average life expectancy is increasing, maximum life span has remained unchanged.

_____ 9. Although older people are more susceptible to disease, they tend to recover faster from most illnesses.

_____ 10. The importance of lifestyle factors in contributing to longevity is underscored by studies of the long-lived.

Progress Test 2

Progress Test 2 should be completed during a final chapter review. Answer the following questions after you thoroughly understand the correct answers for the Chapter Review and Progress Test 1.

Multiple-Choice Questions

1. People tend to view late adulthood more negatively than is actually the case because
   a. they are afraid of their own impending death.
   b. of the tendency to categorize and judge people on the basis of a single characteristic.

c. of actual experiences with older people.

d. they were taught to do so from an early age by their parents.

2. An important demographic change in America is that

a. ageism is beginning to diminish.

b. population growth has virtually ceased.

c. the median age is falling.

d. the number of older people in the population is increasing.

3. Which of the following is MOST likely to be a result of ageism?

a. the participation of the elderly in community activities

b. laws requiring workers to retire by a certain age

c. an increase in multigenerational families

d. greater interest in the study of gerontology

4. Heart disease and cancer

a. are caused by aging.

b. are genetic diseases.

c. are examples of secondary aging.

d. have all of these characteristics.

5. What percentage of the elderly are in nursing homes or hospitals?

a. less than 1 percent   c. 10 percent

b. 3 percent   d. 25 percent

6. Regarding the body's self-healing processes, which of the following is NOT true?

a. Women have a stronger immune system.

b. Given a healthy lifestyle, cellular errors accumulate slowly, causing little harm.

c. Aging makes cellular repair mechanisms less efficient.

d. Women who postpone childbirth have less efficient cellular repair mechanisms.

7. Most gerontologists believe that

a. slowing the rate of senescence would decrease the incidence of many diseases.

b. the senses don't inevitably become less acute as we age.

c. homeostasis occurs more quickly with each passing decade after age 20.

d. some of the body's systems develop increased organ reserve during late adulthood.

8. The oldest age to which a human can live is ultimately limited by

a. cellular aging.

b. the maximum life span.

c. the average life expectancy.

d. the Hayflick limit.

9. Cardiovascular disease is the leading cause of death for

a. men.

b. women.

c. both men and women.

d. neither men nor women; cancer is the leading cause of death.

10. Each time a cell duplicates

a. the genetic clock is reset.

b. the telomere is shortened.

c. the Hayflick limit is reached.

d. telomerase is released.

11. In studies of three regions of the world known for the longevity of their inhabitants, the long-lived showed all of the following characteristics EXCEPT

a. their diets consisted mostly of vegetables.

b. they were spared from doing any kind of work.

c. they interacted frequently with family members, friends, and neighbors.

d. they engaged in some form of exercise on a daily basis.

12. Which of the following best describes the population of older adults?

a. Most would not want to live to 100.

b. About 10 percent experience primary aging.

c. Most are suffering from one or more chronic illnesses.

d. Most are quite happy, healthy, and active.

13. The view of aging as a process by which the body and its parts deteriorate with use and with accumulated exposure to environmental stresses is known as the _____ theory.

a. programmed senescence

b. genetic clock

c. cellular aging

d. wear-and-tear

14. In most nations, the dependency ratio is about

a. 2:1.   c. 1:2.

b. 3:1.   d. 1:3.

15. In humans, average life expectancy varies according to all of the following EXCEPT

a. historical factors.

b. ethnic factors.

c. cultural factors.

d. socioeconomic factors.

Matching Items

Match each term or concept with its corresponding description or definition.

Terms or Concepts

_____ 1. young-old
_____ 2. old-old
_____ 3. glaucoma
_____ 4. cataracts
_____ 5. universal design
_____ 6. elderspeak
_____ 7. compression of morbidity
_____ 8. oxygen-free radicals
_____ 9. Hayflick limit
_____ 10. primary aging
_____ 11. secondary aging
_____ 12. osteoporosis
_____ 13. dependency ratio

Descriptions or Definitions

a. the universal changes that occur as we grow older
b. limiting the time a person is ill
c. the number of times a cell replicates before dying
d. unstable atoms with unpaired electrons that damage cells
e. a condescending way of talking to older adults
f. the majority of the elderly
g. thickening of the lens of the eye
h. the minority of the elderly
i. principles that create settings and equipment that can be used by everyone
j. age-related changes that are caused by health habits, genes, and other conditions
k. the buildup of fluid that damages the optic nerve
l. comparison of the number of self-sufficient people to the number of children and elderly
m. fragile bones disease

Key Terms

Using your own words, write a brief definition or explanation of each of the following terms on a separate piece of paper.

1. ageism
2. elderspeak
3. demographic shift
4. dependency ratio
5. young-old
6. old-old
7. oldest-old
8. universal design
9. primary aging
10. secondary aging
11. acute illness
12. chronic illness
13. compression of morbidity
14. osteoporosis
15. wear-and-tear theory
16. genetic clock
17. cellular aging
18. Hayflick limit
19. calorie restriction
20. maximum life span
21. average life expectancy

ANSWERS

CHAPTER REVIEW

1. ageism; self-esteem; self-fulfilling prophecy

2. cognitive competence; stereotype threat

3. exercise; circulation; digestion; brain

4. diminishes

5. elderspeak

Like babytalk, elderspeak uses simple and short sentences, exaggerated emphasis, slower talk, higher pitch, and repetition.

6. is

7. demography; demographic shift

8. centenarians; 100

9. pyramid; largest; smallest

a. Each generation of young adults gave birth to more children than just enough to replace themselves.

b. About half of all children died before age 5.

c. Those who lived to be middle-aged rarely survived diseases like cancer or heart attacks.

10. fewer births; survival; rectangle

11. technology

12. dependency ratio

13. are not

14. young-old

15. old-old; oldest-old; a small minority; is not; optimal; usual; impaired (pathological)

16. **c.** is the answer.

a. Although Loretta is probably a developmental psychologist, that category is too broad to be correct.

b. Behaviorism describes her *approach* to studying, not *what* she is studying.

d. Demographics is the study of populations.

17. **b.** is the answer.

a. An ageist is a person who is prejudiced against the elderly.

c. People who are "old-old" have social, physical, and mental problems that hamper their successful aging.

d. A gerontologist is a person who studies aging.

18. **d.** is the answer.

19. selective optimization with compensation

20. social construction; biological; grounded theory

21. slowly; dark

22. cataracts; lens; glaucoma; fluid; optic nerve; macular degeneration; retina

23. compensation; hearing loop

24. universal design

25. slows; weaken; volume; 60; neocortex; hippocampus; prefrontal cortex

26. primary aging; secondary aging; environmental; illnesses; is not

27. slower; efficient; more; more

28. cortisol, C-reactive protein, blood pressure, waist-hip ratio, and insulin resistance

29. acute illness; chronic illness; chronic illness

30. cardiovascular disease; risk; age

31. compression of morbidity

32. porous; calcium; strength; osteoporosis; primary; secondary; smoking; alcohol; calcium; weight-bearing exercise

33. **d.** is the answer.

a., b., & c. All of these are true of sleep patterns among older adults.

34. wear-and-tear; machine; is

Each body has a certain amount of energy and strength; for example, women who have never been pregnant tend to live longer than other women. People who are overweight tend to sicken and die at younger ages. One breakthrough of modern medical technology is replacement of worn-out body parts.

35. DNA; genetic clock

36. cells; cell replacement; copying

37. Hayflick limit

38. telomeres; shorter

39. calorie restriction; sirtuins

40. **c.** is the answer. In this example, excessive use of the muscles of the arm and shoulder has contributed to their "wearing out."

41. former Soviet Union; Pakistan; Ecuador; verifiable birth or marriage records

a. Diet consists mostly of fresh vegetables and herbs.

b. Work continues throughout life.

c. Families and community are important.

d. Exercise and relaxation are part of the daily routine.

42. maximum life span; 122; average life expectancy; the number of years the average newborn in a population group is likely to live

43. historical; cultural; socioeconomic; death; 76; 81

PROGRESS TEST 1

Multiple-Choice Questions

1. **b.** is the answer.

a. This is gerontology.

c. This is progeria.

d. This is the wear-and-tear theory.

2. **c.** is the answer.

3. **c.** is the answer.

a., b., & d. These are examples of secondary aging.

4. **a.** is the answer.

5. **b.** is the answer.

a. Cataracts are caused by a thickening of the lens.

c. This disease involves deterioration of the retina.

d. Myopia, which was not discussed in this chapter, is nearsightedness.

6. **b.** is the answer.

7. **a.** is the answer.

b. In fact, free radicals damage DNA, rather than vice versa.

c. The immune system compensates for, but is not directly affected by, damage to cellular DNA.

d. This genetic disease occurs too infrequently to be considered a *direct* result of damage to cellular DNA.

8. **c.** is the answer.

9. **a.** is the answer.

b. & c. According to the genetic clock theory, time, rather than genetic damage or hormonal abnormalities, regulates the aging process.

d. The genetic clock theory makes no provision for environmental alteration of the genetic mechanisms of aging.

10. **c.** is the answer.

11. **d.** is the answer.

12. **b.** is the answer.

13. **d.** is the answer.

a. This is the body's system for defending itself against bacteria and other "invaders."

b. Secondary aging is caused not only by genes but also by health habits and other influences.

c. This is a metaphor for the distribution of age groups, with the largest and youngest group at the bottom, and the smallest and oldest group at the top.

14. **b.** is the answer.

15. **c.** is the answer.

True or False Items

1. T

2. F   The number is much lower.

3. F   Although our population is aging, the terms *old-old* and *young-old* refer to degree of physical and social well-being, not to age.

4. T

5. F   This is the Hayflick limit.

6. T

7. T

8. T

9. F   Older people tend to recover more slowly from illnesses than younger people do.

10. T

PROGRESS TEST 2

Multiple-Choice Questions

1. **b.** is the answer.

2. **d.** is the answer.

a. Ageism is prejudice, not a demographic change.

b. Although birth rates have fallen, population growth has not ceased.

c. Actually, the median age is rising.

3. **b.** is the answer.

4. **c.** is the answer.

a. & b. Over time, the interaction of accumulating risk factors with age-related weakening of the heart and relevant genetic weaknesses makes the elderly increasingly vulnerable to heart disease.

5. **b.** is the answer.

6. **d.** is the answer. The text does not discuss the impact of age of childbearing on a woman's cell repair mechanisms. However, it does note that women who have never been pregnant live longer.

7. **a.** is the answer.

b. All the senses become less acute with each passing decade after age 20.

c. Homeostasis occurs more slowly as we age.

d. Organ reserve declines throughout adulthood.

8. **b.** is the answer.

a. This is a theory of aging.

c. This statistic refers to the number of years the average newborn of a particular species is likely to live.

d. This is the number of times a cultured cell replicates before dying.

9. **c.** is the answer.

10. **b.** is the answer.

11. **b.** is the answer. In fact, just the opposite is true.

12. **d.** is the answer.

13. **d.** is the answer.

   a. & b. According to these theories, aging is genetically predetermined.

   c. This theory attributes aging and disease to the accumulation of cellular errors.

14. **c.** is the answer.

15. **b.** is the answer.

Matching Items

1. f	5. i	9. c	13. l
2. h	6. e	10. a	
3. k	7. b	11. j	
4. g	8. d	12. m	

KEY TERMS

1. **Ageism** is a prejudice in which people are categorized and judged solely on the basis of their chronological age.

2. **Elderspeak** is a babyish way of speaking to older adults, using simple sentences, a slower rate, higher pitch, and repetition.

3. A **demographic shift** is a shift in the proportions of the population of various ages.

4. The **dependency ratio** is an estimate of the proportion of the population that depends on care from others.

5. Most of America's elderly can be classified as **young-old,** meaning that they are healthy and vigorous, relatively well-off financially, well integrated into the lives of their families and communities, and politically active.

6. Older people who are classified as **old-old** are those who suffer physical, mental, or social problems in later life.

7. Elderly adults who are classified as **oldest-old** are dependent on others for almost everything.

8. **Universal design** is the creation of equipment and settings that can be used by everyone, whether able-bodied or not.

9. **Primary aging** refers to the universal and irreversible physical changes that occur as people get older.

10. **Secondary aging** refers to changes that are more common as people age but are caused by health habits, genes, and other influences that vary from person to person.

11. An **acute illness** is one that is sudden and severe.

12. A **chronic illness** is one that is gradual and ongoing.

13. Researchers who are interested in improving the health of the elderly focus on a **compression of morbidity,** that is, a limiting of the time any person spends ill or infirm.

14. **Osteoporosis** is a disease in which low bone mass leads to increasingly fragile bones.

15. According to the **wear-and-tear theory** of aging, the parts of the human body deteriorate with use as well as with accumulated exposure to pollution and radiation, unhealthy foods, drugs, disease, and other stresses.

16. According to one theory of aging, our genetic makeup acts, in effect, as a **genetic clock,** triggering hormonal changes, regulating cellular reproduction and repair, and "timing" aging and the moment of death.

17. **Cellular aging** refers to the cumulative, damaging effect of stress and toxins on body cells over time.

18. The **Hayflick limit** is the maximum number of times that cells cultured from humans and animals divide before dying.

19. **Calorie restriction** is the practice of limiting dietary energy intake in an effort to slow down aging.

20. The **maximum life span** is the maximum number of years that a particular species is genetically programmed to live. For humans, the maximum life span is approximately 122 years.

21. **Average life expectancy** is the number of years the average newborn in a particular population group is likely to live.

24 CHAPTER

Late Adulthood: Cognitive Development

Chapter Overview

This chapter describes the changes in cognitive functioning associated with late adulthood. The first section describes neurological and other reasons for impaired cognitive development during late adulthood. The second section reviews usual changes associated with the information-processing system, providing experimental evidence that suggests declines in older adults' control processes, including their retrieval strategies. Despite some inevitable decline, real-life conditions provide older adults with ample opportunity to compensate for the pattern of decline observed in the laboratory. It appears that, for most people, cognitive functioning in daily life remains essentially unimpaired.

The main reason for reduced cognitive functioning during late adulthood is the development of neurocognitive disorders, the subject of the third section. This pathological loss of intellectual ability can be caused by a variety of diseases and circumstances; risk factors, treatment, and prognosis differ accordingly.

The final section of the chapter makes it clear that cognitive changes during late adulthood are by no means restricted to declines in intellectual functioning. For many individuals, late adulthood is a time of great aesthetic, creative, philosophical, and spiritual growth.

What Will You Know?

The text chapter should be studied one section at a time. Before you read, preview each section by skimming it, noting headings and boldface items. Then read the sections, one at a time, keeping these questions in mind.

1. How does the brain simultaneously grow and shrink in old age?
2. What kinds of memory are least apt to fade in old age? What kinds are the most apt to fade?

3. What is the difference between these four terms: Alzheimer, senility, dementia, and neurocognitive disorders?
4. What gains in cognition occur in late adulthood?

Chapter Review

When you have finished reading the chapter, work through the material that follows to review it. Completing the sentences and answering the questions will enable you to answer the "What Have You Learned?" questions at the end of the text chapter. Scattered throughout the Chapter Review are Study Tips, which explain how best to learn a difficult concept, and Think About It discussions and Applications, which help you to know how well you understand the material. Check your understanding of the material by consulting the answers at the end of the chapter. Do not continue with the next section until you understand each answer. If you need to, review or reread the appropriate section in the textbook before continuing.

The Aging Brain

1. During adulthood, neurons and dendrites _____ (grow/do not grow). This is particularly true in two areas of the brain: the _____ region and the _____ .

State the evolutionary perspective on why neurogenesis occurs during adulthood.

2. Senescence reduces production of

_____ including

_____ , _____ ,

_____ , and

_____ . Other changes in the

brain include a decrease in _____

_____ , thinning of

_____ , and a reduction in the

_____ _____ .

Together, these changes result in an over-

all brain _____ that

is evident in _____

_____ , _____ ,

and _____ .

3. In addition to a reduction in

_____ , brain aging is also

accompanied by decreased _____ ,

especially in the _____ and in the

_____ _____ .

In every part of the brain, the volume of

_____ matter is reduced,

causing many people to have to use their

_____ _____ to

understand events.

4. A person's past _____ and cur-

rent _____ may correlate with

neurological functioning in late adulthood. In

particular, higher _____ and

_____ status correlate with less

cognitive decline. One possible explanation for

this relationship that has received support is that

is high-SES people generally begin late adulthood

as _____ _____

than low-SES people. Another is that intel-

lectually gifted people possess a protective

_____ that keeps their minds

active.

5. Compared with younger adults, older adults use

_____ (more/fewer) parts of

their brains to solve problems.

6. Older adults often find _____

particularly difficult.

7. Because she has trouble screening out distractions and inhibiting irrelevant thoughts, 70-year-
old Lena is likely to
   a. have suffered a mini-stroke.
   b. be at increased risk of developing dementia.
   c. experience typical age-related declines in
   control.
   d. have some type of reversible dementia.

8. Which of the following tasks would an older
adult probably find the most difficult to perform?
   a. reading aloud
   b. following a recipe
   c. reading while walking
   d. riding a bicycle

Information Processing After Age 65

9. In order for stimuli to become information that is perceived, they must cross the

   _____ _____ .

10. The _____ -

   _____ approach separates cog-

   nition into four steps: _____ ,

   _____ , _____ ,

   and _____ .

11. Reduced sensory input impairs cognition because
some information is simply_____ .

12. Once information is perceived, it must be placed

   in _____ _____ .

13. Recall of learned material, which is called

   _____ memory, shows

   _____ (more/less) loss than rec-

   ognition memory (_____ memo-

   ry).

14. The memory deficit in which we forget the

   origin of a fact is _____

   _____ . Remembering

   to do something in the future, called

   _____ memory, also fades with

   age. A crucial aspect of this type of memory is the

   ability to _____ .

15. Working memory has two interrelated functions:

   to temporarily _____ informa-

   tion and then to _____ it.

16. Many experts believe that the underlying impairment of cognition in late adulthood involves

_____ _____ , often called the _____ function of the brain.

17. The final step in information processing is _____ , which is usually _____ in daily life.

18. In the Seattle Longitudinal Study, beginning at about age _____ , older adults began to show significant declines in the five "primary mental abilities": _____ _____ , _____ , _____ , _____ , _____ , _____ , and _____ _____ .

19. The idea that cognition should be measured in realistic settings that test real-life skills is called _____ _____ .

20. Most older adults _____ (do/ do not) consider memory problems a significant handicap in daily life.

STUDY TIP Age-related changes potentially affect every aspect of memory. Make a chart that summarizes typical changes that occur at each stage of the information-processing model (input, programming, storage, output).

Input

Memory

Control processes

Output

APPLICATIONS:

21. Marisa's presentation on "Reversing the Age-Related Slowdown in Thinking" includes all of the following points EXCEPT
   a. regular exercise.
   b. avoiding the use of anti-inflammatory drugs.
   c. cognitive stimulation.
   d. consumption of antioxidants.

22. Which type of material would 72-year-old Jessica probably have the greatest difficulty remembering?
   a. the dates of birth of family members
   b. a short series of numbers she has just heard
   c. the first house she lived in
   d. technical terms from her field of expertise prior to retirement

Neurocognitive Disorders

23. Although pathological loss of intellectual ability in elderly people is often referred to as _____ , a more precise term for this loss is _____ , which is defined as _____ _____ . This term has been replaced in _____ with the term _____ _____ , which can be either _____ or _____ , depending on the severity of symptoms.

24. A recent research study reported that about _____ percent of people 70 years of age and older in the United States had some form of major neurocognitive impairment. More older _____ (men/women) are diagnosed with NCDs than _____ (men/women).

25. The most common cause of NCD is _____ _____ . This disorder is characterized by abnormalities in the _____ _____ , called _____ and _____ , which destroy normal brain functioning.

26. Plaques are formed from a protein called _____-_____ ; tangles are twisted masses of threads made of a protein called _____ within the neurons. Plaques and tangles proliferate in Alzheimer disease in the _____ of the brain.

27. Physiologically, the brain damage that accompanies this disease _____ (does/ does not) vary with the age of the victim.

28. With age, Alzheimer disease (AD) becomes _____ (more/no more/less) common.

29. When Alzheimer disease appears before age 60, the person either has _____ or has inherited one of three genes:

    _____ , _____ , or _____ . In this case, the disease usually reaches the last phase within _____ years.

30. The most frequent forms of AD are poly-genetic, with _____ and _____ among the genes that increase the risk.

31. The second major cause of NCD is a _____ , or _____ _____ _____ .

    This condition occurs because an obstruction of the _____ _____ prevents a sufficient supply of blood from reaching the brain. Repeated events such as these may produce _____ _____ , which involves even more destruction of brain tissue.

32. Unlike the person with Alzheimer disease, the person with VaD shows a _____ (gradual/sudden) drop in intellectual functioning.

33. Another category of NCDs, called _____ _____ _____ , originates in brain areas that regulate emotions and social behavior. These areas include the _____ and the _____ _____ .

34. Other neurocognitive disorders cause a progressive loss of _____ control. The most common of these dementias results from _____ _____ , which produces muscle tremors or rigidity. This disease is related to the degeneration of

neurons that produce the neurotransmitter _____ .

35. In a related form of neurocognitive disorder, round deposits of protein are found throughout the brain. The main symptoms of this NCD, called _____ _____ , include visual _____ , momentary loss of _____ , and loss of _____ .

36. Other causes of NCD that usually begin before age 65 include _____ _____ , _____ _____ , severe _____ _____ , and the last stages of syphilis and AIDS.

37. Brain plasticity _____ (continues/does not continue) throughout life. For this reason, _____ may build brain capacity as well as prevent age-related loss. However, for most neurocognitive disorders, _____ is not certain and _____ is not yet possible.

38. The most common cause of reversible neurocognitive disorder is _____ . Other causes include _____ , _____ , _____ _____ , _____ _____ , and _____ .

39. Symptoms of NCD can result from drug _____ that occur when a person is taking several different medications. This problem is called _____ .

STUDY TIP Complete the following chart of the main causes or types of neurocognitive disorders and their defining characteristics.

Cause or type of neurocognitive disorder	Defining Characteristics
Alzheimer disease	proliferation of plaques and tangles in the cerebral cortex
Vascular dementia	
Frontal lobe disorders	
Parkinson disease	
Lewy bodies	

APPLICATIONS:

40. Leland's parents are in their 70s, and he wants to do something to ensure that their cognitive abilities remain sharp for years to come. As a friend, what would you encourage Leland to suggest that his parents do?
    a. They should take long walks several times a week.
    b. They should spend time reading and doing crossword puzzles.
    c. They should go to a neurologist for regular checkups.
    d. They should do a. and b.

41. Concerning the public's fear of Alzheimer disease, which of the following is true?
    a. A serious loss of memory, such as that occurring in people with Alzheimer disease, can be expected by most people once they reach their 60s.
    b. From 70 to 90, the incidence of Alzheimer disease rises from about 2 percent to almost 30 percent.
    c. Alzheimer disease is much more common today than it was 50 years ago.
    d. Alzheimer disease is less common today than it was 50 years ago.

42. Lately, Wayne's father, who is 73, harps on the fact that he forgets small things such as where he put the house keys; he also has trouble eating and sleeping. The family doctor diagnoses Wayne's father as
    a. being in the early stages of Alzheimer disease.
    b. being in the later stages of Alzheimer disease.
    c. suffering from major neurocognitive disorder.
    d. possibly suffering from depression.

New Cognitive Development

43. According to Erik Erikson, older adults are more interested in _____ than younger adults and, as the "social witnesses" to life, are more aware of the _____ of the generations.

44. According to Abraham Maslow, older adults are more likely to achieve _____-_____ .

45. Many people become more appreciative of _____ and _____ _____ as they get older.

46. Many people also become more _____ and _____ than when they were younger.

47. One form of this attempt to put life into perspective is called the _____ _____ , in which the older person connects his or her own life with the future.

48. One of the most positive attributes commonly associated with older people is _____ , which is defined as "an expert knowledge system dealing with the conduct and understanding of life."

APPLICATIONS:

49. Developmentalists believe that older people's tendency to reminisce
    a. represents an unhealthy preoccupation with the self and the past.
    b. is an underlying cause of age segregation.
    c. is a necessary and healthy process.
    d. is a result of a heightened aesthetic sense.

50. Sixty-five-year-old Lena is becoming more reflective and philosophical as she grows older. A developmental psychologist would probably say that Lena
    a. had unhappy experiences as a younger adult.
    b. is demonstrating a normal, age-related tendency.
    c. will probably become introverted and reclusive as she gets older.
    d. feels that her life has been a failure.

Progress Test 1

Multiple-Choice Questions

Circle your answers to the following questions and check them with the answers at the end of the chapter. If your answer is incorrect, read the explanation for why it is incorrect and then consult the text.

1. In the information-processing approach, cognition is impaired if information does not cross
   a. working memory
   b. long-term memory.
   c. the control processes.
   d. the sensory threshold.

2. Because of deficits in sensory input, older people may tend to
   a. forget the names of people and places.
   b. be distracted by irrelevant stimuli.
   c. miss details in a dimly lit room.
   d. reminisce at length about the past.

3. The two basic functions of working memory are
   a. storage that enables conscious use and evaluation of information.
   b. temporary storage and processing of sensory stimuli.
   c. automatic memories and retrieval of learned memories.
   d. permanent storage and retrieval of information.

4. Holding material in your mind for a minute or two requires which type of memory?
   a. working memory
   b. priming

c. long-term memory
d. beta-amyloid

5. Strategies to retain and retrieve information are part of which basic component of information processing?
   a. sensory threshold
   b. working memory
   c. control processes
   d. long-term memory

6. The plaques and tangles that accompany Alzheimer disease usually begin in the
   a. temporal lobe.
   b. frontal lobe.
   c. hippocampus.
   d. cerebral cortex.

7. During late adulthood, each of the following occurs EXCEPT
   a. neural fluid decreases.
   b. myelination thins.
   c. the corpus callosum is reduced.
   d. cerebral blood circulates more rapidly.

8. When using working memory, older adults have particular difficulty
   a. performing several tasks at once.
   b. picking up faint sounds.
   c. processing blurry images.
   d. recalling the meaning of rarely used vocabulary.

9. The most common cause of reversible neurocognitive disorder is
   a. a temporary obstruction of the blood vessels.
   b. genetic mutation.
   c. overmedication.
   d. depression.

10. Neurocognitive disorder refers to
    a. irreversible loss of intellectual functioning.
    b. the increasing forgetfulness that sometimes accompanies the aging process.
    c. abnormal behavior associated with mental illness and with advanced stages of alcoholism.
    d. a genetic disorder that doesn't become overtly manifested until late adulthood.

11. Which of the following diseases does NOT belong with the others?
    a. Huntington disease
    b. syphilis
    c. multiple sclerosis
    d. vascular dementia

12. Alzheimer disease is characterized by
   a. a proliferation of plaques and tangles in the cerebral cortex.
   b. a destruction of brain tissue as a result of strokes.
   c. rigidity and tremor of the muscles.
   d. an excess of fluid pressing on the brain.

13. Vascular dementia and Alzheimer disease differ in their progression in that
   a. vascular dementia never progresses beyond the first stage.
   b. vascular dementia is marked by sudden drops and temporary improvements, whereas decline in Alzheimer disease is steady.
   c. vascular dementia leads to rapid deterioration and death, whereas Alzheimer disease may progress over a period of years.
   d. the progression of Alzheimer disease may be halted or slowed, whereas the progression of vascular dementia is irreversible.

14. Medication has been associated with symptoms of neurocognitive disorder in the elderly for all of the following reasons EXCEPT
   a. standard drug dosages are often too strong for the elderly.
   b. the elderly are often unaware of the effects of combining alcohol with medication.
   c. drugs may have the side effect of causing confusion and depression.
   d. the intermixing of drugs can sometimes have detrimental effects on cognitive functioning.

15. The primary purpose of the life review is to
   a. enhance one's spirituality.
   b. produce an autobiography.
   c. give advice to younger generations.
   d. put one's life into perspective.

True or False Items

Write T (true) or F (false) on the line in front of each statement.

_____ 1. As long as their vision and hearing remain unimpaired, older adults are no less efficient than younger adults at inputting information.

_____ 2. Reduced sensory input impairs cognition by increasing the power of interference.

_____ 3. More areas of the brain are activated in older people.

_____ 4. A majority of the elderly feel frustrated and hampered by memory loss in their daily lives.

_____ 5. In studies of problem solving in real-life contexts, the scores of older adults were better than those of younger adults.

_____ 6. The majority of cases of NCD are organically caused.

_____ 7. Alzheimer disease is partly genetic.

_____ 8. Parts of the brain shrink during late adulthood.

_____ 9. Late adulthood is often associated with a narrowing of interests and an exclusive focus on the self.

_____ 10. According to Maslow, self-actualization is actually more likely to be reached during late adulthood.

Progress Test 2

Progress Test 2 should be completed during a final chapter review. Answer the following questions after you thoroughly understand the correct answers for the Chapter Review and Progress Test 1.

Multiple-Choice Questions

1. During late adulthood, the volume of the brain's _____ is reduced. As a result, many older adults have to use their _____ to understand events.
   a. white matter; gray matter
   b. corpus callosum; working memory
   c. gray matter; cognitive reserve
   d. prefrontal cortex; hypothalamus

2. Which of the following most accurately characterizes age-related changes in working memory?
   a. The ability to screen out distractions and inhibit irrelevant thoughts declines.
   b. Storage capacity declines while processing efficiency remains stable.
   c. Storage capacity remains stable while processing efficiency declines.
   d. Both storage capacity and processing efficiency remain stable.

3. Which of the following plausible hypotheses for the connection between high SES and high intellect has the greatest amount of research support?
   a. High-SES people began late adulthood with more robust and flexible minds.
   b. Keeping the mind active is protective.
   c. High-SES people generally have better medical care than low-SES people.
   d. High-SES people are better able to avoid pollution and drugs.

4. A patient has the following symptoms: blurred vision, slurred speech, and mental confusion. The patient is probably suffering from
   a. Alzheimer disease.
   b. vascular dementia.
   c. Huntington disease.
   d. Parkinson's disease.

5. In general, with increasing age the control processes used to remember new information
   a. become more efficient.
   b. become more complex.
   c. become more intertwined.
   d. become simpler and less efficient.

6. At the present stage of research into cognitive development during late adulthood, which of the following statements has the greatest support?
   a. There is uniform decline in all stages of memory during late adulthood.
   b. Long-term memory shows the greatest decline with age.
   c. Working memory shows the greatest decline with age.
   d. The decline in memory may be the result of the failure to use effective encoding and retrieval strategies.

7. Regarding the role of genes in Alzheimer disease, which of the following is NOT true?
   a. Some people inherit a gene that increases their risk of developing the disease.
   b. The frequency of the APoE4 gene that increases the risk of Alzheimer disease varies from place to place.
   c. When Alzheimer disease appears before age 60, the cause is usually not genetic.
   d. Alzheimer disease is a multifaceted disease that involves multiple genetic and environmental factors.

8. Older adults often find which type of task particularly difficult?
   a. reading aloud
   b. reading silently
   c. multitasking
   d. walking smoothly

9. Regarding ecological validity and memory testing, which of the following is NOT true?
   a. Traditional tests of memory measure cognitive abilities that are valued by younger people.
   b. When real-life situations are tested, older people sometimes outperform younger people.

   c. In real life, prospective memory is better among older people than among younger people.
   d. In laboratory tests, prospective memory is better among older people than among younger people.

10. Neurocognitive disorders
    a. are more likely to occur among the aged.
    b. have no relationship to age.
    c. cannot occur before the age of 60.
    d. are an inevitable occurrence during late adulthood.

11. The most common neurocognitive disorder is
    a. Alzheimer disease.
    b. vascular dementia.
    c. Parkinson's disease.
    d. alcoholism and depression.

12. Organic causes of neurocognitive disorder include all of the following EXCEPT
    a. Parkinson's disease.
    b. multiple sclerosis.
    c. Huntington disease.
    d. leukemia.

13. The psychological illness most likely to be misdiagnosed as neurocognitive disorder is
    a. schizophrenia.
    b. anxiety.
    c. personality disorder.
    d. depression.

14. On balance, it can be concluded that positive cognitive development during late adulthood
    a. occurs only for a small minority of individuals.
    b. leads to thought processes that are more appropriate to the final stage of life.
    c. makes older adults far less creative than younger adults.
    d. is impossible in view of increasing deficits in cognitive functioning.

15. A key factor underlying the older adult's cognitive developments in the realms of aesthetics, philosophy, and spiritualism may be
    a. the realization that one's life is drawing to a close.
    b. the despair associated with a sense of isolation from the community.
    c. the need to leave one's mark on history.
    d. a growing indifference to the outside world.

Matching Items

Match each definition or description with its corresponding term.

Terms

_____ **1.** delirium
_____ **2.** working memory
_____ **3.** control processes
_____ **4.** frontal lobe disorders
_____ **5.** neurocognitive disorder
_____ **6.** Alzheimer disease
_____ **7.** vascular dementia (VaD)
_____ **8.** Parkinson disease
_____ **9.** beta amyloid
_____ **10.** life review
_____ **11.** tau

Definitions or Descriptions

a. protein that makes up plaques
b. temporarily stores information for conscious processing
c. strategies for retaining and retrieving information
d. severely impaired thinking, memory, or problem-solving ability
e. memory loss and confusion that disappears in hours and days
f. caused by a temporary obstruction of the blood vessels
g. caused by a degeneration of neurons that produce dopamine
h. putting one's life into perspective
i. characterized by plaques and tangles in the cerebral cortex
j. brain disorders that do not directly involve thinking and memory
k. protein that makes up tangles

Key Terms

1. ecological validity
2. neurocognitive disorders (NCDs)
3. Alzheimer disease (AD)
4. plaques
5. tangles
6. vascular dementia (VaD)
7. frontal lobe disorder
8. Parkinson's disease
9. Lewy bodies
10. polypharmacy
11. self-actualization
12. life review

ANSWERS

CHAPTER REVIEW

1. grow; olfactory; hippocampus

According to an evolutionary perspective, the complex social interactions of human led to new brain development during adulthood.

2. neurotransmitters; dopamine; glutamate; acetylcholine; serotonin; neural fluid; myelin; corpus

callosum; slowdown; reaction time; talking; thinking

3. speed; size; hypothalamus; prefrontal cortex; gray; cognitive reserve
4. health; habits; education; vocational; quicker thinkers; openness
5. more
6. multitasking
7. c. is the answer.

   a., b., & d. Lena's symptoms are not indicative of any type of neurocognitive disorder.

8. c. is the answer. Older adults find it particularly difficult to combine a motor task and a cognitive task—such as reading while walking.
9. sensory threshold
10. information-processing; input, storage, programming, output
11. missed
12. working memory
13. explicit; more; implicit
14. source amnesia; prospective; shift the mind quickly from one task to another
15. store; evaluate
16. control processes; executive

17. output; verbal

18. 60; verbal meaning; spatial orientation; inductive reasoning; number ability; word fluency

19. ecological validity

20. do not

21. **b.** is the answer. In fact, *use* of anti-inflammatory drugs may help sustain cognitive functioning in old age.

22. **b.** is the answer. Older individuals are particularly likely to experience difficulty holding new information in mind, particularly when it is essentially meaningless.

    a., c., & d. These are examples of long-term memory, which declines very little with age.

23. senility; dementia; severely impaired judgment, memory, or problem-solving ability; DSM-5; neurocognitive disorders; major; mild

24. 14; women; men

25. Alzheimer disease; cerebral cortex; plaques; tangles

26. beta-amyloid; tau; hippocampus

27. does not

28. more

29. trisomy-21; APP; presenilin 1; presenilin 2; three to five

30. SORL1; ApoE4

31. stroke; transient ischemic attack (TIA); blood vessels; vascular dementia or multi-infarct dementia

32. sudden

33. frontal lobe disorders; amygdala; frontal lobes

34. motor; Parkinson's disease; dopamine

35. Lewy body; hallucinations; attention; inhibition

36. Huntington disease; multiple sclerosis; head injury

37. continues; exercise; prevention; cure

38. depression; malnutrition; dehydration; brain tumors; physical illness; overmedication

39. interactions; polypharmacy

40. **d.** is the answer. While **c.** might be something they should do, the most important things are for them to get exercise and maintain activities that promote cognitive stimulation.

41. **b.** the answer.

c. & d. The text does not indicate the existence of cohort effects in the incidence of Alzheimer disease.

42. **d.** is the answer.

    a., b., & c. The symptoms Wayne's father is experiencing are those of depression, which is often misdiagnosed as neurocognitive disorder in the elderly.

43. arts, children, and the whole of human experience; interdependence

44. self-actualization

45. nature; aesthetic experiences

46. reflective; philosophical

47. life review

48. wisdom

49. **c.** is the answer.

    d. This would lead to a greater appreciation of nature and art, but not necessarily to a tendency to reminisce.

50. **b.** is the answer.

PROGRESS TEST 1

Multiple-Choice Questions

1. **d.** is the answer.

    a. Working memory is involved only if information crosses the sensory threshold.

    b. & c. Long-term memory, which contains the knowledge base, includes information that is stored for several minutes to several years.

2. **c.** is the answer.

    a. & d. The sensory register is concerned with noticing sensory events rather than with memory.

    b. Age-related deficits in the sensory register are most likely for ambiguous or weak stimuli.

3. **a.** is the answer.

    b. These are the functions of sensory memory.

    c. This refers to long-term memory's processing of implicit and explicit memories, respectively.

    d. This is the function of long-term memory.

4. **a.** is the answer.

    b. Priming involves use of a clue to jog one's memory.

    c. Long-term memory includes information remembered for years or decades.

d. Beta-amyloid is the protein that makes up the plaques in the tissues surrounding neurons.

5. **c.** is the answer.

6. **c.** is the answer.

7. **d.** is the answer. Cerebral blood circulates more slowly in the older brain.

8. **a.** is the answer.

   b. & c. These may be true, but they involve sensory memory rather than working memory.

   d. Memory for vocabulary, which generally is very good throughout adulthood, involves long-term memory.

9. **d.** is the answer.

10. **a.** is the answer.

11. **d.** is the answer. Each of the other answers is an example of a neurocognitive disorder that occurs before age 65.

12. **a.** is the answer.

    b. This describes multi-infarct dementia.

    c. This describes Parkinson's disease.

    d. This was not given in the text as a cause of neurocognitive disorder.

13. **b.** is the answer.

    a. Because multiple infarcts typically occur, the disease *is* progressive in nature.

    c. The text does not suggest that MID necessarily leads to quick death.

    d. At present, Alzheimer disease is untreatable.

14. **b.** is the answer.

15. **d.** is the answer.

True or False Items

1. F The slowing of perceptual processes and decreases in attention associated with aging are also likely to affect efficiency of input.

2. T

3. T

4. F Most older adults perceive some memory loss but do not feel that it affects their daily functioning.

5. T

6. T

7. T

8. T

9. F Interests often broaden during late adulthood, and there is by no means exclusive focus on the self.

10. T

PROGRESS TEST 2

Multiple-Choice Questions

1. **c.** is the answer.

2. **a.** is the answer.

3. **a.** is the answer.

4. **b.** is the answer.

5. **d.** is the answer.

6. **d.** is the answer.

   a. Some aspects of information processing, such as long-term memory, show less decline with age than others, such as working memory.

   b. & c. The text does not indicate that one particular subcomponent of memory shows the *greatest* decline.

7. **c.** is the answer. When Alzheimer disease appears before age 60, the cause is almost always genetic.

8. **c.** is the answer. Particularly difficult for the elderly are tasks such as walking and reading that combine motor and cognitive skills.

9. **d.** is the answer. In laboratory tests, but not in real life, prospective memory is better among young people than among older people.

10. **a.** is the answer. Although age is not the key factor, it is true that NCD is more likely to occur in older adults.

11. **a.** is the answer.

    b. MID is responsible for about 15 percent of all neurocognitive disorders.

    c. & d. Compared to Alzheimer disease, which accounts for about 70 percent of all neurocognitive disorders, these account for a much lower percentage.

12. **d.** is the answer.

13. **d.** is the answer.

14. **b.** is the answer.

    a. & d. Positive cognitive development is *typical* of older adults.

    c. Pragmatism is one characteristic of wisdom, an attribute commonly associated with older people.

15. **a.** is the answer.

b. & c. Although these may be true of some older adults, they are not necessarily a *key* factor in cognitive development during late adulthood.

d. In fact, older adults are typically *more* concerned with the whole of human experience.

Matching Items

1. e	**5.** d	**9.** a
2. b	**6.** i	**10.** h
3. c	**7.** f	**11.** k
4. j	**8.** g	

Key Terms

1. **Ecological validity** is the idea that cognition should be measured in realistic settings that involve real-life abilities.

2. **Neurocognitive disorders (NCDs)** are severe impairments of intellect that are irreversible and caused by organic brain damage or disease.

3. **Alzheimer disease (AD),** a progressive disorder that is the most common cause of neurocognitive disorder, is characterized by plaques and tangles in the cerebral cortex that destroy normal brain functioning.

4. **Plaques** are clumps of the protein beta-amyloid found in the tissues surrounding neurons.

5. **Tangles** are twisted threads of the protein tau found within neurons.

6. **Vascular dementia (VaD),** which accounts for about 15 to 20 percent of all neurocognitive disorders, occurs because an infarct, or temporary obstruction of the blood vessels (often called a stroke), prevents a sufficient supply of blood from reaching an area of the brain. It is characterized by sporadic and progressive loss of brain functioning; also called *multi-infarct dementia.*

7. **Frontal lobe disorder** is deterioration of the amygdala and frontal lobes that may cause 15 percent of all neurocognitive disorders.

8. **Parkinson's disease** is a chronic, progressive disease that is characterized by muscle rigidity or tremors, and sometimes dementia, and is related to the degeneration of neurons that produce dopamine.

9. **Lewy bodies** are deposits of a brain protein that interfere with neural communication and cause neurocognitive disorders.

10. **Polypharmacy** is the situation in which elderly people are prescribed several medications, the interactions of which can result in symptoms of dementia.

11. The final stage in Abraham Maslow's hierarchy of needs, **self-actualization** is characterized by increased aesthetic, creative, philosophical, and spiritual understanding.

12. In the **life review,** an older person attempts to put his or her life into perspective by recalling and recounting various aspects of life to members of the younger generations.

Late Adulthood: Psychosocial Development

25
CHAPTER

Chapter Overview

There is great variation in development after age 65. Certain psychosocial changes are common during this stage of the life span—retirement, the death of a spouse, and failing health—yet people respond to these experiences in vastly different ways.

Individual experiences may help to explain the fact that theories of psychosocial aging, discussed in the first section of the chapter, are often diametrically opposed. The second section of the chapter focuses on the challenges to generativity that accompany late adulthood, such as finding new sources of achievement once derived from work. In the third section, the importance of marriage, friends, neighbors, and family in providing social support is discussed, as are the different experiences of married and single older adults. The final section focuses on the frail elderly—the minority of older adults, often poor and/or ill, who require extensive care.

What Will You Know?

The text chapter should be studied one section at a time. Before you read, preview each section by skimming it, noting headings and boldface items. Then read the sections, one at a time, keeping these questions in mind.

1. Do older people become more pessimistic or optimistic as time goes by?
2. Do most elderly people want to move to a distant, warm place?
3. What do adult children owe their elderly parents?
4. Is home care better than nursing home care?

Chapter Review

When you have finished reading the chapter, work through the material that follows to review it. Completing the sentences and answering the ques-

tions will enable you to answer the "What Have You Learned?" questions at the end of the text chapter. Scattered throughout the Chapter Review are Study Tips, which explain how best to learn a difficult concept, and Think About It discussions and Applications, which help you to know how well you understand the material. Check your understanding of the material by consulting the answers at the end of the chapter. Do not continue with the next section until you understand each answer. If you need to, review or reread the appropriate section in the textbook before continuing.

Theories of Late Adulthood

1. Theories that emphasize the active part that individuals play in their own psychosocial development are _____ theories.

2. The most comprehensive theory is that of _____ , who called life's final crisis _____ versus _____ .

3. At this stage, past crises, particularly _____ versus_____ _____ , reappear when the usual pillars of the self-concept crumble.

4. The importance of maintaining their sense of _____ may lead to behaviors such as _____ _____ , which is the tendency to cling to familiar _____ . The DSM-5 now recognizes _____ _____ when these urges and behaviors become hazardous.

5. According to _____
_____ theory, older people prioritize their _____ regulation by
seeking familiar social contacts.

6. Some people cope successfully with
aging through _____
_____ _____
_____ , which is the idea that
individuals set their own _____ ,
assess their own _____ , and then
figure out how to accomplish what they want to
achieve despite the _____ and
_____ of later life.

7. The general personality shift known as the
_____ _____
refers to the tendency of elderly people to perceive, prefer, and remember positive experiences more than negative ones. In addition, with
age there is less distance between what people
hope for themselves (the _____
_____) and how they per-
ceive themselves (the _____
_____).

8. Theorists who emphasize _____
maintain that _____ forces
limit individual _____ and
direct life at every stage. Stratification by
_____ , _____ ,
and _____ often leads to
_____ that makes it difficult
for people to break free from social institutions that assign them to a particular path. The
most harmful effect of stratification may be
_____ . Another form of this phenomenon focuses on _____ ,
reflecting how industrialized nations segregate
the oldest generation.

9. According to _____ theory,
in old age the individual and society mutually withdraw from each other. This theory is
_____ (controversial among/
almost universally accepted by) gerontologists.

10. The opposite idea is expressed in
_____ theory, which holds that
older adults remain socially active. According

to this theory, if older adults do disengage, they
do so _____ (willingly/unwill-
ingly).

11. The dominant view is that the more
_____ the elderly play,
the greater their _____
_____ and the longer their lives.

12. The most recent view of age stratification is that
_____ (neither theory/both theo-
ries) fit(s) everyone.

13. Two other categories of stratification that
are especially important in late adulthood are _____ and
_____ . Another stratification
theory, which draws attention to the values
underlying the gender divisions promoted
by society, is _____ theory.
According to this theory, _____
policies make later life particularly burdensome
for women.

14. One example of stratification by
_____ involves the accumulation
of health disparities as people age. This phenomenon, which is called _____ ,
creates a high _____
_____ in the form of medical
problems such as _____ and
_____ .

APPLICATIONS:

15. An advocate of which of the following theories
would be most likely to agree with the statement, "Because of their more passive style of
interaction, older people are less likely to be chosen for new roles"?
a. disengagement   c. self
b. integrity   d. positivity

16. Professor Martin states that "membership in
certain groups can place the elderly at risk for a
number of dangers." Professor Martin evidently
is an advocate of which theory of psychosocial
development?
a. self theories   c. positivity
b. stratification   d. integrity

17. When elderly Mr. Flanagan reflects on his life, he remembers mostly good times and experiences. This selectivity in thinking is called
    a. the positivity effect.
    b. respite care.
    c. aging in place.
    d. disengagement.

18. Jack, who is 73, looks back on his life with a sense of pride and contentment; Eleanor feels unhappy with her life and that it is "too late to start over." In Erikson's terminology, Jack is experiencing _____ , while Eleanor is experiencing _____ .
    a. generativity; stagnation
    b. identity; emptiness
    c. integrity; despair
    d. completion; termination

Activities in Late Adulthood

19. The employment rate for older workers has _____ (increased/decreased) in the past 10 years. This _____ (is true/is not true) in every nation.

20. Most people retire during the decade of their _____ . Those most likely to stay employed after this age are _____ _____-_____ workers and _____ .

21. A major problem with retirement is inadequate _____ , especially for how to spend _____ . Retirement correlates with illness when it is precipitated by _____ _____ . Retirement correlates with mental decline when it leads to _____ from cognitive challenge.

22. Many older adults stay busy by _____ . The benefits to the individual of doing so include good _____ and less _____ .

23. Compared with younger adults, older, retired adults are _____ (more/less) likely to feel a strong obligation to serve their communities. One reason is that _____ may discourage volunteering. Another is the absence of organizational strategies for _____ older volunteers. A third possible reason is that some older adults are too

_____-_____ . Finally, research surveys may not take into consideration volunteer work such as

_____ .

24. Most elderly people prefer to _____ (relocate when they retire/age in place).

25. Rather than moving, many elderly people prefer to remain in the neighborhoods in which they raised their children, thus creating _____ _____ retirement communities.

26. Religious faith _____ (increases/remains stable/decreases) as people age. Religious involvement correlates with _____ and_____ health.

27. By many measures, the elderly are more _____ active than any other age group. Compared to younger people, the elderly are more likely to _____ .

28. The idea that the elderly vote as a bloc _____ (is/is not) confirmed by the data.

APPLICATIONS:

29. When they retire, most older adults
    a. immediately feel more satisfied with their new way of life.
    b. engage in a variety of social activities.
    c. have serious, long-term difficulties adjusting to retirement.
    d. disengage from other roles and activities as well.

30. The one MOST likely to agree with the statement, "Older adults have an obligation to help others and serve the community," is
    a. an employed middle-aged adult.
    b. a retired older woman.
    c. a retired older man.
    d. an emerging adult.

31. Beyonce's mother wishes to age in place. This means that she
    a. plans to continue working as long as possible.
    b. wishes to remain in her home even after her health begins to decline.
    c. plans to move back to her childhood home.
    d. will do each of these things.

Friends and Relatives

32. The phrase _____ _____ highlights the fact that the life course is traveled in the company of others.

33. Elderly Americans who are married tend to be _____ , _____ , and _____ than unmarried people their age.

Give some possible reasons that marriages may improve with time.

34. Because more people are living longer, more older people are part of _____ families than at any time in history. Sometimes, this takes the form of a _____ family, in which there are more _____ than in the past but with only a few members in each generation.

35. The idea that adult children are obligated to care for their aging parents is called _____ _____ . This idea _____ (is/is not) found equally in every culture.

36. Today, when one generation needs help, assistance typically flows from the _____ (younger/older) generation to their _____ (parents/children) instead of vice versa.

Identify several factors that influence the relationships between parents and their adult children.

37. By age 65, _____ (what percent?) of all U.S. elders are grandparents.

38. Grandparent–grandchild relationships take one of four forms: _____ , _____ , _____ , or _____ _____ .

In the past, grandparents _____ (almost always/never) lived with the family of one of their grandchildren; today, most _____ (do/do not).

39. Most contemporary grandparents seek the _____ role as they strive for the love and respect of their grandchildren while maintaining their own _____ .

40. Grandparents are most likely to provide surrogate care for infants who are _____ - _____ or school-age boys who are _____ , for example.

41. Social workers often seek grandparents for _____ _____ _____ .

42. Approximately _____ percent of adults over age 75 in the United States have been married. This _____ (is/is not) the most married cohort in history.

43. Those who have never married tend to be _____ (quite content/lonely and unsupported).

44. Having a partner and children _____ (is necessary/is not necessary) for happiness in old age.

45. In buffering against stress, having at least one close _____ is crucial.

46. Successful aging requires that people keep themselves from becoming _____ .

THINK ABOUT IT The text notes that contemporary grandparents follow one of four approaches to dealing with their grandchildren. Which approaches were followed by your grandparents? Why? What factors likely influenced their approach?

APPLICATION:

47. Of the following, who is most likely to be actively involved with Facebook, Twitter, and other social networking sites?
   a. 25-year-old Maya
   b. 45-year-old Seth
   c. 55-year-old Angela
   d. 65-year-old Eliot

The Frail Elderly

48. Elderly people who are physically infirm, very ill, or cognitively impaired are called the

_____   _____ .

49. The crucial sign of frailty is an inability to perform the _____ , which comprise five tasks: _____ ,

_____ , _____ ,

_____ , and _____ .

50. Actions that require some intellectual competence and forethought are classified as

_____ . These include such

things as _____ .

51. There _____ (are/are not) cultural differences in care for the frail elderly.

52. Family caregivers for the frail elderly often experience substantial _____ .
Expectations for how the elderly should be cared for _____ (vary/do not vary) significantly from one culture to another.

53. The frail elderly are particularly vulnerable to

_____   _____ .

Most cases of elder maltreatment

_____ (involve/do not involve)

family members.
Identity three conditions under which elder abuse is likely.

   a. _____

   b. _____

   c. _____

54. Many older Americans and their relatives feel that _____

_____ should be avoided

at all costs. An intermediate form of care is

_____   _____ ,

which provides some privacy and indepen-

dence, along with some _____

supervision. Another form of care, called

_____   _____ ,

involves elderly people who live near each other and pool their resources.

THINK ABOUT IT Think of a close frail elderly friend or relative who is currently a part of your life, or once was. How did this person's daily activities and living arrangement change as he or she grew older?

APPLICATIONS:

55. Claudine is the primary caregiver for her elderly parents. The amount of stress she feels in this role depends above all on
   a. how frail her parents are.
   b. how much support she feels she receives from others.
   c. her relationship to her parents prior to their becoming frail.
   d. her overall financial situation.

56. Wilma's elderly mother needs help in taking care of the instrumental activities of daily life. Such activities would include which of the following?
   a. bathing
   b. eating
   c. paying bills
   d. all of these activities

Progress Test 1

Multiple-Choice Questions

Circle your answers to the following questions and check them with the answers at the end of the chapter. If your answer is incorrect, read the explanation for why it is incorrect and then consult the text.

1. According to disengagement theory, during late adulthood people tend to
   a. become less role-centered and more passive.
   b. have regrets about how they have lived their lives.
   c. become involved in a range of new activities.
   d. exaggerate lifelong personality traits.

2. The intermediate form of elder care that provides some of the privacy and independence of living at home, along with some medical supervision, is
   a. family care.
   b. a naturally occurring retirement community.
   c. a nursing home.
   d. assisted living.

3. In concluding her presentation on the frail elderly, Janet notes that each of the following is true EXCEPT that
   a. the frail elderly are usually over age 85.
   b. the frail elderly usually are not severely disabled.
   c. the crucial indicator of frailty is the inability to perform the activities of daily life.
   d. there are marked cultural differences in care for the frail elderly.

4. Grandparents who entertain and "spoil" their grandchildren in ways the parents would not are classified as
   a. remote grandparents.
   b. companionate grandparents.
   c. involved grandparents.
   d. surrogate grandparents.

5. Compared with emerging adults, older adults are characterized by each of the following EXCEPT that they
   a. view lack of broadband access as a significant disadvantage.
   b. are less connected to the Internet.
   c. avoid social networking.
   d. own fewer computers.

6. One study found that caregiving African Americans are _____ than other ethnicities.
   a. more likely to be depressed
   b. more likely to be lonely
   c. equally likely to be depressed and lonely
   d. less likely to be depressed

7. The idea that individuals set their own goals, assess their abilities, and figure out how to accomplish what they want to achieve during late adulthood is referred to as
   a. disengagement.
   b. selective optimization with compensation.
   c. positivity.
   d. age stratification.

8. After retirement, the elderly are likely to
   a. pursue educational interests.
   b. become politically involved.
   c. do volunteer work because they feel a particular commitment to their communities.
   d. perform any of these activities.

9. Which of the following theories does NOT belong with the others?
   a. disengagement theory
   b. feminist theory
   c. activity theory
   d. self theory

10. *Weathering* refers to
    a. the accumulation of health disparities with age.
    b. social forces related to an older person's social stratum.
    c. role confusion during late adulthood.
    d. the tendency of older adults to remember their favorite life experiences.

11. Which cultures emphasize family responsibility and respect for the aged?
    a. North American
    b. South American
    c. Asian and African
    d. European

12. In general, during late adulthood the FEWEST problems are experienced by individuals who
    a. are married.
    b. have always been single.
    c. have long been divorced.
    d. are widowed.

13. Which of the following would NOT be included as an activity of daily life?
    a. eating
    b. bathing
    c. dressing
    d. using the telephone

14. Which of the following is true of compulsive hoarding during late adulthood?
    a. People usually stop hoarding after a short time.
    b. People compulsively save things from when they were younger.
    c. It is always a sign of a more serious psychological problem.
    d. It is a sign of identity confusion.

15. Which of the following most accurately expresses the most recent view of developmentalists regarding stratification by age?
    a. Aging makes a person's social sphere increasingly narrow.
    b. Disengagement is always the result of ageism.
    c. Most older adults become more selective in their social contacts.
    d. Older adults need even more social activity to be happy than they did earlier in life.

True or False Items

Write T (true) or F (false) on the line in front of each statement.

_____ 1. Preschool girls are more likely to live with grandparents than rebellious school-age boys are.

_____ 2. Women are more likely than men to adjust to the death of a partner.

_____ 3. Married elderly people tend to live longer than unmarried ones.

_____ 4. Religious faith increases with age.

_____ 5. Older adults do not understand the social concerns of younger age groups.

_____ 6. Most developmentalists support the central premise of disengagement theory.

_____ 7. In the United States, the rate of volunteering decreases with age.

_____ 8. Most older people suffer significantly from a lack of close friendships.

_____ 9. Nearly one in two older adults makes a long-distance move after retirement.

_____ 10. Financial and emotional assistance typically flows from the younger generation to the older generation.

Progress Test 2

Progress Test 2 should be completed during a final chapter review. Answer the following questions after you thoroughly understand the correct answers for the Chapter Review and Progress Test 1.

Multiple-Choice Questions

1. Critics of disengagement theory point out that
   a. older people want to substitute new involvements for the roles they lose with retirement.
   b. disengagement usually is not voluntary on the part of the individual.
   c. disengagement often leads to greater life satisfaction for older adults.
   d. disengagement is more common at earlier stages in the life cycle.

2. A beanpole family is one that consists of
   a. fewer generations with fewer members than in the past.
   b. fewer generations with more members than in the past.
   c. more generations than in the past but with only a few members in each generation.
   d. more generations with more members than in the past.

3. What percentage of elderly people say they are abused?
   a. less than 1 percent   c. 10 percent
   b. about 5 percent   d. 25 percent

4. In the United States, over the past 20 years the number of nursing home residents has
   a. increased.
   b. decreased.
   c. stayed about the same.
   d. increased more for women than for men.

5. Following retirement, most elderly people
   a. relocate to a sunny climate.
   b. spend less time on housework and unnecessary chores.
   c. prefer to age in place.
   d. move in with their children.

6. Protective factors that act as buffers for the elderly include
   a. personality and social setting.
   b. financial resources and age.
   c. attitude and social network.
   d. none of these act as buffers.

7. The idea that older people seek familiar social contacts who reinforce their generativity, pride, and joy is most directly expressed in
   a. self theory.
   b. socioemotional selectivity theory.
   c. stratification theory.
   d. disengagement theory.

8. Regarding caring for the frail elderly, which of the following is NOT true?
   a. In the United States, a middle-aged son or daughter is usually the caregiver.
   b. Family caregivers experience substantial stress.
   c. The rate of depression among caregivers varies from culture to culture.
   d. Not all caregivers feel overwhelmed.

9. Which of the following would NOT be included as an instrumental activity of daily life?
   a. grocery shopping   c. making phone calls
   b. paying bills   d. taking a walk

10. One of the most important factors contributing to life satisfaction for older adults appears to be
    a. contact with friends.
    b. contact with younger family members.
    c. the number of new experiences to which they are exposed.
    d. continuity in the daily routine.

11. Of the four approaches to grandparenting, which of the following is often forced on the elder because of circumstances?
    a. involved grandparenting
    b. remote grandparenting
    c. companionate grandparenting
    d. surrogate parenting

12. In general, the longer a couple has been married, the more likely they are to
    a. be happier with each other.
    b. have frequent, minor disagreements.
    c. feel the relationship is not equitable.
    d. do all of these things.

13. Which of the following is NOT true regarding long-term marriages?
    a. Married elders tend to be healthier than those who never married.
    b. Absolute levels of conflict and emotional intensity drop over time.

c. Marriages generally change for the better in late adulthood.
d. Marriages improve in late adulthood, unless one spouse becomes seriously ill.

14. Grandparents who live near their grandchildren and see them daily are classified as
    a. remote grandparents.
    b. companionate grandparents.
    c. involved grandparents.
    d. surrogate parents.

15. According to Erikson, achieving integrity during late adulthood above all involves
    a. the ability to perceive one's own life as worthwhile.
    b. being open to new influences and experiences.
    c. treating other people with respect.
    d. developing a consistent and yet varied daily routine.

Matching Items

Match each definition or description with its corresponding term.

Terms

_____ 1. disengagement theory
_____ 2. self theories
_____ 3. naturally occurring retirement community
_____ 4. positivity effect
_____ 5. activity theory
_____ 6. stratification theories
_____ 7. activities of daily life (ADLs)
_____ 8. instrumental activities of daily life (IADLs)
_____ 9. assisted living
_____ 10. allostatic load
_____ 11. filial responsibility

Definitions or Descriptions

a. theories such as Erik Erikson's that emphasize self-actualization
b. an elderly accumulation of health problems that make a person vulnerable to disease
c. eating, bathing, toileting, walking, and dressing
d. living arrangement that combines independence and medical supervision
e. theory that people become less role-centered as they age
f. actions that require intellectual competence and forethought
g. tendency for elderly people to perceive, prefer, and remember positive experiences
h. theories such as feminist theory and critical race theory that focus on the limitations on life choices created by social forces
i. theory that elderly people become socially withdrawn only involuntarily
j. a neighborhood whose population is mostly retired people who moved there when they were younger
k. the obligation of adult children to care for their aging parents

Key Terms

Using your own words, write a brief definition or explanation of each of the following terms on a separate piece of paper.

1. self theories
2. integrity versus despair
3. compulsive hoarding
4. socioemotional selectivity theory
5. positivity effect
6. stratification theories
7. disengagement theory
8. activity theory
9. age in place
10. naturally occurring retirement community (NORC)
11. filial responsibility
12. frail elderly
13. activities of daily life (ADLs)
14. instrumental activities of daily life (IADLs)

ANSWERS

CHAPTER REVIEW

1. self
2. Erik Erikson; integrity; despair
3. identity; role confusion
4. self; compulsive hoarding; possessions and objects; hoarding disorder
5. socioemotional selectivity; emotional
6. selective optimization with compensation; goals; abilities; limitations; declines
7. positivity effect; ideal self; real self
8. stratification; social; choices; gender; ethnicity; SES; stereotyping; financial; ageism
9. disengagement; controversial among
10. activity; unwillingly
11. roles; life satisfaction
12. neither theory
13. gender; ethnicity; feminist; social
14. ethnicity; weathering; allostatic load; hypertension; obesity
15. **a.** is the answer.

b. Integrity is the positive side of Erikson's crisis in old age.

c. Self theories emphasize the quest for self-actualization.

d. The positivity effect is the tendency to remember positive images and experiences more than negative ones.

16. **b.** is the answer. "Groups" are the social "strata" that this theory focuses on.

a. & d. These theories emphasize the efforts of the individual to reach his or her full potential.

c. The positivity effect is the tendency to remember positive images and experiences more than negative ones.

17. **a.** is the answer.
18. **c.** is the answer.

a. This is not the crisis of late adulthood in Erikson's theory.

b. & d. These are not crises in Erikson's theory.

19. increased; is true
20. 60s; nonunionized low-wage; professionals
21. planning; time; poor health; disengagement
22. volunteering; health; depression
23. less; ageism; recruiting; training; self-absorbed; daily caregiving and informal helping
24. age in place
25. naturally occurring
26. increases; physical; emotional
27. politically; vote in elections, write to their representatives, and identify with a political party
28. is not
29. **b.** is the answer.

a. Although the text does not say this specifically, the discussion of the many activities engaged in by elderly people suggests a strong level of satisfaction.

d. There is much evidence that conflicts with disengagement theory.

30. **a.** is the answer.
31. **b.** is the answer.
32. social convoy
33. healthier; wealthier; happier

One reason is that all the shared contextual factors tend to change both partners in similar ways, bringing them closer together in memories and values. Also, older couples generally have learned how to disagree and actually consider their conflicts to be discussions. And, they become interdependent over time.

34. multigenerational; beanpole; generations

35. filial responsibility; is

36. older; children

Assistance arises from need and from the ability to provide. Frequency of contact is related to geographical proximity, not affection. Love is influenced by the interaction remembered from childhood. Sons feel stronger obligation; daughters feel stronger affection.

37. 85

38. remote; involved; companionate; surrogate parenting; almost always; do not

39. companionate; independence (autonomy)

40. drug-affected; rebellious

41. kinship foster care

42. 96; is

43. quite content

44. is not necessary

45. confidant (companion)

46. socially isolated

47. **d.** is the answer.

  a., b., & c. Social networking sites have fewer participants at every age older than the 15- to 25-year-old range.

48. frail elderly

49. activities of daily life (ADLs); eating; bathing; toileting; dressing; transferring from a bed to a chair

50. instrumental activities of daily life (IADLs); shopping, paying bills, driving a car, taking medications, and keeping appointments

51. are

52. stress; vary

53. elder abuse; involve

  a. the caregiver suffers from emotional problems or substance abuse

  b. the care receiver is frail, confused, and demanding

  c. the care location is isolated

54. nursing homes; assisted living; medical; village care

55. **b.** is the answer.

56. **c.** is the answer.

  a. & b. These are examples of "activities of daily life."

PROGRESS TEST 1

Multiple-Choice Questions

1. **a.** is the answer.

   b. This answer depicts a person struggling with Erikson's crisis of integrity versus despair.

   c. This answer describes activity theory.

   d. Disengagement theory does not address this issue.

2. **d.** is the answer.

3. **b.** is the answer.

4. **b.** is the answer.

5. **a.** is the answer.

6. **d.** is the answer.

7. **b.** is the answer.

   a. This is the idea that the elderly withdraw from society as they get older.

   c. Positivity refers to the tendency to remember positive events more than negative events.

   d. According to this theory, the oldest generation is segregated from the rest of society.

8. **d.** is the answer. Contrary to earlier views that retirement was not a happy time, researchers now know that the elderly are generally happy and productive, spending their time in various activities.

9. **d.** is the answer. Each of the other theories can be categorized as a stratification theory.

10. **a.** is the answer.

11. **c.** is the answer.

12. **a.** is the answer.

13. **d.** is the answer. Using the telephone is an *instrumental activity of daily life*.

14. **b.** is the answer.

   d. In fact, compulsive hoarding can be seen as a sign of self theory.

15. **c.** is the answer.

True or False Items

1. F Rebellious boys and drug-addicted infants are more likely to live with grandparents.
2. T
3. T
4. T
5. F In fact, older adults are willing to vote against the interests of their own group if a greater good is at stake.
6. F In fact, disengagement theory has *few* serious defenders.
7. T
8. F Most older adults have at least one close friend and, as compared with younger adults, are less likely to feel a need for more friendships.
9. F A minority of older adults moves to another state.
10. F Aid flows in the opposite direction.

PROGRESS TEST 2

Multiple-Choice Questions

1. **a.** is the answer.

   b. If disengagement were *not* voluntary, this would not be a choice of the elderly.

   c. & d. Neither of these answers is true, nor a criticism of disengagement theory.

2. **c.** is the answer.
3. **b.** is the answer.
4. **b.** is the answer.
5. **c.** is the answer.
6. **c.** is the answer.
7. **b.** is the answer.

   a. NORCs are communities of retired people whose population had moved there when they were younger.

   c. & d. ADLs and IADLs are measures of an older adult's ability to function on his or her own.

8. **a.** is the answer. In the United States, an elderly spouse is usually the caregiver.
9. **d.** is the answer.
10. **a.** is the answer.

b., c., & d. The importance of these factors varies from one older adult to another.

11. **d.** is the answer.
12. **a.** is the answer.

   b. & c. The longer a couple has been married, the *less* likely they are to have frequent disagreements or feel that the relationship is not equitable.

13. **d.** is the answer. Generally, older spouses accept each other's frailties and tend to each other's needs with feelings of affection.
14. **c.** is the answer.
15. **a.** is the answer.

Matching Items

1. e	5. i	8. f	11. k
2. a	6. h	9. d	
3. j	7. c	10. b	
4. g			

KEY TERMS

1. **Self theories** such as Erik Erikson's theory focus on how adults make choices, confront problems, and interpret reality in such a way as to express themselves as fully as possible.

2. The final stage of development, according to Erik Erikson, is **integrity versus despair,** in which older adults seek to integrate the unique experiences with their vision of community.

3. **Compulsive hoarding** is the sometimes hazardous urge to accumulate familiar possessions that tends to increase with age.

4. According to **socioemotional selectivity theory,** older people prioritize their emotional regulation by seeking familiar social contacts.

5. The **positivity effect** is the tendency for elderly people to perceive, prefer, and remember positive experiences and images more than negative ones.

6. **Stratification theories** emphasize that social forces limit individual choices and affect the ability to function in late adulthood.

7. According to **disengagement theory,** aging results in role relinquishment, social withdrawal, and passivity.

8. **Activity theory** is the view that older people remain active in a variety of social spheres and become withdrawn only unwillingly.

9. Many elderly people prefer to **age in place** by remaining in the same home and community, even after their health declines.

10. A **naturally occurring retirement community (NORC)** is a neighborhood or apartment complex whose population is mostly retired people who moved to the location as younger adults and never left.

11. **Filial responsibility** is the idea that adult children are obligated to care for their aging parents.

12. The **frail elderly** are the minority of adults over age 65, and often over age 85, who are physically infirm, very ill, or cognitively impaired.

13. In determining frailty, gerontologists often refer to the **activities of daily life (ADLs),** which comprise five tasks: eating, bathing, toileting, dressing, and transferring from a bed to a chair.

14. The **instrumental activities of daily life (IADLs)** are actions that require some intellectual competence and forethought, such as shopping for food, paying bills, and taking medication.

Death and Dying

Epilogue Overview

Death marks the close of the life span—a close that individuals must come to terms with, both for themselves and for their loved ones. Indeed, an understanding and acceptance of death is crucial if life is to be lived to the fullest.

The first section focuses on how dying is viewed throughout the life span, in different cultures and religions, and at different points in history. The next section discusses hospice and other forms of palliative care designed to help the terminally ill patient to die "a good death."

Although the concept of an unvarying sequence of stages among the dying is not universally accepted, the pioneering work of Elisabeth Kübler-Ross was instrumental in revealing the emotional gamut of terminally ill patients and the importance of honest communication.

The final section deals with changing expressions of grief and how people can be aided in the process of recovery.

What Will You Know?

The text chapter should be studied one section at a time. Before you read, preview each section by skimming it, noting headings and boldface items. Then read the sections, one at a time, keeping these questions in mind.

1. Why is death a topic of hope, not despair?
2. What is the difference between a good death and a bad one?
3. How does mourning help with grief?

Epilogue Review

When you have finished reading the Epilogue, work through the material that follows to review it. Completing the sentences and answering the ques-

tions will enable you to answer the "What Have You Learned?" questions at the end of the text Epilogue. Scattered throughout the Epilogue Review are Study Tips, which explain how best to learn a difficult concept, and Applications, which help you to know how well you understand the material. Check your understanding of the material by consulting the answers at the end of the Epilogue. Do not continue with the next section until you understand each answer. If you need to, review or reread the appropriate section in the textbook before continuing.

Death and Hope

1. (Table Ep.1) Briefly describe five changes in death over the past 100 years.

2. In ancient times people were buried with tools, signifying belief in a/an _____ .

3. Dying children often fear that death means _____ . For this reason, telling children that the deceased person is sleeping or in heaven _____ (is/is not) helpful.

4. According to _____
_____ _____ ,
people adopt cultural values and moral principles in order to cope with their fear of death.

5. Adolescents and emerging adults control their anxiety about death by _____
_____ .

6. A major shift in attitudes about death occurs when adults become responsible for _____ and _____ . From age 25 to 60, terminally ill adults worry about _____ .

7. Adult attitudes about death are often _____ . For instance, people fear travel by _____ more than by _____ . Older adults may engage in _____ _____ as they try to leave something meaningful for later generations.

8. During late adulthood, anxiety about death _____ (increases/decreases). Many developmentalists view acceptance of one's own mortality during late adulthood as a sign of _____ _____ .

9. Some people who survive a serious illness report having had a _____-_____ _____ in which they left their bodies. These experiences often include _____ elements.

_____

STUDY TIP Death has various meanings, depending partly on a person's age. Write a sentence describing a typical young child's understanding of death. Do the same for an adolescent, an adult, and a person who is terminally ill.

_____

Choices in Dying

10. A *good death* is one that is _____ , _____ , and _____ and that occurs at _____ , surrounded by _____ and _____ . Because of modern medical techniques, a swift and peaceful death is _____ (more/less) difficult to ensure today than in the past.

11. A major factor in our understanding of the psychological needs of the dying was the pioneering work of _____ .

12. Kübler-Ross's research led her to propose that the dying go through _____ (how many?) emotional stages. In order, the stages of dying are _____ , _____ , _____ , _____ , and _____ .

13. Another set of stages of dying is based on _____ hierarchy of needs, which are _____ needs, _____ , _____ , and _____ , _____ , and _____-_____ . He later suggested a sixth stage, _____-_____ .

14. Other researchers typically _____ (have/have not) found the same five stages of dying occurring in sequence.

15. The institution called the _____ provides care to terminally ill patients. The first modern institution of this type was opened in London by _____ .

16. Medical care that is designed not to treat an illness but to relieve pain and suffering is called _____ _____ .

17. The least tolerable physical symptom of fatal illness is _____ . Physicians once worried about causing _____ if pain relievers such as _____ were given too freely. Pain medication for dying patients may have the _____ _____ of reducing pain while _____ .

18. Historically, death was determined by _____ . In the late 1970s, physicians decided that death occurred when _____ _____ ceased.

19. All competent individuals have the legal right to control decisions related to life-prolonging treatments, including _____ _____ , in which a seriously ill person is allowed to die naturally, and _____ _____ , in which someone intentionally acts to terminate the life of a suffering person. Usually, if a patient prefers to die naturally, the order _____ is placed on that person's hospital chart.

20. Active euthanasia is _____ (legal/illegal) in most parts of the world. When a doctor provides the means for someone

to end his or her own life, it is referred to as

_____-_____

_____ .

21. In the United States, the state of _____ has allowed physician-assisted suicide since 1994 but under very strict guidelines. Many critics fear that legalizing euthanasia or physician-assisted suicide will create a

_____ _____

in which societies begin hastening death. Since that time, concerns that physician-assisted suicide might be used more often with the old and the poor _____ (have/have not) been proven to be well-founded.

22. A description of what people want to happen as they die is called a(n) _____

_____ . Some people make a(n)

_____ _____

to indicate what medical intervention they want if they become incapable of expressing those wishes. To avoid complications, each person should also designate a _____

_____ _____ ,

someone who can make decisions for them if needed. Proxies _____ (do/do not) guarantee a problem-free death. One problem is that _____

_____ may disagree with the proxy; another is that proxy directives may be _____ by hospital staff.

APPLICATIONS:

23. The terminally ill patient who is convinced his laboratory tests must be wrong is probably in which of Kübler-Ross's stages?

  a. denial   **c.** depression
  b. anger   **d.** bargaining

24. Dr. Welby writes the orders DNR (do not resuscitate) on her patient's chart. Evidently, the patient has requested

  a. a living will.   **c.** active euthanasia.
  b. passive euthanasia. **d.** an assisted suicide.

25. Armand has directed his lawyer to prepare a document specifying that he does not want to be kept alive by artificial means. His lawyer is creating

  a. a health care proxy. **c.** a double effect.
  b. grief work.   **d.** a living will.

26. The doctor who injects a terminally ill patient with a lethal drug is practicing

  a. passive euthanasia.
  b. active euthanasia.
  c. an assisted suicide.
  d. an act that became legal in most countries in 1993.

Affirmation of Life

27. An individual's deep sorrow in response to a sense of loss is called _____ .

28. About _____ percent of all mourners experience _____ grief, a type of grief that impedes the person's future life because of lingering sorrow or

_____ _____ _____ .

29. As rituals diminish, problems such as

_____ _____

may become more common. This is a situation in which a bereaved person is

_____ .

30. Modern life also increases the incidence of

_____ _____ , in

which the bereaved are _____ .

31. Another problem is _____

_____ , in which circumstances such as _____ and _____ interfere with the grief process.

32. The ceremonies and behaviors that comprise the public response to a death are called _____ . These ceremonies are designed by _____ to channel _____ toward _____ of life.

33. A crucial factor in mourning is people's search for _____ in death. The normal reaction at first is intense, with a strong desire to assess _____ . Emotions gradually ease as the person engages in

_____ _____ .

34. (A View from Science) Early studies _____ (underestimated/overestimated) the frequency of pathological grief. Researchers now know that _____ has a major effect on grief and mourning.

35. In recent times, mourning has become more

_____ , less _____ ,

less _____ , and less

_____ .

36. List two steps that others can follow to help a bereaved person.

a. _____

b. _____

APPLICATIONS:

37. Following 30-year-old Ramón's unexpected and violent death, which of the following individuals is most likely to experience disenfranchised grief?

a. Kent, his unmarried partner

b. Janet, the younger sister with whom he has not been in touch for years

c. his father, who divorced Kent's mother two years earlier

d. his biological mother, who put Kent up for adoption when he was a baby

38. Which of the following statements would probably be the most helpful to a grieving person?

a. "Why don't you get out more and get back into the swing of things?"

b. "You're tough; bear up!"

c. "If you need someone to talk to, call me any time."

d. "It must have been his or her time to die."

39. Dr. Robins is about to counsel her first terminally ill patient and his family. Research suggests that her most helpful strategy would be to

a. keep most of the facts from the patient and his family in order not to upset them.

b. be truthful to the patient but not his family.

c. be truthful to the family only, and swear them to secrecy.

d. honestly inform both the patient and his family.

Progress Test 1

Circle your answers to the following questions and check them with the answers at the end of the epilogue. If your answer is incorrect, read the explanation for why it is incorrect and then consult the text.

Multiple-Choice Questions

1. Passive euthanasia is best described as

a. care designed to relieve pain and suffering.

b. a situation in which treatment relieves pain while at the same time hastening death.

c. a situation in which a person is allowed to die naturally.

d. a situation in which someone takes action to bring about another person's death.

2. Which of the following themes about death was NOT apparent in known ancient societies?

a. Actions during life affect destiny after death.

b. An afterlife was assumed.

c. Prayers and offerings were delivered in part to prevent the spirit of the dead from haunting the survivors.

d. Death was viewed as a form of punishment.

3. Kübler-Ross's stages of dying are, in order,

a. anger, denial, bargaining, depression, acceptance.

b. depression, anger, denial, bargaining, acceptance.

c. denial, anger, bargaining, depression, acceptance.

d. bargaining, denial, anger, acceptance, depression.

4. Most adults hope that they will die

a. with little pain.

b. with family and friends.

c. swiftly.

d. in all of these ways.

5. *Hospice* is best defined as

a. a document that indicates what kind of medical intervention a terminally ill person wants.

b. mercifully allowing a person to die by not doing something that might extend life.

c. an alternative to hospital care for the terminally ill.

d. providing a person with the means to end his or her life.

6. Palliative care refers to

a. heroic measures to save a life.

b. conservative medical care to treat an illness.

c. efforts to relieve pain and suffering.

d. allowing a terminally ill patient to die naturally.

7. Adolescents and emerging adults are more likely than other age groups to die in suicides, accidents, and homicides in part because they

a. are easily influenced by others.

b. control their anxiety about death by taking risks.

c. have poor relationships with their parents.

d. cannot establish an identity.

8. Which of the following is a normal response in the grief process?

a. experiencing powerful emotions

b. culturally diverse emotions

c. a lengthy period of grief

d. All of these are normal responses.

9. A double effect in medicine refers to a situation in which

   a. the effects of one drug on a patient interact with those of another drug.

   b. medication relieves pain and has a secondary effect of hastening death.

   c. family members disagree with a terminally ill patient's proxy.

   d. medical personnel ignore the wishes of a terminally ill patient and his or her proxy.

10. Near-death experiences

   a. often include angels and other religious elements.

   b. occur more often following serious injuries than serious illnesses.

   c. occur in most people who come close to dying.

   d. have all of these characteristics.

True or False Items

Write T (true) or F (false) on the line in front of each statement.

_____ 1. Hospice care is affordable to all who need it.

_____ 2. Subsequent research has confirmed the accuracy of Kübler-Ross's findings regarding the five stages of dying.

_____ 3. Studies have found that doctors spend less time with patients who are known to be dying.

_____ 4. Following the death of a loved one, the bereaved can best ensure their psychological health and well-being by increasing their social contacts and the number of activities in which they are involved.

_____ 5. To help a bereaved person, one should ignore the person's depression.

_____ 6. Researchers agree that the hospice is beneficial to the dying person and his or her family.

_____ 7. Physician-assisted suicide is legal almost everywhere in the world.

_____ 8. Hospices administer pain-killing medication but do not make use of artificial life-support systems.

_____ 9. In the long run, the bereavement process may have a beneficial effect on the individual.

_____ 10. Fear of death increases in late adulthood.

Progress Test 2

Progress Test 2 should be completed during a final review of the Epilogue. Answer the following questions after you thoroughly understand the correct answers for the Epilogue Review and Progress Test 1.

Multiple-Choice Questions

1. Kübler-Ross's primary contribution was to

   a. open the first hospice, thus initiating the hospice movement.

   b. show how the emotions of the dying occur in a series of clear-cut stages.

   c. bring attention to the psychological needs of dying people.

   d. show the correlation between people's conceptualization of death and their developmental stage.

2. In recent times, mourning has become all of the following EXCEPT

   a. more private.   c. more complicated.

   b. less emotional.   d. more religious.

3. Which of the following is NOT a limitation of hospices?

   a. Most insurance plans will not pay for hospice care unless the patient has been diagnosed as terminally ill.

   b. Hospice care can be very expensive.

   c. In a hospice facility, a friend or relative is encouraged to stay with the patient.

   d. The dying typically do not receive skilled medical care.

4. A health care proxy is most accurately described as a(n)

   a document that indicates what medical intervention an individual wants if he or she becomes incapable of expressing those wishes.

   b. person chosen by another person to make medical decisions if the second person becomes unable to do so.

   c. situation in which, at a patient's request, someone else ends his or her life.

   d. indication on a patient's chart not to use heroic, life-saving measures.

5. As a result of ongoing police investigations, the bereaved members of a murder victim's family may be at increased risk of experiencing

   a. absent grief.   c. incomplete grief.

   b. disenfranchised grief. d. a good death.

6. Research reveals that Kübler-Ross's stages of dying
   a. occur in sequence in virtually all terminally ill patients.
   b. do not occur in hospice residents.
   c. are typical only in Western cultures.
   d. make feelings about death seem much more predictable and universal than they actually are.

7. Living wills are an attempt to
   a. make sure that passive euthanasia will not be used in individual cases.
   b. specify the extent of medical treatment desired in the event of terminal illness.
   c. specify conditions for the use of active euthanasia.
   d. ensure that death will occur at home rather than in a hospital.

8. My people believe that people should die on the floor, surrounded by family, who do not eat or wash until the funeral pyre is extinguished. I am
   a. African.   c. Hindu.
   b. Muslim.   d. Native American.

9. Ritual is to emotion as
   a. grief is to mourning.
   b. mourning is to grief.
   c. affirmation is to loss.
   d. loss is to affirmation.

10. Healing after the death of a loved one is most difficult when
    a. the death is a long, protracted one.
    b. the bereaved is not allowed to mourn in the way or she wishes.
    c. a period of grief has already elapsed.
    d. no other mourners are present.

Matching Items

Match each term or concept with its corresponding description or definition.

Terms or Concepts

_____ 1. DNR
_____ 2. hospice
_____ 3. living will
_____ 4. passive euthanasia
_____ 5. double effect
_____ 6. physician-assisted suicide
_____ 7. palliative care
_____ 8. grief
_____ 9. bereavement
_____ 10. complicated grief
_____ 11. terror management theory
_____ 12. advance directives

Definitions or Descriptions

a. hospice treatment that relieves suffering and safeguards dignity
b. an alternative to hospital care for the terminally ill
c. lingering sorrow or contradictory emotions following a death
d. a document expressing a person's wishes for treatment should he or she become terminally ill and incapable of making such decisions
e. providing the means for a terminally ill patient to end his or her life
f. idea that people adopt cultural values in order to cope with their fear of death
g. the sense of loss following a death
h. allowing a seriously ill person to die naturally by withholding medical intervention
i. situation in which a pain-relieving drug also hastens the death of a terminally ill patient
j. an individual's response to the loss of a loved one
k. hospital chart order to allow a terminally ill patient to die naturally
l. statements of what people wish to happen when they die

Key Terms

Using your own words, write a brief definition or explanation of each of the following terms on a separate piece of paper.

1. terror management theory (TMT)
2. hospice
3. palliative care
4. double effect
5. passive euthanasia
6. DNR (do not resuscitate)
7. active euthanasia
8. physician-assisted suicide
9. slippery slope
10. advance directives
11. living will
12. health care proxy
13. grief
14. complicated grief
15. absent grief
16. disenfranchised grief
17. incomplete grief
18. mourning

ANSWERS

EPILOGUE REVIEW

1. Death occurs at a later age, takes longer, and more often occurs in hospitals. The major causes of death have also shifted from infectious diseases, and people now are more aware of cultural and religious diversity.
2. afterlife
3. being abandoned by the people they love; is not
4. terror management theory
5. taking risks
6. work; family; leaving something undone or leaving family members alone
7. irrational; plane; car; legacy work
8. decreases; mental health
9. near-death experience; religious
10. quick; painless; peaceful; home; friends; family; more
11. Elisabeth Kübler-Ross

12. five; denial; anger; bargaining; depression; acceptance
13. Maslow's; physiological; safety; love; acceptance; respect; self-actualization; self-transcendence
14. have not
15. hospice; Cecily Saunders
16. palliative care
17. pain; addiction; morphine; double effect; speeding up death
18. listening to the heart; brain waves
19. passive euthanasia; active euthanasia; DNR (do not resuscitate)
20. illegal; physician-assisted suicide
21. Oregon; slippery slope; have not
22. advance directive; living will; health care proxy; do not; family members; ignored
23. a. is the answer.
24. b. is the answer.

    a. A living will is a document expressing how a person wishes to be cared for should he or she become terminally ill.

    c. This is when a person *intentionally acts* to end another's life.

    d. In this situation, a person provides the means for another to take his or her own life.
25. d. is the answer.

    a. A health care proxy is a person chosen to make decisions for a person unable to do so.

    b. Grief work is the experience and expression of strong emotions on the death of a loved one.

    c. In the double effect, pain is eased but death is hastened.
26. b. is the answer.
27. grief
28. 10; complicated; contradictory emotions
29. absent grief; not expected or allowed to go through a mourning period
30. disenfranchised grief; not allowed to mourn publicly
31. incomplete grief; suicides; murders
32. mourning; cultures; grief; reaffirmation
33. meaning; blame; grief work
34. overestimated; personality
35. private; emotional; religious

36. **a.** Be aware that powerful, complicated, and culturally diverse emotions are likely.

    b. A friend should listen and sympathize, never implying that the person is too grief-stricken or not grief-stricken enough.

37. **a.** is the answer.

    b., c., & d. Because each of these individuals is biologically related to Ramón, none is likely to be excluded from mourning his death.

38. **c.** is the answer.

    a., b., & d. These statements discourage the bereaved person from mourning.

39. **d.** is the answer.

PROGRESS TEST 1

Multiple-Choice Questions

1. **c.** is the answer.

   a. This describes palliative care.

   b. This is the double effect that sometimes occurs with morphine and other opiate drugs.

   d. This is active euthanasia.

2. **d.** is the answer.

3. **c.** is the answer.

4. **d.** is the answer.

5. **c.** is the answer.

   a. This is a living will.

   b. & d. These are forms of euthanasia.

6. **c.** is the answer.

7. **b.** is the answer.

8. **d.** is the answer.

9. **b.** is the answer.

10. **a.** is the answer.

    b. & c. Near-death experiences, which occur in some people who are dying, are no more likely to occur following a serious injury than an illness.

True or False Items

1. F Hospice care is too expensive for most.

2. F Later research has not confirmed Kübler-Ross's findings that the emotions of an individual faced with death occur in orderly stages.

3. T

4. F The psychological well-being of the bereaved depends above all on their being able to openly express their grief.

5. F A friend should listen, sympathize, and not ignore the mourner's pain.

6. F Hospices have significant benefits, but some people are critical of them in part because they deny hope to the dying and because they are expensive.

7. F These practices are *illegal* throughout most of the world.

8. T

9. T

10. F Just the opposite is true.

PROGRESS TEST 2

Multiple-Choice Questions

1. **c.** is the answer.

2. **d.** is the answer. In recent times, mourning has become less religious than formerly.

3. **d.** is the answer. Hospices generally *do* provide patients with skilled medical care.

4. **b.** is the answer.

   a. This is a living will.

   c. This is voluntary euthanasia.

   d. This refers to DNR.

5. **c.** is the answer.

   a. Absent grief occurs when people cut themselves off from the community and customs of grief and mourning.

   b. Disenfranchised grief occurs when bereaved people are not permitted to mourn publicly.

   d. A good death is one that is swift and painless and that occurs in the company of loved ones.

6. **d.** is the answer.

   b. & c. There is no evidence that hospice residents experience different emotional stages than others who are dying or that these stages are a product of Western culture.

7. **b.** is the answer.

8. **c.** is the answer.

9. **b.** is the answer. Mourning refers to the ceremonies and rituals that a religion or culture prescribes for bereaved people, and grief refers to an individual's emotional response to bereavement.

10. **b.** is the answer.

   a. & c. In such situations, death is expected and generally easier to bear.

   d. This issue was not discussed.

Matching Items

1.	k	5.	i	9.	g
2.	b	6.	e	10.	c
3.	d	7.	a	11.	f
4.	h	8.	j	12.	l

KEY TERMS

1. According to **terror management theory (TMT),** people adopt cultural values and moral principles in order to cope with their fear of death.

2. A **hospice** is an institution in which terminally ill patients receive palliative care to reduce suffering.

3. **Palliative care,** such as that provided in a hospice, is care that relieves the patient's suffering and provides support and guidance to his or her family.

4. A **double effect** is a situation in which medication has the intended effect of relieving a dying person's pain and the secondary effect of hastening death.

5. **Passive euthanasia** involves allowing a seriously ill person to die naturally by withholding medical interventions.

6. **DNR (do not resuscitate)** is a written order from a physician that no attempt should be made to revive a dying patient if he or she suffers cardiac or respiratory arrest.

7. **Active euthanasia** involves a person taking action to end another person's life in order to relieve suffering.

8. A **physician-assisted suicide** is one in which a doctor provides the means for a person to end his or her life.

9. A **slippery slope** is an argument that a given action will start a chain of events that will end in an undesirable outcome.

10. **Advance directives** describe what people want to happen as they die and after they die.

11. A **living will** is a document that specifies what medical intervention a person wants if he or she becomes incapable of expressing those wishes.

12. A **health care proxy** is a person chosen to make medical decisions for someone else if the second person becomes unable to do so.

13. **Grief** refers to the deep sorrow that people feel at the death of another.

14. **Complicated grief** occurs when a death impedes a person's future life because of lingering sorrow or contradictory emotions.

15. **Absent grief** occurs when people cut themselves off from the community and customs of grief and mourning.

16. **Disenfranchised grief** occurs when bereaved people are prevented from mourning publicly by cultural customs or social restrictions.

17. **Incomplete grief** occurs when circumstances, such as a criminal investigation, interfere with grieving.

18. **Mourning** refers to the ceremonies and rituals that a religion or culture prescribes for bereaved people.

Appendix B
More About
Research Methods

Appendix B Overview

The first section describes two ways of gathering information about development: library research and using the Internet. The second section discusses the various ways in which developmentalists ensure that their studies are valid.

Appendix B Review

When you have finished reading Appendix B, work through the material that follows to review it. Completing the sentences and answering the questions will help you to know how well you understand the material. Check your understanding of the material by consulting the answers at the end of Appendix B. Do not continue with the next section until you understand each answer. If you need to, review or reread the appropriate section in the textbook before continuing.

Make It Personal

1. Before asking questions as part of a research assignment, remember that observing _____ _____ comes first.

2. Before interviewing someone, you should _____ the person of your purpose and assure him or her of _____ .

3. Research studies that may be published require that you inform the college's _____ _____ _____ .

Read the Research

4. Four journals that cover human development are

   _____ ,

   _____ ,

   _____ , and

   _____ .

5. The best journals are _____ - _____ , which means that scientists other than an article's authors decide if it is worthy of publication.

6. Two good handbooks in development are _____ and

   _____ .

7. Two advantages of using the Internet to learn about development are

   a. _____

   b. _____

8. Two disadvantages of using the Internet are

   a. _____

   b. _____

9. To help you select appropriate information, use general topic lists, called _____ , and _____ , which give you all the sites that use a particular word or words.

Additional Terms and Concepts

10. To make statements about people in general, called a _____ , scientists study a group of research _____ , called a _____ .

11. When a sample is typical of the group under study—in gender, ethnic background, and other important variables—the sample is called a(n) _____ _____ .

12. Ideally, a group of research participants constitute a _____ _____ , which means that everyone in the population is equally likely to be selected. To avoid _____ _____ , some samples are _____ and trace development of some particular characteristic in an entire cluster.

13. In a _____ study, researchers begin with a group of participants that already share a particular characteristic and then look "backward" to discover other characteristics of the group.

14. Every researcher begins by formulating a _____ . They also learn what other scientists have discovered about the topic and what _____ might be useful and _____ in designing research.

15. When the person carrying out research is unaware of the purpose of the research, that person is said to be _____ to the hypothesized outcome.

16. Researchers use _____ _____ to define variables in terms of specific, observable behavior that can be measured precisely. This is useful not only in _____ research but also in _____ research.

17. Journal articles that summarize past research are called _____ .

18. A study that combines the findings of many studies to present an overall conclusion is a _____ .

19. Researchers often report quantitative analyses that measure _____ _____ , which indicates whether or not a particular result could have occurred by chance.

20. The statistic that indicates how much of an impact the independent variable had on the dependent variable is _____ _____ .

Progress Test

Circle your answers to the following questions and check them with the answers on page 344. If your answer is incorrect, read the explanation for why it is incorrect and then consult the text.

1. A journal article that summarizes past research is
   a. *Psycscan: Developmental Psychology.*
   b. *Child Development Abstracts and Bibliography.*
   c. *Developmental Psychology.*
   d. a review article.

2. Which of the following is NOT one of the journals that publish research on human development?
   a. *The Developmentalist*
   b. *Developmental Psychology*
   c. *Human Development*
   d. *Child Development*

3. Which of the following is a disadvantage of conducing Internet research?
   a. You can spend hours sifting through information that turns out to be useless.
   b. Anybody can put anything on the Internet.
   c. There is no evaluation of bias on Internet sites.
   d. Each of these is a disadvantage of Internet research.

4. To say that the study of development is a science means that developmentalists
   a. use many methods to make their research more objective and more valid.
   b. take steps to ensure that a few extreme cases do not distort the overall statistical picture.
   c. recognize the importance of establishing operational definitions.
   d. do all of these things.

5. The entire group of people about whom a scientist wants to learn is called the
   a. reference group.
   b. sample.
   c. representative sample.
   d. population.

6. A researcher's conclusions after conducting a study are not valid because a few extreme cases distorted the results. In designing this study, the researcher evidently failed to pay attention to the importance of
   a. sample size.   c. representativeness.
   b. "blindness."   d. all of these things.

7. Rachel made a study of students' opinions about different psychology professors. She took great care to survey equal numbers of male and female students, students who received high grades and students who received low grades, and members of various minorities. Clearly, Rachel wished to ensure that data were obtained from a
   a. population.
   b. "blind" sample.
   c. representative sample.
   d. comparison group.

8. A person who gathers data in a state of "blind-ness" is one who
   a. is unaware of the purpose of the research.
   b. is allowing his or her personal beliefs to influence the results.
   c. has failed to establish operational definitions for the variables under investigation.
   d. is basing the study on an unrepresentative sample of the population.

9. Which of the following is an example of a good operational definition of a dependent variable?
   a. walking
   b. aggression
   c. 30 minutes of daily exercise
   d. taking steps without support

10. The technique of combining the results of many studies to come to an overall conclusion is
    a. meta-analysis.
    b. effect size.
    c. a prospective study.
    d. a retrospective study.

11. For a psychologist's generalizations to be valid, the sample must be representative of the population under study. The results must also be
    a. statistically significant.
    b. derived from participants who are all the same age.
    c. large enough.
    d. none of these things.

12. The particular individuals who are studied in a specific research project are called the
    a. independent variables.
    b. dependent variables.
    c. participants.
    d. population.

13. A research study that begins with participants who share a certain characteristic and then "looks backward" is a
    a. prospective study.
    b. retrospective study.
    c. meta-analysis.
    d. representative sample.

14. A research study that begins with participants who share a certain characteristic and then "looks forward" is a
    a. prospective study.
    b. retrospective study.
    c. meta-analysis.
    d. representative sample.

15. Summarizing the results of his research study, Professor Schulman notes that "the effect size was zero." By this she means that the
    a. independent variable had no impact on the dependent variable.
    b. independent variable had a large impact on the dependent variable.
    c. dependent variable had no impact on the independent variable.
    d. dependent variable had a large impact on the independent variable

Key Terms

Using your own words, write a brief definition or explanation of each of the following terms on a separate piece of paper.

1. population
2. participants
3. sample
4. representative sample
5. blind
6. operational definition
7. meta-analysis
8. effect size

Answers

APPENDIX B REVIEW

1. ethical standards
2. inform; confidentiality
3. Institutional Review Board (IRB)
4. *Developmental Psychology; Child Development; Developmental Review; Human Development*
5. peer-reviewed
6. *Handbook of Child Psychology; Handbook on Aging*
7. **a.** Virtually everything you might want to know is on the Internet.

    b. The Internet is quick and easy to use, any time of the day or night.
8. **a.** There is so much information available on the Internet that it is easy to waste time.

    b. Anybody can put anything on the Internet.
9. directories; search engines
10. population; participants; sample
11. representative sample
12. random sample; selection bias; prospective
13. retrospective
14. hypothesis; methods; ethical
15. blind
16. operational definitions; quantitative; qualitative
17. reviews
18. meta-analysis
19. statistical significance
20. effect size

PROGRESS TEST

1. **d.** is the answer.
2. **a.** is the answer.
3. **d.** is the answer.
4. **d.** is the answer.
5. **d.** is the answer.
6. **a.** is the answer.

    b. "Blindness" has no relevance here.

    c. Although it is true that a distorted sample is unrepresentative, the issue concerns the small number of extreme cases—a dead giveaway to sample size.
7. **c.** is the answer. Rachel has gone to great lengths to make sure that her student sample is typical of the entire population of students who takes psychology courses.
8. **a.** is the answer.
9. **d.** is the answer.

    a., b., & c. Each of these definitions is too ambiguous to qualify as an operational definition.
10. **a.** is the answer.
11. **a.** is the answer.
12. **c.** is the answer.

    a. These are the factors that a researcher manipulates in an experiment.

    b. These are the outcomes that a researcher measures in an experiment.

    d. It is almost always impossible to include every member of a population in an experiment.
13. **b.** is the answer.
14. **a.** is the answer.
15. **a.** is the answer.

    b. In this case, the effect size would be a number close to 1.0.

    c. & d. Independent variables impact dependent variables, and not vice versa.

KEY TERMS

1. The **population** is the entire group of individuals who are of particular concern in a scientific study.
2. **Participants** are the people who are studied in a research project.
3. A **sample** is a group of individuals who are drawn from a specific population.
4. A **representative sample** is a group of research participants who reflect the relevant characteristics of the population being studied.
5. **Blind** is the situation in which data gatherers and sometimes their research participants are deliberately kept unaware of the purpose of the study in order to avoid unintentionally biasing the results.
6. An **operational definition** is a precise description of the specific, observable behavior that will constitute the variable being studied so that another person will know whether it occurred.
7. **Meta-analysis** is a research technique in which the results of many studies are combined to produce one overall conclusion.
8. **Effect size** is a statistical measure of how much impact an independent variable had on a dependent variable in a research study.